CW01281368

The Design of
Virtual Environments

The Design of
Virtual Environments

Rory Stuart

McGraw-Hill
New York San Francisco Washington, D.C. Auckland Bogotá
Caracas Lisbon London Madrid Mexico City Milan
Montreal New Delhi San Juan Singapore
Sydney Tokyo Toronto

McGraw-Hill
A Division of The McGraw·Hill Companies

Library of Congress Cataloging-in-Publication Data

Stuart, Rory
    The design of virtual environments / by Rory Stuart.
       p.   cm.
    Includes index.
    ISBN 0-07-063299-5 (h)
    1. Human-computer interaction. 2. Virtual reality. I. Title.
QA76.9.H85S79 1996
006—dc20   95-51656
                                                                                CIP

Copyright © 1996 by The McGraw-Hill Companies, Inc. Printed in the United States of America. Except as permitted under the United States Copyright Act of 1976, no part of this publication may be reproduced or distributed in any form or by any means, or stored in a data base or retrieval system, without the prior written permission of the publisher.

1 2 3 4 5 6 7 8 9 FGR/FGR 9 0 0 9 8 7 6

ISBN 0-07-063299-5

The acquiring editor of this book was Jennifer Holt DiGiovanna, the book editor was Kellie Hagan, and the executive editor was Robert E. Ostrander. The production supervisor was Katherine G. Brown. This book was set in ITC Century Light. It was composed by TAB Books.

Printed and bound by Quebecor Printing, Fairfield, Pennsylvania.

McGraw-Hill books are available at special quantity discounts to use as premiums and sales promotions, or for use in corporate training programs. For more information, please write to the Director of Special Sales, McGraw-Hill, 11 West 19th Street, New York, NY 10011. Or contact your local bookstore.

Product or brand names used in this book may be trade names or trademarks. Where we believe that there may be proprietary claims to such trade names or trademarks, the name has been used with an initial capital or it has been capitalized in the style used by the name claimant. Regardless of the capitalization used, all such names have been used in an editorial manner without any intent to convey endorsement of or other affiliation with the name claimant. Neither the author nor the publisher intends to express any judgment as to the validity or legal status of any such proprietary claims.

> Information contained in this work has been obtained by McGraw-Hill from sources believed to be reliable. However, neither McGraw-Hill nor its authors guarantee the accuracy or completeness of any information published herein and neither McGraw-Hill nor its authors shall be responsible for any errors, omissions, or damages arising out of use of this information. This work is published with the understanding that McGraw-Hill and its authors are supplying information but are not attempting to render engineering or other professional services. If such services are required, the assistance of an appropriate professional should be sought.

MH96
0632995

For more information about other McGraw-Hill materials, call 1-800-2-MCGRAW in the United States. In other countries, call your nearest McGraw-Hill office.

In memory of Albert R. Teichner. A family friend since my childhood, he nurtured my interest in science and gave me the first book I read on artificial intelligence. A science-fiction writer, he had a greater breadth and depth of knowledge on a wider range of topics than anyone else I've known. His love of learning was contagious.

Contents

Acknowledgments   xiii
Preface   xv
Introduction   xix

Part 1   Defining the Requirements

Chapter 1. Defining the User, Task, and Environment   3

- Who Is the User?   3
  - Single vs. Multiple Users   4
  - Remote vs. Proximate Users   5
  - Novices vs. Experts   6
  - User Aptitude   7
  - Individual Physiological Differences   7
  - Users with Disabilities   7
- Defining the Task   8
  - Categories of Virtual Environment Applications   8
- Defining the Environment   13
  - The Physical Environment   13
  - The Work Environment   14
  - The Social Environment   14
- Questions   15

Chapter 2. Human Capabilities and Performance   17

- Visual Perception   19
  - Basics of Visual Perception   19
  - Monocular Depth Cues   21
  - Oculomotor Cues   23
  - Binocular Disparity and Stereopsis   24
  - Additional Cues with Motion   24
  - Relative Importance of Depth Cues   24
  - Field of View   25
  - Resolution   26
  - Color Perception   27

Brightness and Contrast	27
Visual Cues and Performance	28
Implications for Virtual Environments	28
Auditory Perception	29
Basics of Auditory Perception	30
Types of Listening	32
Auditory Localization	32
Implications for Virtual Environments	35
Haptic Perception	35
Tactile Perception	36
Force and Kinesthetic Perception	38
Implications for Virtual Environments	39
Olfactory Perception	40
Basics of Olfactory Perception	40
Why Use Olfactory Perception?	42
Implications for Virtual Environments	42
Vestibular Sense	43
Vestibular Illusions and Adaptation	44
Implications for Virtual Environments	44
Comparing the Senses	44
Motor Capabilities	47
Hands and Arms	47
Locomotion	51
Speech Production	52
Eye Movement	53
Facial Movement and Expressions	54
Sensory Interactions	54
Implications for Virtual Environments	55
Sensory Adaptation	55
Implications for Virtual Environments	56
Cognitive Capabilities and Issues	56
Implications for Virtual Environments	57
Affect	57
Implications for Virtual Environments	58
Recommended Display and Control Performance	59
Questions	59

Chapter 3. Requirements for VE Applications   63

Sociability and Connectivity	64
Veridicality	64
Immersion, Engagement, and Presence	65
Quantifying Immersion	67
Mixed Immersion Systems	67
Resolution	68
Reconfigurability	68
Responsiveness	69
Stability	69
Robustness	70
Viewpoint	70
Virtual Egocenter	70
Viewpoints: Egocentric vs. God's Eye	70
Representation of the User	71

Degree of Virtuality and Integration in a Real Environment	72
Registration	73
Input/Output Bandwidth	73
Multisensory Requirements	74
Interactivity	74
Navigation Techniques	74
Physics of the Virtual Environment	76
Autonomy	77
Locus of Control	77
Choice of Representation	78
Calibration and Customization	79
Safety, Health, and Hygiene	80
Cybersickness	80
Visual Impairment	81
Auditory Damage	82
Disease Transmission	82
Awareness of the Environment	82
Burns, Shocks, and Skin Irritation	83
Injury from Motion Displays	83
Other Common Requirements	84
Cost	84
Size and Weight	84
Application-Specific Requirements	92
Questions	93

Part 2 Designing the System

Chapter 4. Input Technologies — 97

Position Tracking	98
The Role of Position Tracking	99
Active vs. Passive Systems	100
Inside-Out vs. Outside-In Configuration	100
Technologies	100
Issues and Requirements	104
Evaluation	106
Instrumented Gloves and Suits	106
Technologies	109
Issues	110
Evaluation	110
Locomotive Input	111
VACTORs	113
Technologies	113
Issues	114
Evaluation	114
Eye Tracking	114
Technologies	115
Issues	115
Evaluation	116
Biosignal Processing	117
Technologies	117
Issues	117

       Evaluation   118
    Haptic Devices   118
       Technologies   118
       Issues   119
       Evaluation   119
    Gesture Recognition and Predictive Tracking Software   119
       Gesture Recognition   119
       Predictive Tracking and Filtering of Tracker Data   120
    Speech Recognition   121
       The Role of Speech   122
       Speech-Recognition Approaches and Challenges   122
       Issues   124
       Evaluation   124
    Integrating Input Technologies   125
    Questions   125

Chapter 5. Output Technologies   127

    Visual Displays   127
       Image Generation   128
       Image Sources   131
       Optical Systems   134
       Issues and Requirements   140
       Evaluation   142
    Acoustic Displays   142
       Audio Sources   143
       Synthesis of Auditory Localization Cues   146
       Auditory Presentation Technologies   148
       Super-Localization   149
    Force and Tactile Feedback   149
       Tactile Display Technologies   151
       Force Display Technologies   153
       Temperature   154
    Olfactory Display   154
    Locomotive Displays   155
    Inertial Displays   155
    Questions   156

Chapter 6. Computational and Supporting Technologies   157

    System Architecture   158
       Real-Time Requirements and Minimizing Latency   162
       Single-Processor vs. Multiprocessor Systems   164
    Hardware Requirements   164
       Processing and Memory   164
       Cost, Size, and Durability   165
    Software Requirements   165
       The Operating System   166
       Interrupt-Driven vs. Polled Systems   167
       Virtual World Database   168
       Programmer Interface and Toolkits   169
       Device Drivers   170
       Simulation   170
       Modeling   171
       Cross-Platform Compatibility   171

Networking	172
Expert System Components	173
Questions	173

Chapter 7. Objects, Behaviors, and Interactions — 175

Objects	175
Behaviors	176
Interactions	177
Movement	177
Selection	179
Manipulation	179
Scaling	179
Virtual Widget and Menu Interaction	180
Modification of Object and World Properties	180
Object Creation	180
Questions	180

Chapter 8. Design Trade-Offs — 181

General-Purpose vs. Special-Purpose VE Systems	181
Degree of Encumbrance and Choice of "Flavors"	181
Degree of Customizability for the Individual User	182
Responsiveness vs. Image Quality vs. World Complexity	182
Sharing Resources vs. Bandwidth	183
Optimization vs. Cross-Platform Compatibility	183
Specific Technologies	183
HMD Trade-Offs	184
Tracker Trade-Offs	184
Acoustic Display Trade-Offs	185
Physical vs. Virtual Devices	186
Questions	186

Part 3 Evaluating the System

Chapter 9. System Performance — 189

Total Latency	189
Display Update Rate	191
Synchronizing Spatial and Temporal Cues	191
Robustness and Fault Tolerance	192
Registration	192
Working Volume	193
Questions	193

Chapter 10. Usability — 195

Evaluation Processes	195
Videotape Analysis	199
Automatic Data Collection	199
Think-Aloud Protocol	199
Likert-Like Questionnaires	200
Open-Ended Interviews	201

xii   Contents

        Physiological Monitoring   201
        Alternatives to Usability Studies   201
    Factors to Measure   202
        Task Completion   202
        Errors   203
        Task Completion Time   204
        Learning   204
        Workload   204
        Novice vs. Expert Behavior   206
        Subjective Impressions   206
        Cybersickness   206
        Other Physiological After-Effects   207
    Questions   207

Chapter 11. Value for Task and Application   209

    Online Performance   210
    Offline Training and Rehearsal   210
    Online Comprehension   210
    Offline Learning and Knowledge Acquisition   211
    Online Design   211
    Entertainment   211
    Communication   211
    Tools for Researching Human Perceptual-Motor Capabilities   212
    Questions   212

Chapter 12. Using the Results of the Evaluation   213

    System Performance   213
    Usability   214
    Value for the Task and Application   215
    Questions   216

Chapter 13. Conclusion   217

    The Design Process   217
    The Design Team   217
    Tools and Implementation Technology   218
    Future Research and Development   219

Appendix   221
Glossary   235
Bibliography   251
Author Index   261
Subject Index   267
About the Author   275

Acknowledgments

I would like to thank the people who provided help and support in a variety of ways. First of all, my position at NYNEX Science & Technology, where I currently lead the Virtual Reality Project, has permitted me to work in the areas of virtual environments and other human-computer interface technologies for the past several years. I want to thank NYNEX and all those at Science & Technology for their support. I also want to single out two people whose support has been especially crucial. I'd like to thank my technical director, Debbie Lawrence, for her support of this work, and for all I've learned from her about usability testing. And I especially want to thank my laboratory director, John Thomas, who has been more instrumental than anyone else in my working in this field, and has provided continued support for my efforts, as well as collaboration on papers and many creative ideas.

The genesis of this book was a thesis I wrote in the course of earning a degree from the Department of Computer Science and Information Systems at Pace University, and I want to thank the faculty at Pace. Two people there were especially helpful: Dr. Susan Merritt, Dean of the Department of Computer Science and Information Systems at Pace, who was my thesis advisor and who gave me nine months' worth of valued feedback on it; and Dr. Allen Stix, whose discussions with me led to the original idea for the thesis, and whose excellent classes (as well as support and encouragement) were invaluable. Thanks also to Dr. Narayan Murthy, Chairman of the Department of Computer Science and a member of my thesis committee. A useful forum for exchanging ideas was provided by a year-long seminar on virtual environments at Pace. My thanks to the members of this group, which included Ron Frank and Dr. Frank Lo Sacco of the Pace faculty, and a fellow graduate student, John Crawbuck.

Colleagues at other laboratories and universities have provided many of the ideas and much of the work on which this book is built. Of course, there are too many to list here and a partial list risks offending those who aren't included. But I would especially like to single-out Steve Ellis, Tom Piantanida, Beth Wenzel, Steve Feiner, Myron Krueger, and Rick Satava. Each gave me ideas, information, or help that made a real difference at various points in my career. Thanks also to Keith Fredericks, Steve Bryson, David Meyer, Leonard Trejo, John Thomas, Arden Strasser, Ron Azuma, John Martin, and David Burgess, who gave me feedback on specific book-related questions.

Finally, I want to thank the people involved in the publication of this book as a finished work: Carl Machover and the staff at McGraw-Hill, especially Jennifer Holt DiGiovanna and Stacey Spurlock. And my wife, Elizabeth H. H. Stuart, for her warm support and graceful good humor.

Preface

When I became interested in virtual environments, the readily available references on the subject were few and far between. There was one book on the subject, Myron Krueger's original *Artificial Reality*, and the pertinent research papers were scattered among journals and conference proceedings from a variety of disciplines. I began to search for these papers in proceedings from conferences such as ACM's SIGCHI and SIGGRAPH, the annual conferences of SPIE, the Acoustical Society of America, and the Human Factors Society, and appreciated the occasional attempt at an overview, such as James Foley's October 1987 *Scientific American* article (Foley 1987). But there was little available to bring the relevant knowledge together, let alone to assist me in actually designing or building a virtual environment (VE) system.

I missed the first conference devoted to the field, Human Machine Interfaces for Teleoperators and Virtual Environments, sponsored by NASA Ames Research Center, ONR, and IBM and held in Santa Barbara, California in March 1990. (An earlier 1987 conference on Spatial Displays and Spatial Instruments, also associated with NASA Ames, might also vie for the title of "first" conference in the field, though it had a heavy emphasis on visual displays, where the 1990 conference dealt with the full range of sensory modalities.)

I did participate in the First Conference on Cyberspace, held two months later in June 1990 at the University of Texas at Austin and sponsored by the university's School of Architecture and Department of Computer Sciences. It featured a remarkably diverse group of people—perhaps the most diverse group I have ever been a part of at *any* conference—and, while many interesting ideas were exchanged, people came from such different backgrounds that, at times, they seemed to be speaking different languages and simply failing to communicate with each other. Moreover, with the interesting ideas and philosophies presented, there was little that was sufficiently concrete to prove useful in actually designing a system (although, in fairness, this was not the goal of the conference).

The attention to virtual environments in conferences devoted to fields such as computer-human interaction, computer graphics, and acoustics and the number of conferences devoted exclusively to virtual environments both grew rapidly in the early 1990s (I chaired three of the Virtual Reality Systems conferences myself in

New York City). With a sudden rush of attention in the popular media, the attention to the field grew perhaps even more rapidly than did its technical evolution, but there was noteworthy progress to report. And with the publication of *Presence: Teleoperators and Virtual Environments* by The MIT Press, the field had a quality technical journal of its own.

Meanwhile, starting with a journalist's first-person account of the field for the public (nontechnical) audience (Rheingold 1991) and a book created from papers presented at the previously mentioned 1987 conference on Spatial Displays and Spatial Instruments and edited by Stephen R. Ellis, head of the Spatial Perception and Advanced Displays Lab at NASA Ames (Ellis, 1991), the number of books devoted to virtual environments began to grow.

In spite of the rapid proliferation of conferences and books devoted to virtual environments, I still felt there was a gap when it came to sources for designing a virtual environment system or application (I'll elaborate on this application vs. system distinction in a moment). As leader of a project in this area at NYNEX Science & Technology, Inc., I noticed this gap as it related to our own VE design decisions and, when I would give tutorials or participate in seminars, I found the same need expressed by others. This book is my attempt to address this need; the field is a relatively young one, and there are still many unanswered questions, but this book is intended to provide you with the information and the help that's available in designing a virtual environment system, given our present knowledge.

Note that, in many places, I speak about designing a virtual environment *system* and *application* almost interchangeably. This is certainly not how most people are accustomed to thinking if they've been designing conventional computer applications. For conventional applications, the designer is often presented with a very clearly defined system—for example, a certain kind of UNIX workstation with keyboard and mouse running a specified operating system, windowing system, etc.—and given the task of designing an application (such as a statistical package, text editor, spreadsheet program, or mail reader) that will run on this system and can be used to accomplish certain specified tasks. In such a case, the designer doesn't have to pay any attention to system-level choices such as the choice of input devices, displays, or operating system.

In building a virtual environment application, the situation is quite different. There isn't a single standard system (or even a few standard systems) for which applications are built. Although a few vendors are creating software packages for VE that can be ported between certain machines, there's still little cross-platform compatibility. So if you realize you've chosen your hardware and platform poorly after you write software, you'll have to rewrite your software to work with different hardware. And it isn't at all clear whether a limited number of common systems that suffice for all applications will emerge in the near future. Therefore, in designing an application using virtual environments, the designer is by necessity also designing (or at the least selecting) a system.

A personal challenge for me in writing a book about such a rapidly evolving field was to do so in such a way that it wouldn't quickly become out of date. I recall, for example, getting one of the best early books on virtual environments (Kalawsky 1993) and feeling bad for its author because, by the time of its publication, much of the device-specific discussion throughout the book was about an earlier generation of equipment that was no longer current. Although future readers might be amused by the primitive states of some of these 1995 technologies, I thought it more useful to communicate issues and principles that will remain salient rather than describe soon-to-be historical artifacts.

In attempting to meet this challenge, I've followed two strategies. First, throughout the book I generally discuss technologies, principles, and requirements, not specific products. Second, although I provide an appendix that offers some information on specific vendors and products that was current at the time of publication, I am offering a more extensive current collection of information on vendors and products. I'm also offering a very extensive and periodically updated bibliography (which would have filled more than half of this book if included in its entirety) and current contact information for virtual environment researchers and developers.

If you're interested in this bibliography of VE literature, contact information for VE researchers and developers, and information about commercially available VE technologies and who manufacturers them (as well as when they were last updated, prices, and available formats), send me a self-addressed, stamped envelope marked "list of available VE updated" at the following address:

Rory Stuart
P.O. Box 391
Pomono, NY 10970-0391
USA

Please also send any comments, corrections, requests, or suggestions to this address as well.

Introduction

Why design virtual environments (VEs) and why read a book that discusses their design? If you're reading this book, you should have in mind the goal of designing a system that will permit its user(s) to solve a problem or accomplish a task more effectively than would be possible without the system. Without this goal, design is probably not the issue on which you should focus. For example, if you simply want to put together a system to demonstrate virtual reality (VR), you should get a commercially available system that comes with demos, or build a simple low-end system using one of the available books on "garage VR" as your guide. However, if you want to create a system that will permit its users to solve a problem or perform a task more effectively than would be possible through other means, then the *design* of the system and the VE it produces is crucial, and you have a challenging task ahead of you. The design of virtual environments (VEs) and the systems that generate them call upon knowledge from a wide variety of disciplines, including (but not limited to) mechanical, electrical, optical, and acoustical engineering, human factors, perceptual psychology, and computer science. This book presents an approach to use in this design process, and will provide you with much of the information you'll need from the many relevant disciplines (with pointers to sources for further information, which you might need in some cases).

In this introduction I'll lay the groundwork for the rest of the book, discussing what VEs are, and I'll provide a description of the "flavors" of VE systems, the applications for which they can be used, a brief summary of the field's history, an introduction to the iterative design process and explanation of why it's recommended, and an outline of the book's content as well as suggestions for its use. If your background in these areas is strong, you might want to skim it; if, on the other hand, you're completely unfamiliar with any of these areas, you'll want to use the other sources referenced in the book to strengthen your knowledge and review more than this book can provide.

What Are Virtual Environments?

What are virtual environments? There are a great many definitions offered by different researchers. In spite of this, nearly everyone agrees that certain current systems provide virtual environments; the contention is whether other systems, which share some features (and differ in others), should be included within the definition. Another point of contention is in terminology; in general, the popular press uses the term *virtual reality*, while the scientific community, in part to distance itself from the press and in part because a virtual environment doesn't necessarily try to replicate reality, prefers *virtual environments*. While you should be aware that the definition I give is mine rather than one held in common by everyone in the field, this definition will include the salient points of most other definitions.

An *environment* is that which surrounds you, the set of conditions and objects you can perceive and with which you can interact. A *virtual environment* is an interactive computer-generated environment provided by a VE system. (For the sake of consistency, the system that produces a VE should probably be termed a *VE system*, so I'll use this term rather than *VR system* in spite of my nostalgic attachment to the latter term, having been editor-in-chief of one of the early quarterly publications on virtual environments, *Virtual Reality Systems*. When I use *VR* in place of *VE*, it's for a specific reason. For example, *fishtank VR* is the term of choice in the field rather than *fishtank VE*.) An example of the basic architecture for a virtual environment system is shown in Figure I.1.

There are a range of human-computer interfaces that are VE systems. In the most strict sense, a *VE system* is a human-computer interface that provides "interactive immersive multisensory 3-D synthetic environments" (Stuart 1993); it uses position-tracking and real-time update of visual, auditory, and other displays (e.g., tactile) in response to the user's motions to give the user a sense of being "in" the environment, and it could be either a single- or a multiuser system.

Let's examine this definition. By interactive, I mean that the interaction between user and system is guided by the user's input; the level of interactivity in a virtual environment typically permits practically unlimited variation in what occurs in a session between user and system. For example, one typical form of input is movement of the user's head, which is tracked for changes in position and orientation and in turn produces changes in all relevant display modalities in response to this movement. The *practically unlimited variation* that's possible in this case is that user can move his head in any direction at any time (as frequently or infrequently as desired) and the display will respond appropriately.

Please note that, in this type of interactivity and real-time display update, a VE is quite different from what is commonly referred to as a *multimedia system*. Multimedia systems typically have a body of hyperlinked prerecorded and digitized video, audio, text, and graphics, and the user can choose which link (and hence which prerecorded materials) to access next. But there are only fixed choices a user can make, e.g., a scene can be viewed only from certain prerecorded angles.

By *immersive*, I mean that rather than looking at and listening to a display coming from a typical small computer monitor, the display creates the impression that you're inside the environment produced by the computer. Not everyone agrees on the meaning of *immersion*; in a later section, I define it as "the presentation of sensory cues that convey perceptually to users that they're surrounded by the computer-generated environment," and distinguish *immersion* from *engagement* and *presence*.

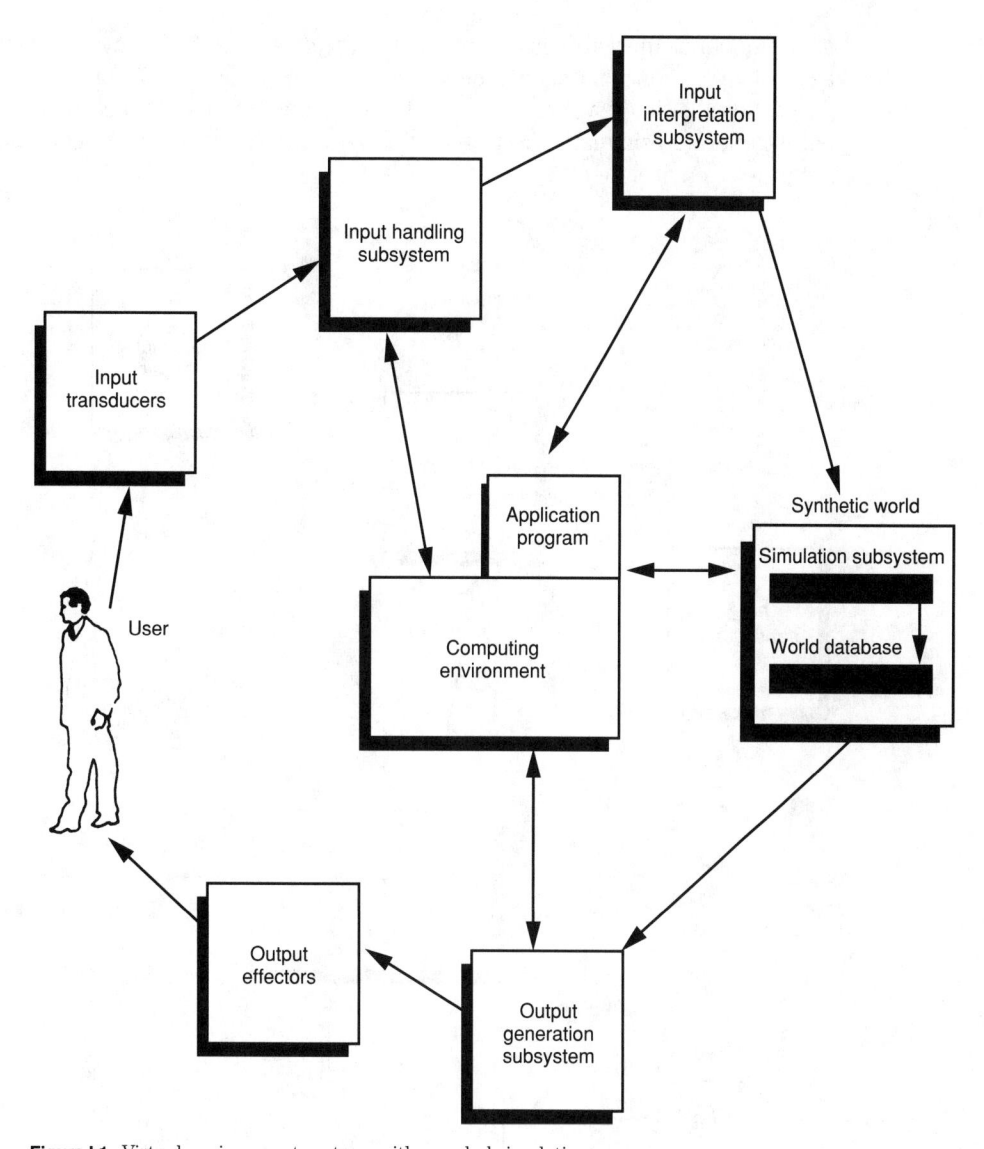

Figure I.1 Virtual environment system, with coupled simulation.

By *multisensory*, I mean that more than one sensory modality is used to display the environment: visual, auditory, haptic, etc.

By *3-D*, I mean that not only does the environment appear to the user to surround him, but cues are also given to convey that it has depth and the user can move through it.

By *synthetic*, I mean that the environment is generated by a computer system (it isn't, for example, prerecorded). A teleoperation system isn't truly synthetic, because multisensory information presented to the user is in fact transduced by a remote robot that mimics the user's motions. Because the human-computer interface of a teleoperation system is essentially identical to that of a VE system (see Figure I.2), teleoperation systems will be included in our discussion, though the engineering of the robot itself won't. Note also that a teleoperation system can integrate computer-generated simulation to transduced data and thus integrate teleoperation with a synthetic environment.

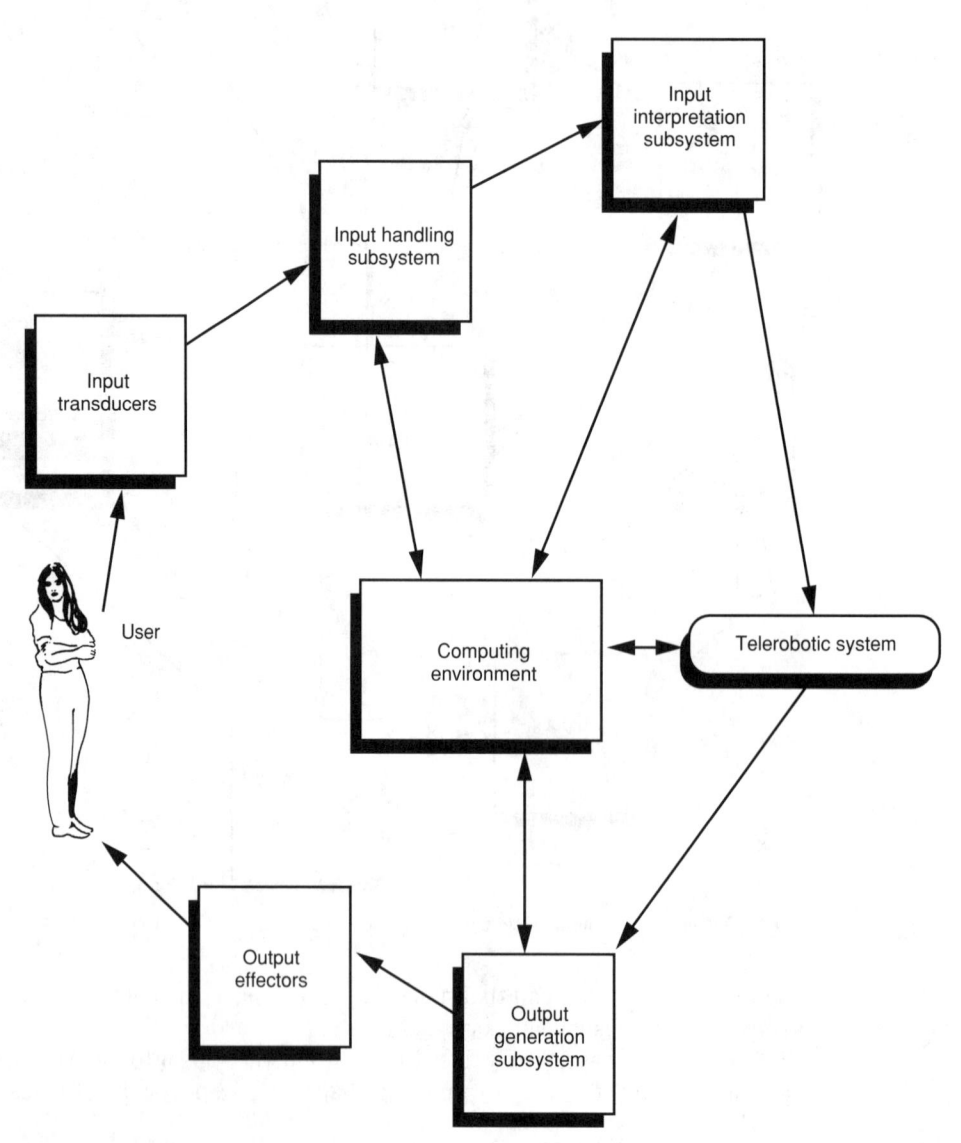

Figure I.2 Teleoperation system.

For another definition that captures some of the crucial elements from a different perspective, Wickens and Baker (1995) define VR as incorporating five features:

- Three-dimensional (perspective and/or stereoscopic) viewing.
- Dynamic display (rather than static images).
- Closed loop (interactive or learner-centered design, where the user is the active navigator as well as the observer).
- Inside-out (ego-referenced) frame of reference. The image of the virtual environment displayed is from the point of view of the user's head as it's positioned in the world.
- Multimodal interaction (via several input techniques and feedback through several sensory modalities).

In this book, I'll also consider interactive systems that have most, but not all, of the properties described in these definitions. Examples of these are systems described as *artificial reality*, *augmented reality*, *fishtank VR*, as well as *teleoperation*. These examples are, however, less immersive (fishtank and artificial reality systems), or the environments presented aren't synthetic (telepresence) or are less synthetic (augmented reality). Figure I.3 shows some of the VE systems that have been created so far.

Standard immersive VE systems using HMDs and BOOMs are shown; both of these block out the surrounding world and present stimuli to the user in response to position and orientation of the user's head—or, in the case of a binocular omni-oriented monitor (BOOM), the position and orientation in which the BOOM is held.

Augmented reality systems superimpose sensory stimuli that are integrated with the surrounding world. Artificial reality systems project the user's image onto a screen and let the unencumbered participant interact with objects in the synthetic world through the actions of the projected image, with respect to the screen objects.

Vehicular simulators provide physical cockpits (often on motion platforms) with images projected on the cockpit's screens, and these images and the motion of the cockpit respond appropriately to the user's manipulation of the cockpit controls.

Fishtank VR systems display head-coupled images on a conventional monitor, and stereoscopy is provided by synchronizing the shuttering of glasses worn by the user with alternate rapid display of left- and right-eye images on the monitor.

CAVE systems surround the user in a room whose walls are projection screens, but in other ways they behave like a fishtank system, i.e., they're coupled to the user's position and orientation and synchronized to shuttered glasses to provide stereoscopy.

Finally, teleoperation systems have human-computer interfaces like those of immersive HMD-based virtual environments, but the user interacts with the real world, as transduced and manipulated by an anthropomorphic robot, rather than a synthetic world.

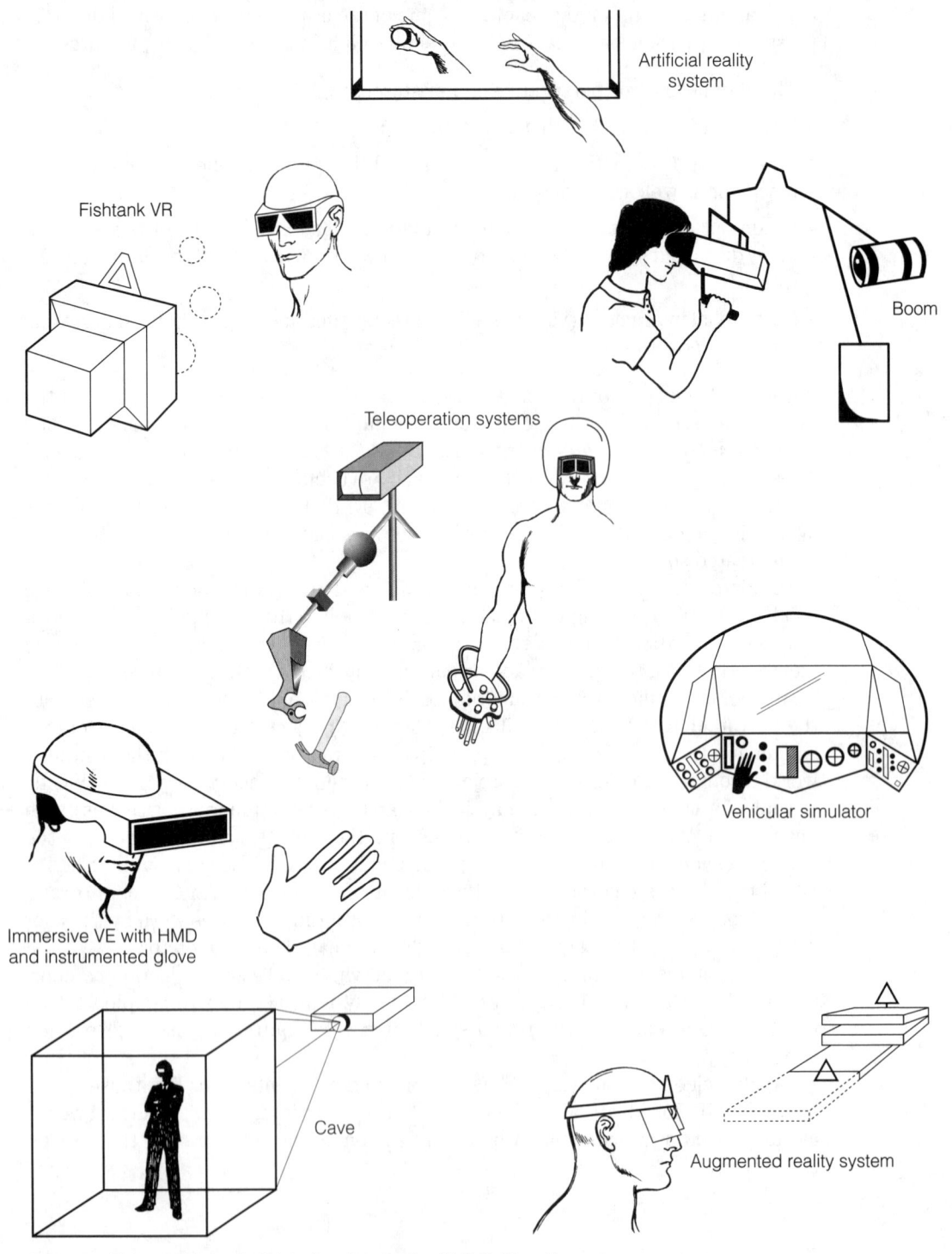

Figure I.3 Types or "flavors" of virtual environments. *(E.H.H. Stuart)*

Applications of Virtual Environments

If you want to design a VE system that permits its users to solve problems or accomplish tasks more effectively than would otherwise be possible, an obvious question to address is: "What are the problems or tasks to which VEs can be applied?" Although this is a young field and new applications continue to be found, the categories of applications discussed in this book should provide you with a framework. Briefly, they're as follows:

Online performance. The VE is used to accomplish tasks in the real (nonsynthetic) world, e.g., via teleoperation.

Offline training and rehearsal. The VE allows you to practice tasks that will later be performed in the real world.

Online comprehension. The user understands or gains insight into the VE while interacting with it.

Offline learning and knowledge acquisition. The user acquires knowledge and experience using the VE that can later be synthesized into more abstract knowledge.

Online design. An individual or collaborative group uses the VE to design objects or environments.

Entertainment. The VE is used solely for the enjoyment it brings the user.

Communication. The VE allows users to share ideas or otherwise communicate.

Tools for research of human perceptual-motor capabilities. The VE is used to isolate and study human performance characteristics.

These categories (expanded from Wickens and Baker 1995, which names the first four) are not without occasional overlap, but they should help you think about the range of possible applications. Examples of each will be given later in the book.

A Brief History of Virtual Environments

Although the goal of this book is to help you design virtual environments rather than to give you a history of the field, a few historical notes will help if you aren't already familiar with the material. You'll want to have some historical perspective on your chosen field, and this section will point you to additional sources.

Several people and groups have been key in the development of virtual reality concepts and technology. Because of its multidisciplinary quality, some of the technologies required for virtual environment were developed by people who didn't have VE systems in mind. And much of the knowledge of human perceptual processes comes from work by perceptual psychologists before computing technology was advanced enough to make implementing VEs a possibility.

One important precursor to virtual environments was early vehicular simulators, particularly flight simulators such as those produced by the Link corporation and used since the 1930s. These early simulators were fully functional instrument panels mounted on plywood boxes that were in turn attached to gimballed motion platforms. The user would sit in the box and could steer the simulator using the controls on the instrument panels; the motion platform would pitch, yaw, and roll in response to this input.

These early simulators draped a hood over the user to block out sensory input from the surrounding world, but they had no auditory or visual display and permitted the user to fly only by instrument. In spite of this, they were found to be of value in training pilots. Pimentel and Teixeira (1993) describe the evolution of flight simulators in the 1950s: video cameras on moving platforms were suspended over scale models of airports, and their motion controlled by the actions of the pilot trainees and the video images displayed to the pilot as a maneuver was practiced. (As they point out, the scale models became more complex and detailed, and this technique is still used for some Hollywood movie special effects.)

The principles of flight simulators were also applied to other vehicular simulators for submarine, air traffic control, air defense, tanks and other surface vehicles (National Research Council 1995). Ivan Sutherland realized that, in place of servo-controlled video cameras and physical models, computer-generated images could be used for flight simulators, and, with David Evans, formed a company named Evans and Sutherland in the late 1960s to manufacture systems to produce interactive computer graphics engines for simulators. By the early 1970s, the military was using flight simulators with computer-generated graphics to train its pilots.

Meanwhile, teleoperation, which was not dependent on computer graphics or digital signal processing performance, has been used since the late 1940s in the first nuclear laboratory experiments and soon after at other remote hazardous sites such as the deep ocean (Durlach and Sheridan 1990).

Another precursor to virtual environments was the Sensorama Simulator, developed by Morton Heilig in the late 1950s and early 1960s. It offered the user a richly multisensory 3-D experience, including a wide field-of-view stereoscopic display with images from adjacent cameras, stereo sound, odors, limited motion (the user's seat vibrating), and wind. In its use of these many sensory modalities, Heilig's entertainment-oriented invention was ahead of its time. It wasn't, however, truly a VE system because it lacked interactivity. The user could, for example, experience a ride through Brooklyn on the back of a motorcycle, but, since the visual and auditory material presented was prerecorded rather than synthesized (computer-generated), the user could only go along for the ride rather than steer through arbitrary paths, look in different directions, and so forth. Heilig also patented an early head-mounted display (HMD), but never succeeded commercially or got the corporate support that would have allowed further evolution of his inventions.

Several people have been called the "father" of virtual environments (Tom Piantanida of SRI quips that he would like to be known as the "godfather" of VE). If any single person deserves this distinction, however, it's Ivan Sutherland. In the mid-1960s, Sutherland made the first system that combined position tracking, a stereo HMD, and a graphics engine that synthesized and displayed to the user a virtual environment, albeit a simple VE (see Sutherland 1968). Sutherland, also noted for his creations in the areas of computer graphics algorithms and custom-made high-performance graphics hardware, had a vision of virtual environments, described in his classic paper on "the ultimate display" (Sutherland 1965), that still hasn't been fully realized 30 years later. Besides his vision, Sutherland created some of the first implementations, including tracking systems using a couple of different technologies and a see-through HMD.

Shortly after Sutherland's innovations and classic publications, Myron Krueger began work at the University of Wisconsin on unencumbered interactive systems that used video to capture the silhouettes of users, process these images, and, via edge detections, let the users interact with a virtual world projected on a large screen (by, for example, "touching" a graphical object). His primary focus was on creating responsive art forms, with emphasis on the way the participants interacted with the system. He called this technology *artificial reality* and, though he intended this term to encompass position-tracked HMD systems such as Sutherland's as well as his own unencumbered systems, the term is now commonly used to describe the Krueger-type system.

Artificial reality systems don't provide stereoscopic viewing, nor do they provide an egocentric viewpoint (*inside-out* in Wickens and Baker's terminology), but they do have their advantages: they don't require any encumbering equipment to be worn, they allow the user's entire body to interact with the virtual world, and they can provide a large working volume. Also, Krueger designed and implemented fairly complex behavioral properties for VE objects before this was done in other systems. For example, his Critter, a graphical creature that responds to users in a variety of ways, was created using conceptual dependency notation, which was created by Roger Shank of Yale University. Conceptual dependency notation is normally used in natural language systems rather than to control Critters; there are 150 states in which a Critter can be. Krueger's various interactive systems spanned more than 20 years and are well described in his book (Krueger, 1991).

Another luminary of VEs who has had great historical impact is Fred Brooks, known also for his book *The Mythical Man-Month* and for his prior work at IBM designing the operating system for the IBM 360 computer series. At the University of North Carolina at Chapel Hill, Fred Brooks and his group have been leaders in the development of multisensory virtual environments that incorporate force displays. Since 1967, Brooks and his colleagues have created a series of Grope systems (Brooks 1988; Brooks, Ouh-Young, Batter, and Kilpatrick 1990) that permit the user to manipulate chemical structures and feel the resulting molecular attractive and repulsive forces using large remote manipulator arms (e.g., the Argonne E-3 remote manipulator). Brooks and his colleagues also developed very high-end graphics engines (the Pixel-Planes series) and have done innovative work on applications such as architectural walk-throughs (Brooks, Airey, Alspaugh, et al. 1992) and visualization for planning radiation therapy. Brooks continues to be a leader in the field, and one of the UNC projects getting a lot of recent attention is the use of VE technology to control a scanning tunnelling microscope (Taylor, Robinett, Chi, Brooks, Wright, Williams, and Snyder 1993).

Tom Furness did early work at Wright-Patterson Air Force Base on an HMD-based system for use by Air Force pilots, known as VCASS (visually coupled airborne systems simulator). Because much of this work was classified, it is less well documented in scientific books and journals than the other historic work described previously (Furness 1986). VE research continues at Wright-Patterson at present, but Furness went on to the University of Washington at Seattle to found and lead the Human Interface Technology Laboratory (HIT Lab), where a group of faculty and students work on VE technology.

The blossoming of work on VE that occurred in the late 1980s was ignited by the mid-80s work at NASA Ames by a group that began with Steve Ellis, his student Michael McGreevy, and Scott Fisher, and grew to include Warren Robinett, Elizabeth Wenzel, and others. McGreevy and Fisher managed to construct a very low-cost HMD using inexpensive parts that could be obtained at a consumer electronics store. Soon, with help from others who joined the group, they managed to create an integrated system (the VIEW, or Virtual Interface Environment Workstation system), which incorporated a position-tracked HMD, a position-tracked instrumented glove that permitted the user to interact with the VE via a graphical image of his hand, a speech recognition system for input, a virtual acoustic display, and the simulation and computational engine required to support all these features (Fisher, Wenzel, Coler, and McGreevy 1988). VE (or *virtual reality*, as coined by Jaron Lanier) began to get more widespread attention and, starting with California-based VPL Research (led by Jaron Lanier), companies were started to commercialize VE technology.

The historical figures mentioned previously were leaders in conceptualizing and implementing early integrated VE systems, but others deserve credit for development of some of the specific interface technologies. Although Ivan Sutherland is thought by many to have produced the first visually coupled HMD, a few HMDs preceded Sutherland's, though they were used to display images from cameras whose direction was controlled by the user's head movement (tracked magnetically) rather than the computer-generated graphics in Sutherland's system. One such system, created by Comeau and Bryan in the early 1960s for Philco Corporation, is described by Kalawsky (1993). Indeed, Ellis (1991) points out that Eric Howlett's LEEP optics system, used commonly in HMDs for VE systems, was first created for a stereoscopic camera system.

Instrumented gloves and suits can be thought of in terms of sensing the bend in joints, tracking the position and orientation of the hand or body, representing these in a virtual environment, and either recognizing gestures or using these hand and body representations to directly manipulate objects in the VE. Sturman and Zeltzer (1994) point to master-slave manipulator arms developed shortly after World War II as an early use of tracked hand motion as input, and MIT's Put That There project of the 1970s as an early example of hand gestures being interpreted as a control device (in that case to indicate graphical objects on a screen and, in combination with speech recognition, move or query those objects). Put That There used a magnetic tracker (made by Polhemus), but didn't use bend sensors.

Early glove systems, such as the Sayre glove developed by Thomas DeFanti and Daniel Sandin at the University of Illinois at Chicago and based on an idea by Rich Sayre, measured finger bending (using flexible tubes along each finger, with light sources at one end and photocells at the other), but didn't measure position and orientation and didn't interpret gestures made with the instrumented glove (it was used as a control device, e.g., to simulate slider functionality). After a couple of other instrumented gloves were prototyped in the early 1980s (a camera-based LED glove at MIT for behavioral animation and a glove for sign language recognition using flex, inertial, and touch sensors by Gary Grimes at Bell Labs), the first commercially produced glove, the DataGlove, was created in 1987 by a team led by Tom Zimmerman (Zimmerman, Lanier, Blanchard, Bryson, and Harvill 1987).

The DataGlove, commercialized by VPL, used fiber optics to measure finger bending, magnetic tracking to measure position and orientation of the hand, a graphical representation of the hand in the VE, and gesture recognition software to permit specific hand gestures to be used for control in the VE (e.g., to "fly" the user forward or backward in virtual space). The DataSuit, also produced by VPL, used similar technology for measuring position and motion of the entire body, but it was an expensive system used by very few, even in the research community. Other instrumented gloves using other technologies to measure finger bending have since been developed and offered commercially. For more on the history of instrumented gloves and the applications for which they've been used, I recommend Sturman and Zeltzer (1994).

There are several early precursors to virtual acoustic displays. The Pseudophone, a mechanical device with two large sound collectors spaced far apart from each other, was used during World War I to attempt to enhance the ability of users to locate enemy aircraft via auditory localization (Durlach 1991). The FLYBAR (Flying by Auditory Reference) system, used since World War II to represent the speed and orientation of planes by panning different tones between the ears of pilots, taught the pilots to fly well and keep a fairly straight course using only an auditory display (Garner 1949). Finally, the Gehring Auditory Localizer, a telepresence approach, used a servo-driven assembly to couple the motion of the user's head to that of a remote anthropomorphic mannequin head with microphones in its ears and a single speaker near it; the user wore headphones and heard the respective sounds captured by the microphones in the mannequin's ears (Calhoun, Valencia, and Furness 1987). The only problem with this system, as Gehring told me, was that occasionally the mannequin's anthropomorphic ears would fall off as a result of all the swinging around on the servo system, and they would have to be replaced!

In part because of their rather intense signal processing demands, virtual acoustic displays have been around for a much shorter time than head-tracked HMDs, and one of the first was created by Scott Foster and Elizabeth Wenzel for the NASA Ames VIEW project (Fisher, Wenzel, Coler, and McGreevy 1988). Using head-related transfer functions (HRTFs) measured by Fred Wightman and Doris Kistler at the University of Wisconsin (Wightman and Kistler placed probe microphones in the ears of subjects in an anechoic chamber and played sounds from different directions to measure HRTFs), Foster and Wenzel were able to synthesize the position-dependent acoustic cues used for auditory localization and, in real time, to respond to the user's position-tracked head movement. The result was a system that let a listener with headphones hear acoustic objects that maintained their apparent positions or trajectories in three-dimensional space regardless of head movement.

Virtual acoustic display systems are now commercially available from Scott Foster's company, Crystal River Engineering, and research systems have been made by others. Refer to Blauert (1983) for an excellent review of auditory localization, and Wenzel (1992) for a review that looks at virtual acoustic display.

Position trackers have a longer history than some of the other technologies of VE, if nonreal-time tracking is included. Meyer, Applewhite, and Biocca (1992) cite the

Plane Survey of the ancient Egyptians (using transits and plumb lines to reestablish boundary markers that annually disappeared when the Nile flooded) as the earliest position tracking, and the use of sextants and compasses by European explorers as another historical use of position tracking.

More recently, position trackers have been used in robotics to facilitate navigation. Sutherland (1968) was the first to use position trackers to control a computer-generated image in real time in response to a user's head movement to create the impression of a VE. Sutherland used mechanical position tracking (a six-degree-of-freedom, or 6-DOF, goniometer) as well as acoustic tracking.

Mechanical tracking has a long history, including use in medical applications and land survey. Magnetic tracking technologies, patented first in the early 1970s by Polhemus, were created with the idea of tracking head position to control visual displays. Optical tracking systems, reportedly discussed in the early 1970s at the University of Utah, weren't implemented successfully until the 1980s and were used, among other things, for biomechanical studies.

I recommend Ellis (1991) as a source for general overview and more information on the history of VE.

The Iterative Design of Virtual Environments

The design philosophy espoused in this book is generally known as *iterative design*. Iterative design has been used in designing many types of human-computer interfaces, and follows principles recommended by John Gould and Clayton Lewis at IBM since the 1970s (Gould and Lewis 1983). So this design methodology is nothing new in the field of computer-human interaction, although there are some special challenges to applying this approach to VEs, which I'll discuss. If you aren't already familiar with iterative design, this section will describe it; be certain you understand it before proceeding with this book. As Gould and Lewis pointed out, the principles seem obvious once they're stated, but this doesn't mean that people are accustomed to following them.

Gould and Lewis begin with the premise that a system designed for people to use must be easy to learn, easy and pleasant to use, and useful. In the case of VEs, let me add to their premise the requirement that the system be safe to use. Gould and Lewis's methodology to achieve these goals requires the following:

- That the designers understand who the users will be, in terms of their attitudes, behaviors, and cognitive and anthropometric characteristics, and in terms of the work they will accomplish using the system.
- That the design team work closely with a group of representative users starting early in the design process.
- That prototypes are created early in the development process and that these prototypes are used to evaluate the design by measuring the performance and reactions of intended users as they try to use the prototypes to carry out their work.
- That the results of this evaluation are used to redesign the system, the problems identified in the evaluation corrected in the redesign, and the redesigned system prototyped and again evaluated. This process is iterative, so the cycle of design, prototype, and evaluate must be repeated until the evaluation shows the design to be a success by all selected criteria.

As mentioned previously, the iterative design methodology might seem obvious, but in many cases it isn't followed. Gould and Lewis found that, although designers mentioned goals (such as making a system easy to use), they fell short in several areas:

- They often didn't have a process to meet the goals they set forth.
- They didn't have sufficient direct and early contact with intended users to adequately understand them or the tasks they would perform with the system, and didn't sufficiently involve them in the design process.
- They demonstrated a prototype to users to sell it, rather than to empirically measure the users carrying out their work with the prototype.
- They didn't use the results of empirical evaluation in redesign.
- They didn't allow sufficient iterations to achieve satisfactory results.

Gould and Lewis found that the iterative design methodology was not used because of the following:

- User diversity was underestimated.
- Designers mistakenly believed that they could adequately figure out how a task should be done through their "power of reason," without involving the intended users.
- Designers correctly realized that users hadn't considered some of the options for doing their jobs more effectively, but didn't convey these options in a way that users could understand and react to.
- Design guidelines, though useful, were mistakenly believed to be sufficient.
- Designers believed that, with respect to the user interface, they were supposed to "get it right the first time," although this rarely proves to be possible, and they tended to "freeze" the user interface too early in the development process.
- Concern that iterative design methodology would lengthen the development process was used as a reason not to apply it. (Gould and Lewis point out alternatives that can reduce this issue; they also note that user testing will happen in any case—if not during the design process, later in the "customer's office" where the cost of design problems are much greater to all involved parties.)
- Iteration was mistakenly believed to be nothing more than an expensive form of fine-tuning when, in fact, it's necessary to ensure that the design process leads to the creation of a useful and usable system.

Why should this iterative design methodology be applied to the design of VE systems, how should it be applied, and what are the special challenges in applying it to virtual environments? Virtual environments are a particularly challenging design problem. Unlike most current human-computer interfaces, there are rather severe design trade-offs, e.g., between responsiveness, world complexity, and the quality of the images and sounds rendered. In the case of responsiveness, the perceptual capabilities of users make for much more demanding requirements than in other systems in order to minimize latency to the point where it isn't an obstacle to usability.

Given the current state of computational power and VE I/O technology, and these severe design trade-offs, Bryson (1994) has noted that the design of virtual environments must be both top-down and bottom-up, since poor design in either direction can make the application a failure. The iterative process permits both top-down design and a feedback cycle that provides many of the advantages of bottom-up design. Bryson also notes that, up until the present, the success of most virtual environment projects have been due to one or two people on the development teams who mastered all levels of the system. Whether you end up functioning as one of these "wizards" or as part of a successful team, the iterative design approach should prove useful.

There are additional special challenges in the design of VEs. Many individual differences that would be irrelevant to other kinds of human-computer interfaces, such as the distance between the user's eyes (interpupillary distance) or the shape of the user's outer ears (pinnae), affect the success of VE systems.

There are more levels of design required for VEs than for most other human-computer interfaces. In the typical human-computer interface, the input and display technologies are already a given, and the designer has to be concerned with content and interaction. For VEs, the "flavor" of system is an issue; the choice of sensory modalities and what information should be displayed through each is an issue; the objects, behaviors, and interactions in the VE must be determined; system architecture must be selected, with repercussions in terms of performance kept in mind; and there are a great many decisions to be made about input technologies (e.g., whether an HMD with wider field of view or higher resolution should be selected) and output technologies (e.g., how speech input and gesture should interact).

Finally, there is a smaller body of experience for VEs than with conventional human-computer interfaces, and hence more uncertainty about some of the design decisions. Thus, even more than with conventional human-computer interfaces, it's a mistake to assume that the designer will get it entirely right on the first try.

The iterative design process, as applied to the design of VEs, is illustrated in Figure I.4. As illustrated in this figure, the designer should begin by defining as clearly as possible the requirements of the system, as well as the user, task, and environment issues mentioned by Gould and Lewis. This includes:

- Defining the human capabilities and performance as pertinent to the system to be designed.
- Defining the users, the tasks they'll perform with the system, and the environment (in several senses of the word, as will be discussed) in which the system will be used.
- Defining various, generally important requirements (some functional, others practical).
- Defining requirements that are specific to the application.

The next step is to attempt to design the system based on the defined requirements; designing or choosing the input, output, and computation technologies; and the system architecture, objects, object behaviors, and interactions in the VE.

Define requirements

- Define human capabilities & performance (see chapter 2)
- Define user/task/environment (see chapter 1)
- Define functional requirements common to virtual environments (see chapter 3)
- Define other common (practical) requirements (see chapter 3)
- Define application-specific requirements (see chapter 3)

Design system

- Design/choose input technologies (see chapter 4)
- Design/choose output technologies (see chapter 5)
- Design/choose computation technologies & architecture (see chapter 6)
- Design objects/behaviors & interactions (see chapter 7)

Prototype system

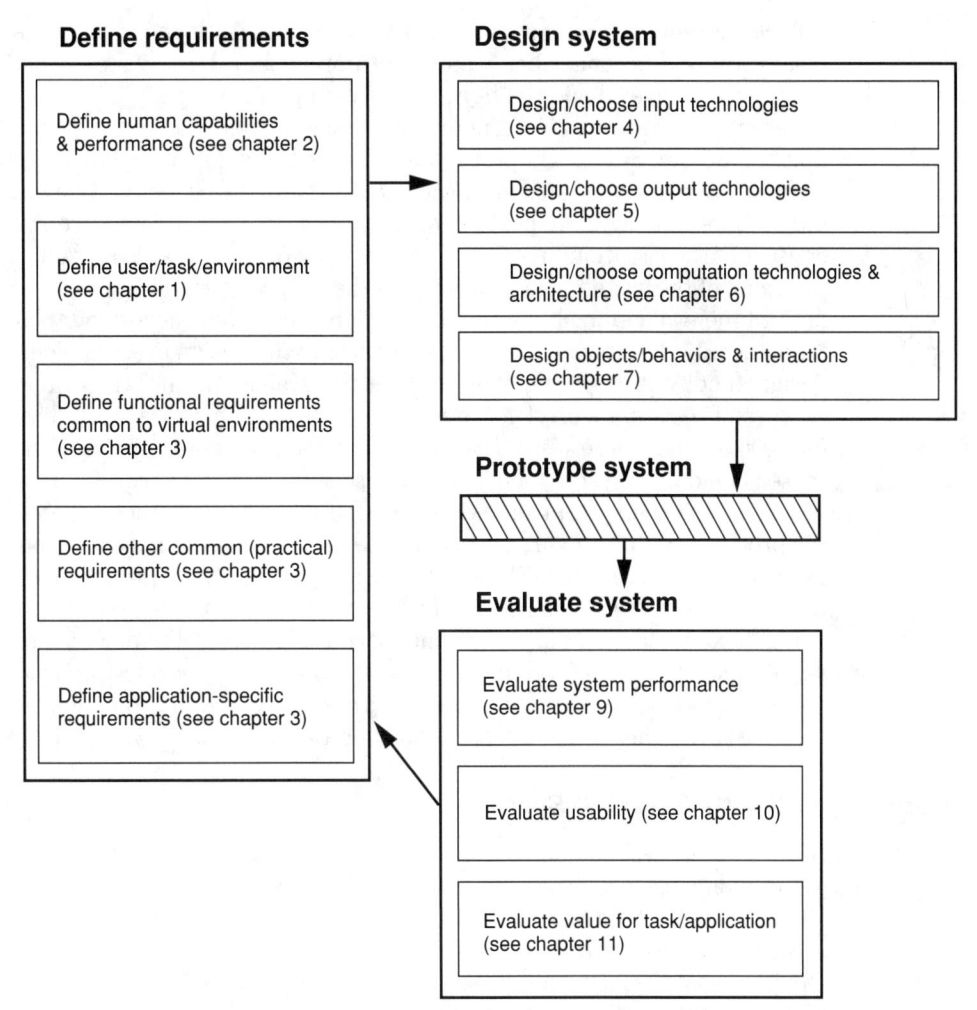

Evaluate system

- Evaluate system performance (see chapter 9)
- Evaluate usability (see chapter 10)
- Evaluate value for task/application (see chapter 11)

Figure I.4 The iterative design process applied to the design of virtual environments.

With this first pass at a design, the system should be prototyped. The details of how to prototype a system are outside the scope of this book; if you choose a particular package, vendors typically provide detailed material for creating prototypes. If you or others you're working with plan to prototype without using an existing package, it's assumed that you already have sufficient programming experience to implement your first-pass design. Choose your hardware platform carefully since, given the current lack of device-independent standards for VEs, you could end up spending a lot of time rewriting your software for a different platform. In terms of the graphics algorithms to be used, refer to the classic *Computer Graphics: Principles and Practice* by Foley, van Dam, Feiner, and Hughes (1990).

Once you've successfully prototyped the system, you'll use the prototype to evaluate the system performance, usability, and value for the target application. In terms of system performance, make sure to distinguish those places where the prototype reflects system performance that will be shared by a deployed application, and those places where differences between the prototype and the way a deployed system is put together have a major influence on system performance.

Very poor performance of the prototype should alert you to the possibility either that the design was poorly prototyped or that the deployed system might actually have similarly unacceptable performance. Evaluate the usability by having representative users actually try to perform tasks with the system; if they can do so within the context of the situation in which they'll actually perform the tasks, you can evaluate the value of the system in accomplishing these tasks.

Until the evaluation shows the design to be acceptable according to all these criteria, feed the results of the evaluation back into the design process. Then iterate the design, modify the prototype, and repeat the evaluation until the evaluation shows successful results. Figure I.4, however, doesn't tell the entire story. The evaluation might show that there were problems in the requirements definition, in which case these should be corrected, but it might also show problems with the system design, in which case the system should be redesigned to address these problems, or that the prototype didn't adequately instantiate the design, in which case prototype problems should be corrected. Thus, not only must you identify problems in the evaluation, but you must also identify and correct their causes.

Don't expect that, by simply reading this book and using the power of reason, you'll successfully design a VE on the first pass. No book could credibly promise that, given the current knowledge and experience with VEs. Instead, use the information in this book to narrow the design space, and the iterative design methodology to "get it right."

Position and Orientation in 3-D Space

Because there will be so much discussion in the book of navigation and interaction in three-dimensional space, this is just a brief introduction to the subject of thinking about and describing 3-D space.

Start by considering a point or solid object in space. It can change its position, moving forward, back, side to side, and up and down. Its position is described in terms of a three-axis coordinate system, where the axes are X, Y, and Z. In addition to changing position, it can change its orientation, or *attitude*. An easy way to think of orientation is in terms of what are known as Euler angles: yaw, pitch, and roll.

Picture the object as an airplane on which you're a passenger (see Figure I.5). Yaw would be movement around a vertical axis; such movement would keep the floor of the plane level, but change the direction in which it was pointing, e.g., from north to east. Pitch would be movement around a lateral axis running from wing tip to wing tip; such movement would make the nose rise or fall with respect to the tail. Roll would be movement along the longitudinal axis running from nose to tail; such movement would make one wing rise or fall with respect to the other. Notice that, if you were seated in a precise spot in the center of the plane, one point, such as the tip of your nose, could be experiencing changes in orientation—yaw, pitch, and/or roll—without changing position at all. (Bryson, 1994, points out that Euler angles are actually concatenated, so that rotations around each axis must be done in the correct order.)

Applying this idea to a human head (which is essentially a solid object), the common way to describe X-Y-Z yaw, pitch, and roll is shown in Figure I.6. In addition to

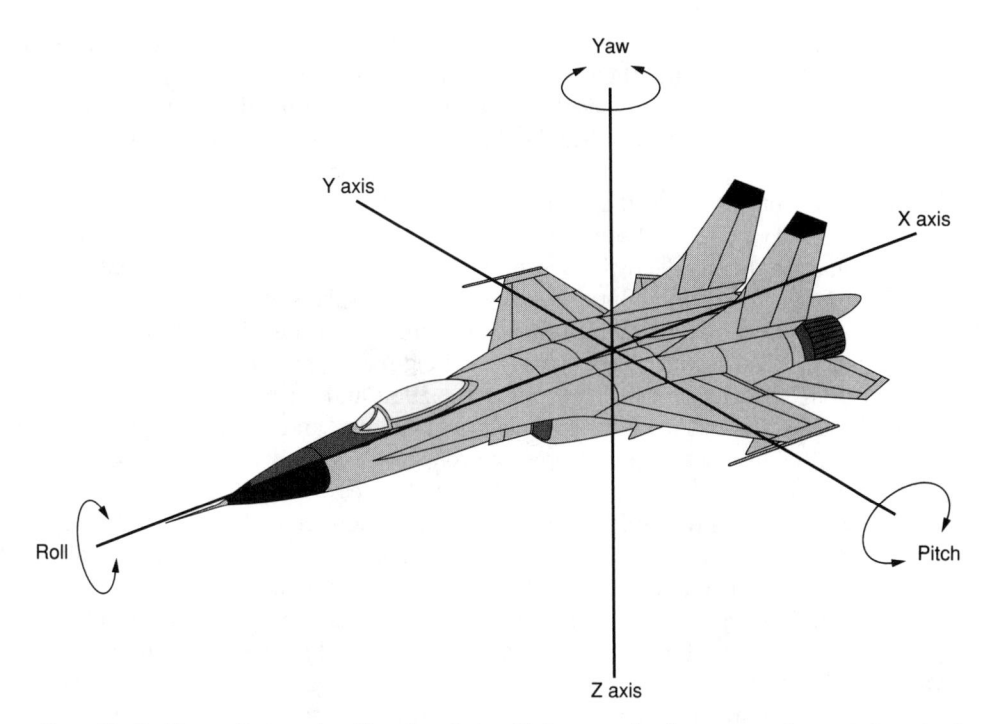

Figure I.5 Position and orientation. Note the relationship between the three axes and yaw, pitch, and roll.

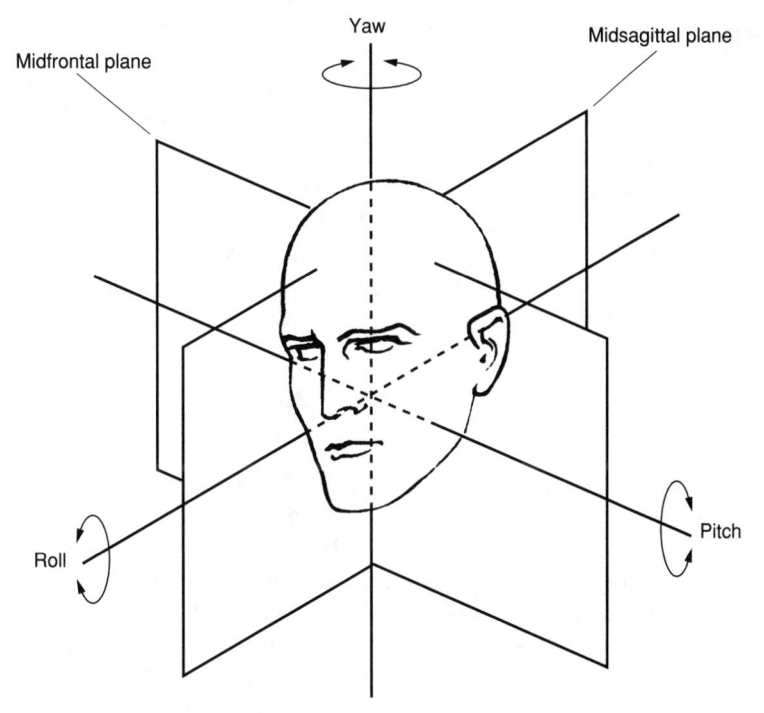

Figure I.6 Position and orientation for a person, showing the midsagittal and midfrontal planes.

the X, Y, and Z axes around which yaw, pitch, and roll can occur, two planes, the midsaggital plane and the midfrontal plane are shown.

In thinking about objects in 3-D space, keep in mind that not all objects are solid. Consider, for example, the human hand: an individual point on the hand, or an individual joint of a finger can be adequately described in terms of X-Y-Z yaw, pitch, and roll, but this isn't sufficient to describe the hand as a whole. The fingers can be thought of as a collection of solid segments that move around joints, so you could describe the hand either explicitly by describing the angle of bend along each joint or by describing the position and orientation of each of these solid segments (from which the joint angles could be derived if necessary). More complicated still is describing the motion of a nonrigid surface, such as the breathing-related motion of the abdomen.

If you can think clearly about position and orientation in terms of X-Y-Z, yaw, pitch, and roll as described, then your understanding of position and orientation is sufficient for the design process. You should also be aware that the terms *azimuth* and *elevation* (used in disciplines such as cartography, astronomy, and surveying) are commonly used to describe the direction from the observer of objects in 3-D space. If an arc is drawn along the horizon, the point where a vertical circle from a point in question intersects this arc is its azimuth, and the vertical distance up from the horizon to the point is its elevation (in astronomy the arc would be measured from the south point, and in navigation it would be measured from the north point). Thus, referring back to Figure I.6, if you're upright and your head orientation changes in terms of yaw, you'll be facing a different point in azimuth. If your head orientation changes in terms of pitch, you'll be facing a different point in elevation.

When it comes to implementation, the details of alternative description systems become crucial. Although I've discussed orientation in 3-D space in terms of Euler angles, there are other ways to describe it, such as via rotation matrices, direction cosines, or quaternions. Bryson (1994) points out, for example, that different position tracking devices offer different formats for describing orientation. Each descriptive technique has its advantages and disadvantages, and you might want to consider gimbal lock, the number of bytes of data required to describe orientation, and the efficiency of calculations, as well as the formats that chosen devices use, in making decisions. But, as a designer, the details of these descriptive formats need not concern you. I mention them only as a "heads up" to readers who are implementors as well as designers; look into these alternative formats if you aren't already familiar with them.

Using This Book

Given the iterative design process and the many challenges in designing a VE system, how should you use this book? First, I recommend that you read the book from cover to cover to become familiar with all of the issues, requirements, and technologies to be considered in the design process, as well as the design trade-offs and the evaluation techniques to be used. After this initial reading, the book can serve as a reference, so if you're working on a VE design project you can find specific material pertinent to that project, as well as pointers to additional references on the topic.

Part one

Part one of the book describes the four major considerations for defining requirements. The first is to identify whom the user(s) of the system will be, the task(s) that will be performed with the system, and the environment in which it will be used, so the relevant criteria in these areas are described in chapter 1. The second consideration is in the area of human capabilities and performance, so there's a discussion of relevant aspects of human perception (including visual, auditory, and tactile perception) and motor capabilities in chapter 2. The third consideration is the common issues that must be addressed and the requirements that need to be specified, such as sociability, responsiveness, and registration; there are quite a few of these, and they are described in chapter 3. Many of these are requirements that must be addressed on a system level. For example, to meet the responsiveness requirement, you must consider the cumulative contribution to system latency, not merely the latency introduced individually by the tracker, renderer, or display devices. Finally, in chapter 3 there's also a discussion of application-specific requirements.

The designer, in facing the numerous design trade-offs and decisions, such as choice of system architectures, choice of input and display technologies, and choice of interaction techniques and object design, should use the requirement definition achieved from the material in part one of this book in order to make these choices. Don't be surprised if the first pass at defining these requirements isn't entirely adequate. In many cases, more research and experience with VEs is necessary to fully define all the requirements for certain tasks. For example, a high-level requirement for a visualization system for network or financial planning might be to maximally facilitate the recognition of patterns and anomalies in complex network or financial data. In spite of reasoned arguments that an immersive (as well as multisensory) display might aid in this, empirical studies don't yet show whether immersive systems are superior for these types of visualization. While there are questions that haven't yet been adequately answered, you can use the requirements as defined in part one to at least narrow the design space.

Part two

Part two provides a guide to meeting the requirements defined in part one through system design, the selection and integration of optimal technologies, and the choice of objects, object behaviors, and interactions in the VE. It's necessary to know the strengths and weaknesses of available technologies to determine how best to meet functional requirements, and this section describes input and output technologies, as well as computational issues. In particular, chapter 4 discusses input technologies, chapter 5 addresses output technologies, and chapter 6 reviews computational and supporting technologies. Chapter 7 discusses objects, behaviors, and interactions in the virtual environment, and chapter 8 focuses on design trade-offs.

Part three

Based on a definition of requirements and a choice of technologies and design to meet these requirements, you can prototype a system. How to then evaluate that prototype? More specifically, how to answer these three questions:

- What are meaningful metrics for evaluating the integrated system's performance from a system point of view?
- What are metrics for evaluating usability of the interface?
- What are metrics for determining the value for the task/application?

There is much to gain by using metrics to evaluate how well the system meets the requirements of the application (quantitatively as well as qualitatively), and this often isn't done when prototypes are built. The evaluation criteria and approaches are described in part three of this book. The results of this evaluation are then used to refine the requirements definition, to revise the design, and/or to correct problems in the prototype. When evaluation of the most recent iteration produces satisfactory results, the design process is completed and the system can be implemented and deployed.

Appendix

As discussed in the preface, an appendix provides information on vendors who offer technology for the deployment of VE systems, available at the time of writing (mid to late 1995). It's included as a practical aid with the realization that it will quickly become dated, but I invite you to get the more extensive periodically updated information on vendors and products offered at the back of the book.

• • • • • •

Bryson (1994) has made the observation that "we have no overall predictive theory that tells us how to design a virtual reality interface to solve a particular application problem, though we have some experience and a few theoretical insights." Although I don't claim that this document is such an "overall predictive theory," it is a guide that can direct you, the designer, to the essential problems that must be solved and technologies that can address these problems. And it is an approach, through iterative design, to solving the problems for a given application, even when there isn't an overall predictive theory that guarantees results without testing.

If you haven't yet acquired the range of knowledge encompassed in this book, you'll design or select systems based on what's commercially available rather than what's required to successfully build an application, and there's a great risk in doing this. Although a demonstration prototype might result, it won't lead to an application that will truly be useful to its users. By helping you specify the requirements of a VE system in terms of defining the functional requirements for a given application, meeting these requirements through the selection of appropriate technologies and system design, and using metrics to evaluate how well the system meets the requirements, I hope that this book will promote better designed VE systems.

Questions

- In what ways does my definition of virtual environments differ from that of Wickens and Baker? What are examples of interfaces you can imagine that would be considered VEs according to these definitions, but aren't included in the examples of "flavors" of systems (fishtank VR, augmented reality, etc.) given in the text?
- What are the advantages and costs of using the iterative design methodology that's described? What would be the advantages and costs of not using this methodology? Can you give examples of situations where it would be a wise decision not to use it?
- Notice yaw, pitch, and roll in your everyday life. For example, notice how you move your own head. When do you yaw, pitch, or roll it? Are there certain tasks you do in which you wouldn't need to change your head's orientation in one or more of these ways? If a VE system with head tracking didn't measure one of these degrees of freedom, do you think it would have any impact on your performing one of these tasks? What would you want to happen to the visual and auditory display if you did change your head's orientation in a degree of freedom that wasn't measured?
- Imagine an "overall predictive theory" that would describe the design to be used in a VE in order to solve any given application problem. What would such an "overall predictive theory" have to consist of? What are examples of such predictive theories in other domains? (After you've read the remainder of this book, you might want to come back to this question and note the areas in which our current knowledge is inadequate to provide such a theory for VEs.)

Part 1

Defining the Requirements

You can specify many requirements of a VE application a priori by using the material in this section. Although you might not correctly identify all functional requirements the first time through this process, you can use the requirements you can identify in designing the system, in order to narrow the design space. This section will describe categories of VE applications and some of the crucial functional requirement areas to address in building systems that meet the needs of these applications.

In order to define functional requirements, it's first necessary to know four kinds of things:

- *Who are the users of the specific application and what are their experiences, aptitudes, motivations, and needs?*
- *What is the task and what is required to do it?*
- *What is the environment in which the application will be used, and what is the context in which the task will be done?*
- *What are the basic perceptual, cognitive, motor, and affective capabilities of humans?*

Once you answer these questions, it's necessary to consider and define requirements pertaining to issues that are common to applications of virtual environments as well as requirements that are application-specific. Once you define the requirements, use part two of this book to design a VE system that meets the requirements for the given application.

This part is organized into three chapters. The first discusses identifying and understanding the user, task, and environment; the second summarizes the basic perceptual, cognitive, and motor capabilities of humans, commenting on affect and the implications of these capabilities on the design of virtual environments; and the third delineates specific issues common to virtual environments that generally have to be addressed when defining functional (and other) requirements, as well as application-specific requirements.

Chapter 1

Defining the User, Task, and Environment

Defining the user, task, and environment is essential in specifying appropriate technology for human-computer interaction in general and in creating usable systems. This is no less the case (and perhaps more so) for VE systems in particular. There are several criteria for performance, and defining the user, task, and environment can contribute to evaluation criteria.

On one level, the usability of the interface itself is an issue, and can be evaluated according to criteria such as error rates, task-completion times, workload, and user subjective assessment (via Likert-like questionnaires and responses to open-ended questions). On another level, the effectiveness of the interface for the task in question is an issue. Does it, for example, use information representation and display techniques that permit new understanding of complex data used in a planning problem? Or does it facilitate a teleoperation task being accomplished with less frequent errors and reduced training requirements? Finally, consider the value of the interface in the work environment in which the users actually perform the task in question.

In a recent keynote address, Steve Ellis of NASA Ames made the observation that, even when the technology matures, there might not be a general VE interface that's ideal for all tasks. He gave the example of trade-offs in turning off head roll in different applications, some of which don't require the user to make such motions (Ellis 1993).

Who Is the User?

In designing and implementing virtual environments, no less than in building other human-computer interfaces, human factors research indicates the importance of "knowing the user." The classic mistake in interface design is the implicit (and often very mistaken) assumption that the users will be like the system builders in all pertinent ways. This mistake can lead to designing a system that requires expertise to use and offering it to users who will give up or find an alternative before ever acquiring this expertise. Conversely, users who spend a great deal of time with a system will become frustrated if it doesn't provide "power user" features that let them be faster and more effective in performing their tasks.

The novice/expert distinction is only one such distinction that must be made in defining the users of a proposed VE system. Others are whether the system will be used by one or many users, where the users will be located with respect to the system and each other, and whether users with disabilities will be a target audience for the system.

Single vs. multiple users

For the single vs. multiple user parameter, you should identify the number of people who use the physical hardware and the number of people who simultaneously interact in the virtual environment. With respect to users of the physical hardware, a pilot with an advanced cockpit display only he uses might have an HMD with customized interpupillary distance, custom-fitted instrumented gloves, a speaker-dependent speech recognizer, and perhaps even a virtual acoustic display using the pilot's own head-related transfer function (HRTF). A system that several people use might have adjustable HMD and gloves, speaker-independent speech recognition or a speaker-dependent system with multiple user-specific speech databases, and a virtual acoustic display with a generic HRTF. For a system to be demonstrated to a very large number of users (e.g., a museum display) HMD and gloves would have to be sturdy and it might be unrealistic to expect users to be able to adjust and calibrate HMDs and gloves, so a "one size fits most" approach (or offering a few sizes, e.g., for children and adults) would be necessary; other concerns such as hygiene (transmission of germs on the i/o devices) would also have to be considered.

With respect to the number of people who simultaneously interact in the virtual environment, many current systems support only single users, but it's important for many applications to be able to permit multiple users to simultaneously share and interact in the virtual environment.

There are a number of issues that arise with multiparticipant virtual environments; some are specific to whether the users are proximate or in remote locations (these will be discussed in the next section); some are in the realm of decisions on interaction techniques (e.g., if multiple users select and attempt to move an object in different directions at the same time, what will happen?); and some are related to computational complexity (i.e., the demands of dealing with the large number of viewpoints and interactions involved).

In terms of complexity, the largest-scale distributed interactive simulation has been SIMNET, a system whose development was led by the Defense Advanced Research Projects Agency (DARPA, now ARPA). SIMNET permits interoperation for simulated war games of a network of tank and helicopter simulators, and has supported as many as 1,000 simultaneous participants. This is a far greater number of simultaneous participants than there have been yet in shared virtual environments accessed via HMD/position-tracked systems, but the technical problems are similar.

SIMNET work has led to the development of protocols (distributed interactive simulation, DIS) that were adopted by the IEEE as standards for this type of simulation (Hardy and Healy 1993). There's a significant effort by the military at present to develop the next generation of multiuser, distributed, interactive, simulated war games. In order for software to be appropriately designed, it must be determined whether the application will support multiple users and shared virtual environments.

Wexelblat (1993) lists six of the problems to be solved in computer-supported cooperative work (CSCW) systems:

- How much data will be shared?
- Who will have control over input and output and for how long?
- How will users communicate with each other?
- How will users know what other users are doing?
- What parts of the system will users see at any one time?
- How will users know what other users are seeing and how does what others see compare to what they see?

VE systems make some of these problems more simple than in conventional CSCW systems (e.g., a shared text editor). For example, users can know what other users are doing by seeing a representation of them and their actions in the virtual environment. However, VE systems might make some of these problems more complex to solve. For example, it's possible to represent data in different customized ways for each user in the virtual environment, but this could make it particularly difficult to let users know what other users are seeing, hearing, and feeling without switching to the representations being used by the other collaborators.

Remote vs. proximate users

Where will users be located with respect to the system? If the application supports multiple users, will they be proximately or remotely located? With users distant from the system, networking is a necessity, not simply an option. The distance involved affects the choice of transmission media, which should be considered early in the design process. If transmission time is long enough to be of consequence, it could introduce additional difficulties that must be addressed.

An example is the recent work described by Carol Stoker (1993) in teleoperation of a robot located in the Antarctic by an operator at NASA Ames Research Center in California. In this work, a model of the remote environment permits the operator to interact without the negative effects on performance of significant time delays. This model is modified as it's found to diverge from the transduced distant environment. It should be noted that this approach is reasonable only because, in this case, the remote environment (within an ice-covered lake) is so static. Transmission delay in multiuser distributed interactive simulations such as SIMNET also presents challenges. For example, if one user moves a tank but another user at a distant location (who hasn't yet received information that the tank has been moved) fires artillery at its "former" location and succeeds at blowing it up, how should this transmission delay-related conflict be resolved?

Another multiuser issue raised by Thomas and Stuart (1993) is that a system that permits user-system speech for speech recognition as well as user-user speech should have a way to distinguish these. (They suggest a virtual position in space for the system so that the user can indicate he's addressing the system rather than another user via head position and orientation.)

Novices vs. experts

In comparing the needs of novices and experts, there are obvious marked differences. The concern for novices is generally ease of first-time use, clarity of what the user can and can't do (e.g., via "affordances"), and recoverability from error. For the expert user, more focus tends to be on the "power" the system provides: high functionality, speed with which users can accomplish routine tasks, and flexibility of the system to accommodate the needs of expert users (e.g., to let users customize the way an interaction is accomplished). In addition, expert users might spend a great deal of time with a system or use it for very demanding tasks, so issues such as workload must be considered. Many current virtual environment systems are demonstration-of-concept systems whose primary audience is made up of first-time users, and the emphasis has therefore been on ease of use rather than high functionality.

Developers often have a deep knowledge and understanding of a system by the time it's prototyped and evaluated with representative users, and are surprised to witness the usability problems these novice users experience. They're tempted to add an enormous number of features to a system, and lose perspective on how difficult the presence of these features can make the system. If the interface is too difficult to use, novices might never spend enough time with it to gain expertise; if it's easy to use but offers little functionality, novices might not use it after the first few successful experiences.

The "holy grail" of interface design is to offer ease of use for the novice, high functionality for the expert, and a system that facilitates the novice-to-expert shift. This goal is desirable in virtual environment systems no less than in other computer-human interfaces. Stuart (1993b) makes a case that, for some applications, support of virtuoso performance by users (analogous to virtuoso instrumental technique of a member of an improvisational jazz ensemble) might be warranted. For expert users to put in the effort required to attain such virtuosity, however, the rewards in terms of the performance possible must be great.

Experts might adapt perceptually to the system from spending a great deal of time with it, and this should be taken into account. In the realm of speech synthesis, for example, users become better at comprehending synthesized speech with practice, and it's anecdotally reported that visually impaired users who rely on speech synthesizers to read electronic text documents to them learn to understand the synthesizers at the fastest rate at which manufacturers set performance. As users can adapt to aspects of the system, the system can be designed to adapt to the user—in this case, speeding up synthesis as users have more sessions with the system.

The other side of the increased time that experts spend using a system and their perceptual adaptation to it is that harmful effects of this adaptation, if any, might appear where they wouldn't in novices. Although they haven't been reported with respect to virtual environment systems, repetitive stress disorders are one example of the type of harmful effect that should be considered for experts, though they wouldn't be found in novices.

User aptitude

As observed by Stuart and Thomas (1991), users have different aptitudes and, although much of the human performance research has been done on young male fighter pilots, it's an ill-advised assumption that all users will, for example, be equally good at 3-D visualization. Standardized tests, such as those developed by the Johnson O'Connor Institute in New York City, can measure a variety of different aptitudes, and might be pertinent in making decisions about the design of virtual environments for users with common aptitudes. It has also been suggested that, because of the multimodal interaction that virtual environment systems support, systems can support the types of customization that would let users tailor them to their aptitudes. For example, a user who's better at understanding certain kinds of abstract information presented through sonification than through visual display could control the choice of display modalities.

Individual physiological differences

There are numerous individual differences that are pertinent to the use of virtual environments. These include age and age-related performance (such as age-related changes in visual accommodation and capability to hear high frequencies), interpupillary distances, individual dark-focus distances (which result in objects appearing to be farther away than they are because users tend to focus at this distance rather than at optical infinity), differences in tolerance of accommodation/vergence mismatches, differences in HRTFs and auditory localization capability as well as pitch and rhythmic perception, and differences in susceptibility to motion sickness (in particular, simulator-like sickness).

Users with disabilities

Users with physical disabilities can use virtual environment technology to represent information that wouldn't otherwise be available to them, or to control devices in the world with unimpaired motor capabilities. Synesthetic representation, described in Stuart and Urdang (1992), is the representation of information normally perceived through one sensory modality via another modality.

Stuart and Urdang also describe an approach for allowing a visually impaired user to navigate through an unfamiliar city by using a virtual acoustic display integrated with real-world sounds (with the virtual acoustic display presenting information about the location of landmarks that would normally be perceived visually), in combination with a geographic information system. For users with disabilities, such synesthetic representation might be a necessity rather an option.

Using virtual environment technology to allow motorically impaired users to control devices is being investigated presently, for example, at Loma Linda Medical Center. For more information on the special needs of users with disabilities and the work on virtual environment systems to address these needs, I recommend the proceedings of a series of conferences: "Virtual Reality and Persons with Disabilities," held by California State University at Northridge.

Defining the Task

Task definition is essential to specifying requirements for a virtual environment application. You should identify the goals of the application, the tasks that will be required to achieve those goals, and how the tasks will be accomplished in the virtual environment. This section will describe categories of tasks for which virtual environments can be designed, and examples in each of these categories.

Once the task is defined, a task analysis can be performed and used to specify requirements. Although some of this task analysis will be used to determine requirements as they relate to issues common to VE systems (see chapter 3), other identified requirements might be unique to the application in question. An example of application-specific requirements that resulted from a task analysis is given by Levison and Pew (1993) in the last section of chapter 3, *Application-Specific Requirements*.

Note that an application might in fact involve a very large number of different tasks, so this section is describing categories of applications more than categories of individual tasks used for the applications. A lower-level description of these tasks, which are common to many virtual environment applications and their requirements, is given by Wickens and Baker (1995). These tasks include search, navigation, manipulation, perception and inspection, and learning.

I'll resist the temptation to describe an exhaustive set of current and proposed applications because they generally fit into the categories listed in the previous paragraph. But to give a few examples suggesting the range of these, consider the following:

- The simulation of self-rescue maneuvers by astronauts separated from a spacestation using a hand-held thruster. Thirty separation scenarios were used to judge feasibility, time, and fuel needed for self-rescue, as well as assessing whether attitude hold capability was required (Brody, Jacoby, and Ellis 1992).
- Architectural walk-throughs: creating models of buildings that haven't yet been constructed, and letting prospective users respond to the design. This application has been described in numerous papers, and is summarized by Brooks, Airey, Alspaugh, et al. (1992).
- Enhanced air-traffic control displays that give auditory cues regarding the locations of pilots and their aircraft (Wenzel 1992).

Categories of virtual environment applications

Wickens and Baker (1995) divide the tasks for which virtual environments can be designed into four categories: online performance, offline training and rehearsal, online comprehension, and offline learning and knowledge acquisition. Online performance means applications where the operator uses the virtual environment as an interface for manipulating the nonsynthetic world; a typical example of this is in teleoperation tasks. Offline training and rehearsal refers to the use of virtual environments for practicing tasks (such as maneuvering a spacecraft or performing a surgical procedure) that will then be performed in the real world. Online comprehension is applications in which the task is to understand or gain insight into the virtual environment with which the user is interacting while the interaction is occurring (e.g., the chemist might gain an insight about the way molecules can be docked, or the geologist understand something about a planetary surface). Offline learning and knowledge acquisition means applications in which the user should acquire knowledge that will be be employed later in a more abstract form.

There are four categories of use of virtual environments that don't fit into the Wickens and Baker classification:

- Online design, where the virtual environment interface is used for designing objects and environments displayed by the system.
- Entertainment, where the goal of the environment is the experiential pleasure the user gets from it.
- Communication, where the goal is for multiple users to use the environments as media or tools so they can communicate.
- Tools for research on human perceptual-motor capabilities.

All eight of these categories are summarized in Table 1.1.

Online performance. In online performance, the user uses the virtual environment to accomplish tasks, generally in the real world. Wickens and Baker's examples in this category are mostly teleoperation tasks, and indeed this is one of the areas where the most work has been done in developing applications (there's a rich teleoperation literature; see McGovern 1991 and the numerous publications by A. Bejczy).

Teleoperation can be useful because the environment in which the task must be done is hazardous (e.g., undersea, in space, or in radioactive or otherwise toxic areas); because the interface gives intuitive and precise control (see the work by Taylor, et al. on control of a scanning tunneling microscope); or because the user is at a remote location from the site at which the work must be done and can't get there in time to carry out the work in person (e.g., telepresence surgery, discussed by Satava 1993). But I believe that two other categories of online performance tasks are important:

- Using virtual environment technology to enhance or augment the user's physical capabilities. Examples include people with disabilities using the technology to interact with the world around them—see papers presented at California State University at Northridge's conference on "Virtual Reality and Persons with Disabilities" and Weghorst, et al. (1994)—or people using the technology to augment their physical abilities in other ways, e.g., the work of Gershenfeld and Machover with YoYo Ma on the Hypercello Project (Gershenfeld 1991, Paradiso and Gershenfeld in press).
- Using augmented reality interfaces to perform tasks that are local to the user, e.g., installation and repair (Feiner, MacIntyre, and Seligmann 1992).

TABLE 1.1 Categories of Virtual Environment Applications

Category of application	Purpose	Criteria for success	Crucial issues	Examples
Online performance	Use VE to manipulate nonsynthetic world	Successful performance of task in nonsynthetic world	Transmission time/delay, mapping between human and robot motion, etc.	Teleoperation in hazardous environments, telepresence surgery, control of scanning tunnel microscope
Offline training and rehearsal	Use VE to practice activities that will be done in nonsynthetic world	Positive transfer to performance in nonsynthetic world	Representation of training task, avoidance of negative transfer, maximization of positive transfer	Surgical simulation, Hubble Space Telescope repair, flight simulation, simulated war games, sports simulation, airplane marshalling
Online comprehension	Gain insight into VE while interacting with it	Insights gained (especially insights that could not have been gained otherwise)	Design choices (e.g., sensory modalities) to facilitate recognition of patterns and anomalies	Molecular docking (e.g., GROPE), financial visualization, network planning, planning of radiation therapy for cancer treatment
Offline learning and knowledge acquisition	Acquire knowledge from VE to be synthesized for later use	Successful acquisition and synthesis of knowledge and understanding	Representation of information	Virtual windtunnel, virtual physics laboratory, virtual planetary exploration
Online design	Use VE for design of objects or environments	Good designs produced	Creation and modification of objects and environments from within the VE, collaboration issues	(limited true online design) Matsushita kitchen design, Northrop F-18 fighter jet redesign and Boeing aircraft design, automobile design
Entertainment	Use VE for the purpose of experiential pleasure	User enjoys the experience	LBE: safety, hygiene, throughput Personal systems: cost, ease of use	Numerous LBE systems, e.g., W Industries Virtuality, Battletech
Communication	Use VE as media or tools with which to communicate	VE facilitates effective communication	Synchronous vs. asynchronous, representation of user	Few synchronous communication applications exist
Tools for research on human perceptual-motor capabilities	Use VE to study human capabilities	Isolate perceptual/motor phenomena to be studied	Control of system performance, repeatability, flexibility	Study of auditory localization, intersensory interactions, role of stereopsis

The primary goal of an online performance application is simply the effective performance of the task. Above all else, the application must be designed to support this. The success or failure of an online performance application is generally straightforward to measure. Wickens and Baker (1995) note that these applications should provide good closed-loop perceptual/motor performance (fast reaction, minimal errors, and stable tracking of moving targets), high situational awareness, and low workload or cognitive effort.

Offline training and rehearsal. Although the descriptive phrase is perhaps misleading (since the training and rehearsal actually occurs online), offline training and rehearsal describes using virtual environments to practice tasks that will later be performed in the real world, or offline. There's a wide range of potential domains that can use virtual environments for offline training and rehearsal. Examples include surgical simulators (see Bostrom, Singh, and Wiley 1993, and Rosen 1991), flight simulators (there's too large a body of literature to cite, but refer to the work on how recent human factors affect flight simulator display by Kleiss and Hubbard 1993), simulated war games (e.g., SIMNET, for which a large body of literature exists: Calvin, et al. 1993), and sports simulators (several reported, but not much is yet described in the scientific literature; see Andersson 1993).

In these and other offline training and rehearsal applications, the primary goal of the application is to give the user experience that will effectively transfer to a real-world task.

Online comprehension. Online comprehension, where the goal is to understand or gain insight into the virtual environment while interacting with it, is exemplified by the much-discussed GROPE system created at the University of North Carolina at Chapel Hill for molecular docking (see Brooks, et al. 1990). This system permits a chemist to manipulate molecules and explore the ways they can be docked. Clearly, there's no particular value to docking virtual molecules except in the insight it gives the chemist about how to combine real molecules. In addition, you wouldn't expect a chemist who failed to dock molecules in a virtual environment to later acquire any insight from the experience; the understanding is usually gained while in the virtual environment (although later insights are possible). Other examples of online comprehension applications include using virtual environments for financial visualization (Feiner and Beshers 1990) and network planning.

Offline learning and knowledge acquisition. In virtual environment applications for offline learning and knowledge acquisition, the user is meant to acquire knowledge and experience by using a system, and later synthesize it into more abstract knowledge. For example, a student using a virtual physics laboratory can control physical parameters such as friction, atmospheric drag, the coefficient of restitution for elastic bodies, and the magnitude and direction of gravity (Loftin 1993), and see what effects these have. Through this cumulative experience, the student should be able to attain a greater understanding of physical properties, which will in time be useful in understanding more about real-world physics.

The distinction between online comprehension applications and offline learning and knowledge acquisition applications isn't always entirely clear—for example, users of some applications could gain insight either while using the virtual environment system or later when synthesizing the experiences—but examples of applications that could fall into the latter category include a system for virtual planetary exploration being developed at NASA Ames (McGreevy 1993) and a simulation of computational fluid dynamics known as the Virtual Windtunnel (Bryson and Levit 1992).

Online design. Online design involves an individual or collaborative group of users designing objects or environments using the virtual environment system. In many cases, where virtual environments are currently used in design, the design is accomplished away from the virtual environment system, and then the virtual environment system is used to visualize the results of the design effort. Examples include the redesign of the Northrop F-18 fighter jet and recent work at Boeing. In these cases, using a virtual environment system could be included in the category of online comprehension applications, described previously.

However, in some current applications, such as the kitchen design application at Matsushita in Japan, users select from available objects (in this case, kitchen appliances) and design a kitchen layout from within the virtual environment. This is a simple example of online design. ISAAC, a research system built at UNC Chapel Hill, goes further by permitting users to employ a variety of direct and indirect manipulation techniques to not only position and orient objects in the VE, but also scale them (Mine 1995a).

A more sophisticated type of online design, which can be termed VE-CAD, involves not merely positioning and sizing objects, but creating objects from within the virtual environment. 3DM, also created as a research system at UNC Chapel Hill, permits the creation of simple geometric objects from within the VE (Butterworth et al. 1992). Conceptual Design Space, a research system built to study the interactive design of architectural spaces from within VEs (Bowman 1995) provides a ground covered with vertices you can select and, by indicating a height for each vertex, create three-dimensional objects (such as walls and ceiling). Future systems could permit highly skilled users to collaboratively design from within VEs with sophisticated gestural languages (see Stuart 1993b), but currently only rudimentary VE-CAD is incorporated into research systems.

Entertainment. Virtual environments for entertainment are *autotelic*, which means they have no purpose except for the enjoyment they bring. Entertainment systems can be single- or multiuser, and can be designed for home use or for use in public places (e.g., arcade). Because their purpose is simply the enjoyment of the user, entertainment applications don't have some of the more stringent demands associated with applications for online performance or offline training and rehearsal. Perhaps this is why current low-end systems have succeeded and are becoming most widespread in the area of entertainment. On the other hand, because it isn't easy to define what people will enjoy before the fact, it's especially difficult to specify requirements for entertainment systems without going through several iterations of prototyping and evaluation.

Communication. In a way, virtual environments are like telephones; people were particularly bad at predicting what the telephone would be used for before it became widespread, and it has turned out to be used for all sorts of communication (via speech) between people. Like online comprehension, virtual environments can be used to bring insight to users while they're in the environment. When using virtual environments for communication, however, the aim of the interface is to facilitate transfer of knowledge (and other types of communication) between users, rather than insight about the environment itself. The virtual environment is simply the medium for communication between users.

Communication applications can be either asynchronous or synchronous. If they're asynchronous they can be used to communicate the design of a building to prospective clients via architectural walk-through or to reconstruct the scene of a crime from available evidence and communicate this reconstruction to jurors. In this case they're often indistinguishable from online comprehension applications, but if they're synchronous they clearly belong in this category of their own.

At present, most VE applications have had as their focus the content of the environment or the interaction between user and system rather than communication between users. However, communication applications could become more widespread in the future. Although there are no successful communication applications yet, further discussion of VE technology as a medium for communication is provided by Biocca (1992).

Tools to research human perceptual-motor capabilities. Virtual environments developed as tools for research into human perceptual-motor capabilities have very specific requirements that depend on which human performance characteristics are studied. In general, however, they should give the researcher a high degree of control over specific parameters in the modalities to be studied. For example, for many virtual environments, a virtual acoustic display subsystem with synthesis of a single acceptable generic head-related transfer function is adequate. But, for a research system that studies the effects of interaural intensity difference, interaural time difference, pinna filtering on externalization and localization of audio sources, or the effects of modifying cues to attempt to produce superlocalization, the researcher must be able to adjust individual parameters of the audio display.

Defining the Environment

You can define the environment in which the application is used in several ways, as the physical, work, and social environment. If you're designing a VE system, it's important to consider each type of environment early in the design process, and not wait until a great deal of work has been done only to discover that one of these issues is an unexpected surprise that will affect whether your system is useful. In fact, issues with respect to any of these three types of environments that are not conducive to the VE system being designed could be of sufficient importance to entirely preclude the success of the system.

The physical environment

The physical environment is the space in which the system is used, and includes such elements as the amount of available space, lighting, noise, temperature, power supply, network access, and whether it's necessary to be aware of hazards. Some types of VE systems don't require a great deal of physical space, but others, for example a CAVE or typical vehicular simulator, require a rather large dedicated space. Physical characteristics of the space might also be significant. For example, if there's a great deal of metal present, it can affect the accuracy of magnetic tracking systems.

Physical environments tend to be an especially great challenge in augmented reality applications, where the user moves through the real world with the system, and synthetic display is combined with real-world input. Lighting isn't generally important for HMD-based systems that block out the surrounding physical environment, but it's important to understand the lighting situation in the environment in which an augmented reality system will be used in order to plan the display technology and effectively combine synthetic and nonsynthetic images. Similarly, if real-world sounds and synthetic sounds are to be integrated, the designer of the system must be aware of ambient noise levels in the environment and take into account the effect they'll have in masking synthetic sounds.

You should also consider temperature in terms of its impact both on the technology and on the user (especially, for example, if the user is expected to wear an HMD or a large full-body suit in a hot environment). You must determine the availability of a power supply and network access if they're required. And, if the physical environment is one in which the user must be aware of hazards, you must take this into account; some VE technologies are remarkably effective at keeping their users unaware of things going on around them in the physical world.

The work environment

Another type of environment to be considered is the work environment, which is the context in which the application is used with regard to the user's other job functions. For example, are the developers imagining that users will get all "suited up" without realizing that they have to respond to frequent phone calls and get pulled away from work to handle administrative functions? The term *work environment* perhaps isn't the best descriptive term, since even in the case of using an entertainment system at home, you need to consider the effects of interruptions.

In the case of the work environment of a fighter pilot who's using an augmented reality display, an element of the work environment that should be considered is that the pilot should be able to eject from the aircraft if it malfunctions or is hit by enemy fire. Meyer, Applewhite, and Biocca (1992) give an example of a mechanical tracking device used by the Israeli military that was based on rods connected at one end to the pilot's helmet, and at the other end to the cockpit, but it wasn't deployed because of G force and seat ejection problems. As another example, a VE system for stock traders that cut them off from the action around them on the floor of a stock exchange wouldn't be useful if information they gathered from hearing, speaking with, and watching other traders was crucial.

The social environment

Finally, you must consider the social environment—the attitudes, habits, and expectations of the social climate in which the application will be used. The social environment might affect the use of the system either negatively or positively. Would the social climate in which the user works support the use, for example, of HMDs? For certain groups of users, the social climate might preclude use of HMDs; for others, such as young users of entertainment systems in public arcades, HMDs are probably desirable, even if they're a prop with little functionality (e.g., no position tracking and no stereoscopy).

What of the case where a VE system would be useful to a group of users, but the social climate doesn't support the use of such a system? Perhaps, if some members of the group adopt the technology and demonstrate its value, the social environment will change through time to make the technology more accepted. But a social environment that's initially not accepting of the technology presents a barrier to its adoption and use that you need to consider before developing the system.

Questions

- Do you agree with Steve Ellis that there might never be a general VE interface? What capabilities and properties would a general VE system have to have?
- You get an RFP (request for proposals) for a VE system that would permit biathletes to train in a simulation of the Olympic course. What are some specifications about the users, their environment, and the simulated event that you would need to know to intelligently respond to this RFP?
- What special needs would elderly users of a VE system have?
- How can you, as the designer of a VE application, determine the physical environment in which your system will be used and which characteristics of this environment will be crucial to its design? How can you determine the characteristics of the work environment and the social environment? What lessons can you learn from the position-tracking system for Israeli military pilots that wasn't employed because of seat ejection problems?
- How do you handle transmission delay in a teleoperation system if the environment is changing rapidly in the robot's location? How do you resolve transmission delay-related conflicts in multiuser systems where users are in remote locations?
- What are some of the behaviors that an expert user might want in a VE system that wouldn't be appropriate for a novice user?

Chapter 2

Human Capabilities and Performance

There are several reasons to consider basic human perceptual, cognitive, and motor capabilities in designing virtual environments for any application, and various reasons are reflected in the different approaches that several authors have taken.

First, you can use perceptual and motor capabilities to determine the range within which input and output technologies should perform. Certainly, they can help define an upper boundary; it isn't useful, for example, to specify a visual, auditory, or tactile display with much greater resolution than the human user is capable of perceiving, or an input device that captures movement at a resolution finer than the user can control. Perceptual and motor capabilities can also help define certain minimum requirements, such as the frame rate required for flicker fusion or the frequency range required for auditory localization.

Second, if you view a human as a model information processor and the human-computer interaction as a problem of information transfer, then you can think of the human senses as informational channels, each with different possible rates of information transfer.

Third, from a more qualitative perspective, you can look at the issue not as how to exchange the most information in the least time between human and computer, but as how (and through what sensory modalities) to best represent and display information to facilitate understanding, promote the recognition of patterns and anomalies, and convey gestalt to the user.

Fourth, you must consider issues such as intersensory interactions, adaptation, and factors contributing to simulator-like sickness (cybersickness) in order to design a system that best fits the user and is safe for that user, both while using the VE and afterwards.

Finally, and less frequently discussed, the nature of the system might have an effect that, though important, would never be revealed by thinking of the user as a model information processor. An engaging system that uses many of the user's perceptual, cognitive, and motor capabilities might reduce distractions from the task, increase motivation, and hence have other positive benefits (e.g., increase time on task). The question this raises is whether you can predict anything about a system's affective influence based on how it addresses the user's capabilities. If so, this could contribute to a specification of requirements and to system design; if not, you could evaluate effective measures only after the fact. (Although, with iterative design, this doesn't mean that such an evaluation can't contribute to the final design of the system.)

Perceptual dimensions have been classified according to several schemes. Boff & Lincoln (1988) review some of the major dimensions, such as Stevens' metathetic/prothetic distinction, Erickson's topographic/nontopographic distinction, and Helmholz's analytic/synthetic distinction. Prothetic (or quantitative) dimensions vary in intensity but not in quality, and are exemplified by brightness, warmth, loudness, and pressure; metathetic (or qualitative) dimensions vary in quality and are exemplified by pitch, taste, position, and color. Topographic dimensions are believed to be neurally encoded in the brain in an orderly spatial way, and are exemplified by visual and tactile position; nontopographic dimensions don't have this orderly spatial encoding, and are exemplified by taste, warmth, and color. Analytic dimensions are those in which distinct values on the dimension don't fuse into a single percept when combined, and are exemplified by auditory pitch; synthetic dimensions are those that, when combined, fuse into a single percept, and are exemplified by color (e.g., from light of different wavelengths).

Human motor control encompasses both the control of movement and the maintenance of stability. Motor capabilities are responsible for almost all types of input we're capable of supplying to human-computer interfaces (the exceptions, e.g., using brain-evoked response potential as input, will also be discussed). Motor control tends to be described more with respect to a type of activity engaged in (e.g., reaching and grasping) than with respect to the components of the body used (e.g., hand and arm movement). This is probably because, unlike perceptual activities, which can be attributed to isolated sensory systems (e.g., vision and the eyes, audition and the ears), motor activities often involve multiple parts of the body.

Motor activities include grasping and manipulating things with the hands, moving the arms to reach for things, using the legs for locomotion via walking, cycling, climbing, etc., moving the eyes, drawing, writing, and typing, making facial expressions, and producing speech. Although a variety of motor activities and capabilities will be discussed, note that there are other motor activities that aren't relevant to VE input that will not be covered (e.g., bodily functions such as breathing).

Let's first consider the different modes of perception (visual, auditory, tactile, and kinesthetic, with some mention of olfactory and vestibular) and motor activity (manual dexterity and other movement-related capability of the limbs, speech production, and eye movement) and their implications in the design of virtual environment systems.

We'll focus on human sensory capabilities and perceptual cues, but it's important to note that, for all of our sensory systems, it's knowledge of the world and not just raw sensory data that we use in forming models of objects and environments that we perceive. The observation that "seeing is an active, constructive process utilizing considerable nonvisual information, some of which is in a Kantian sense *a priori* knowledge" (Ellis 1991b, p.10) can be applied also to auditory and haptic perception. In fact, as some perceptual cues are described, you'll notice that they're most effective when the perceiver compares a sensory stimulus to the stimulus expected from a known source; a visual cue to the distance from the observer of a truck down the highway is the observer's knowledge about the size of trucks, for example. In some cases, knowledge about the user (as discussed in a previous chapter), is useful in estimating what *a priori* knowledge will be brought to bear.

Visual Perception

We gather much of the information about the world we live in through our eyes. This section considers the process of vision and some of the visual parameters that are relevant to virtual environment systems, particularly visual depth perception. There are a number of cues used in visual depth perception, which can be classified into monocular (or extrastereoscopic) cues, oculomotor cues, and stereopsis. Attempts have been made to assess which of these cues are most important, such as the weighted additive model by Wickens, Todd, and Seidler (1989).

Basics of visual perception

In order for human vision to occur, light enters the eye through the cornea, passes through the pupil, lens, vitreous humor, and the nerve fibers and blood vessels at the front of the retina, and triggers nerve impulses generated by the eye's specialized transducers, the photoreceptors (the rods and cones). The iris controls the size of the pupil, hence sensitivity to light; the muscles in the eye control the thickness of the crystalline lens, hence focusing the image on the retina (known as *accommodation*). The fovea is the area of the retina (~1–2° of visual angle in diameter) with the greatest density of cones and the greatest visual acuity (i.e., the ability to discriminate detail).

Humans can see a small range of the electromagnetic spectrum, from approximately 400–700 nm (1 nanometer = one billionth of a meter). Wavelengths below this range (ultraviolet) are absorbed by the lens of the eye (and can cause damage, such as cataracts, with excessive exposure), and those above it (infrared) are felt as heat but don't have enough energy to produce a chemical reaction in the photoreceptors. Within the visible range, different wavelengths of light are perceived as having different colors. Cones are responsible for color vision, and in dim light the visual field appears to be colorless.

The visual system is capable of adapting to a wide range of intensities of light, from ~0.00003–300,000+ candelas per square meter, and is much quicker to adapt to bright light (this is known as *phototropic vision*, which takes just a few minutes) than to dim light (known as *scotopic vision*, which takes about an hour for greatest sensitivity to dim light). Perceived brightness of a narrow beam of light is less when it passes through the edge of the pupil than through the center (the Stiles-Crawford effect). The eye rotates around a center, which is, on average, 13 mm behind the front of the cornea, and it can comfortably rotate ~40° from center. The distance between the pupils of the eyes, known as the *interpupillary distance* (IPD), ranges from 6–76 mm and varies quite a bit in different populations. The IPD for most adult males, for instance, fall in the range of 50–76 mm. IPD measurements are taken with the eyes looking ahead in parallel; *vergence* is the inward or outward rotation of the eyes that occurs so that the lines of sight of the eyes intersect at the distance of the viewed object.

The unit used to express accommodation is the *diopter*, which is the inverse of the distance from the object to the eye in meters. The variable focal length of an average eye is from ~60–~69.4 diopters (16.7–14.4 mm); when focused on an object at infinity, the eye is said to be exerting zero accommodation. At rest (in the dark), the eye does not focus at infinity, but rests on average at ~1.7 diopters, though there's a wide distribution of resting accommodation. Even when you attempt to fixate your eyes on an object, there's a constant small fluctuation in accommodation you're not aware of. In order to change focus when the target distance changes suddenly, it takes ~400 milliseconds for the eye focus response to begin, and ~600 milliseconds more to complete the change.

Accommodation and vergence are normally coupled, and their relationship is expressed as the AC/A ratio, or change in accommodative vergence (in prism diopters) per unit change in accommodation (in diopters). The Donders line shows the AC/A for symmetrical convergence on a target as it approaches the viewer along the midline. The AC/A must be within a certain range in order for binocular vision without double images to be possible, and there are large individual differences in the ability to tolerate accommodation/convergence mismatches (which might lead to discomfort and *diplopia*, or double images). Eye strain is produced by differences of magnification, image distance, brightness, and vertical position in the images that reach the eyes.

There are several types of eye movements, which are responses to different types of stimuli and occur at different speeds. Among the slower types of movement is vergence, which is up to 10° per second, and smooth pursuit of a slowly moving object, which is up to 40° per second and not normally under voluntary control. One faster type of eye movement is saccades, which are a response to peripherally detected motion or decision to change fixation; they're up to 1,000° per second and, with especially high initial acceleration and final deceleration, they can go up to 40,000° per second squared according to Young & Sheena 1975). Another fast type is vestibulo-ocular movement, which is the compensatory movement in the opposite direction of head or body movement that's required to maintain visual fixation; it occurs as is necessary up to 500° per second.

This vestibulo-ocular movement is described as the *vestibulo-ocular reflex*, and it can be suppressed in order to follow a target that rotates with the head. There are a number of interactions between factors affecting this suppression, such as the frequency of the head oscillation and movement in the peripheral background (see Boff and Lincoln 1988, pp. 456–457). The vestibulo-ocular reflex itself can be modified (recalibrated) with repeated exposure to optical distortions or mismatches between movement of the head and movement of the visual scene; two effects of this recalibration are that they can produce headaches and nausea and, when the distortions are removed, it takes a period of time to recalibrate to normal undistorted visual input, and therefore visual impairment and instability when the head is moved might result.

Many man-made sources such as videotapes and fluorescent lights produce pulsed changes in luminance known as *flicker*. If the flicker rate is high enough (the *critical flicker frequency*, also known as the *critical fusion frequency*), the visual target appears steady; this phenomenon is called *fusion*. There are many factors that contribute to sensitivity to flicker, including location in the visual field (greatest sensitivity in the fovea), the observer's state of adaptation (greatest sensitivity when light-adapted), and the luminance of the target and background (greatest sensitivity for high contrast). In average room light, a refresh rate of 60 Hz will appear to be free of flicker (McKenna and Zeltzer 1992). Many factors also influence spatial sensitivity and visual acuity, such as pupil size (acuity is best at intermediate sizes), illumination level (acuity is best at phototropic, i.e., high levels of illumination), position of target in the visual field (acuity is best in the center of the field), and exposure time; in photopic conditions, acuity improves up to 100–200 milliseconds (Boff and Lincoln 1988).

Although in vision we use some of the light that's reflected from objects, bounces around these objects, and reaches our eyes in order to form descriptions of the physical objects from which this light was reflected, Gestalt psychologists point out that we follow well-described principles in visually grouping things, and "fill in" the shapes of partially occluded objects in predictable ways. Thus, we form mental images of objects even when visually perceiving only parts of the objects. A recommended source for more background on visual perception is Cornsweet (1970).

Monocular depth cues

There's rich redundancy of visual depth cues in the nonsynthetic world. The visual cues that are used to perceive depth fall into three categories. The first of these, monocular (extrastereoscopic) cues, don't depend on detection of oculomotor or binocular disparity cues; in other words, they're cues that could be used to determine the distance of an object from the viewer if the viewer used one eye and was insensitive to focusing. The second category, oculomotor cues, are the cues a viewer gets from the muscular feedback in converging and focusing the eyes. The third category, stereopsis, is depth cues produced by binocular disparity, the difference in the image cast by an object on the two eyes. An object might change in depth if the distance from it to the viewer changes (egocentric motion) or it might change in distance from another object along the viewer's line of sight (exocentric motion) (Regan, Kaufman, and Lincoln 1986). A distinction can be made between the perception of absolute distance and relative distance, where relative distance is the ratio of absolute distances, and can be known without the unit of absolute distance being known (Stevens 1991).

The visual depth cues are further described in Wickens (1990), Wickens, Todd, and Seidler (1989), Lipton (1991), and Sedgwick (1988). A number of them, described in the following sections, are as follows:

- Linear perspective
- Interposition
- Textural gradients
- Proximity-luminance covariance
- Aerial perspective

- Shadows
- Highlighting
- Size and past experience
- Height in the visual field

Linear perspective. Linear perspective is the result of an apparent decrease in the size and spacing of elements of an object due to it moving a greater distance from the observer. It's the phenomenon that makes parallel lines (e.g., railroad tracks or the edges of a cube) appear to converge as they recede from the viewer. Although the perceived convergence of parallel lines is a good illustrative instance, linear perspective isn't limited to parallel lines; it also describes the apparent convergence of the component parts of any object as its distance from the viewer increases. Thus, in general, convergence suggests greater distance from the viewer. Linear perspective was reportedly first identified and used by Italian artists in the fifteenth century.

Interposition. Interposition, a monocular cue that's also described as *occlusion*, *obscuration*, and *contour interruption*, is the phenomenon whereby an object closer to the viewer partly obstructs the view of an object farther away from the viewer. When one object occludes another, you know that the occluding object is nearer. This tells you relative position but not absolute distance. If the observer or the objects are moving, this phenomenon is also described as *kinetic occlusion*.

Textural gradients. Many surfaces have patterns of some regularity. For patterns of approximately equal density, such as those of grass in a field or tiles on a floor, textural gradient is used as a cue for depth by letting the viewer use density in the visual field to indicate distance. As these patterns appear more dense, the viewer knows that the area is farther away. J. J. Gibson, for example, first observed that sensitivity to gradients in texture provides cues to the shape and slant of a surface, the relative size and distances of objects touching the surface, and, in the special case of the observer standing on the textured surface, the distance from the observer's feet to the object (Sedgwick 1988).

Proximity-luminance covariance. Areas in a scene that are illuminated more brightly are generally perceived to be closer to the viewer than those more dimly illuminated (Wickens 1990). This is a monocular cue for depth.

Aerial perspective. Aerial perspective, also known as *atmospheric attenuation*, is a monocular cue that gauges relative distance by measuring the scattering and absorption of light by the atmosphere. A nearer object will have more color saturation and brightness contrast; a more distant object will have less of these, and thus appear bluer.

Shadows. Shadows can convey depth as they fall on an object or are cast from the object onto adjacent surfaces. The user then estimates the location of light sources in the scene. Light sources are normally overhead (e.g., sunlight or light from indoor ceiling lights), and the pattern of shadows cues the viewer both to surface characteristics and depth.

Highlighting. Highlighting refers to the way light is reflected off certain (e.g., curved) surfaces, which creates the sense of the three-dimensionality of a scene. This is one of the less frequently discussed depth cues, and applies to a scene only in which such surfaces are present (Wickens 1990).

Size and past experience. Size is a cue to distance in two ways. If the size of two objects in the visual field is known or believed to be the same, apparent size can be a cue for which is closer (the closer object appears larger in the visual field). Size is also an absolute cue to distance if from past experience the viewer knows the actual size of an object. In this case, you can compare the known actual size and perceived size in the visual field to calculate the object's absolute distance from the viewer. The latter is an example of one of the uses of *a priori* world knowledge in perception to which Ellis (1991) refers.

Height in the visual field. Objects that are higher in the visual field are commonly objects that are farther away, and those that are lower in the visual field are commonly closer to the viewer. In fact, this phenomenon is related to accustomed position with respect to the horizon, so an object that's higher in the visual field appears to be closer to the horizon and hence farther away. However, an object that's still higher (above the horizon) appears closer to the viewer; the higher an object appears above the horizon, the higher in the visual field the object is and the closer to the viewer it appears to be. This is a cue that has perhaps been given especially great attention due to its significance for aircraft pilots. Also known as *elevation*, height in the visual field is a cue both for relative and for absolute distance.

Oculomotor cues

Oculomotor cues are those in which the state of muscular tension in the viewer's visual system is used to determine the depth of viewed objects. Two oculomotor cues for depth are recognized. In *accommodation*, the state of the muscles that control focus of the eye's lens is used; in *vergence*, the state of the muscles that point the eyes inward or straight ahead is used. Although these cues are considered relatively weak in determining depth, especially depth of objects that aren't close to the observer, they're of concern because they're normally coupled but must be decoupled in current HMDs, and individuals vary in how well they can handle this decoupling. The oculomotor cues, combined with the binocular disparity used in stereopsis, make up what Wickens (1990) collectively describes as *observer-centered cues* because they rely on properties of the visual system itself, and they're useful only in perceiving the depth of objects within approximately 10 meters of the observer.

Accommodation. Accommodation is the physical stretching and relaxing of the lens of the eye that's caused by the eye muscles when you focus on an image. The depth of an image that can be focused is influenced by distance and by the size of the pupil (which in turn is influenced by the scene's lighting and the viewer's emotional state). The range of accommodation decreases with age, thus the widespread need for reading glasses by people as they reach middle age. The state of the eye muscles in stretching or relaxing the lens is a cue for the depth of the object on which the observer is focused. Accommodation is apparently useful only in gauging the depth of objects within approximately two meters of the observer (Schiffman 1990).

Vergence. Vergence is the rotation of the eyes (i.e., their movements in opposite directions) so the images of a viewed object fall on corresponding portions of the two retinas due to intersecting lines of sight at the distance of the viewed object. These movements are normally done in order to fuse the image of objects, whether they're near to or far from the observer. Convergence is the rotation of the eyes in the inward direction, corresponding to viewing a closer object. Muscular feedback on the current state of vergence is an oculomotor cue to the depth of the viewed object.

Binocular disparity and stereopsis

Because the two eyes are spatially separated, in our normal viewing of the world, images that reach them are different. The difference in these images is known as *binocular disparity*; for obvious geometric reasons, binocular disparity is greatest for very close objects and least for very distant objects. You can produce the effect of stereopsis in virtual environments by displaying appropriately different images to the two eyes of the observer. Naturally, this effect requires using the correct geometry, presenting greater binocular disparity for objects that are close to the observer than for those that are farther away. Although those who are not perceptual psychologists commonly think of stereopsis as the sole source of depth information, it is in fact primarily important only in close viewing situations (as with other observer-centered cues, for objects within ~10 meters), as there's little binocular disparity for objects that are distant from the observer. Also, when the different images that reach the two eyes aren't properly fused, binocular rivalry might occur, in which the visual system suppresses one of the two images.

Additional cues with motion

Motion gives additional cues about the distance of objects. Relative motion is a clear cue as to the distance of things from a viewer as the viewer moves—objects that are nearer move more in the visual field, and objects that are farther from the viewer move less in the visual field. A clear example of this is that, as you drive down a highway and look out of the side of the car's window, the distant mountain peaks move very little, while the closer telephone poles move by quickly. This is commonly described as *motion parallax*. Another type of motion cue is the rotation of objects, commonly used in some computer displays to visualize 3-D objects. Relative motion is an important depth cue, especially useful (in the case of motion parallax) for distant objects for which stereopsis doesn't provide good cues.

Relative importance of depth cues

Empirical studies and models (e.g., the weighted additive model by Wickens, Todd, and Seidler 1989) have examined and predicted the relative importance of visual depth cues. One important point to note is that the salience of depth cues might not be associated with the cost of presenting them to the user of a virtual environment system. In other words, a cue could be dominant and yet be less costly (computationally or in terms of display technology) than another much less dominant cue. Highlights of the findings about the relative importance of cues are as follows:

- The weighted additive model holds up fairly well, but the presence of motion tends to violate the model.
- Stereopsis, interposition, and motion parallax are the most dominant cues in the model.
- Texture gradient, proximity-luminance covariance, and perspective are not as strong but are of some importance, especially in combination with the stronger cues.
- Past experience and highlighting are quite weak, with the former dominated by perspective and occlusion and the latter perhaps not worth the current effort and computational overhead to incorporate in virtual environment displays.

Piantanida (1993) notes how important the interaction between cues is and, for example, how poor a display that puts flat texture in combination with parallax is, as it can produce undesirable visual illusions. Another key finding by Wickens, et al. is that the strength of cues is apparently somewhat task-dependent. More research is needed in this area.

Although visual perception of distance is better with multiple visual depth cues, Foley (1991) notes that, under most cue conditions, there are still systematic errors in the estimation of depth. He also suggests that, because our perceptual-motor system is well adapted to making adjustments for these systematic errors, if a system allows interaction that provides feedback, it isn't necessarily advisable to attempt to present cues in a way that prevents these normal systematic perceptual errors.

Looming is the rapid change in angular size and textural density that produces behavior such as avoidance reactions that indicate that the viewer perceives the object drawing near (Regan, Kaufman, and Lincoln 1986). This behavior is an empirical way to gauge the success of visual displays in conveying a sense of realism and presence in the virtual environment. Other approaches are depth salience studies (in which observers subjectively rate depth of scenes that use different depth cues) and cue conflict studies (in which conflicting cues are presented and the subjective depth estimation by the observer indicates which cues are stronger).

Field of view

The field of view (or *visual field*) is that part of space you see without moving your eyes or head. The normal field of view is illustrated in Figure 2.1. Each eye has an individual field of view of ~150° horizontally. Together, their horizontal fields overlap in the center, and this area of overlap is called the *binocular field of view*; it's the area in which stereoscopy occurs, and is the region of central vision. The area of overlap between the eyes is, on average, ~120°, with ~30–35° monocular vision on each side, for a total combined horizontal field of view of ~180–200°. (These estimates vary some; see Hezel and Veron 1993 versus Kalawsky 1993.) The vertical field of view, which is the same for one eye or two, is variously estimated at 120° (Kalawsky 1993) or 135° (Hezel and Veron 1993). In order to see with maximum resolution, you must use eye, head, and body movements to keep viewed objects within the foveal region.

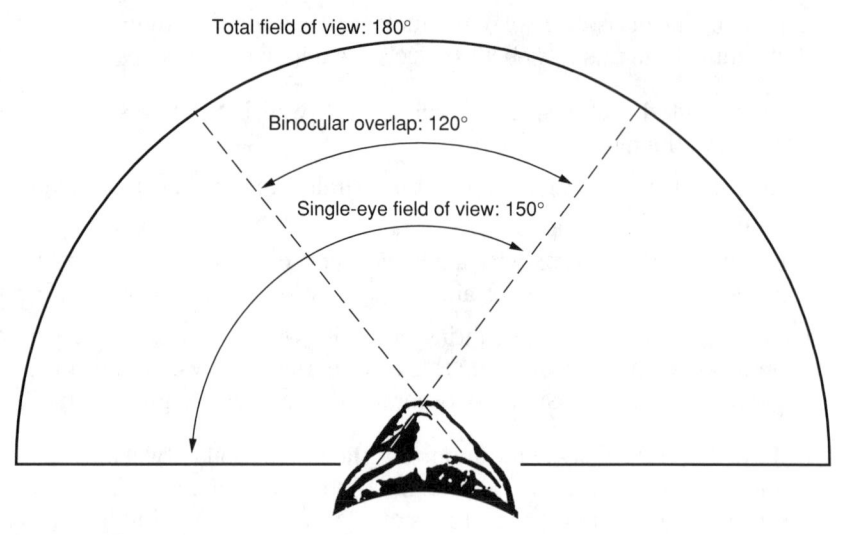

Figure 2.1 Field of view.

Both the visual angle subtended and the resolution (number of scan lines in this case) have been found to be positively correlated with recognition of vehicular targets on CRT displays (Boff and Lincoln 1988). A wider FOV display permits both a greater visual angle to be subtended by displayed objects and more objects to be displayed with given visual angles.

Resolution

As noted previously, foveal vision (the ~1–2° of the visual angle in diameter for the area of the retina known as the fovea) has the greatest spatial resolution of the human visual system, and this is a limiting resolution of ~1 arc min. A 1 arc min resolution allows you to distinguish discernible detail of 0.01 inch at a distance of three feet. Estimates of foveal resolution are the most commonly cited, and this is the highest resolution of which the eye is capable. Visual acuity worsens some with movement of the visual target.

The retina can be described in terms of regions, with successive belts out from the central fovea, including the parafovea, perifovea, peripheral areas, and ora serrata (extreme periphery), as described by Wyszecki and Stiles (1982). Visual resolution decreases for visual targets as they increase in distance from the point of fixation (i.e., from foveal vision). Olzak and Thomas (1986) show a linear relationship between distance from fixation in degrees and minimum angle of resolution in arc mins, ranging from approximately one arc min at 0 degrees (similar to the foveal resolution estimate) to approximately six arc mins at 20 degrees from fixation. (This is for phototropic vision; the situation for scotopic vision, less relevant for virtual environments, is that there's a central blind spot, with maximum acuity at four degrees from fixation and a decrease in acuity at greater angles.)

A similar linear decrease in resolution, with increasing distance of images from the area on the retina in which foveal vision is produced, is described by Anstis (1974).

The reasons for the reduced resolution in peripheral vision cited by Olzak and Thomas are the reduction in density of cones, with increasing distance from the center of the fovea, and the decreased size of the cortical representation for peripheral areas. An implication of this gradient of resolution is that a visual display that can control what's displayed to the fovea and what's displayed peripherally doesn't have to have as high a resolution in the peripheral areas to approach the limits of visual acuity.

Color perception

Color is the subjective experience of light within the part of the electromagnetic spectrum we can perceive. The sensation of color is largely the product of the wavelength of the light perceived, known as its *hue*. Color sensation is also affected by brightness (the perceptual quality associated with the light's intensity) and saturation (the perceptual quality associated with the purity of wavelength of the light; the addition of other wavelengths decreases saturation).

Hue, brightness, and saturation interact. For example, the Bezold-Brücke shift is the change in hue associated with a change in intensity, in which increased intensity causes violets and blue-greens to appear more blue, and yellow-reds and yellow-greens to appear more yellow. Although we consistently use different names to describe the colors perceived from different wavelengths, there are many colors we can discriminate and yet describe by the same name. In other words, there are more discriminable colors than there are names we associate with them.

There are several theories of color perception. The trichromatic receptor theory (also known as the Young-Helmholz theory) holds that there are three types of cones, each maximally sensitive to light in a particular spectral region, and that the extent to which these three types of cones are differently excited permits perception of all hues. The opponent-process theory similarly holds that there are three types of cones, but postulates different sensitivities (blue-yellow, green-red, and black-white) and holds that each type of cone can respond in one of two antagonistic ways, with opponent neural processes from these responses producing the perception of color. A detailed account of empirical findings and the resulting identified principles of color perception is provided by Cornsweet (1970), with a good more general overview of theories provided by Schiffman (1990).

Brightness and contrast

As noted previously, the visual system is capable of adapting to a wide range of intensities of light, from ~0.00003–300,000+ candelas per square meter, but the time required for adaptation through this range is too great to make it practical for use in display technologies. In particular, the time to adapt to scotopic (dim) intensity light is too great to be usable.

In studies with aircraft simulators, operator performance at identifying whether silhouettes of stationary aircraft were diving or climbing was studied with respect to different contrasts and resolution of visual displays. Not surprisingly, performance was better with a high resolution and higher rather than lower contrast; in these studies, a 25:1 target-to-background luminance contrast proved better than lower contrasts (Boff and Lincoln 1988). Since there are many variables in studies such as these (e.g., performance might depend on orientation of aircraft or the particular objects displayed, and might change with different uses of color and inclusion), the main conclusion to be drawn is that visual displays must provide enough resolution and luminance contrast to allow the user to detect a significant feature of objects in the environment when necessary.

Visual cues and performance

There has been considerable research on the effects of stereoscopic display on performance of "toy" tasks. Liu, Tharp, and Stark (1992) examined the effects of presenting two depth cues, occlusion and disparity (individually and in combination), on performance of a simulated telerobotic task. In their experimental tracking task, which required subjects to use joysticks to keep a solid ball within a box that moved unpredictably through virtual space, the subjects used HMDs with a small (~22°) FOV, and had to move their heads to keep the box within their fields of view. It was found that either occlusion (in which a subject using bioptic display determines where to move by whether the box occludes the ball or the ball occludes the box) or disparity (in which a subject using stereoscopic display determines where to move via stereoscopic depth cues) permitted fairly good and almost equivalent performance, and that combining them improved performance only slightly. With experience, they found less difference in performance, and suggest that this was due to secondary depth cues (such as the relative size of the ball and box) that the subjects learn to use. Using the same system with both the same and another task, they found that for the 3-D tracking task, display update rates affected task performance, with performance level plateauing at 10–20 Hz, and performance degraded below that level (Tharp, Liu, French, Lai, and Stark 1992).

Color is an example of a feature that users subjectively prefer (and have come to expect and demand with even conventional computer displays), but which, for many tasks, doesn't produce observed improvements in performance.

Implications for virtual environments

To visually present a virtual world so it's perceived as the real world is perceived, we could imagine an "ideal" HMD with a total horizontal field of view (FOV) of 180°, each eye having a 150° FOV, a binocular overlap of 120° (30° nonoverlapping peripherally for each eye), and a vertical FOV of 135°. This HMD would display at the limiting resolution of the human visual system, i.e., ~1 arc min, producing discernible detail amounting to 0.01 inch at a distance of three feet. It would display the range of discernible colors, and wouldn't have distortions and optical aberrations (Hezel and Veron 1993). In addition, all normal depth cues would be incorporated, and visual-vestibular cues would be synchronized as they are normally. Finally, the HMD would be lightweight and comfortable to use, and viewed objects would maintain stability in the presence of eye movements.

This collection of characteristics is well beyond the capabilities of any current systems, but it provides an upper limit beyond which there's no reason to strive. Since there are trade-offs, for example, between FOV and resolution, although it would be possible to build an HMD with an FOV wider than the normal human FOV, there wouldn't be any point in doing so because it would create unnecessarily poor resolution. Conversely, there wouldn't be any point in designing an HMD with better than ~1 arc min resolution and an extremely narrow FOV, since resolution this great couldn't be perceived by the user. Hezel and Veron (1993) examined current HMDs and suggested goals that are somewhat less than those of the hypothetical "ideal" HMD, with the following specifications: 140° horizontal FOV, 100° vertical FOV, 70° binocular overlap, resolution of 2–3 arc min, and 32,768 colors.

It's also important, when addressing the visual perception system, to coordinate stereoscopic depth cues. As noted previously, Piantanida points out how poor a display that puts flat texture in combination with parallax is, and the undesirable visual illusion it can lead to. He also points out that it's possible to adapt to a system's visual distortion, but it's much easier if the system gives the same distortion all the time. Although over the course of time you can learn to adapt to state-dependent distortion almost instantly (as you do when taking eyeglasses on and off), the adaptation process starts out being a slower one before you've had a great deal of experience switching between the states—and this can result in difficulty not only in adapting to using an HMD but also to readapting to seeing without the display. There are individual differences in how well people adapt to problems with visual displays (Piantanida 1993).

One implication of the nature of foveal versus peripheral vision, which is of possible significance for future displays, is that the high resolution and perception of color present in foveal vision isn't found in peripheral vision. Foveal vision represents a relatively small part of the FOV and, if it were possible to have sufficiently fast and accurate eye tracking and change in the display, presenting a dynamic high-resolution insert that's always presented to the area of foveal vision would be an alternative to making a high-resolution HMD through its full FOV.

Because of the individual differences in interpupillary distance, a display that presents different images to each eye must match the IPD of the user, either by being suited to a wide range of IPDs or by being adjustable. Individual differences in susceptibility to accommodation/vergence mismatches is another source of potential problems. In some cases, you can even measure who will best be able to adjust to a system. Alternately, in order to avoid this problem, you could explore engineering approaches to keep these mismatches from happening.

Finally, keep in mind that there are alternatives to presenting material visually. For example, a recent book edited by Kramer (1993) examines auditory representation of information, called *sonification*, and its advantages in some cases to visual presentation.

Auditory Perception

The information-gathering and situational awareness we gain through the sense of audition is perhaps less obvious than that from our sense of vision, but there are strong motivations to more extensively and effectively use audition in human-computer interfaces than has commonly been done. This section considers the process of auditory perception and some of the parameters that are relevant to virtual environment systems (or *virtual acoustic displays*, as VE auditory presentations are described). I'll focus especially on auditory localization; it's interesting that, unlike visual depth perception, in which cues have been understood for quite a while, one of the most important cues in auditory localization (pinna filtering) has been identified and understood only recently.

Basics of auditory perception

The outer ear, middle ear, and inner ear all play roles in human hearing. The outer ear (including the *pinna*, which is the visible portion of the ear outside of the head), collects sound received in the form of air vibrations (rapid changes in air pressure). This is converted to mechanical vibrations in the middle ear, where vibrations of the tympanic membrane produce vibrations in three small attached bones (the *ossicles*), which in turn transmit the vibrations to the inner ear's cochlea. The *cochlea* is spiral-shaped, filled with fluid, and contains a membrane known as the *basilar membrane*. The motion of the fluid inside the cochlea causes the basilar membrane to vibrate, and these hydrodynamic vibrations are transduced to nerve impulses by the hair cells that line the membrane.

Sound is the propagation of pressure variations (waves) through a surrounding medium. Sounds have acoustical properties (which I'll distinguish from their psychoacoustical characteristics), including *amplitude* (the magnitude of the pressure variations), *frequency* (the rate at which the pressure varies), and *phase* (when these waves fall in time). Complex sounds also have many spectral components, and the presence and relative amplitude of these components determine the sound's *timbre* (its quality or tone color, e.g., its brightness and nasality). Sounds are attenuated as they travel through a medium, and they can be reflected off of objects in their path.

Like visual adaptation to a wide variety of intensities of light, the auditory system has some adaptive mechanisms, such as loudness adaptation and the *acoustic reflex*, which is a protective contraction of inner-ear muscles that prevents damage to hearing from high-intensity sounds, but also causes temporarily reduced auditory sensitivity. The auditory system is also sensitive to a huge range of sound intensities; the most intense sound at 2 kHz that can be tolerated is one trillion times the intensity of the weakest sound that can be heard.

Visual stimuli can be static (i.e., remaining until eye movements put them in the line of sight), but sounds necessarily have a temporal component. Sounds tend to drop out of our conscious awareness if they're too constant, but changes in sound (such as an unexpected change in the sound of an automobile's engine) draw attention. And, while vision *requires* that our eyes be directed towards something for us to see it, we perceive sounds coming from sources in all directions.

There's a distinction between acoustical descriptions of sounds and their psychoacoustical descriptions. Frequency is an acoustical description and is easily measurable (e.g., with an oscilloscope); pitch is the psychoacoustical description of a subjective impression that generally corresponds fairly closely to frequency, but is affected by a number of factors such as loudness (sine waves under 1 kHz are perceived as getting lower in pitch as they get louder; those above 1 kHz are perceived as getting higher in pitch as they get louder) and timbre (sounds that are bright in timbre, i.e., have more high harmonics, are perceived as higher in pitch than are less bright sounds of the same frequency). Similarly, the psychoacoustical term *loudness* is a subjective impression that generally corresponds to what is acoustically described as amplitude, but loudness is affected by other factors, such as frequency (the Fletcher-Munson curve shows equal loudness contours for sine waves; as a generalization, sounds with frequencies between 1 kHz and 5 kHz sound louder than those of equal amplitude but above or below these frequencies) and bandwidth (within a frequency region of about one third of an octave, known as a *critical band*, the energy of different sounds are summed). For more information, see Buxton, Gaver, and Bly 1989.

Bark is a hearing-related scale for frequency, and the audible frequency spectrum can be divided into 24 discrete crucial bands each of 1 Bark (HEAD Acoustics 1990). A good introduction to psychoacoustics with further description of equiloudness contours and other phenomena is provided in Lindsay and Norman (1972).

While we can use our knowledge of psychoacoustics to accurately predict whether a single sound in a controlled setting can be detected, it becomes more complex when there are multiple simultaneous sounds and sound sources, as is so often found in the real world. Some sounds can obscure spectral components of other sounds, which is known as *masking*. In general, louder sounds mask softer sounds and lower-frequency sounds mask higher-frequency sounds; masking tends to happen especially between sounds in the same critical band. Masking might even happen between sounds that aren't simultaneous but immediately precede or follow one another.

For more on masking, as well as more psychoacoustical tips relevant to auditory displays, I recommend Buxton, Gaver, and Bly (1989); for mathematical functions used to predict psychophysical measures from acoustical measures, see HEAD Acoustics (1990).

Environments typically have numerous sounds within the range of our hearing, and these sounds originate from many sources. They combine into complex mixtures of acoustic energy, yet we manage to retrieve from this complex mixture mental descriptions of the sources by perceptually grouping them into discrete "objects." This process is known as *auditory scene analysis* and is described quite thoroughly by Bregman (1990). The process of auditory scene analysis is in place quite early in the human development process; Bregman gives the example that even babies don't insert imitations of cradle squeaks that happen simultaneously with their mother's voice when they try to imitate the mother's voice, so thus must be able to distinguish the squeaks as not being part of the perceptual "object" formed by the mother's voice.

Auditory stream segregation is the process of grouping sequential sounds (such as a series of tones) into a single perceived event; it depends on the rate at which the sounds occur, the differences in their timbres and frequencies, and the apparent location of their sources. Bregman points out that auditory stream segregation as well as *spectral integration* (the grouping and association with their sources of different spectral components of simultaneously heard complex sounds) depend on fairly constant tendencies of sound in the everyday world, such as the tendency for sounds to be continuous, move through space at fairly smooth rates along paths, and have components that begin and end together. Along the lines of Ellis's (1991b) notion that vision depends in a Kantian sense on *a priori* knowledge about the world, our ability to perform stream segregation seems to depend on our world knowledge as well as our experiences with certain familiar sounds.

Types of listening

In much of the work on auditory perception, the focus is on abilities such as discriminating between different pitches, rhythms, or melodies. Bill Gaver describes this as *musical listening* and maintains that we don't normally listen to events in the world in the same way we listen to music. For example, if we hear a pebble hit a can or a pot fall to the ground, we don't listen to the musical attributes of these sounds (their pitch, rhythm, timbre, or melody and harmony); rather we listen in an "everyday" way, in which our attention is focused on the attributes of the sound's source. So, in these examples, we'd notice how large and how full the can was and how hard the rock was thrown, or how heavy and how full the pot was, not what pitches they made. In Stuart (1993c), I cite an anecdote about a jazz musician who had such good "ears" that he immediately exclaimed "C#" when the shoe of his colleague squeaked; the point is that this is *not* how most of us listen to the squeaking of shoes or other everyday sound events.

Gaver (1986), describing his work as a "psychology of everyday listening," organizes everyday sounds into a taxonomy, describing characteristic effects of different object properties such as size (which is related to frequency and bandwidth), and force (which is related to amplitude); he also includes in this taxonomy descriptions of liquid sounds such as dripping (which reveals attributes of the liquid, such as its viscosity and density, and of the object the liquid strikes) and splashing, as well as aerodynamic sounds and the sounds of vibrating solids.

Musical listening capabilities can be incorporated into auditory displays, e.g., in representing abstract data through sonification. As Gaver's work has shown, everyday listening capabilities can also be used; for example, sounds can be associated with objects so that users perceive attributes of the objects as they would perceive attributes of objects in their everyday listening.

Auditory localization

The ability of humans to perceive the location of a sound's source from the acoustic energy that reaches the ears depends on several factors, and it's important to understand these in order to be able to create displays that give their listeners the impression of sounds located in space that remain in their positions or trajectories regardless of movement by the listener. These cues are interaural level difference, interaural time difference, pinna filtering, reflection/reverberation, and Doppler effects.

Interaural level difference. The exploration of how humans localize sound has gone on since long before anyone envisioned synthetically generating localization cues via a computer. Venturi, late in the 18th century, proposed that the difference in volume of the sound reaching the two ears was used for localization; his experimental design involved circling subjects in an open field at a distance of 40 meters and playing occasional notes on his flute. (This and other early experiments are described in Gulick, Gescheider, and Frisina 1989.) This cue is *interaural level difference* (ILD). In the simple case that a sound's source is near one side of the listener's head, it's easy to see that the sound level reaching the ear on that side would be louder than that reaching the other ear, as the head itself would obstruct and attenuate sound waves, and that ILD could identify the sound's source as being on the one side.

Interaural time difference and phase difference. Subsequently, Thomson proposed a phase hypothesis and Mallock suggested a time difference hypothesis (Gulick, et al. 1989 provides a good historical account). The latter cue is known as *interaural time difference* (ITD). Unlike light, which travels at such a high speed that you couldn't use it as a perceptual cue, sound travels in air at approximately 344 meters per second, slow enough that the difference in the time it arrives at two points (your two ears) can be used perceptually to identify the location of the sound's origin. Note also that the speed at which a sound travels is the same regardless of its frequency, complexity, or intensity. In the simple case that a sound's source is near one side of a listener's head, the sound will reach the ear on that side before it reaches the ear on the far side of the head, and this ITD is the time it takes the sound to travel around the head from ear to ear.

Phase difference between sounds reaching the two ears depends both on the distance of the sound source from the ears and on the frequency of the sound. For example, a given phase difference would be observed for sounds of different frequencies at different points in azimuth around the listener's head. Also, an ambiguity is observed for a continuous tone of higher frequency, where the same phase difference is produced by sounds in corresponding positions on opposite sides of the listener's head.

Duplex theory. Diotic stimuli (the same in both ears) and dichotic stimuli (different to each ear) have been used in studies, and both monaural and interaural processing have been examined. Durlach (1991) describes a theory that was popular until recently, known as *duplex theory*. Duplex theory postulates that the cues used for localization depend on the bandwidth and frequency of a sound source; this theory ascribes localization of broadband signals in all frequencies to time and phase difference, and localization of narrowband signals to intensity difference if the signal is above 1,500 Hz and phase difference if it's below 1,500 Hz.

Two phenomena, however, aren't explained by duplex theory. One is the ability to localize sounds by using only one ear. The other is the lack of externalization of sounds played through headphones where appropriate intensity, time, and phase differences are introduced; people report that the sounds do *not* seem to be coming from outside of their heads—although, as mentioned, externalization remains a controversial issue. (See Durlach, et al. 1992, for a discussion of this issue.)

Pinna filtering and head-related transfer functions. The missing cue for localization, *pinna filtering*, was discovered only within the past 30 years (although it was suggested by a demonstration by W. B. McLean in 1959). Batteau and others experimentally observed the importance of the pinna (the outer ear) in localization (see Batteau

1967), and it was observed that even people who are deaf in one ear are commonly able to localize sounds. In essence, the pinna acts as a filter that distorts incoming sound signals depending on their direction and distance in a way that permits the listener to decipher the direction/distance information. Blauert (1983) gives an excellent presentation on this pinna-related transfer function, and notes that the acoustical effect of the pinna is based on reflection, shadowing, dispersion, diffraction, interference, and resonance. As the entire head affects the incoming sound signal, this direction-dependent filtering is called the *head-related transfer function* (HRTF).

Frederic Wightman and Doris Kistler of the University of Wisconsin at Madison have performed the leading work in measuring HRTFs, using probe microphones with subjects in anechoic conditions (see Wightman and Kistler 1989a and 1989b). Many, if not most, of the research and commercially available virtual acoustic displays at the time of this writing use the HRTF from one of their subjects. An alternative used by some (in part because HRTFs measured with probe microphones are difficult to obtain), is to use HRTFs measured with an anthropomorphic mannequin head. This approach permits more repeated measurements, as the mannequin is a tireless subject. In using HRTFs, whether obtained from human subjects or anthropomorphic mannequins, an issue of concern is individual differences. People vary in their ability to localize sound sources, and there's a question whether performance will deteriorate if they use an HRTF that isn't their own. This will be discussed in the section *Synthesis of auditory localization cues* in chapter 5.

Complex (nonanechoic) acoustic environments. Although much of the work on auditory localization has focused on individual stationary sound sources heard by stationary listeners in an anechoic environment, these conditions aren't representative of most listening conditions in our everyday world, where the situation is far more complex. This complexity (as illustrated by Durlach and Colburn 1978) arises from reverberations (sounds bouncing off surfaces and the reflected sound reaching the listener after the initial signal), the presence of multiple, simultaneous sound sources, and the movement of sound sources and of the listener.

Reverberations are one of the few auditory cues for distance, and perhaps the best cue for absolute distance (Mershon and King 1975), though they make it more difficult to determine direction. You might wonder how all the temporally separated reflected sounds that reach your ears are perceptually fused into a single source (we're rarely consciously aware of reverberations). This phenomenon, in which the first arriving signal in a reverberating sound sequence takes perceptual precedence (and hence known as the *precedence effect*) was described by Wallach in 1939. Multiple sound sources can result in masking, in which one sound is less audible due to the presence of another sound simultaneous or close in time to the first sound (a sound can be masked by another sound that follows it quickly, as well as by one that precedes it or occurs simultaneously).

Cues for motion. The previous discussion addresses auditory localization at one point in time. Listeners typically move their heads to better localize the source of a sound, and this moves a fixed sound to different positions with respect to the listener. In combination with the listener's vestibular cues for self-motion, head movement aids in localization, particularly in disambiguating between possible source locations. You can similarly identify the motion of a moving sound source by comparing localization cues the source produces from moment to moment.

Two specific cues used to identify the motion of an auditory source relative to a user's position are changing volume and Doppler shift, known as the *Doppler effect* (Schiffman 1990). If the intensity of a sound gradually increases, the sound is perceived to be approaching; if its intensity gradually decreases, it's perceived to be moving away from the listener. Thus, a change in volume can be used in virtual acoustic display to convey motion.

The Doppler shift, named for Christian Doppler, the Austrian physicist who first identified it, is the apparent change in frequency of waves that occurs as the result of the relative motion between the source and the observer. In the case of sound, it's the apparent shift in pitch that's observed, for example, as a fast-moving ambulance with its siren on approaches and then passes you. The Doppler shift is the result of successive sound waves, though moving at a constant rate, originating from a changing center and therefore bunching up in front of their moving source, thus having smaller distances between them, a resulting increase in frequency, and a perceived rise in pitch. The Doppler shift can also be used in virtual acoustic displays to convey the motion of a virtual sound source.

Implications for virtual environments

Auditory display has obvious value for numerous applications, and has been largely underused (see Stuart 1993c). Unlike force and tactile perception, it allows transduction of information about distant objects not in contact with the observer and, unlike visual perception, the information perceived can come from any direction, not just the visual field of the observer. As auditory perception permits quick response to changes in stimuli, it has been suggested that, in virtual environments as in the real world, the ears can guide the eyes (direct the eyes to a point of interest).

Another strength of auditory perception is that you can simultaneously monitor multiple sound sources that are spatially distributed, known as the *cocktail party effect*. The auditory perception system is good at detecting changes while not directing attention to unvarying sounds; therefore, it can be effective in tasks that involve monitoring. The auditory perception system's ability to take in large rates of data and its sensitivity to temporal events also motivate its use in virtual environment systems.

Although the ILD and ITD cues are easy to synthesize, HRTFs are more complex, as are room characteristics such as reverberation. I'll discuss the synthesis of these cues in a section in chapter 5: *Synthesis of auditory localization cues*.

Haptic Perception

Haptic perception is a rather complex subject that includes the very different mechanisms of tactile (or cutaneous) perception (including perception of temperature), and kinesthetic/force perception. Tactile perception depends on cutaneous sensitivity, which includes the ability to detect mechanical, thermal, and electrocutaneous stimuli at the surface of the skin, and is produced through stimulation of receptors in the skin. Force perception and kinesthetic perception are closely related, and are produced by receptors in the muscles, joints, and tendons. Kinesthetic perception is perception of movement, position, and torque of the limbs and other body parts. Force perception depends on sensitivity to the muscular opposition that resists mechanical forces. Although these two terms describe very similar things, *kinesthetic perception* describes the perception a conductor has of his/her hand waving through the air or the perception a tennis player has of the motion of a backstroke, and *force perception* describes the perceptions one has when pushing against a door to try to open it or when squeezing a piece of fruit to determine its ripeness.

Kinesthetic perception may be divided into two types: a passive type, in which you experience your limbs being moved by an external force (e.g., a mechanical piece of equipment or another person), and an active type, in which the movement is self-induced. The passive type is said to produce only afferent information (the product of sensory input), while the active type produces both afferent and efferent information (the brain's transmitted neural impulses that produce motor movement). Motion, in addition to being active or passive, can be whole-body or part-body. The term *haptic perception* describes the combination of tactile and kinesthetic/force perception, and can be similarly passive or active.

Tactile perception

Cutaneous sensitivity is the product of numerous types of cutaneous receptors, located under the surface of the skin. These receptors are sensitive to different types of stimulation and are found in varying concentrations in different areas of the body. In particular, a distinction is made between areas of skin that are covered by hair and those that aren't (the latter is known as *glabrous skin*), and there are different receptors associated with each of these two types. Of the roughly two square meters of skin on the average adult, 10% is glabrous and 90% is covered by hair.

The receptor systems can be grouped either by their anatomical similarities or by their functional similarities. Anatomical classification groups receptors with similar configurations of nerve fibers (basket endings, spindle-shaped capsules, encapsulated receptors, etc.), while functional classification groups them by their type of sensitivity (to displacement, velocity, acceleration, or jerks) and their adaptive characteristics (slowly or rapidly adapting). For example, the glabrous skin of the fingertips has SA I (slowly adapting type 1), SA II (slowly adapting type 2), RA (rapidly adapting), and PC (Pacinian) receptors. Chang, Tan, Eberman, and Marcus (1993) note that the receptors respond differently to different experimental stimuli and speculate that the SA I system precisely detects object shape, the SA II system detects lateral skin stretch, the RA system detects transient dynamic events, and the PC system detects vibration.

Stimulation to cutaneous receptors can be mechanical, thermal, or electrical. Although there are no special receptors for electricity, the bioelectrical nature of nerve impulses makes it possible to mimic mechanical or thermal stimuli through electrocutaneous stimulation, which is often used in perceptual experiments. Because of the biophysical properties of the skin, cutaneous stimulation generally involves a large number of cutaneous receptors, as the skin carries the stimulation over an area greater than the area of contact. Spatial resolution therefore isn't very fine for cutaneous stimuli. Spatial and temporal summation have been found to occur with tactile perception, which results in a fusion of tactile information that allows you to very rapidly identify physical objects by touch, and in the interaction between separate stimuli that follow each other closely in time.

An example of the variation in tactile perception over different parts of the body due to varying receptor types and concentrations is demonstrated by the ability to distinguish a two-point touch from a one-point touch in different areas of the body. This "two-point resolution" varies from ~1 mm at the fingertip to 60 mm at the thigh (Boff and Lincoln 1988). Another example is in absolute thresholds for one type of touch (applying a mechanical stimulus, the von Frey hair), which were found to vary from 5 mg on the noses, cheeks, and upper lips of females to 355 mg on the large toes of males (Sherrick and Cholewiak 1986). Boff and Lincoln (1988) also note that individual differences in many measures of tactile perception are large. Some contact with the skin is completely undetectable. For example, Srinivasan (1990) points out that the slip of a smooth glass plate on the skin cannot be detected. However, remarkably small features are detectable, such as a grating that's 0.06 micron high (which is sufficient to cause a response in the Pacinian corpuscles).

Tactile stimulations can be classified as *step function* (a displacement held for one or more seconds), *impulse function* (a displacement of shorter duration), or *periodic function* (repeated brief displacements). The von Frey hair, for example, is a calibrated filament used to study perception of step function stimuli. Much of the work on tactile display has focused on using a vibratory stimulus as an aid to people with disabilities. Much of this research is relevant to using tactile display for virtual environments, and Sherrick and Cholewiak (1986) provide a good overview of the work that has been done with respect to spatial and temporal acuity, adaptation, and masking. They also discuss research on the application of tactile display to vigilance and tracking tasks.

Interesting experiments in tactile perception have been carried out in the context of representing visual images through tactile display for visually impaired users. White, et al. (1970) tested a device that processed the images received by a television camera and displayed them by controlling an array of 400 tactile vibrators on the back of the user. Based on the intensity of light in each part of the image, the corresponding vibrator would be activated or inactivated; the camera was panned across a scene and the user's task was to identify objects in it. White et al. found that users could identify many common objects using this tactile display, and could even make good assessments of depth (in this case, the relative positions of objects on a table) using monocular depth cues contained in the image. This experiment provides insights into the capabilities of tactile perception; just keep in mind that you can use tactile displays in this way for users who are *not* visually impaired.

One other type of cutaneous perception that has been less considered with respect to virtual environments is the perception of temperature (when VE researchers speak of tactile feedback, they often don't consider temperature display as fitting within the category). Sensitivity to temperature (warmth and cold) and temperature change is dependent on what area of the body is stimulated (areas of greatest sensitivity are the forehead, forearm, and back), and sensitivity increases as the area of stimulation increases. In addition, there's adaptation to temperature, and sensitivity to temperature change is related to the rate of change, with the threshold constant for rates of change of 0.1°C/sec and greater, but greater temperature change required to be perceptible at lower rates of change (Boff and Lincoln 1988).

Force and kinesthetic perception

Kinesthetic perception is produced by sensory receptors that detect information about joint angles and muscular length and tension. Kinesthetic awareness includes awareness of the position of the parts of the body, their direction and rate of movement, and the force produced by muscular contractions. Although some of the same receptors are involved, different mechanisms are employed to detect the static position of limbs, their movement, and the force developed by a muscle and associated effort (Clark and Horch 1986). Human fingers are fairly sensitive to force and pressure variations, and Shimoga (1993a) reports that a force step of 0.5 Newton or pressure variation of 0.2 N/cm2 can be detected. A wide range of frequency of forces can be perceived, up to chattering at 300–400 Hz and fine vibrations at 5,000–10,000 Hz.

Rosenberg (1993) has suggested that haptic percepts be decomposed into their salient sensory features in order to design haptic displays. For example, he decomposes the percept of contact with a rigid wall into the initial dynamic surface contact, the quasi-static interaction with the hard surface, and the final dynamic release of the surface, and associates the respective qualities of crispness, hardness, and cleanness with these stages. His experiments with a limited number of subjects have suggested that all three qualities must be conveyed effectively for the subjects to experience a convincing haptic percept of a wall.

Researchers at EXOS, Inc., a company that manufactures force feedback displays, found that the information on force and tactile perception in the available literature was insufficient to define the requirements for their haptic displays, and they performed original research to help define these requirements. Among their findings (described in Chang, Tan, Eberman, and Marcus 1993) are that:

- Perception of joint angles is more accurate in proximal joints (those closer to the torso) than in distal joints; at the shoulder joint the just noticeable difference (JND) was 0.8°, and at the wrist and elbow it was 2.0°.

- Pressure resolution is greater as a function of the area of contact; pressure JND decreased from 15.6% to 3.7% as the contact area increased from 0.20 inch squared to 3.14 inches squared. Force was felt mainly around the perimeter of the circular contact area, suggesting the sensitivity of the haptic perceptual system to pressure gradients.

- 140 lb/inch is required to simulate the stiffness of a rigid object.

- Controllable force increases from 3.72 lbs from the most distal joint of the fingers to 23.02 lbs from the most proximal (the shoulder), and subjects have better control of force output from the more proximal joints.

- Manual dexterity decreases with fatigue from weight applied to the elbow.

Shimoga (1993a) also notes the clearly asymmetrical input/output capabilities of the human hand, i.e., that it can transmit motion commands to a handmaster at a maximum frequency of 5–10 Hz, but it requires force feedback signals at a frequency of at least 20–30 Hz.

An extensive overview on tactile perception is contained in Sherrick and Cholewiak (1986), and an overview of kinesthesia is provided by Clark and Horch (1986). Further discussion of force and tactile perception, in the context of displays for virtual environments, as well as pointers to a wealth of addition sources of information, can be found in Shimoga (1993a, 1993b).

Implications for virtual environments

Tactile and force feedback are important for certain tasks. There has been more research on the value of force feedback than on tactile feedback, though Shimoga (1993b) mentions a couple of findings that suggest the value of tactile displays. Tactile displays have been perhaps most developed for and used by people with disabilities in non-VE contexts, for example, in tactile vision substitution systems and tactile auditory substitution systems (reviewed in Kaczmarek and Bach-y-Rita (1995). Kaczmarek and Bach-y-Rita also point out that, with more than 10,000 parallel channels (receptors), a large amount of information can be processed by the tactile system if that information is effectively presented.

Shimoga (1993a) reviews results by several researchers on the value of teleoperation systems that use force feedback to the wrist and fingers. He notes that force feedback to the operator's wrists reduces the task completion time, energy consumption, number of errors, and magnitudes of contact forces. Although less supporting research on force feedback to the fingers has been done, he hypothesizes that similar advantages would result from it. He suggests that, because lack of finger forces worsens performance on some tasks (e.g., stiff astronaut gloves that dull users' sense of grasping and insertion forces, which result in them doing worse on pegboard dexterity tests), by analogy dexterity would be improved by being able to feel finger forces.

In spite of the information and references cited, researchers such as Margaret Minsky have noted that haptic perception is one of our least understood senses. There has been limited work incorporating haptic displays into virtual environments, but more work on force displays (thanks in part to the efforts at the University of North Carolina, as well as work in the area of teleoperation).

Brooks, Ouh-Young, Batter, and Kilpatrick (1990) note performance gains from enhancing visual displays with haptic perception for certain tasks (the display they studied was a force display without a tactile component). They found performance enhancements of 2.2 times for a simple manipulation task and 1.7 times for a complex molecular docking task. They speculate that applications for which haptic displays will prove most valuable are those where a visual display of the data is difficult, complex force fields are important to performance, and education (understanding of information) is a goal.

Olfactory Perception

Olfactory perception is the perception of odor, using the sense of smell. It's striking that many standard references on human perception and performance (e.g., Boff and Lincoln 1988, and Boff, Kaufman, and Thomas 1986) don't include sections on olfaction, and many of the easily available references on the subject tend to be less rigorous and technical than those in the fields of visual, auditory, and haptic perception (although there certainly are technical articles on olfaction, e.g., in *Annals of Otology, Rhinology, and Laryncology* and *Electroencephalography and Clinical Neurophysiology*). The sense of smell (as well as the sense of taste) has been used so little in computer-human information displays that many of the studies that pertain to it (e.g., by the perfume industry or by neurobiologists and the medical community) haven't even been examined by most of us in the field of human-computer interaction.

Although gustation, the sense of taste, gives us chemical information as does olfaction, the sense of taste is normally applied to what we eat rather than to acquisition of awareness of our environment (ignoring here infants who puts every object within reach into their mouths, to the consternation of parents). Even with respect to food, many of the qualities we commonly attribute to taste are actually perceived by us due to their odors. So, although neither taste nor smell have been used in notable VE systems at present, I'll examine olfactory perception here because of the promise of olfactory displays for some applications, whereas gustation won't be further considered. One other sense that provides chemical information but won't be further discussed is known as *common chemical sense* or *trigeminal chemoreception*, and is characterized by the sensitivity of mucosal surfaces to chemical irritants such as pepper. Even those with *anosmia*, the complete absence of a sense of smell, can experience trigeminal chemoreception.

Often funded by perfume companies, which are secretive about their work, research at labs such as the Monell Chemical Senses Center in Philadelphia has produced results that could be helpful in the development of olfactory displays for virtual environments. At a recent medical conference (Medicine Meets Virtual Reality II, San Diego, California in 1994), Myron Krueger made a plea for research into incorporating olfaction in virtual environments and has since reportedly been working in this area.

Basics of olfactory perception

Olfaction, the sense of smell, allows us to gather information about chemical events in our environment, whether they occur near or far away. The *olfactory epithelium*, or *olfactory mucosa*, is an area high in the nasal cavity that has specialized tissue sensitive to odor. This area is approximately one square inch in total size (divided into the two sides of the nasal cavity), and includes approximately ten million olfactory receptor cells, each with dendritic knobs attached to hair-like cilia that are embedded in the moist mucosa.

There are theories of olfaction, but none is fully agreed upon. The "lock and key" theory holds that there are specific receptor sites that fit the geometric shapes of each type of molecule we can smell. While it's true that many molecules with similar geometries have similar odors, research has not revealed receptors of this specificity. Another theory maintains that olfactory receptors are sensitive to different broader categories of stimuli, so a particular odor will cause a variety of them to trigger and the perception of the specific odor depends on the resulting pattern of neural activity. This theory allows a given receptor to be activated by a variety of odors, which seems to correspond to the available experimental evidence.

The odors that serve as chemical stimuli for olfaction must be volatile (so at least some of their molecules are vaporized), they must be soluble in water and lipids (in order to penetrate the film over our olfactory receptors), and they must be chemicals that we're capable of perceiving with our olfactory receptors (we're capable of perceiving an especially large number of organic compounds).

There have been many attempts to classify odors (analogous to the primary colors with respect to visual stimuli), but there's more disagreement than agreement about what the basic categories are. Cater (1992) defines the basic categories as caprylic (goaty), fragrant, acid, and burnt (in this, he's using the Crocker-Henderson system cited in Schiffman 1990). Ackerman (1990) describes them as minty, floral, ethereal (e.g., pears), musky, resinous (e.g., camphor), foul, and acrid. Henning (cited in Schiffman 1990) organizes the basic odors—putrid, ethereal, resinous, burned, spicy, and fragrant—into a triangular "smell prism" along whose surfaces lie intermediate odors. Given the difficulty of coming to any agreement on the classification of "primary" odors, it might turn out to be impossible to find a small number of odorants that can be combined in different ways to approximate the smells of the large variety of substances to which we're sensitive.

The intensity of an odor is proportional to the number of molecules that interact with the olfactory receptors, and hence it's proportional to the concentration of molecules in the air. Our olfactory systems are capable of perceiving a huge range of intensities of stimuli: Cater (1992) notes that humans can identify odor over a range of 100 dB. We're remarkably good at detecting odors in very sparce concentrations; in the case of some substances, we can detect their presence in smaller concentrations than can most laboratory procedures. There are considerable individual differences in this sensitivity, though, some of which are associated with age (people tend to lose olfactory sensitivity as they reach old age, with anosmia found in nearly half of the people over 80 years old who have been tested), gender (females are generally more sensitive to odors than are males, and the sensitivity of sexually mature females to some odors varies through the course of their menstrual cycle), and personal habits (nonsmokers are more sensitive to odors than are smokers).

In contrast to the threshold sensitivity of olfaction, temporal sensitivity to odors is poor, and response times for olfaction are quite slow. It can require successive olfactory stimuli presented at 20- to 60-second (or greater) intervals for them to be resolved into separate odors (similarly, stimuli for taste must be presented at intervals of 30 seconds or greater to be resolved).

Adaptation and masking are also present with olfaction. Olfactory adaptation results in desensitization to an odor with continued exposure to it. Olfactory masking is the decrease in sensitivity to one odor caused by exposure to another odor, and can occur when the masking odor is present in much greater concentrations. In some cases a combination of odors can result in the odors still being individually identifiable; in other cases the odors blend to create a new hybrid odor.

I recommend a chapter by Schiffman (1990) on olfaction, which has been a valuable source for much of the material in the brief introduction offered here. Schiffman also provides pointers to many of sources in the technical literature on olfaction.

Smells have been claimed to not create percepts, and, because the olfactory receptors send neural impulses to the brain's olfactory bulb (or smell center), which in turn sends signals straight to the limbic system, the sense of smell is said to need no interpreter (Sowa 1984). The memory for olfactory stimuli has been found to be more stable with the passage of time than the memory for visual stimuli, and olfactory memory seems to be tied especially closely to the emotions (Schiffman 1990).

Why use olfactory perception?

Why would incorporating olfactory display be useful in a virtual environment? For some types of what I describe as online performance tasks and offline training tasks, the usefulness of olfactory display seems clear. In the case of an online performance task such as teleoperation, it could be useful to display to the operator the smells associated with the state of equipment (e.g., overheating), and smells of the environment in which the remote robot is operating. For offline training tasks, olfactory displays could prove useful for veridicality. One can imagine that olfactory veridicality might be helpful in training systems for fire fighters or emergency rescue teams. Similarly, some diseases, such as the one that affects infants and is known as maple syrup urine disease, are recognized by their smell.

The oft-noted ability of odors to evoke memories and moods suggest they might be useful even in offline training tasks where the odors in the environment in which the real task is performed aren't themselves a crucial source of information. At the previously mentioned recent medical conference, a surgeon commented on how important he felt the smells of surgery were to getting him into the appropriate mood and frame of mind; providing similar smells in a surgical training system might prove helpful in transferring the experience to the real world.

Implications for virtual environments

There's much to learn about olfactory perception in order to use it effectively in computer-human interfaces. Anecdotal observations suggest its value for certain applications. Implementation also presents challenges that could be solved with a better understanding of perception. For example, if there are in fact a set of "primary" odors that can be combined to create the effect of other odors, implementation of olfactory displays might be a less daunting challenge. Olfactory perception is clearly not the best modality for presenting quickly changing, temporally significant information, but, in general, so little has been examined about the topic that there's little else that can be said at this time.

Vestibular Sense

The vestibular system senses movements of the head rather than information about the external world. The nonauditory labyrinthine organs embedded in the bone on each side of the head consist of the three vestibular canals, which are used to sense rotations of the head, and the otolith organs, two small sack-shaped organs known as the *utricle* and the *saccule*, which sense gravity and linear accelerations of the head. The canals and otolith organs are connected, and they're filled with the endolymph fluid. Head rotations cause endolymph to lag behind the walls of the canals, in the direction opposite that in which the head is rotating, and this is used to sense head rotation.

The canals form three pairs. Members of a pair are roughly but not exactly parallel, and pairs are roughly but not exactly at right angles, thus no plane of head rotation stimulates only one of the pairs. Both otolith organs have membranes (*macula*) with cilia that protrude into a gelatinous structure (*statoconia*) that contains calcite crystals. This structure has a higher specific gravity than the surrounding fluid, and tilting or linear acceleration of the head cause it to be displaced. This displacement is the mechanism used to sense this tilting or linear acceleration (Howard 1986).

We usually respond to stimuli from the vestibular system without consciously attending to it, and are generally conscious of it only when its normal functioning is disturbed. We use the combination of our visual and kinesthetic perception and our vestibular sense in order to maintain our posture. Our vestibular and visual systems are tightly coupled, and objects that we look at maintain their perceptual constancy as we move, in part because our eyes move in the opposite direction of our head rotation (the vestibulo-ocular reflex).

As Piantanida (1994) points out with respect to eye-movement, there are two major theories of eye-movement control: the outflow (efferent copy) model and the inflow (feedback) model. The inflow model holds that rotation of the eyes, produced by extraocular muscles, produces afferent signals to the higher visual centers that the eye is moving; since time is required to generate and process these afferent signals, there's some lag between eye movement and change in the retinal image. The outflow model holds that a copy of the efferent signal that causes the eye movement is sent to the higher visual centers and prepares them for the changes in retinal image that will be produced by the eye movements *before they occur*.

An experimenter who temporarily paralyzed (curarized) his extraocular muscles found that, when he willed his eyes to move in one direction, the world appeared to move in the opposite direction, and Piantanida points out that this offers support for the efferent model. The efferent model implies the intolerability of lag between eye movement and change in the retinal image. It's also likely that, if the efferent model is correct for eye movement, it's also correct for head movement and the corresponding processes that maintain perceptual constancy.

Vestibular illusions and adaptation

Numerous vestibular illusions have been observed. They're typically observed by stimulating the vestibular system in the absence of visual cues, and include effects such as the inversion illusion (of being upside down when in zero gravity), cross-coupling (as the body rotates around a vertical axis, tilting the head forward produces the illusion of falling to one side) and postrotatory sensations (after prolonged rotation, deceleration produces the illusion of turning and falling in the opposite direction). For more on vestibular illusions, see Boff and Lincoln (1988).

These vestibular illusions haven't generally been useful in virtual environments because they require that the person be moved in order to perceive these illusions (and most VE systems, other than vehicular simulators, don't included motion platforms). Visual-vestibular interactions can also produce a variety of illusions in addition to the purely vestibular illusions mentioned previously. The manufacturers of motion platform systems also report that, in entertainment applications where precisely veridical movement isn't required, certain combinations of motions in concert with visual cues can be used to fool the user into thinking other motions actually occurred.

The vestibular system is also capable of much long-term adaptation, such as recovery from motion sickness on extended ocean voyages and adaptation to conflicting cue-producing stimuli such as spectacles that reverse and invert scenes. Currently, a relatively small number of people have spent extended amounts of time in virtual environments, and little research has been done on adaptation to conflicting cues.

Implications for virtual environments

The vestibular system can be used in a positive sense in motion platform systems, where the motion of the platform (e.g., vehicular simulator) mimics the motion cues the user would receive in the real vehicle. As most virtual environment systems (except vehicular simulators) don't incorporate motion platforms, the vestibular illusions in the previous section don't come into play. It's significant that motion platform vendors have "tricks" for fooling users because it's less expensive and less difficult from an engineering perspective to make a motion platform with fewer degrees of freedom, and this might suffice for applications where a higher level of motion veridicality is not required.

A major reason the vestibular sense has been of concern to the field of virtual environments is that conflicts between vestibular sense and other sensory channels (particularly visual perception) has been thought to play a role in simulator-like sickness, or *cybersickness* (for more on this, see chapter 10). A better understanding of simulator-like sickness should indicate more about the conflict between the vestibular and other senses and, perhaps, suggest solutions.

Comparing the Senses

Several authors have compared the human senses as informational channels. An early such comparison is made by Mowbray and Gebhard (1961). Following the previous discussion of the individual senses, refer to Table 2.1 (created by Wulfeck and

TABLE 2.1 Characteristics of the Senses

Parameter	Vision	Audition	Touch	Taste and smell	Vestibular
Sufficient stimulus	Light: radiated electromagnetic energy in the visible spectrum	Sound: vibratory energy, usually airborne	Tissue displacement by physical means	Particles of matter in solution (liquid or aerosol)	Accelerative forces
Spectral range	Wavelengths from ~400 to ~700 nm (violet to red)	20–20,000 Hz	>0 to <400 pulses per second	Taste: salty, sweet, sour, bitter Smell: fragrant, acid, burnt, caprylic	Linear and rotational accelerations
Spectral resolution	120–160 steps in wavelength (hue) varying from 1–20 nm	~3 Hz for 20–1,000 Hz; 0.3% above 1,000 Hz	~10 percent change in number of pulses per second		
Dynamic range	~90 dB (useful range); for rods = 0.000032–0.0127 cd/m^2, for cones = 0.0127–31,830 cd/m^2	~140 dB (where 0 dB = 0.0002 dyne/cm^2)	~30 dB (0.01–10 mm displacement)	Taste: ~50 dB (0.00003 to 3% concentration of quinine sulfate) Smell: 100 dB	Absolute threshold is ~0.2 deg/sec
Amplitude resolution	Contrast = 0.015	0.5 dB (1,000 Hz at 20 dB or above)	~0.15	Taste: ~0.20 Smell: 0.10–50 dB	~0.10 change in acceleration
Acuity	1 min of visual angle	Temporal acuity (clicks) ~0.001 sec	Two-point acuity ranges from 0.1 mm (tongue) to 50 mm (back)		
Response rate for successive stimuli	~0.1 sec	~0.01 sec (tone bursts)	Touches sensed as discrete to 20/sec	Taste: ~30 sec Smell: ~20–60 sec	~1–2 sec; nystagmus might persist to 2 min after rapid changes in rotation
Reaction time for simple muscular movement	~0.22 sec	~0.19 sec	~0.15 sec (for finger motion if finger is the one stimulated)		
Best operating range	500–600 nm (green–yellow) at 34.62–68.52 cd/m	300–6,000 cps at 40–80 dB		Taste: 0.1–10% concentration	~1 g acceleration directed head to foot

TABLE 2.1 Characteristics of the Senses (Continued)

Parameter	Vision	Audition	Touch	Taste and smell	Vestibular
Indications for use	1. Spatial orientation required 2. Spatial scanning or search required 3. Simultaneous comparisons required 4. Multidimensional material presented 5. High ambient noise levels	1. Warning or emergency signals 2. Interruption of attention required 3. Small temporal relations important 4. Poor ambient lighting 5. High vibration or g forces present	1. Conditions unfavorable for both vision and audition 2. Visual and auditory senses 3. Detection of fine surface irregularities	1. Parameter to be sensed has characteristic smell or taste (e.g., burning insulation)	1. Gross sensing of acceleration information

Table adapted from *Psychological Principles in System Development* by Robert M. Gagne, © 1962 by Holt, Rinehart, and Winston, Inc. and renewed 1990 by Robert M. Gagne. Reproduced by permission of the publisher.

Zeitlin, 1962) as a useful summary comparison of the senses. Boff and Lincoln (1988) cite this table and offer the following caveats about it:

- Many of the parameters interact. They give the example that, while the value for visual acuity of 1 min. arc is nominal, visual resolution is much poorer for low contrast, low luminance, nonstandard test patterns, some spectral distributions, and short presentation times, or under conditions of vibration.

- There are significant individual differences not expressed in these values, and it could be important to take these into account in system design.

Boff and Lincoln (1988) compare reaction time (RT) to stimuli presented in different sensory modalities, and observe that the most rapid RTs were to optimally presented auditory or tactile stimuli (110–120 msec). The RT to optimally presented visual stimuli was slower (150 msec), and visual and auditory cues that were lower in intensity produced slower RTs. For example, the RT to a small, brief, dim, visual stimulus is 500 msec, and the RT to an auditory stimulus near the threshold of hearing is 350 msec.

Kaczmarek and Bach-y-Rita (1995) cite studies suggesting that maximal rates of information flow both at the receptor level and after processing. At the receptor level these maximal rates are 10^7 bits per second for the eye, 10^6 bits per second for the skin, and 10^5 bits per second for the ear. After processing, the stream of tactile information, for example, is reduced to 2–56 bits per second (compared to 40 bits per second for understanding speech and 30 bits per second for reading).

In the next section, I'll discuss motor capabilities. Because of how the different senses perceive and what is described as the *perceptual-motor integration problem*, the choice of display modality can have an important effect on user performance of motor tasks. For example, Hirose, Hirota, and Kijima (1992) studied the effects of different virtual environment displays on object manipulation performance. This type of performance is particularly important in what are called *online performance tasks*. Hirose et al. examined the use of cues such as stereoscopy, motion parallax, and force display on users' performance at inserting a virtual cylinder into a virtual pin and curved platform. They found that stereoscopy, subject-induced motion parallax, and force feedback (especially boundary constraints) were helpful for task performance.

Motor Capabilities

Hands and arms

Many human motor control tasks that involve the hands are not limited to the use of just the hands, i.e., arm motion from the elbow and shoulder joints is also incorporated. For example, time-related measurements such as maximum tapping speed have been studied but, in the case of tapping, the maximum speed found was for tapping movement originating from the subjects' right elbows. However, I'll begin by discussing the motor capabilities of the hands themselves. Human fingers can exert momentary forces of 30–50 Newtons and sustained forces of 4–7 Newtons. The hand can exert force commands at the rate of 5–10 Hz, although it can perceive forces at a much higher rate (Shimoga 1993a). Joints connect the metacarpal region of the hand to the proximal phalange (or first digit) of the fingers, as well as to the succeeding digits (the medial phalange and the distal phalange). The kinematics of the fingers are rather complex, and they're discussed by Speeter (1992).

Hand strength, measured with a hand dynamometer, has been tested for different segments of the population and is rather variable even within a population segment. For example, U.S. Air Force males, 18–25, had a maximum squeeze ranging from 90–203 lbs; for U.S. civilian males ages 20–30, the 5th percentile was 74 lbs, while the 95th percentile was 142 lbs.

Hand size was also somewhat variable; hand length in adult males ranged from 7.0 inches (5th percentile) to 8.2 inches (95th percentile), with the 50th-percentile male hand length being 7.6 inches. For adult females, hand length ranged from 6.4 inches (5th percentile) to 7.4 inches (95th percentile), with the 50th percentile at 6.9 inches. By contrast, hand length of six-year-olds ranged from a 5th percentile of 4.6 inches (males) and 4.5 inches (females) to a 95th percentile of 5.7 inches (males) and 5.4 inches (females). Hand breadth and thickness also vary and have been measured for male and female populations of different ages (Woodson 1981).

As many virtual environment systems use instrumented gloves to capture the user's manual input (although gloveless gesture recognition is also possible, through processing of video input), the size of users' hands needs to be considered; in the case of dexterous handmasters, which provide force feedback to the user's hands, hand strength should also be considered. Given the use of instrumented gloves as input devices in VEs, it's interesting to observe that there has been some human factor research on how wearing gloves affect the performance of control operations

(Boff and Lincoln 1988). These studies are of limited applicability for most virtual environment applications for the following reasons:

- The tasks studied consist mostly of manipulating physical devices, e.g., the maximum torque that can be applied to rotary switches, or the speed of operating toggle switches, rotary knobs, buttons, and levers.
- The gloves studied were quite different than the instrumented gloves used for virtual environments (the implicit purpose of wearing them had to do with protection, e.g., from hostile environments, such as cold), so the gloves studied were, for example, leather gloves over wool insert gloves.
- The effects of wearing gloves varied considerably based on the characteristics of the gloves worn.

Aimed movements. Many everyday motor activities that can be used in virtual environment, as they frequently are in the nonsynthetic world, involve aimed movements. Examples of these activities include reaching, grasping, pointing, and touching. In a virtual environment, the user might select, grab, or move an object, or reach for it to feel its texture and examine its shape. There's a long history of research by psychologists into aimed movements, especially concerning speed/accuracy trade-offs. A wonderful review of this history, from the pioneering work of Woodworth in the late 1890s (whose interest in the subject was stimulated by his observation that Italian construction workers swung their hammers rapidly and casually, yet rarely missed their intended targets) to the current findings and theories is provided by Meyer, et al. (1990).

Experiments in rapid aimed movement typically involve a series of trials where a part of the subject's body is aligned with a specified location, a new target location is shown (either as a point, line, or region), and the subject tries to move as quickly and accurately as possible from the current location to the target location at a moment cued by a response signal (often an auditory tone). The movement latency is the time between the response signal and the beginning of movement, and the movement duration is the time from the beginning to the completion of the movement. Both movement latency and movement duration, as well as the path of the movement and its endpoint, are measured as a function of independent variables such as target size, distance to the target, and whether the subject's eyes remain open or closed. Two alternative procedures for studying speed/accuracy trade-offs are time-matching movement tasks, in which subjects try to time their movement to reach a target in a specified time, and time-minimization movement tasks, in which subjects try to make their movement to the target in the least possible time.

Paul Fitts observed in the mid-1950s that, if you consider the "index of movement difficulty" to be the logarithmic transformation of target distance divided by target width, there's a linear relationship between movement duration and the index of movement difficulty. This relationship, known as Fitts' Law, is expressed as:

$$T = A + B \log^2\left(\frac{2D}{W}\right)$$

where T is mean movement duration, A and B are constants, D is distance to the target, and W is width of the target. Thus, the time it takes to move the hand to a target is dependent only on the relative precision required, i.e., the target distance/size ratio. This law is frequently quoted in the context of human-computer interaction (see Card, Moran, and Newell 1983); a variation, Schmidt's Law, applies to briefer movement where there's no correction from visual feedback. Although Fitts' law applies to a great variety of movements, including finger, wrist, leg, head, and throwing, this empirically based "law" doesn't provide a theoretical basis for the relationship it describes.

Woodworth, in his pioneering work in the 1890s, postulated that an aimed movement consists of an initial-impulse phase, which is programmed and ballistic, and a current-control phase, in which unintended errors are corrected as the movement proceeds, based on sensory feedback.

Competing theoretical explanations for the relationship described by Fitts' law have attributed it to the initial-impulse phase or the current-control phase. For example, the deterministic iterative-corrections model holds that movement to hit a target consists of a series of discrete submovements guided by sensory feedback, each of a constant proportion of the distance to the target, each requiring the same amount of time regardless of the distance traveled. Thus, this model holds that the logarithmic speed-accuracy trade-off is produced primarily by the current-control phase. One opposing model holds that with faster movement speed there is increased neuromuscular noise, and this affects the initial adjustment required.

The model that most successfully explains empirical results, however, is the stochastic optimized-submovement model proposed by Meyer, et al. (1988), which holds that both phases contribute. This model maintains that there's an initial (primary) submovement directed at the center of a target but that, if this primary movement misses the target due to neuromuscular noise, a corrective secondary submovement occurs based on sensory (e.g., visual or kinesthetic) feedback. Submovements have a gaussian distribution around the target center due to the neuromuscular noise, and the movement time is minimized by a compromise between durations of the submovements. The stochastic optimized-submovement model formulates a more general relation, of which Fitts' Law is a special case where the number of submovements approaches infinity.

Studies of the time and precision of *blind positioning* (in which a subject is shown current and target positions, and then asked to move from the current to the target location with the lights turned out) and of hand movements made with different types of visual feedback have revealed that the error rate is lowest when the hand is always visible, the target remains visible, and the eyes can move freely (Boff and Lincoln 1988).

Grasping. Grasping involves more than movement of the hand to a target: it consists of a transport phase and a grasp phase, and the grasp phase involves wrapping the fingers around the object to be grasped. The maximum separation between the thumb and index finger is greater if a larger object is to be grasped, but it's also greater if the movement to grasp the object is at higher speed (in which case a wider finger positioning increases the chance of successfully grasping the object). It appears that coordinative structures control the interaction of joints in reaching and grasping movements and, similarly, there appear to be coordinative structures for two arms and hands moving at once. A good account of reaching and grasping and this intersegmental coordination is provided by Rosenbaum (1991).

Key-pressing. Key-pressing has been extensively studied, in part for what it reveals about the way the human information processing system works (Card, Moran, and Newell 1983). There have been numerous studies of reaction time, errors, and the timing of keystrokes. Skilled typists routinely produce on the order of 450 keystrokes per minute, but typing is a motor capability seldom used within current virtual environment systems. Since it has been much studied and discussed elsewhere, I won't discuss it further.

Other capabilities. Other capabilities of the hands and arms include writing, drawing, tapping, sign language, sculpting, and playing musical instruments (which, in the case of woodwinds and brass, also require breath control and movements of the lips and tongue—not capabilities often used in human-computer interfaces).

Writing and drawing are physically similar processes, and both are thought to be accomplished via a process in which a series of executable instructions are generated through hierarchical translations from abstract representations in the mind. Several relationships are time-related: the sharper a drawn curve the more the pen slows down when drawing it, equal angles are drawn in equal times (even if the two loops of a figure eight are of radically different sizes the drawing time is equal), and the absolute time but not the relative time to draw letters of the alphabet while writing changes with the size of the letters drawn. A VE system can provide a virtual pen for annotation, and either keep the characters as written or translate them into machine-readable text.

Tapping has been studied mainly with respect to speed. The relationships between maximum tapping speed and age, sex, typing speed, and handwriting speed have been observed (Boff and Lincoln 1988). The fastest mean rate of tapping observed, slightly over 7 taps per second for males, originating with their right elbows, suggests the maximum speed of human motion that would need to be tracked in a virtual environment—except that the distance traveled during each tap wasn't measured.

Sign language is of particular interest to those designing virtual environment systems for users with disabilities. For example, Kramer and Leifer (1989) describe a system that allows users with an instrumented glove to generate sign language gestures that are then converted into synthesized speech.

Like sign language, sculpting and playing musical instruments require the user to develop a set of skills through practice. There's little in the scientific literature on sculpting, but there have been a number of studies of musical performance. Skilled pianists routinely produce "keystrokes" even more rapidly than do skilled typists due to their ability to play multiple notes simultaneously; Rosenbaum (1991) cites the example of playing three notes with each hand, with these chords played at a rate of more than three chords per second, which produces a total "keystroke" rate of nearly 1,100 per minute. Musical performance on a piano involves more than just the sort of motor capabilities used in typing; the timing of the key presses, not just their order and speed, is also important, as is force with which they're hit (and the variety in this force). Musicians are willing to put in a great deal of effort developing specialized motor skills because of the rewards of virtuosity in musical performance. Stuart (1993b) discusses the process of jazz improvisation and the idea that similar highly developed motor skills (as well as improvisation and real-time collaboration) could be taken advantage of in design applications of virtual environments.

Implications for virtual environments. You'll want to consider the range of hand sizes if you're planning to use instrumented gloves; similarly, you also want to consider the range of hand strengths when designing or choosing force feedback devices such as dexterous handmasters. If instrumented gloves must be worn for extended periods of time and if they must be worn while interacting with real-world objects (e.g., in augmented reality applications), the gloves should be sufficiently light and unencumbering to avoid the negative effects of wearing heavy, bulky gloves.

A virtual environment system can take advantage of the fact that the greatest speed of aimed motion results when the minimum of target precision is necessary. Depending on the precision and sample rate of input technologies that capture hand movement, targets (and the precision required to select or manipulate them) can be made large and require imprecise movement. If the input technology's precision of measurement is poor but can be sampled frequently, or the targets can be made small and require precise hand movements (which will naturally slow down the user's hand movements), then you want to choose input technology that captures movement precisely but with a relatively slow sample rate.

If fast and precise hand movements are required (e.g., for teleoperation tasks or virtual environment games such as virtual handball), the perceptual/motor literature suggests that the hand or its graphical representation should remain visible in the virtual environment, as should the target.

The other motor capabilities using the hands and arms (writing, drawing, sculpting, producing sign language, and playing musical instruments) are seldom used in current virtual environment systems, but either these or analogous skilled movements could be used to collaboratively design and communicate in systems of the future.

Locomotion

There are many ways in which human motor capabilities permit us to move ourselves in the real world, including walking, skipping, running, crawling, hopping, and swimming. In addition—if the equipment is available—you can self-locomote via climbing and cycling. Most of these forms of locomotion involve rhythmical repetitive actions, and they're influenced by sensory feedback (such as using optic flow when walking to gauge when the foot will next make contact with the floor). Gait patterns change with the speed of walking/running, and can be recognized when only a few points of light on the leg can be seen. The complexity of walking/running, however, is hinted at by how difficult it is to build robots that walk.

In navigating in the real world, we're accustomed to using our motor capabilities of locomotion to get from place to place. Early researchers believed that humans possess no true spatial memory but rather remember familiar motor response sequences, but this is now thought to be unlikely. The action of self-locomotion gives us feedback that provides a sense of how far we've traveled. Locomotion interfaces, described briefly in chapter 4, allow us to make use of these motor capabilities and the navigation feedback they provide.

Speech production

Speech is a powerful mode of communication for humans, and has been studied by researchers from several disciplines, including linguists, psychologists, speech pathologists, and physiologists. The production of speech is a complex act, which I'll review in only a cursory way, given that its primary relevance to the design of VEs is that humans *can* produce speech and that the user's speech can be used to communicate with other users, as well as to issue commands to and control the VE.

A brief review of the physical production of speech. The production of speech involves controlling the movement by three muscle groups: the articulatory muscles in the head and neck, the muscles of the larynx (which are used in phonation), and the muscles in the chest and trunk (which are used for breathing). The breathing mechanism (specifically, the air flowing out from the lungs) is the source of the speech energy. The vocal cords, through control of the laryngeal muscles, can be brought together to form an obstruction of the path from the lungs to the mouth. The pressure of air from the lungs against the vocal cords pushes them out of the way and, through a combination of the elasticity of the vocal cords and the Bernoulli effect, they then bounce back, only to be pushed out of the way again. The sound of speech is produced by the vocal cords cyclically opening and closing this path, which controls the frequency of produced sound. In fact, this sound production is complicated by the fact that waves other the fundamental ones (e.g., transverse waves) travel through the vocal folds. The articulatory muscles then shape this sound through a variety of mechanisms such as changes in tongue position and shape and changes in lip shape, such as lip-rounding (Fry 1979).

Speech as a communication medium. When analyzed in this way, the production of speech turns out to be a rather complex act, but speech has been described as the most natural communication channel for humans. Among its advantages as a communication medium are that it's a rapid way to convey information and it takes little training (actually, it takes training that practically all users completed when they were young). In addition to the explicit content of speech (the words spoken), additional information can be conveyed by the melody, rhythm, and emphasis, collectively known as *prosody*.

Although naturally occurring speech between humans varies in rhythm and also from speaker to speaker (as well as between speakers from geographic region to geographic region), the rate of communication in human-to-human speech communication is rapid. In terms of information transfer, symbol rates have been estimated at 50 bits per second in speech, as opposed to 30 bits per second for writing with a pen (in shorthand), 30 bits per second for keyboard entry, and less than 10 bits per second for using a mouse (Segan 1993).

Speech in human-computer interaction. Some important considerations for using speech in human-computer interaction are the way we use speech, the assumptions we bring to its use, and the way it interacts with other processes, rather than the physiological characteristics of speech production. Waterworth (1982) has noted the body of experience and expectations that users bring to verbal interactions and Stuart, Desurvire, and Dews (1991) observed behavior by users of a speech-based computer system that suggested they were using a human-human communication model (at least with respect to turn-taking) which can lead to unnecessarily inefficient interaction. Also, speakers might vary their prosody, rate of speech, and choice of words to describe an action or concept. They're accustomed to speaking continuously, using anaphoric references (and other components of natural language that make it difficult for a computer system to understand speech), and communicating nonverbally in parallel with their spoken communication.

Implications for virtual environments. Because speech can be used for an exceptionally high rate of information transfer and because, although a physically complex act, it's a natural communication medium (requiring little training), speech should be incorporated more often in virtual environment systems. Speech can be used both as a means of human-to-human communication (in the case of multiuser virtual environments) and as a means of human-to-computer communication. With the latter, the interface can be designed to maximize efficiency by encouraging a human-to-computer dialogue suited to the capabilities of the recognition system, the demands of the task, and the behavior of the user. Integrating recognition of nonverbal communication with speech recognition could offer further advantages in terms of information transmission rate and naturalness.

Eye movement

Eye movements are often thought of as a mechanism to support visual perception rather than as a motor capability for input to a human-computer interface. Several types of eye movements were discussed in the context of vision, in the section *Basics of visual perception* early in this chapter. These include vergence (up to 10° per second), smooth pursuit of a slowly moving object (up to 40° per second), saccades, which are a response to peripherally detected motion or decision to change fixation (up to 1,000° per second, with especially high initial acceleration and final deceleration, and up to 40,000° per second squared according to Young and Sheena, 1975), and vestibulo-ocular movement, which is the compensatory movement in the opposite direction of head or body movement that's used to maintain visual fixation (as necessary, up to 500° per second). Through the use of eye-tracking technologies, eye movements can also be detected and used as input. This has proven especially helpful for users with motor disabilities.

Implications for virtual environments. The speed of vestibulo-ocular movement is fast, which is one reason why latency in adjusting the visual display of a head-tracked system in response to user motion is so apparent and can create problems. The use of eye tracking as a control technology is reasonable given the speed of slow-pursuit eye movements. However, using eye tracking to determine changes in the point of regard and, for example, to display the foveal region at higher resolution than other areas in the display might be difficult given the high rate of movement of saccades.

Facial movement and expressions

Facial expression and movement are a powerful mode of communication, especially in the expression of emotion. Facial expressions vary widely in duration (from several seconds to as briefly as 40 milliseconds). Although there has been much research on the perception of facial expression, there has been little on its production. Facial expressions can be studied in terms of their appearance, the muscular (electromyographic) activity that produces them, or the emotions they convey. Electromyography reveals that facial expressions can be produced by single facial muscles or by the activity of several muscles. Rosenbaum (1991) discusses the muscular and neural control of facial expressions, as well as their association with emotions.

Many current virtual environment systems have display devices (such as HMDs or BOOMs) that obscure the face of the user from others and, particularly in communication through shared virtual environments, the information conveyed through facial expression is lost. An exception to this is those systems that use VACTOR technology (discussed in chapter 4), which measure facial movement and use it to control animations (e.g., displaying facial expressions and movement on animated cartoon-like characters that represent users in the virtual environment).

Sensory Interactions

The senses, in concert, allow us to perceive the world, be it a virtual world or the real world. There are numerous sensory interactions that can be used to the benefit of the virtual environment design, and ignored only at the risk of detrimental effects. Although there are more of these interactions than can be described in detail here, I'll provide a couple of examples and direct you to sources for more information.

One relationship between visual perception and auditory localization is the *ventriloquist effect*, which describes the result of conflicts between visual and auditory localization cues, which is that vision has a powerful and dominating effect on the localization of sound. In other words, sound will appear to originate from a source other than that suggested by auditory cues if a sufficiently compelling visual source for the sound is presented. This is why ventriloquism is possible (Warren, Welch, and McCarthy 1981), and it might also account for some of the front-to-back errors subjects make when they attempt to localize sounds in purely auditory virtual environments. We're used to being able to see a source for sounds and might be more prone to believe the source is behind us if none is visible.

Vision also tends to dominate when there are conflicts between visual and haptic cues. For example, when describing a straight rod that they both touched and viewed through prisms that made it appear to be curved, subjects reported that the rod both looked and felt curved (Rosenbaum 1991).

The vestibulo-ocular reflex, described earlier, involves the interaction of head or body movement and eye movement. This reflex produces the compensatory eye movement in the opposite direction of head or body movement that's required to maintain visual fixation.

Using virtual environments to study human perceptual-motor capabilities might facilitate the study of conflicting sensory information and sensory interactions between vision, audition, proprioception, and the haptic senses; in turn, new information on these interactions that's acquired through such research could help in the design of virtual environments. An excellent source on sensory interactions is Welch and Warren (1986). See also Bertelson and Radeau (1981).

Implications for virtual environments

You can use sensory interactions to create effects not otherwise possible due to limitations in display technologies. By using the ventriloquist effect, you could create a system with inadequate virtual acoustic display (or none at all) that produce the effect of sound originating from visible sources by providing compelling visual cues. On the other hand, sensory interactions can cause difficulties. In the case of the ventriloquist effect, a sound whose spatial cues indicate that it's in front of the listener might be perceived as coming from behind if there isn't a visual source in the virtual front location from which the sound originates. Scaling errors, in which a given motion results in a difference in the degree to which cues to the visual, auditory, and haptic systems change, are also a problem and should be avoided if possible.

Sensory Adaptation

The human sensory systems are capable of a surprising degree of adaptation. We can adapt to a large range of distortions (beyond the scope of this book)—even, for example, flipping the visual field. While this plasticity of the human sensory systems is impressive, it comes at a price; when adaptation to altered sensory input occurs, a period of readaptation to normal sensory input must follow. With training, this adaptation/readaptation process can become more rapid for a given distortion (as it does when we become accustomed to using new prescription glasses). And this plasticity allows users to tolerate some of the limitations and distortions in current virtual environment displays. But the period of readaptation might cause difficulties following use of the virtual environment system (see the section *Visual Impairment* in chapter 3). In addition, adaptation to certain types of distortion is difficult (Welch 1978).

There have been studies of the degree of adaptation to some specific problems in virtual environment displays. Ellis, Tyler, Kim, and Stark (1992) studied three-dimensional pursuit tracking with misalignment between the axes of the perspective display and those of the control devices (which were rotated from those of the display). Using two different types of input devices, joysticks and an instrumented glove, they found that simultaneous adaptation to a variety of display-control misalignments was possible with practice. A recommended source for more information on sensory adaptation is a classic book by Welch (1978), which presents both an overview on sensory adaptation and numerous specific research findings.

Implications for virtual environments

Although users can adapt to many types of distortions if given sufficient time, readaptation to normal sensory input also takes time, and this might cause problems (e.g., if the user has to operate a vehicle or engage in potentially dangerous activities after using the virtual environment system). Where possible, the human plasticity and capability to adapt to sensory distortions should not be taken advantage of in virtual environments.

Cognitive Capabilities and Issues

Many of the issues regarding cognitive capabilities and their significance in defining requirements for virtual environments are similar to issues with other types of human-computer interfaces. For example, you should consider working memory and long-term memory characteristics. The model information processor view (described by Card, Moran, and Newell 1983) sees working memory as mental operations processing the representations produced by the perceptual system as well as returning the results; working memory is the activated part of long-term memory. Long-term memory stores all of a person's available knowledge.

In terms of human-computer interface design, there are limits to the amount of information that can be held in working memory and the time in which it can be held there. *Chunking*, in which smaller units of information are grouped into larger units, permits more information to be held in working memory, but it's dependent on the way information is presented and the contents of long-term memory. Card, Moran, and Newell (1983) give as a simple example the difficulty of holding (and being able to repeat back) the character string BCSBMICRA in short-term memory and the greater ease of doing so with the character string CBSIBMRCA, especially if this is recognized and "chunked" into CBS IBM RCA.

To the extent that a user needs to keep information in short-term memory to use a virtual environment (e.g., to respond to options presented through speech synthesis), it's advisable to present the information in a way that both takes into account the limits (temporal and size) of working memory and facilitates appropriate chunking. Card, Moran, and Newell (1983) summarize studies of the decay rate of working memory and describe it approximately in a series of formulas. They note that, with more items in working memory, decay rate is faster, e.g., one chunk can be retained for 73 (73–226) seconds, but three chunks can be retained for only 7 (5–34) seconds. They note that you normally use both working memory and long-term memory to repeat something a few seconds after hearing it, but that techniques can be used to separate these systems, such as presenting a long series of digits, unexpectedly stopping, and noting the number of digits immediately preceding the stop point.

In the case of long-term memory, retrieval of information is difficult if there aren't adequate associations for the information to be retrieved or if the associations are also tied to memory chunks that are similar to the information to be retrieved. Thus, the interface designer should avoid negative transfer (in which associations with previously stored information causes interference in learning to do a new task or use a new system), and should provide rich associations to information that must be recalled from long-term memory.

Learning (the process of modifying behavior, acquiring knowledge, or developing skills through experience or training) is pertinent to VEs in terms of both learning to use the virtual environment itself and learning the skills and subject matter that the VE application is intended to convey. The issue of negative transfer suggests that you must be careful when expecting the user of a virtual environment system to learn things where the appearance is like that of doing the real-world task, but the behavior is different. This needs to be examined especially in terms of tasks categorized as *offline rehearsal*, as users of the virtual environment system are at risk of learning behaviors that won't work correctly in doing the task in the real world. A good introduction to theories of learning, a field too large to discuss extensively here, is provided by Lindsay and Norman (1972).

In terms of providing rich associations to facilitate recall of information from long-term memory, virtual environments are especially well-suited to providing a variety of associations not possible with other human-computer interfaces, due to the multisensory and spatial qualities of virtual environments.

Other cognition-related recommendations that apply to virtual environments as they do to a wide variety of other human interfaces (such as affordances) are discussed in Norman (1988). Of special concern to the designer of virtual environments are cognitive issues that have *not* been examined with respect to other types of human-computer interfaces. In particular, the issue of how users represent space and determine their position in the space is important, as is examining the best ways to aid users in this regard. Psotka, Davison, and Lewis (1993) discuss the user's sense of self-position in space based on cues from the images displayed (this is discussed further in the *Virtual egocenter* section in chapter 3), and Regian, Shebilske, and Monk (1992) have addressed cognitive issues pertaining to learning spatial tasks in virtual environments. Further discussion of task-specific cognitive issues pertinent to virtual environments can be found in Wickens and Baker (1995).

Implications for virtual environments

Like designers of other computer-human interfaces, virtual environment designers should keep in mind cognitive issues such as working memory, retrieval of information from long-term memory, and learning. Further research might reveal more cognitive issues, such as those noted previously, that are of particular concern to virtual environments.

Affect

Most of the focus in the field of human-computer interaction is on usability (ease of use, ease of learning, performance) and the user is treated as a computer-like model information processor (Card, Moran, and Newell 1983). Yet, as Carroll and Thomas (1988) point out, the affective nature of users and their relationship to interfaces has not been given sufficient attention. In particular, they distinguish between the concepts of *ease* and *fun* and observe that, while ease implies simplicity, things that are considered fun are often expected to (and then found to) have some moderate complexity. They point out that, for example, while the Lisa system was described as a breakthrough in ease of use and ease of learning, a study they describe showed that this wasn't the case, and yet Lisa-style interfaces have been a big success; they suggest that this is because people find them more fun to use. They also describe an analysis of Adventure, an adult navigational game. Some of its characteristics, which included spatiality, interactiveness, and feedback, were sources of intrinsic motivation that they found to draw players into the game. Intrinsic motivation is important to consider; experiences that are intrinsically motivating and fun are likely to motivate people to try things they wouldn't otherwise try, and to spend more time on a task. That time might, in turn, result in learning and the development of greater skills.

Implications for virtual environments

In addition to spatiality, interactiveness, and feedback, which they describe as being sources of intrinsic motivation in at least one game application, Carroll and Thomas suggest other characteristics of interfaces that could make them more fun, such as using novel stimulation through the incorporation of different media, using emotion-arousing metaphors, and adapting to the user so that complexity increases as the user gains expertise. Virtual environments necessarily incorporate spatiality, interactivity, and the use of different media (or different modalities); well-designed ones also give feedback through multisensory displays. Although the use of metaphor is probably appropriate only in some systems (e.g., those for visualization of abstract data) and not others (e.g., some teleoperation systems) and the use of adaptive virtual environment interfaces isn't yet common, there's certainly reason to believe that well-designed virtual environment applications can be intrinsically motivating and fun. The popular excitement over even the primitive virtual environments available to the public in current arcade games is confirmation of this, although scientific studies of virtual environments and user affect have yet to be done.

Stuart and Thomas (1991) suggest, for example, that the intrinsically motivating qualities of virtual environments might be important for educational applications. A cautionary note is offered, however, by Peter Lewis, who has noted a long history of mistaken prognostications about the revolutionary effect of new technologies (from the blackboard to television to the computer), including Thomas Edison's prediction that motion pictures would make the classroom such an exciting place for students that it would be a problem to get them to leave.

In addition to the significance of affective issues in terms of intrinsic motivation, time on task, and learning, there are applications for virtual environment technology in which modifying affect might itself be a goal. Examples include role playing, conflict resolution, empathy training, psychotherapeutic applications, and entertainment. With respect to entertainment, consider the efforts that are made to influence the viewers' moods; Warren Robinett, a prominent researcher in virtual environments who worked at NASA and the University of North Carolina at Chapel Hill, has recently founded a virtual reality entertainment company and has stated publicly that his goal is to create within the next two years a virtual environment that makes its users cry.

Recommended Display and Control Performance

The results of much perceptual and motor research have been presented in this chapter, with pointers to sources for further information that might be useful/applicable for some applications. While there's much to learn about perception and human motor control as well as cognition and affect as they apply to virtual environments, Steve Ellis of NASA Ames Research Center has come up with some general recommendations for the performance required of VE input and output technologies, based on the available perceptual and motor research (Ellis 1994). He points out that these are neither minimal, maximal, nor optimal performance parameters, and that their wide variability reflects both the need for further research and requirements that are application-specific. He gives the example that, depending on the application, the operator might have to use focal or peripheral vision. Tables 2.2 and 2.3 on pages 60 and 61 show the parameters he recommends as "points of reference for future research."

Although these general parameters are a useful starting point, you should use the iterative design process described in this book to come up with more specific parameters for the application being designed.

Questions

- Can you think of examples where your *a priori* knowledge about known sources for sensory stimuli could be misleading in a virtual environment?
- What visual cues for depth would you use most if the objects you're looking at are far away and you aren't moving? What if they're near and you aren't moving?
- What are some advantages of auditory perception over visual perception? Disadvantages? What are the advantages and disadvantages of force and tactile perception?
- Think of a scenario where you'd want to be able to display a large amount of data to the user's senses in a VE, yet also have the user simultaneously input information to the system. What conflicts can you see between different ways of displaying the data and different input methods?

TABLE 2.2 Display Performance Requirements

Display type	Transmission delay	Bandwidth	Resolution	Dynamic range	Signal/noise
Visual (monocular)	20–100 msec	20–100 Hz	2 arcmin/pixel within 5° central vision	8-bit grayscale/color 60° field	25:1 contrast ratio
Visual (stereoscopic)	100 msec	0.1–5 Hz	2 arcmin/pixel within central vision	30° stereo overlap; 30° field overlap; 2° disparity range; 0.1–6-meter angle convergence	120:1 disparity ratio
Tactile	5 msec	0–10 kHz	10–100-micron vibration; 1–2 mm spatial resolution	8 bits	200:1 RMS ratio
Kinesthetic/force	20 msec	50–100 Hz	0.1 Newton	20N @ DC to 1N @ 10 Hz; 6 bits 1–10 cm	64:1 RMS ratio
Audio (sound)	1 msec	20 Hz–20 kHz	Frequency 0.02–3 Hz, power 2 dB	16 bits; 60 dB	40:1 RMS ratio
Audio (directional sound)	50–500 msec	3–6 Hz	Relative direction: 1° @ 5° C.E.P.; Absolute direction: 20–30°	4π steradians	20–30:1 solid angle ratio
Vocal (synthetic speech)	10–100 msec	1.5–2 words/sec	90–95% recognition in 50,000-word vocabulary	Potentially unlimited	

SOURCE: Stephen R. Ellis, NASA Ames Research Center (Ellis, S.R. 1994)

TABLE 2.3 Control Performance Requirements

Display type	Transmission delay	Bandwidth	Resolution	Dynamic range	Signal/noise
Manipulative (mice, joysticks, pedals, trackers, etc.)	10 msec	3–10 Hz 100 Hz for force reflection	0.2 joint angle 1–4 bits/dof (discrete control)	Range: exoskeleton limb motion 20N @ DC to 1N @ 10 Hz	200:1 RMS ratio
Vocal (speech recognition)	1–2 sec	1–2 words/sec	<5% probability of misrecognition	20,000 words	100:1 RMS ratio

SOURCE: Stephen R. Ellis, NASA Ames Research Center (Ellis, S.R. 1994)

Chapter 3

Requirements for VE Applications

There are a number of functional requirements that must be considered when designing practically all virtual environment applications. These requirements, though they're of varying importance depending on the application in question, must at least be addressed when designing most applications and systems. This section describes 22 of these common issues:

- Sociability and connectivity
- Veridicality
- Immersion/engagement/presence
- Resolution
- Reconfigurability
- Responsiveness
- Stability
- Robustness
- Viewpoint
- Representation of the user
- Degree of virtuality/integration with the real world
- Registration
- I/O bandwidth
- Multisensory requirements
- Interactivity
- Navigation techniques

- Physics of the virtual environment
- Autonomy
- Locus of control
- Choice of representation
- Calibration and customization
- Safety, health, and hygiene

In addition, other nonfunctional issues common to virtual environment applications—cost, size, and weight—should be considered. Finally, application-specific requirements should be taken into account.

Sociability and Connectivity

Sociability is the capability of a system to permit multiple users to share a virtual environment. This is often thought of in terms of users sharing a common physical workspace as well as a common virtual environment. It puts demands particularly on the computational resources and on the position tracking system, which must be able to track multiple objects and track over a sufficiently large working volume that multiple users can fit and work in it.

Connectivity addresses the issue of multiple users being at physically remote locations; it's the ability for sites or users to connect on the network in order to share a virtual environment. An everyone-to-everyone architecture (like the telephone network) provides a high-connectivity system; other architectures (like cable television) provide less connectivity. The demands on a system with users at remote locations are somewhat different than those of a system where users share a physical workspace. For example, it might use local CPUs and position tracking systems that don't track many objects or support large working volumes. However, the network must support exchange of information between the users (e.g., their position coordinates and interactions), and deal with transmission time and synchronization.

Veridicality

Veridicality describes the accuracy with which the virtual environment reproduces real objects, the user's interactions, and the environment it models. In the case of a virtual environment for surgical training, for example, veridicality would describe how closely the simulated organ on which the student surgeon practices resembles the real organ. Is its visual appearance (size, shape, color, texture) accurately reproduced? Are the haptic sensations that the user gets when working on it similar to those a surgeon would get when working on a real organ? Is its behavior like that of the real organ: its response to manipulation, the way it distends, bleeds, etc.? Resolution, responsiveness, and stability are all related to veridicality but are more a product of the way objects in the database are presented to the user and less the result of the properties they have; these performance-related properties are discussed as separate requirements.

Note that, contrary to a common implicit assumption, maximizing veridicality isn't necessarily desirable for all applications. For example, in a visualization task, well-chosen distortions and exaggerations might facilitate the recognition of patterns and anomalies. Fairchild (1993) discusses the intentional reduction of perceived complexity in virtual environments for visualization tasks by using the laws of perspective, fish-eye views, and what he describes as *degree of interest distortion*; these are, in a sense, intentional reductions in veridicality.

Other distortions, caused by system components rather than intentional introduction by designers, might be problematic for some applications and aren't always simple to measure. For example, in the case of transduced visual images (e.g., in teleoperation), orthostereoscopic display refers to the accurate correspondence of size, shape, and relative position of displayed objects to real-world objects, and it more generally describes a display in which all angles of sight from the scene to be displayed are duplicated by the display device, with straight lines appearing straight, objects at their correct azimuth and elevation, and correct perspective.

In the case of virtual environments, orthostereoscopy is manifested, for example, by the constancy of object size, shape, and relative position as viewers move in their head-tracked HMD. There are several challenges to orthostereoscopic display in virtual environments (e.g., see Robinett and Rolland 1992, and Howlett 1990). For example, there's a need to accurately determine line-of-sight angles (necessary to correctly match the graphics to the optical system) and to correctly use off-center perspective projection. Also, although optical distortions in HMDs are difficult to directly measure, if correction for these distortions is important for an application, they can be calculated through computational models (Robinett and Rolland 1992) or through clever subjective judgment techniques (Ellis and Nemire 1993).

Another veridicality issue is mapping the user's motions to movements in the virtual environment. In magnitude, either this mapping can be 1:1 or motions can be amplified. More complex is the case where the VE interface controls a robot rather than a simulation. Even an anthropomorphic robot is, at least in some ways, different than its human operator. Therefore, for example, motions by the user's hands must be transformed to motions by the robot's hands, which are necessarily different. In turn, the forces sensed by the robotic hands from contact with objects in its environment must be transformed to forces applied via force feedback devices to the user's hands. For a discussion of the transformation from the user's hand motion to motion by the robot's hand, see Speeter (1992).

Immersion, Engagement, and Presence

The terms *immersion* and *presence* are often used to mean the defining characteristics of the user interfaces provided by VE systems, yet there has been a great deal of ambiguity and disagreement concerning these expressions. At scientific conferences, it isn't uncommon to hear heated arguments regarding how immersive a certain system is, for example, and then realize that those engaged in the arguments mean entirely different things by *immersion*. In this section, I'll offer my own definition and description of *immersion*, *engagement*, and *presence*, which I see as three distinct phenomena. I believe that, if adopted by researchers in this field, these definitions would help reduce some of the current miscommunication on these subjects.

I define *immersion* as the presentation of sensory cues that convey, perceptually, to users that they're surrounded by a computer-generated environment. Thus, immersion is an objectively quantifiable phenomenon that can be described by measures such as visual field of view, auditory localization cues, directions from which force reflection can be displayed, and the range of orientations supported by tracking. A computer-generated display can be captivating or boring, but the extent to which it's immersive can be described by these objective measures. (Admittedly, this is somewhat simplified in the case of auditory externalization, since there's still debate about what cues produce the phenomenon and some individual differences that come into play.) There's also a temporal component to immersion (discussed later) since, in addition to instantaneous FOV, a virtual environment that lets users change position and orientation and continue to receive visual cues that they're surrounded by a virtual environment is more immersive than one that merely presents a wide instantaneous FOV.

I define *presence* as the subjective sense by users that they're physically in a virtual environment. Although this is a subjective measure, it's also somewhat quantifiable (Wells 1989). For example, if a large virtual object is hurled at the user, the user's response to this visual looming (such as involuntary movement to avoid being "hit") can be measured. Adaptation could play a role in the sense of presence. For example, early silent motion film watchers who saw things coming towards them on the screen in D.W. Griffith movies and panicked experienced a greater sense of presence in a movie theater than do present-day film-goers, who have experienced enough films that they've adapted and no longer behave as did the early viewers.

I define *engagement* as the subjective sense by users of being deeply involved and occupied with what they're doing. This involves paying attention to the immediate experience and not being distracted by thoughts of other things; it can be associated with losing track of time, and has been described as the sense of *flow*. A highly immersive virtual reality system could, for example, be less engaging than a well-written novel, but no matter how well-written the novel the experience of reading it wouldn't be described as *immersion* as it's defined here.

According to these definitions, immersion is an objective and very much quantifiable phenomenon, engagement is entirely subjective, and presence is also subjective, but perhaps more quantifiable as suggested by the work of Wells (1989).

The need for immersion and its value for specific tasks has been much debated. Many current immersive virtual environments have sufficient problems (e.g., low-resolution visual displays and latency) that there hasn't been much empirical evidence that immersion has any value for the tasks studied. In one offline training and rehearsal task, that of learning airplane marshalling, it was suggested that immersion was necessary for the sense of fear it created (Bletter 1993). As virtual environment technologies (HMDs in particular) improve, it's hoped that research will clarify the benefits, or lack thereof, of immersion.

Quantifying immersion

If you consider immersion, as defined above, as an objective phenomenon, you can consider quantifying it. There are some problems with trying to do so and, while I won't offer solutions to all of these problems, I will suggest some issues to consider.

Intuitively, immersion is fairly standard regardless of what sensory modality perceives it. If you're standing in front of a movie set, you'll see the set in front of you, hear the sound of the actors' voices coming from the set as they rehearse their lines, and be able to reach out and feel the surface of a couch or grab a chair from the set. (Similarly, if you're in the middle of a desert during a windstorm, the wind will whip the sand against you from all directions and you'll hear and see it on all sides.) Yet to objectively quantify immersion, the different cues to the sensory modalities must be measured in appropriately different ways.

If you think of immersion as "surroundedness," then the degree of immersion required of a force feedback subsystem would describe the range of directions from which force could be exerted and on how much of the user's body these forces could be exerted. This would be similar for any user. But describing the degree of auditory immersion provided by a virtual acoustic display would require quantifying the localization cues, and research shows some individual differences in how people respond to synthesized localization cues (Wenzel 1992).

Further, there's a temporal element to immersion. *Panorama* is the expression used by Cruz-Neira, Sandin, DeFanti, Kenyon, and Hart (1992) to describe the ability of the display to surround the viewer, incorporating the viewer's head movement. This is in contrast to FOV, which doesn't incorporate the temporal element and head movement. Thus, for visual displays you need to consider whether an HMD with a narrow FOV (and a magnetic tracker) that lets the user look around and see the virtual environment in all directions is more or less immersive than an HMD with a wide FOV (and optical tracker) that displays a larger instantaneous image of the virtual environment but doesn't let users look behind themselves.

A reasonable quantitative description of a system's immersiveness might specify visual, auditory, and haptic immersion, and distinguish static and temporal properties.

Mixed immersion systems

Having distinguished immersion in different sensory modalities, I'd like you to consider the idea of mixed immersion virtual environments—a concept I've espoused but that hasn't been implemented widely yet. You can take advantage of the strengths of the different senses by combining nonimmersive and immersive displays. For example, you can use a fishtank VR system to view nodes and links of a complex network, which is seen stereoscopically in high resolution in front of the user. As the user navigates through this network, distant nodes and links are approached as other nodes and links pass behind (and out of sight of) the user. Now, the user has lost situational awareness and the ability to monitor the nodes and links behind him. However, if an immersive virtual acoustic display is used, activity in those nodes and links that are now lost to view can be represented through audio display (sonification), and the user can keep track of this activity while focusing attention on the visible nodes and links. This idea is illustrated in Figure 3.1.

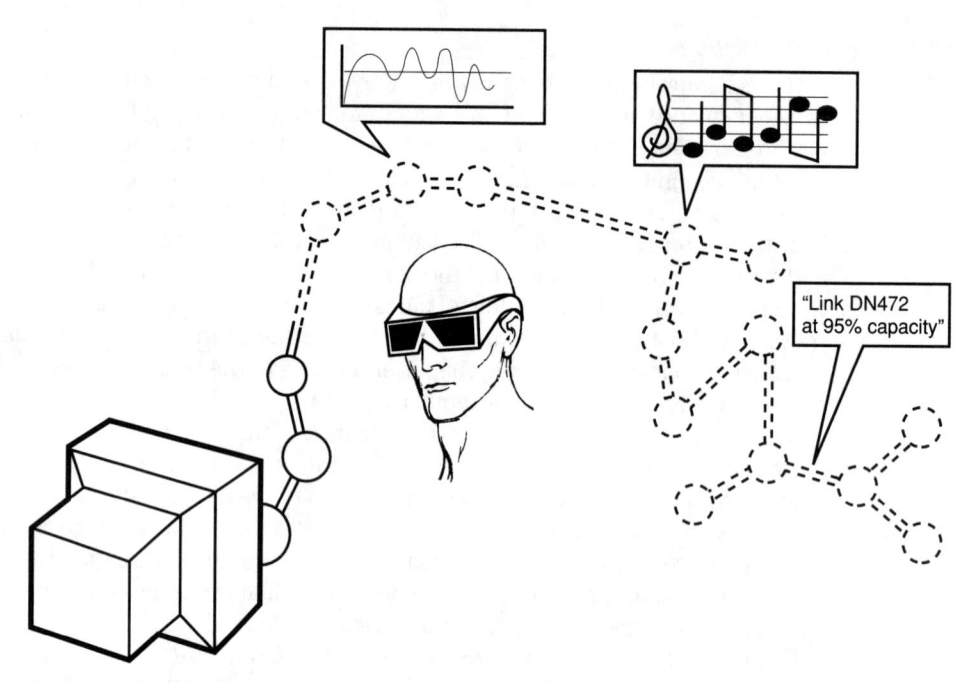

Figure 3.1 Mixed immersion system. Note the combination of immersive virtual acoustic display with a "fishtank" visual display. *(E.H.H. Stuart)*

Resolution

Resolution is a virtual environment's level of precision and detail. From the user's point of view, it has to do with the visible detail of the visual display (e.g., pixel density), and analogous precision and detail in the audio and force/tactile display, as well as how small a motion the user can make that will be detectable by the system.

Reconfigurability

Reconfigurability is the ability of a system to be modified. How much time and effort is required to reconfigure the environment if it's necessary to do so? Can a system built for one application be easily modified to be used for another application? Conventional flight simulators have physical control panels and displays in their cockpits, and are therefore not easily reconfigured. A fusion interface for cockpit simulation, like that being developed at Wright Patterson Air Force Base (Haas and Hettinger 1993) combines real and virtual cockpit controls; the virtual controls can be reconfigured in software, but a modification of the real controls requires that a new unit be physically created. An immersive VE system that excludes sensory input from the real world might permit a programmer to modify code using a text editor and then recompile the code objects in the environment in order to modify them (move, change in color, size, shape, and texture, etc.), or it might simply require user input (e.g., gestures or speech) in order to change the objects.

Responsiveness

Responsiveness is the ability of a system to minimize the time between a user's input and the system's response. *Lag* (also referred to as *latency*) is the total delay time between a user action and the system response; the more responsive a system is, the lower its latency. Lag is the cumulative effect of delays caused by each system component required to generate the system response, and these delays are typically introduced by the data rate and update rate of position trackers and other input devices; the time spent by the host computer in processing tracker position, running the simulation, and rendering the graphical, sonic, and tactile images (i.e., the *update rate* of the computer); the time required for synchronization in multiprocessor systems; the refresh rate of display devices (this is significant for visual and force/tactile displays, less so for auditory displays via headphones); and cumulative transmission time (which is particularly significant in networked systems, e.g., teleoperation). A good overview on the components of latency, as well as techniques to reduce it, is provided by Wloka (1995).

A commonly cited figure for the overall lag that's acceptable is less than 0.1 second (van Dam 1994). However, this is a very rough guideline that's directed at visual perception and should be defined based on the application. For example, much less lag might be acceptable in a game of virtual squash, which requires you to track a fast-moving object. Held and Durlach (1991) note a decrease in the adaptation of eye-hand coordination to prism displacement from very short delays, though not from delays of 0.06 second or less under their experimental conditions. The subjective impression of their subjects was that, with short delays, the viewed hand appeared as though it were being dragged through a viscous medium but, at delays of greater than 0.2 second, the viewed image of the hand was no longer associated with the real moving hand.

Update rate (frame rate, in the case of visual displays) might be of concern beyond its contribution to latency. To highlight the distinction, consider that a system could, for example, have a very high frame rate, yet not reflect changes due to actions by the user for a considerable number of frames (i.e., have considerable lag). Or there might be low latency in all other components up to the generation and display of images, in which case the frame rate would be the limiting factor in system responsiveness. In the visual domain, too low a frame rate can produce the impression of a series of snapshots rather than an environment in which the user is present, in which case increasing the frame rate would be desirable even if there's enough latency to be of concern. Burdea and his colleagues (Burdea and Coiffet 1994) have studied the time it takes a subject to grasp a moving target in a virtual environment as a product of the graphics refresh rate, and found that below 14 frames per second the performance degraded radically, while above it the performance was close to that in the real world.

Stability

Stability, which must be considered largely because of problems in position tracking technologies, refers to the lack of jitter or oscillation in the position of objects in the virtual environment. Stability is especially important for the category of tasks that Wickens and Baker (1995) describe as online performance, such as using virtual environments for telepresence surgery or to control a teleoperated robot in a hazardous environment. Stability is a system performance issue that can be objectively measured.

Robustness

The environment in which the VE system is run can be considered when defining requirements for robustness. Robustness is a measure of the system's ability to withstand the conditions in which it's used. For a position tracking system, this might mean an environment that's challenging in terms of signal interference (e.g., metallic objects with respect to magnetic tracking systems and noise such as jangling keys in the case of an ultrasonic tracking system).

For the computer hardware, conditions such as heat in the environment could be a challenge. For instrumented gloves, rough handling by users (e.g., at a public-access display) might challenge robustness, as might impact from dropping or mishandling for HMDs. Robustness in terms of network connections is of clear importance in an application such as telepresence surgery.

In the case of an augmented reality system for advanced cockpit display, failure in the weakest link in the system could be disastrous for the pilot, so it's important in an application like this to examine robustness of the entire system. For future wireless HMDs, robustness in the face of interference from environmental sources will be important for some applications.

Viewpoint

Viewpoint describes how users perceive their location. The following sections consider the different possible viewpoints.

Virtual egocenter

Psotka, Davison, and Lewis (1993) introduced the notion of a *virtual egocenter* and point out that, in many visual media, the user must adopt an alternate ego, i.e., a sense of location in virtual space that's only accidentally in the user's real space. This is because cues given indicate a perspective in space different than that of the viewer. Two issues that arise are how maintaining two egocenters will affect performance and whether (as Psotka, et al. suggest) the compatibility between these egocenters is an issue in the user's sense of presence (which they refer to as *immersion*) in the virtual environment.

Viewpoints: egocentric vs. God's eye

From what viewpoint or viewpoints will the user perceive the virtual environment? Howard (1991) distinguishes frames of reference within which scenes can be viewed: egocentric viewpoints, which are defined with respect to some part of the viewer's body, and exocentric viewpoints, which are defined with respect to external coordinate systems. Teleoperator systems are almost always viewed egocentrically, from transducers in the anthropomorphic robot. An example of an exocentric viewpoint is known as a *God's eye viewpoint*, which lets the user view the entire scene from above it.

An exocentric viewpoint, in which observers can view themselves or a representation of themselves within the scene, is used in artificial reality systems (also sometimes described as *mirror worlds*). Users see a projected image of themselves on a screen and, through movement, control that image and use it to interact with virtual objects (or other users) also projected on the screen. There has been little research on the advantages and disadvantages of this approach, although it seems clear that there might be some advantages to a first-person perspective for online performance tasks and for offline training and rehearsal tasks.

Although the choice of appropriate viewpoints is application-specific, one alternative is to allow the user to choose from multiple viewpoints. An engineer visualizing signal quality strength in a mobile cellular network could traverse the terrain either from the perspective of a user driving along a road and engaged in a cellular telephone conversation, or from a God's eye view, floating above the terrain and observing the signals transmitted from several cell sites. Similarly, a pilot practicing in a flight simulator could view the environment from the perspective of the virtual cockpit while engaged in maneuvers, and then switch to a God's eye perspective and replay the maneuvers, watching them from a fixed point in space.

Representation of the User

How are users visually represented to themselves and others sharing the virtual environment? In the case of an anthropomorphic teleoperated robot, the user sees the robot's body, as transduced by its visual sensors. In many current single-user virtual environments, the only representation of the user is a graphical representation of one of the user's hands, which reflects hand movement captured by an instrumented glove. In this type of system, if you look down at where your body should be, there's nothing there. This isn't a problem in many single-user applications, but in some the representation of the user's body is important.

Esposito (1993) gives the example of using virtual environments at Boeing to design aircraft; a representation of the user's body is important so the engineer can get a sense of how difficult it is to reach certain parts of the planned aircraft for maintenance. Allowing users to see themselves while performing maintenance maneuvers on the modeled aircraft gives engineers the only available feedback, as force and tactile displays aren't currently sophisticated enough to be practical for this application.

Representing the user is especially an issue in multiuser virtual environments. Benford et al. (1995) refer to this as *user embodiment*, and point out the information it can provide to other users, for example, in terms of user location, identity, activity, attention, and availability. How do you recognize who the other participants are and what they're doing? Is the user represented as an icon, as is the case in an early version of a system where users appear as different colored monoliths (Fahlen, Stahl, Brown, and Carlsson 1993)? In this case, much of the potential nonverbal communication between users is lost. Can the communicative function of facial expressions be conveyed? This is possible through technology that senses facial expressions and movement (discussed in the *VACTORs* section in chapter 4).

Another issue is how closely the representation of users match their real body dimensions, position, and movement; this is relevant to systems such as the Boeing system mentioned previously and also for interaction between users in multiuser systems. Benford et al. (1995) give examples of user embodiment in current systems, and point out other issues such as truthfulness (whether the embodiment of the user is an accurate portrayal or allows the user to be deceptive) and efficiency (the computational resources required to implement the user embodiment).

Degree of Virtuality and Integration in a Real Environment

The concept of *degree of virtuality* refers to the extent to which sensory input perceived by the user is synthetic (computer-generated) or nonsynthetic (real). The maximum degree of virtuality is where all that can be perceived by the user is the synthetic world. If sufficiently veridical, this would result in a system along the lines of Ivan Sutherland's "ultimate display." In such a system, all the visual, auditory, tactile, and other sensory input accessible by the user would be computer-generated. Changes in such a virtual environment would require changes only in the software.

Exclusion of real-world sensory input isn't necessarily desirable in some cases. Augmented reality systems have a lower degree of virtuality, since real-world objects and events are experienced by the user, with computer-generated text, graphics, and sound superimposed. Augmented reality systems typically permit direct input from the real world, e.g., with see-through HMDs (Feiner, MacIntyre, and Seligmann 1992), but they can also transduce and display the real-world data, e.g., by capturing video via a camera mounted on the user and combining in the HMD display the video and computer-generated images (Lion, Rosenberg, and Barfield 1993; Bajura, Fuchs, and Ohbuchi 1992).

Existing augmented reality prototypes often leave little doubt as to what is real and what is virtual, as the synthetic part of the presentation is about the real part (Feiner, MacIntyre, and Seligmann 1992), for example showing text and line diagrams superimposed on objects. But this isn't always necessarily the case; Haas and Hettinger (1993) at Wright Patterson Air Force Base are developing "fusion interfaces" that combine real and virtual control devices in a cockpit. Another case where this distinction must be clear, but isn't necessarily is in the landing displays described by Pavel (Pavel, et al 1993). A still lesser degree of virtuality is found in vehicular simulators, which typically have entirely real cockpits or cabins and control devices combined with computer-generated images on visual display panels, or "windows."

In some cases, augmented reality systems need to, in a sense, increase the degree of virtuality to be effective. Although you could simply superimpose computer-generated graphics on real-world images, this might result in conflicting visual cues to confuse or misinform the user.

Bajura, Fuchs, and Ohbuchi (1992) found that, in an experiment in which ultrasound echography data was superimposed on the image of a pregnant woman viewed with an augmented reality system, the ultrasound images appeared to be pasted on top of her rather than inside her, unless further virtual imagery was added in the form of a shaded polygonal pit ("virtual hole") imposed on her abdomen. In this case, the additional synthetic imagery solved one problem—the ultrasound images now appeared to be appropriately inside the abdomen—but it created a new problem: all real images in the direction of the virtual hole (including those in front of it) were hidden. However, the problem could be avoided by incorporating range finding from the HMD and using it to determine what should and should not be displayed. This example is given here, however, to provide an example of an issue that arises when certain degrees of virtuality are used.

Teleoperation typically has little or no degree of virtuality at all in the sense that all the information presented is transduced from the real world, although at a remote location. There's nothing in the software that can change the characteristics of the world displayed; a change in the world would require that the remote robot actually physically change things in its vicinity. It is possible, however, to create a sort of augmented reality/teleoperation hybrid in which synthetic information is merged with the robot's transduced information. Another interesting case is that described by Stoker (1993) of modeling data about a physical terrain in which a remote robot is operating and displaying this modeled data in order to deal with the problem of transmission time (in this case, the time required for transmission between NASA Ames in California and a teleoperated robot in Antarctica).

The notion of *degree of virtuality* is intended to be more a qualitative than a quantitative concept. It's useful in considering design trade-offs, such as that between the greater realism of physical cockpit control devices and more inexpensively and quickly reconfigured virtual devices.

Registration

Meyer, Applewhite, and Biocca (1991) define *registration* as "the correspondence between a physical position and orientation and a reported position and orientation." In general, it's the accuracy with which the virtual environment's geometry corresponds to that of the real world. Registration is an especially important factor in augmented reality interfaces that use see-through HMDs, since the superimposed text and graphics must appropriately match external objects in the real world.

Feiner, MacIntyre, and Seligmann (1992) discuss registration in the context of a test-bed application for end-user maintenance and repair of a laser printer. More recent work by Feiner's group at Columbia University, in collaboration with NYNEX Science and Technology, has focused on using see-through HMDs to install and maintain telephone cross boxes. Here, registration is particularly crucial since the cross box contains a very large number of closely-packed pairs (posts), and registration must be accurate enough to permit the user to readily distinguish which pair the text and graphics in a see-through HMD refers to.

Input/Output Bandwidth

I/O bandwidth refers to the amount of information that must pass (or that can pass) from the user to the system and from the system to the user. I/O bandwidth can be broken down into the bandwidth from the system to each of the user's sensory modalities and from the user's motor modalities to the system; it can also be viewed cumulatively. The amount of redundancy between information presented in different display modalities should also be considered.

Multisensory Requirements

The specification of multisensory requirements should describe in which modalities the virtual environment is to be displayed. Are visual display, auditory display, force display, and tactile display needed? What about other modalities, such as temperature and olfactory display? How much and what types of things must be displayed through each modality?

The presentation of redundant information has been found to decrease reaction time in some experimental tasks; the redundancy can consist of repeating a signal, displaying the signal in different ways to a single sense (e.g., visual text and graphics), or simultaneously presenting the information to different sensory modalities (Boff and Lincoln 1988).

Interactivity

There are two "flavors" of interactivity that are pertinent to virtual environments. The first is interactivity as it pertains to any human-computer interface. Brenda Laurel (1986a and 1986b) has identified three variables that describe this flavor of interactivity: frequency (how often the user can interact with the system), range (how many choices are available), and significance (how much effect the choices have).

The second flavor of interactivity is unique to virtual environments: the tight coupling of head-tracked (and other) user input with multisensory display, so users perceive themselves as present in the environment. This latter flavor of interactivity distinguishes a virtual reality system from Sensorama, the virtual reality precursor by Morton Heilig (1955) and from a super-3D-HDTV system (Stuart and Thomas 1991).

The former flavor of interactivity hasn't been used in many virtual reality systems created to date. User modification of the virtual environment from within the environment has often been quite limited, and I've described (Stuart, 1993b) a class of applications for which virtual environments could be useful if they supported a different type of interaction from within the environment. The interaction in VEs is described further in chapter 7.

Navigation Techniques

How do you get from place to place in the virtual environment? Tracking the position of the user allows some movement in the VE via corresponding movement in the physical world. For additional movement and movement over a greater distance, users can employ different techniques for a variety of styles of navigation. The required user input for this larger-scale movement might be via gestures, speech input, or input devices. The styles of possible navigation are described by Fairchild (1993) as falling into five categories:

- Relative motion
- Absolute motion
- Teleportation
- Hyperspace
- Transformation

These navigation styles are described in Table 3.1.

Although Fairchild addresses styles of navigation in the sense of what kinds of motion are possible from one location to another, another issue is the type of display techniques used to allow the users to orient and locate their position in the virtual environment. Brooks (1988) speaks of the value he has observed in simultaneously giving users both a view of the virtual world and one or more auxiliary map views, and the tendency for users to begin by using map navigation and increasingly switch to scene navigation as they learn the topography of the virtual world. Yet another issue is the choice of input methods for navigation. These are summarized in Table 3.2.

TABLE 3.1 Navigation Styles

Navigation technique	Description	Speed	Accuracy	Issues
Relative motion	Get to a place via a sequence of steps from where you are (as in the nonsynthetic world)	Slow	Good	Familiar because of its use in the real world
Absolute motion	Point to a location on a map in order to go there	Fast	Poor	Requires knowing map location beforehand
Teleportation	Go directly to a place that can be named	Fast	Good if location can be accurately described	Requires knowing and being able to describe location
Hyperspace	Follow hyperlinks from object to object	Fast (if the path of links is fairly direct)	Good	Requires the objects in the VE be hyperlinked (which makes sense only if their relationship is important)
Transformation	Move the objects with which the viewer wants to interact to his/her position, rather than moving the viewer's viewpoint	Depends on how it is accomplished	Depends on how it is accomplished	Little explored to date

TABLE 3.2 Input Methods for Navigation

Input method	Description	Example
Tracked head and body movement	Self-movement with respect to position-tracking device(s)	Boeing system for airplane design (Esposito 1993)
Selection of map location	Point to location on virtual map to move to a location in the VE	Seldom used, but map navigation is described by Brooks 1988
Physical input devices, cockpits	Manipulate haptic device or physical cockpit controls to control motion	Wright Patterson Air Force Base "fusion interface" system (Haas and Hettinger 1993)
Virtual controls	Manipulate virtual controls to control motion	Super Cockpit system (Furness 1986)
Eye tracking	Look at the place to which you want to go	None yet integrated in VE systems
Gesture	Use gesture recognition to "fly" to location	Division system using Jim Kramer glove
Speech	Say name of place to which you want to go or navigation command	SRI system (Bletter 1993)
Locomotive device	Use locomotive device to cycle, walk, run, or climb to a location	UNC Chapel Hill treadmill and stationary bike systems (Brooks, et al. 1992)

Physics of the Virtual Environment

The physics of the virtual environment refers to properties such as space exclusion, gravity, friction, and inertia. In the real world, solid objects typically can't simultaneously occupy the same position in space, and this is described as the property of space exclusion. Most current virtual environments don't incorporate this property. The user walks through walls, and the user's hands pass through objects in the virtual world. Brooks (1988) notes the "surprisingly large role" that space exclusion plays in our perception of "realness," and suggests that this should still be a priority in spite of the difficulties in implementing it.

Gravity, friction, and inertia are other physical properties that can be simulated. Although realistically simulating all these properties might be important if maximizing the veridicality is essential, in many cases they aren't necessary and should be considered individually with respect to a specific application of virtual environment technology.

Poston and Fairchild (1993) point out that, while Aristotelean physics aren't as accurate at describing and predicting physical events in the world as are Newtonian physics, there are three advantages to using Aristotelean physics in those VE applications that don't require very close simulation of real-world behavior (as would a flight simulator, for example). These advantages are:

- Aristotelean physics are less computationally demanding to simulate. Poston and Fairchild point out that, with current technology, "correct" physics might be too CPU-costly to implement for many applications.

- Aristotelean physics in many cases are actually a better match to people's intuitive (albeit mistaken) expectations of physical behavior in the real world, and are thus easier to learn and control.
- Because of the computational demands of simulating more realistic physics, objects in a system of a given processor speed that simulates realistic physics tend to move less smoothly than do objects in a system with identical processor speed that simulates Aristotelean physics.

For more on Aristotelean physics and their use in virtual environments, see Poston and Fairchild (1993).

Finally, you might want a system design that allows the user to change the physics of the VE. An example of this is a virtual physics laboratory, designed to help students better understand the laws of physics by letting them alter them and observe the effects on the behavior of objects in the VE (Loftin, Engelberg, and Benedetti 1993).

Autonomy

Autonomy refers not to the ability of users of a virtual environment to act freely in a variety of ways, but to the ability of the objects and processes simulated in the virtual environment to exhibit independent behaviors. In the taxonomy created by Zeltzer (1992), three salient features of VEs are presented in an "autonomy-interaction-presence cube." Zeltzer describes a range in degrees of autonomy, from simple geometric models with no associated procedures to which typical computer graphics techniques, such as affine transformations, can be applied (these have no autonomy), to virtual actors and knowledge-based agents capable of sophisticated behaviors in response to the state of the simulation or actions by its users (these have very high autonomy). Although behaviors of objects that exhibit physics-based properties such as inertia are showing some degree of autonomy, autonomy clearly encompasses a range of properties wider than the physical properties discussed previously in terms of the physics of the virtual environment.

Locus of Control

Locus of control is a meta-issue, in a sense: who creates and controls the content of virtual environments? If you think in terms of other communication media, you can contrast network television and popular cinema, which are created and marketed by a few very large corporations, with electronic bulletin boards, chat lines, and even telephone conversations, where many different individuals control the content through their involvement.

Stuart and Thomas (1991) point out that there's a range of scenarios in terms of the locus of control of virtual environments, and they give the example of educational applications. In between the extremes of centrally controlled (e.g., federal government-controlled) content and content controlled entirely by the individual, they envision several levels (federal, state, local school boards and principals, teachers, parents, and individual students) exerting different degrees of control via various negotiation processes. For example, there might be state educational requirements for mathematical and lingual fluency, federal prohibitions against exposing children to pornography, parental refusal to allow their children exploration of certain things, and the children's own desires to spend their free time in certain kinds of virtual environments.

Although you might want to consider locus of control from this futuristic perspective (i.e., who will control it when it becomes widespread and a part of everyday life), in more immediate terms locus of control is determined by the nature of the application-building toolkits provided (what level of programming skill is required to construct a virtual environment?), the availability of source code, and proprietary/nonproprietary issues. A criterion used, for example by the VEOS team at the Human Interface Technology Laboratory at the University of Washington, was that all software used in their system be nonproprietary (Coco 1993); this gave anyone who used the system (rather than vendors) a greater level of control.

Choice of Representation

The choice of representation of information can be separated from the technology with which the information is displayed. Among the types of representation possible are:

Realistic. A tangible real-world object is represented in the VE to be perceived as nearly identical as possible to its real-world counterpart.

Scale-altered. Real-world objects are represented realistically except that their scale (either in size or in time) is altered. This would let the user examine things not otherwise observable, such as molecules, t-cells and organs within the human body, glaciation during ice ages, and the spin of a curve-ball pitch.

Property-altered. Real-world objects are either represented with altered qualities, e.g, altered laws of physics, transposed pitches, or altered colors and textures, or allow users to move through the VE in ways that wouldn't be possible in the real world. Another sense of property-altered representation is one in which what isn't perceivable without sensory systems (e.g., outside the electromagnetic spectrum we can perceive) is represented within our perceptual range. Robinett (1992), in his taxonomy of synthetic experience, includes technologies such as night vision systems because they map stimuli we can't perceive into a spectrum we can perceive.

Modality-altered. Synesthetic representation is used to map stimuli normally perceived with one sensory modality to another. Synesthetic representation (Stuart 1993a) can be used because one modality isn't available, as it was when a NASA Ames system that didn't have force feedback used an audio display to represent force. (For an empirical comparison of synesthetic representations, see Richard, et al. 1994.) It can also be used to take advantage of the strengths of certain senses. (Note that in the medical condition of synesthesia, from which the idea of synesthetic representation arises, the mapping between modalities for an individual is fixed rather than arbitrarily selectable—see Cytowic 1993 for more on this.)

Iconic. A symbol represents an object or process that either doesn't need to be examined in more detail or can be further examined if the user chooses to deiconify it.

Reified. Abstract concepts are represented in the virtual environment by physical concrete real-world-like objects.

Abstract. Abstract concepts are represented abstractly in the VE, in the sense of abstract art, i.e., not attempting to look, sound, or feel like real-world objects. (Some of these categories were previously described in Stuart and Thomas 1991.)

A particular issue is how to represent intangibles. Intangibles are abstract, such as probabilities, molecules, or financial indicators and have no obvious mapping to perceptual modalities in the real world (e.g., salinity gradients or computational fluid dynamics). Intangibles are also difficult to display in the sensory modality with which they're most naturally associated (e.g., temperature gradients). Although categories of representation—reified, abstract, and property-altered, e.g., synesthetic—are described, this doesn't tell you which category should be used and what specific choice of representation should be used within that category. Brooks (1988) makes the case that, with abstractions, the goal should be to produce as many different representations as possible rather than perfecting one.

Calibration and Customization

How much time and effort is required to set up a system for a given user? How accurate can this setup be? Must components of the system be calibrated once for each user, or must this calibration occur with every use of the system (or even within the course of a single session)? To what extent does the system permit customization by (or for) each user? Customization permits taking into account user preferences to make a more satisfactory system; calibration allows using individual physical characteristics of users to improve accuracy, which is often necessary if you're allowed to make adjustments in I/O devices in order to improve ergonomic fit.

What customization and calibration (and, in the case of speaker-dependent speech recognition or gesture recognition systems, training) have in common is that, in return for their benefits, they exact a cost in set-up and start-up time. Through analysis of the requirements of the application, you'll have the basis to evaluate these trade-offs. A system to train pilots on the use of a new aircraft (where each pilot spends many hours training on the system) might require a level of accuracy that warrants extensive calibration, and adjusting I/O equipment for each individual pilot might offer other benefits for extended use (e.g., reduction in visual fatigue from correct IPD adjustment of the HMD). A location-based entertainment system or museum exhibit that's intended to be used by a large number of users daily, each for a brief session, would typically be much more successful if the least possible amount of time were required for calibration.

Calibration can be done on instrumented gloves and suits, eye-tracking devices, position-tracked HMDs, and other position-tracked I/O devices. Customization might include adjustment of interpupillary distance for HMDs (or graphics in a fishtank VR system to display images for eyes that correctly match the IPD of the user), customization of a virtual acoustic display to match the user's HRTFs, and a host of software choices with regard to representation and sensory modalities to which information is displayed.

Boresighting is the process of determining the offset from a position tracker to a desired point (e.g., one of the user's eyes). This offset determines the required transformation, for example, to present an image from the correct viewpoint to the user's eye. Azuma (1995b) describes a full calibration procedure for an augmented reality system that involves the measurement of the following five values, in the order listed:

- Position and orientation of a real-world object (Azuma used a crate)
- Center of the field of view
- Orientation offset between the tracker and the right eye
- Position offset between the tracker and the right eye
- Field of view

In this case, the boresighting procedure determines the values of both the orientation and position offsets and involves the user sighting through a virtual crosshair and lining up virtual and real colored lines.

One other informal observation I'd like to offer: Beware of the apparent ease and speed with which calibration procedures can be performed when they're demonstrated by vendors and other experts. Calibration procedures for some systems (e.g., instrumented glove recognition and eye tracking) appear easy when demonstrated by experts because they use a wealth of knowledge and experiences (and "tricks"), although they might not be consciously aware of doing so. Try to do the calibration procedure yourself and notice how much they coach you as you do so (notice if they're making suggestions based on rules of thumb they didn't previously articulate, and try to get them to make these rules explicit). Then try to do the calibration procedure without them coaching you (unless an expert will always be there to coach calibration); this will give you a more realistic estimate of the time and effort required for calibration in real use of the system.

Safety, Health, and Hygiene

You must consider safety, health, and hygiene issues when designing a virtual environment. Cybersickness (simulator-like sickness), visual impairment, and hazards in the physical environment of which the user isn't aware (such as tripping on tethers or walking into walls) are addressed in this section.

Cybersickness

Simulator-like sickness (cybersickness) has been observed and studied by the flight simulation community for many years. It's characterized by a variety of motion sickness-like symptoms during use of the interface as well as residual after-effects. These symptoms include nausea, disorientation, stomach awareness, fatigue, and headache; after-effects include ataxia (postural instability), weakness, fatigue, and visual illusions and problems. These symptoms have been studied mostly in the context of flight simulators, which I refer to as an offline training and rehearsal task. If a real-world maneuver caused a pilot to experience motion sickness and the same maneuver causes similar motion sickness in the simulator, this isn't considered to be simulator sickness; it is when the real-world maneuver doesn't cause motion sickness but the simulated maneuver does. For an offline training and rehearsal task, these symptoms are a problem: users might learn to avoid or adapt to them and, in so doing, change the way they perform the task and therefore learn behaviors in flying the airplane that are undesirable.

Residual after-effects can also be a problem, especially for military use of systems, as they might require a longer-than-desired waiting period between when pilots undergo training and are ready to fly a mission. Finally, for virtual environment systems for use by the public, there's a danger that residual after-effects will result in injury to users (e.g., car accidents)—a matter of concern both to those who care about their customers and to those concerned about product liability.

Several theories attempt to explain the cause(s) of cybersickness, including one that attributes it to cue conflicts (such as visual vection without corresponding vestibular cues), another to the lack of learned strategies (or disruptions in strategies) to maintain postural control in the VE, and a less widely cited theory to update rates between 4 and 12 Hz that produce inappropriate eye movements (Piantanida, Boman, and Gille 1993). An overview of causal theories, as well as individual differences and task characteristics that play a role, is provided by Kolasinski (in press).

Although there are some conflicting findings by researchers on simulator sickness, and a lack of studies of cybersickness in virtual environments for tasks other than flight simulation, some observations suggest ways to avoid the problem. Ebenholtz (1992) notes that, while motion sickness is experienced by both sighted and blind people, labyrinthine-defective (LD) individuals, who lack intact vestibular systems, are entirely immune to motion sickness, although these LD individuals can experience vection (illusory impression of self-motion) under conditions in which people with intact vestibular systems would experience both vection and motion sickness. Thus, he concludes that vection and the (optokinetic) visual stimulation that produces it are not in and of themselves the cause of simulator sickness, but must interact with a functioning vestibular system to produce it.

Visual impairment

Researchers from the University of Edinburgh have reported that some commercially available HMDs can be harmful to vision, at least temporarily. People who used the HMDs for as short a period as 10 minutes were found to have temporary deficits in binocular function, particularly heterophoria (Mon-Williams, Wann, and Rushton 1993). The HMDs used in their tests had a number of problems, including poor illumination, poor contrast, and an unusually close working distance; in some cases, the HMDs weren't adjusted for the user's IPD and were apparently not aligned properly. The criticism has been leveled that any display with these problems would cause temporary problems to visual acuity. Users would adapt to it but then have to undergo a period of readaptation to normal visual conditions—the way a person with new glasses has to adapt to both putting them on and taking them off before the process becomes natural.

However, the HMDs used in the Edinburgh studies and the problems associated with them are representative of what many users of public-access VE systems experience. It's common for users to view the HMD under conditions of poor alignment and improper adjustment. Such users also won't use the HMD often enough to adapt to the optical changes from putting it on and taking it off, so these users might indeed experience the effects found in the Edinburgh study, even if they don't reflect anything inherent in the use of HMDs.

More recent studies by the Edinburgh researchers suggest that the variable dissociation of accommodation and convergence in stereoscopic HMDs is one cause of the visual stress they found. One way to eliminate this variable dissociation is to present an identical image to both eyes. In a study using a commercially available binocular (binoptic) HMD that permitted IPD adjustment, they didn't find users experiencing the visual problems noted in their previous studies (Rushton, Mon-Williams, and Wann 1994). Unfortunately, binocular displays don't permit stereoscopy since they don't make use of binocular disparity.

Auditory damage

There's no risk of hearing damage that is unique to virtual acoustic displays, but, like any auditory system, the volume of sound played to the listener should be limited. As with systems that have headphones, it's even more important to limit volume in within-ear monitors that can't be removed as quickly from the user's ears. Fortunately, volume-limiting safeguards are included with commercially available within-ear monitors.

Disease transmission

The issue of disease transmission is another one that's primarily pertinent to public-access virtual environments, in which many users don HMDs and instrumented gloves, or hold pointing devices. Can germs be deposited on the equipment by one user and transmitted to subsequent users? If so, is there a reasonably convenient way in which the maintenance staff at the public site can clean the equipment between users? Alternatively, is there a way to design the equipment so, without cleaning it between users, it won't transmit germs? Unencumbered systems (e.g., artificial reality systems) are one way to entirely avoid the risk of transmitting diseases on surfaces touched by multiple users.

Awareness of the environment

Unlike artificial reality systems, in all current immersive HMD-type virtual environment systems, the user is heavily tethered, with cables running from the HMD, the instrumented gloves, and from other pointing devices. In augmented reality systems using see-through HMDs, these cables are visible to the user. But in typical immersive virtual environments, neither the cables nor other features of the real world (such as walls and chairs) are visible to the user. The safety risk is that of the user tripping on the cables or other obstacles in the local environment, or smashing into walls or furniture.

Several approaches have been used to deal with this hazard. The user can be physically constrained from moving too far by barriers (as is done in W Industries' Virtuality arcade game). Cables can be suspended from the ceiling and a mechanical tracker can impose limits on the range of motion of the user, as was done in an early Ivan Sutherland system (Sutherland 1968). Tricks have been suggested, such as making the world appear to curve as the user moves in a straight direction so the user will always adjust movement to stay within the confines of the physical, real environment. And I'll suggest yet another trick that hasn't yet been implemented: using position tracking sensors to detect the position of the cable, walls, and other obstacles with respect to the user and representing them in the virtual environment, or at least issuing some sort of warning within the virtual environment when the user is approaching a barrier and in risk of injury.

A related hazard exists for augmented reality systems. The user perceives a combination of the synthetic and the real world; if the synthetic stimuli distract too much from the real-world stimuli, the user might fail to notice (hear or see) real-world hazards to be avoided.

Burns, shocks, and skin irritation

Tactile and force displays have safety considerations different than those of display devices for other sensory modalities. Kaczmarek and Bach-y-Rita (1995) point out that pain and burns can be associated with the use of electrodes and vibrators for tactile display, and note three types:

- Electrochemical burns caused by a net flow of ions (preventable if dc current flow at an electrode is kept to a minimum)
- Large thermal burns (unlikely if tactile stimulation is kept below the pain threshold)
- Small black marks of ~0.25 mm in diameter, visible after the "sting" of an electrode (believed to be the result of high-power density in a single conductive pathway)

The risk of electrical shocks, which could induce heart attack if severe enough, can be eliminated by following standard principles of electrical safety when designing tactile displays. Skin irritation from electrotactile display has also been noted as a safety factor by Kaczmarek and Bach-y-Rita, and they recommend that the waveform for electrotactile displays be asymmetric biphasic in shape to minimize this irritation. It should be noted, however, that the irritation was found in trials in which the displays were worn for very extended periods of time (in one study, 10 hours per day for a two-week trial).

Force displays must be designed so they don't exert enough force to damage the user's bones, joints, or soft tissues. This can be done both by limiting the maximum force they can exert and by controlling the direction in which forces can be exerted, taking into account the direction and range of motion possible without injury to the user.

Injury from motion displays

In designing motion displays, you need to keep in mind the risks of whiplash and even a broken neck. If the user's head and neck aren't supported, a relatively small absolute amount of motion can cause damage if it happens too quickly.

Other Common Requirements

You also need to consider the pragmatic requirements of cost, size, and weight when designing a virtual environment system.

Cost

Although it isn't a functional requirement, cost is an issue that could very well determine the viability of an application. The acquisition or deployment of systems might be impossible if their cost is too high for the developer's budget, and applications whose primary purpose is cost-savings might not be viable if their cost is too high.

Cost issues are complicated by the rapid changes in virtual environment technology that are occurring at the time this was written. On the one hand, prices are coming down so quickly for equipment at a given level of performance that some designers claim it's a mistake to make decisions based on current costs since, by the time a system is developed and deployed, the cost of hardware will have decreased dramatically. On the other hand, performance is also improving quickly, and hardware that's purchased now will probably be obsolete within a short time and, even worse, software developed for current hardware might not run on the next generation of hardware since there isn't yet a stable set of standards or a large enough installed user base that vendors feel compelled to provide backward-compatible products. Even if software developed on current hardware does run on the next generation of hardware, you must consider the cost of current hardware in the context of its very short lifetime.

Size and weight

Size and weight have been an area of concern, particularly with respect to HMDs. HMDs that are too heavy and/or poorly balanced quickly cause fatigue in users and can't be worn for long. Size and weight of HMDs are also of concern in applications such as a virtual cockpit display, where the user is in a confined space and must be able to quickly eject from the cockpit in the case of a serious malfunction.

Although few augmented reality applications have been deployed to date, the size and weight of not only the HMD but also the supporting computing hardware are of concern in the case of some of these applications. If users are to walk around using the system, it isn't reasonable to expect them to carry a heavy pack filled with computing equipment (especially while they're engaged in activities such as walking around warehouses or climbing up telephone poles).

Even if system components don't have to be supported by the user's body, their size might have to be considered, depending on the environment in which they're used. The University of North Carolina's GROPE system (Brooks, Ouh-Young, Batter, and Kilpatrick 1990), for example, requires a very large remote manipulator device in order to supply the user with force feedback. Such a device won't fit in the offices of many biochemists. Similarly, CAVE-type systems might simply not fit in available facilities.

Issues common to virtual environments as they relate to different categories of applications and different types of systems are summarized in Tables 3.3 and 3.4.

Requirements for VE Applications 85

TABLE 3.3 Issues Common to Virtual Environments as They Relate to Different Categories of Applications

	Online performance	Offline training and rehearsal	Online comprehension	Offline learning and knowledge acquisition	Online design	Entertainment	Communication	Tools for research on human perceptual-motor capabilities
Veridicality	Usually important	Positive transfer is crucial, veridicality might be important	Might be required	Might be required	Usually important	Not required	Might be required	Not required
Immersion	Often crucial	Might be required	Might be required	Might be required	Might be required	Might be required	Might be required	Depends on experiment
Engagement	Useful	Useful	Useful	Useful	Useful	Crucial	Dependent on participants, not system	Might be required
Resolution	High resolution often crucial	Depends on specific application	Depends on specific application	Depends on specific application	Depends on specific application	Depends on specific application	Depends on specific application	Depends on experiment
Reconfigurability	Not required for many applications	Might be required	Might be required	Might be required	Probably important	Might be required	Might be required	Usually important
Responsiveness	Crucial	Usually crucial	Might be required	Might be required	Probably important	Important for most applications	Might be required	Must be predictable and controllable
Stability	Crucial	Probably important	Preferable, but might be required	Preferable, but might be required	Preferable, but might be required	Preferable, but might be required	Preferable, but might be required	Crucial (to eliminate uncontrolled source of error)
Robustness	Crucial	Preferable, but depends on application	Preferable, but depends on application	Preferable, but depends on application	Preferable, but depends on application	Crucial for location based entertainment	Preferable, but depends on application	Not essential

86   Defining the Requirements

TABLE 3.3 Issues Common to Virtual Environments as They Relate to Different Categories of Applications (Continued)

	Online performance	Offline training and rehearsal	Online comprehension	Offline learning and knowledge acquisition	Online design	Entertainment	Communication	Tools for research on human perceptual-motor capabilities
Viewpoint	Egocentric	Egocentric, though God's-eye "playback" could be useful	Depends on application	Depends on application	Depends on application	Depends on application	Egocentric	Depends on experiment
Representation of user	Generally not relevant	Should be at least as realistic as necessary to avoid distraction and negative transfer	Depends on application	Depends on application	Depends on application	Might be entirely unrealistic and imaginative	Essential, though choice depends on application	Depends on experiment
Registration	Crucial	Might be important if kinesthetic skills are a component of learning	Generally unimportant	Generally unimportant	Depends on application	Generally unimportant	Depends on application	Depends on experiment
Navigation techniques	Relative motion only	Relative motion often preferable, but depends on application	Absolute and relative motion, teleportation, hyperspace, and transformation might all be appropriate	Any navigation technique might be appropriate	Any navigation technique might be appropriate	Any navigation technique might be appropriate	Any navigation technique might be appropriate	Navigation techniques needed only as required by experimental design

Physics of VE	Generally not relevant	Realism might be important	Depends on application	Often irrelevant except, e.g., if simulating forces to test structural stability	Depends on application, but physics are very much unlike real world, often appropriate	Depends on application	Often irrelevant, depends on experiment
Locus of control	In teleoperation, all control is generally with human operator within constraints of robots capabilities	Depends on application	Depends on application	Participants should have control and be able to make modifications	In LBE, entertainment company rather than individual user has control	Locus of control should be flexible, depending on application	Experimenter should be able to make a variety of modifications
Safety issues	Teleoperation: range of motion of human and damage by robot	Positive transfer, so that there are no accidents in doing the task for which the user is training; other safety issues are system-dependent	System-dependent	System-dependent	Disease transmission and other sanitary issues from high throughput of users, cybersickness, poorly adjusted IPD in HMDs resulting in visual problems	System-dependent	Generally minimal given limited duration of use
	Augmented reality for real-time performance: distraction from physical hazards						

TABLE 3.4 Issues Common to Virtual Environments as They Pertain to Different Types of Systems

	VE w/ position-tracked HMD	VE w/ BOOM	Fishtank VR	CAVE	Vehicular simulator	Augmented reality	Artificial reality (mirror world)	Teleoperation
Source material	Synthetic	Synthetic	Synthetic	Synthetic	Synthetic	Synthetic and real world	Synthetic and transduced	Transduced
Working volume	Dependent on tracking system	Small	Small	Dependent on CAVE size	Dependent on simulator size	Dependent on tracking system	Dependent on size/visibility of screens	Varies
Sociability (multiple participants in same physical space)	Possible, depending on tracking systems, cables, etc.	One person	Multiple participants possible, but only one gets the correct experience; Screen display depends on position/orientation of single viewer	Multiple participants possible, but, as w/ Fishtank, only one gets the correct experience	Well suited for multiple participants	Well suited for multiple participants	Well suited for multiple participants	Typically one person
Immersive	High	High	Less immersive	High	High (depending on size of display screens, etc.)	High	Less immersive	High
Resolution	System-dependent (often low unless very high-end)	Generally higher than HMD	High	System-dependent, generally high	High	System-dependent	System-dependent, generally high	System-dependent
Reconfigurability	Excellent	Excellent	Excellent	Excellent	Poor	Excellent	Excellent	System-dependent
Viewpoint	1st person	1st person	1st person	1st person	"1st person" (but actually that of vehicle)	1st person	3rd person	1st person (Robot's transducers)

Requirements for VE Applications

Representation of user	Varies	Generally none	Generally very limited, perhaps a cursor, but user can see own body	Generally none, but user can see own body	None, but user can see own body	None, but user can see own body	Not applicable (the "body" seen is the robot's)
Degree of virtuality	Entirely virtual	Entirely virtual	Display is virtual, but surrounding environment is not excluded	Entirely virtual except user can see him/herself	Mixed: physical cockpit, etc., and user can see him/herself	Mixture of real and synthetic environment;	On screen, video (or processed video) combined with synthetic environment; user can see surrounding world	Entirely real environment as transduced by remote robot
Registration	Not crucial, precision not required	Not crucial, precision not required	Moderately good is preferable	Moderately good is preferable	Not applicable (the user is not position tracked)	Highly crucial, demands are exacting	Moderately good is preferable	Highly crucial, demands are exacting for some applications
Multisensory	Visual/ auditory/ haptic	Visual/ auditory (not well suited for force/ tactile)	Visual; in current systems, audio is generally only stereo; current systems do not use force/ tactile	Force/tactile feedback is problematic; head-coupled visual display	Force/tactile feedback of physical cockpit; synthetic visual and audio display	Visual display has been emphasized, but auditory display is possible	Generally only visual, w/limited audio; virtual acoustic display would be possible w/ wireless headphones; force and tactile are precluded	Transduced video and force are commonly displayed; spatial audio also possible

90　Defining the Requirements

TABLE 3.4　Issues Common to Virtual Environments as They Pertain to Different Types of Systems (Continued)

	VE w/ position-tracked HMD	VE w/ BOOM	Fishtank VR	CAVE	Vehicular simulator	Augmented reality	Artificial reality (mirror world)	Teleoperation
Navigation techniques	All navigation techniques and input methods are possible	All navigation techniques and input methods are possible (though awkward w/ physical devices)	Current systems generally do not support navigation except for head movement, but the range of navigation techniques and input methods would be possible	Usually relative motion (other techniques possible), using wand or input methods other than locomotive devices	Usually relative motion (other techniques possible) using cockpit controls	Relative motion, using position-tracked head and body movement	All navigation techniques possible, input methods other than physical and locomotive devices	Relative motion, using choice of input methods
Calibration and customization	IPD adjustment, individualized HRTFs, calibration of instrumented gloves and suits, and customization of environment possible; other I/O devices (e.g., eye trackers, and biocontrollers) also require calibration	see VE with position-tracked HMD	Shuttered glasses do not require IPD adjustment, but graphics displayed as alternating left- and right-eye images need to be adjusted for user's IPD to produce accurate images; customization of environment is possible	Graphics displayed could be corrected for user's IPD; customization of environment is possible	Generally no calibration required and no customization possible	Very precise calibration required to align displayed objects properly with real-world stimuli; synthetic elements can be customized	Generally no calibration required; customization of environment possible	Calibration of input and display technologies might be required; mapping between human and robot (e.g., movement) is key; customization of this is possible

Safety issues	Cybersickness, tripping on tether, visual problems, etc.	Cybersickness	None known	Simulator sickness (cybersickness)	Distraction from physical hazards by synthetic elements	None known	Visual problems (also, hazards at the robot site)
Cost (current)	Wide range	Medium to high at present	Generally inexpensive	Expensive	Wide range	Medium	Expensive
Size/weight	Varies	Varies (though the BOOM itself is substantial)	Generally light beyond size and weight of conventional computer system and monitor	Large physical space surrounded by projection screens	Very large, very heavy (with motion platform)	Small size and light weight is often crucial	User unencumbered, but large projection screen required	Generally substantial

I've reviewed some requirements and issues that must at least be considered when designing practically all VE systems and applications. Next, we'll consider application-specific requirements.

Application-Specific Requirements

There are many requirements to be identified that aren't common to all VE systems, but are instead specific to a particular application being designed. There are three situations you might encounter in defining these application-specific requirements for a virtual environment system. The first is when a detailed analysis of how users perform a task in the real environment suffices, since users will do the task in a similar way in the virtual environment. The second is when users perform a similar task in the real world, but the virtual environment system will let them do it in essentially different ways, producing requirements that can't be entirely defined from *a priori* knowledge of how the task has previously been done. The third is when the virtual environment application is used for tasks and interactions that are unlike anything done in the real world, so the analysis of current practices by users is of very little value.

Currently, it's surprisingly rare to find analyses of application-specific requirements for virtual environments in published form. A notable exception is Levison and Pew (1993). They analyze using virtual environments for individual combat training, and provide detailed description of the application-specific requirements for this military application. They base their work on 25 tasks and functions from army training documents, and they distinguish three training purposes (combat training proficiency, mission planning and rehearsal, and mission-specific training) and three levels of capability (not needed, desirable but not necessary, and necessary). They also break the application-specific tasks down in terms of whether their requirements are visual, auditory, or haptic, although in some cases they appear to be making unnecessary assumptions about the solutions before they've defined the problems. However, the choice of modality is less arbitrary than it first appears if a criterion is that the modality chosen is the one actually used in the field, and using the same modality is important.

Because this sort of analysis has been so infrequent, at least in the published literature, I'll include their application-specific requirements here as an example of the results of this sort of analysis. They are:

- Assess physical environment with respect to cover and concealment
- Assess suitability of terrain and other aspects of physical environment for troop and vehicle movement
- Assess likelihood of enemy travel paths
- Conduct operations in an urban environment
- Conduct nonurban close-in operations
- Determine status (location, movement, activity, condition) of friendly troops
- Determine status of enemy forces
- Determine status of friendly and enemy vehicles

- Distinguish/identify friendly and enemy forces
- Assess status and effect of weapons
- Recognize and assess status of various battlefield details (barbed wire, obstacles, etc.)
- Read navigation aids
- Command troops via hand and arm signals
- Communicate among trainees
- Command simulated troops
- Be subjected to disruptive effects of battlefield noise
- Receive feedback concerning physical condition of troops
- Perform control and manipulation of weapons, other equipment, and objects (and receive realistic feedback from this)
- Be subjected to physical and cognitive and other limitations of protective and other types of gear
- Perceive a sense of body movement
- Perceive effects of the degraded physical condition of a simulated dismounted infantryman
- Suffer physical and cognitive limitations on performance due to a degraded physical condition

This analysis by Levison and Pew is an example of assuming that what users will do in the synthetic environment is very much like what they would do in the real world. In cases where users will do tasks in essentially new ways or tasks that they aren't currently doing at all, the designer can describe scenarios and identify application-specific requirements necessary to support those scenarios. There are bound to be characteristics of actual use of the system that are different from those in the scenarios or characteristics that were entirely unanticipated by the designer, and this is one place where evaluating users interacting with prototyped systems can lead to iterative redesign in order to support unanticipated functionality requirements.

Like requirements common to virtual environment applications, application-specific requirements could determine characteristics of the virtual environment created as well as of the technology used to display these environments.

Questions

- What are some applications for which you think immersion would be crucial? How could you test the value of immersion?
- What other kinds of mixed immersion systems (besides the one illustrated in Figure 3.1) could prove useful?
- What user elements are important to represent in a VE? How would your answer to this question differ for a communication application, an online performance application, and an online comprehension application?

- When would you choose absolute motion over relative motion as a navigation style in a VE? How many of the navigation styles described would you offer to users in a single VE application?
- Choose an abstract form of information (such as mathematical probabilities or financial trends) and come up with several ways to represent it. What are the advantages and disadvantages of each?
- Develop your own application-specific task analysis for an application other than the one analyzed by Levison and Pew.

Part 2

Designing the System

When you examine what's needed to meet the requirements defined for virtual environments in the preceding section, there are several obvious and some not-so-obvious generalizations you can make. An obvious one is that there must be a variety of special input and output technologies and that they must be effectively integrated to produce a system that conveys the appropriate perceptual stimuli and captures the crucial motor activities. Perhaps less obvious is that, to achieve this, the supporting computation technology must meet performance demands unlike those of all but a very few other types of systems, and that there are trade-offs that developers of non-VE applications seldom confront. Also less obvious is that fulfilling the application-specific requirements for some virtual environment systems might call for very different input and output technologies than for others; at least for now, there are no technologies that meet the needs of all applications.

This section examines input technologies, output technologies, and computation technologies, including software, hardware, and system design, as well as the design of objects and behaviors, and their interactions within the virtual environment.

Chapter 4

Input Technologies

Virtual environment systems are highly interactive, so their input technologies are crucial. The basic input subsystem is shown in Figure 4.1. Perhaps most essential is some form of position tracking. Whether an immersive VE system with HMD, an unencumbered artificial reality system, an augmented reality system, or a teleoperation system, the user's position and motion is tracked through one of a variety of technologies, which will be described in this chapter.

Instrumented suits and/or gloves track position and orientation, but they also measure joint flexion; VACTOR technology measures facial expression; eye-tracking systems measure point of regard; neuro-muscular impulses are among the physiological measures used for input by biosignal processing technologies; and haptic devices range from 3-D mice to cockpit control devices on vehicular simulators, and are controlled by physical contact and manipulation by the user.

Although devices such as position trackers and instrumented gloves and suits output raw data to the computer system about position, orientation, flexion, etc., associated software makes this data usable. Gesture-recognition software associates a higher-level semantic meaning with input from these technologies so, for example, actions can have meaning at the level of "grabbing and pointing." Other software associated with these input technologies "smooths" tracking data to minimize jitter and peforms predictive tracking to reduce lag. Finally, speech-recognition technology, widely researched and implemented in contexts other than virtual environments, can be incorporated into VE systems, with some special refinements and issues to be addressed that are specific to these systems. The final section of this chapter on input technologies discusses the challenge of integrating these input technologies, and some approaches to integration that have been taken in existing systems.

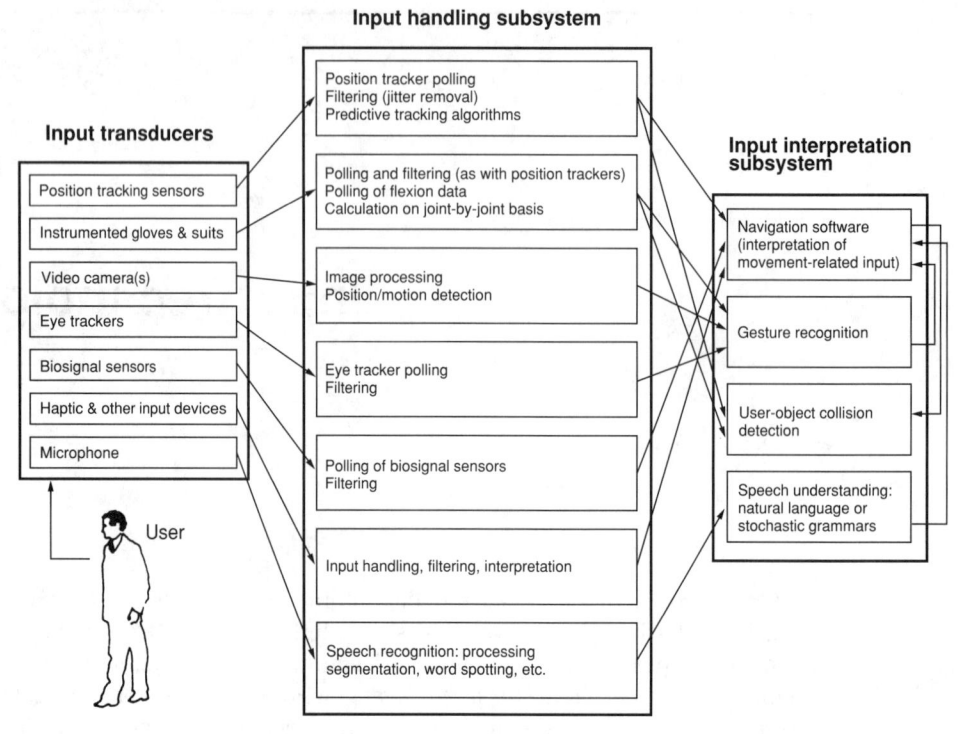

Figure 4.1 Input subsystem.

Position Tracking

In order to provide the users of a VE system with a dynamic sense of immersion (what I've described as *panorama*) and permit interaction through point of view, location, and body movement, position-tracking technology determines the position and orientation of the user. In artificial reality systems, the user's image and motion are captured by video, and signal processing of the video determines the user's position and resulting interaction with the virtual world. In immersive VR systems, position tracking associated with the HMD (head-coupling) allows visual and auditory displays to be updated in response to the user's head motion and orientation. Immersive VE systems with additional position tracking allow further interaction through body movement, including grasping and moving virtual objects via movement of the user's hands and, in some cases, full body movement and interaction (e.g., walking through the world). Augmented reality systems also require that the user's position with respect to physical objects in the real world be determined. In order to permit this interaction, position tracking is an essential core technology that must be included in all VE systems.

Except for artificial reality systems that handle only 2-D input and 2-D display, position tracking for virtual environments uses six coordinates to describe position and orientation. Choosing a reference point as the origin, X, Y, and Z coordinates uniquely describe another point's position. Because objects have volume in space, although the center of an object might correspond to this new point's X, Y, and Z position, three more coordinates are required to describe its orientation. Each of these latter coordinates describe an angle of rotation (sometimes described as Euler angles) about a line parallel to one of the axes of the coordinate system; changes in orientation are commonly referred to as *yaw*, *pitch*, and *roll*. The total number of coordinates needed to describe position and orientation are described as degrees of freedom (DOF).

Although this section will focus on position trackers used for VE systems, there's a history of position tracking that precedes VE, and there are many approaches to position tracking that are used for other tasks but aren't suited to VE. As noted in the Introduction, the ancient Egyptians used transits and plumb lines to determine land boundaries whose markers were washed away by floods, and European explorers used compasses and sextants as early forms of position tracking (Meyer, Applewhite, and Biocca 1991). Biological tracking systems include olfactory tracking by bloodhounds, and auditory tracking by barn owls (see chapter 5); while a form of acoustic tracking is used in some systems (discussed later in this chapter), olfactory tracking isn't used in any known VE system. Practical considerations and the need for resolution and real-time performance prevent some of these non-VE tracking approaches from being applicable to VE systems. Although 6-DOF tracking is used for virtual environments and not found commonly in many other contexts, 2-DOF mechanical tracking of position or motion is common in computer input devices (such as joysticks and mice).

VE-related systems that don't track the user's position typically fall into one of two categories:

Low interactivity. These systems can provide multisensory 3-D displays, but they treat the user as a passive viewer (like Heilig's Sensorama).

Dome or vehicular simulators. These systems can be highly interactive, but their display systems are farther from the user and are necessarily not interactive in the same 3-D way a system with an HMD is. The user can't, for example, look around objects because the system can't detect and respond to the user's position.

The role of position tracking

Position tracking is what permits users to experience being "in" the virtual environment. In the real world, you're accustomed to being able to move your position and orientation in space and, depending on where you move, seeing different views and hearing things from a different listening point. Similarly, you expect to be able to interact with the world by feeling objects, pushing against them, and perhaps grasping and moving them.

Because your visual sensors (eyes) and acoustic sensors (ears) are located on your head, and because visual and auditory displays have been the most developed at present, head tracking is especially common and important in VE systems. Head tracking gives the system the input necessary to interactively update the visual and auditory displays in response to the position and orientation of the user's head. This means that the virtual environment can be visually immersive, for example, without a wide FOV display because users can look around and see themselves as being "in" the synthetic environment wherever they look.

Position tracking in VR systems can be thought of as both head tracking and other types of tracking, most commonly of a 3-D input device such as a 3-D mouse or of a part of the user's body, most commonly (but not limited to) the hand.

Active vs. passive systems

The underlying architecture of position tracking systems comes in two flavors, active and passive. An active system has at least one emitter, which transmits a signal whose properties vary in space, and at least one sensor, which senses the emitted signal and permits calculation of spatial position based on properties of the sensed signal. Active systems can, for example, emit and sense magnetic, ultrasonic, or infrared signals. They can use a pitch/catch approach, in which the signal is transmitted directly from emitter to sensor, or an echo approach, in which the signal is bounced off the object being tracked (as in sonar or radar).

A passive system doesn't use emitters; instead, its sensors detect features of objects or the space they occupy in order to determine their position. Typically, passive systems use video and image-processing technologies to calculate the position and orientation of marked or unmarked objects. Biomedical motion studies are an example of passive position tracking using distinctive markers on objects; robot vision with raw scene analysis is an example of passive tracking without markers (Applewhite 1991).

Inside-out vs. outside-in configuration

Active position-tracking systems can be configured so the object to be tracked has the emitter on it (an "outside-in" configuration) or so the object to be tracked has the sensor on it (an "inside-out" configuration). This distinction is primarily of significance because it affects the sociability (see chapter 3) of a system in which there are multiple objects to be tracked in the same physical space. An inside-out configuration requires adding multiple sensors for multiple objects to be tracked; an outside-in configuration requires the addition of multiple emitters. The presence of multiple emitters requires a technique to distinguish the signals coming from them, e.g., by choosing different frequencies for their signals or coordinating their timing. The need to distinguish between multiple emitters could increase the cost or difficulty of implementation.

Technologies

In principle, any technology that permits the quick determination of the user's position and orientation can be the basis of a position-tracking system. In practice, the most widely used tracking technologies in current VE systems are mechanical, magnetic, acoustic, and optical. These and a fifth technology, gyroscopic, will be described in this section.

Note that you can combine these technologies in a tracking system to overcome the shortcomings of the individual technologies (e.g., "noise" to a magnetic system is of no consequence to an ultrasonic system), although this has been more discussed than implemented so far. Also note that these aren't the only possible technologies that can be used. Zimmerman et al. (1995) discuss electric field sensing, a technology that has been little-used for human-computer interfaces, and also mentions sensing mechanisms such as microwaves (not currently practical because of potential health problems) and triboelectric sensing (detection of static electric charge, which requires that sensed object be electrically charged). Although Zimmerman et al. give examples of using electric field sensing for I/O, and the ability of weakly electric fish to use it shows its potential, I won't discuss this or other possible technologies with which so little have yet been done in terms of VE position tracking.

Mechanical tracking systems. Mechanical tracking systems physically connect the user to the tracker, which is at a known reference point, and mechanically measure the user's position with jointed linkages. Goniometers, developed for medical measurement of the range of motion of joints, were used by Sutherland in his 1968 VE HMD system (Sutherland 1968); a variety of gears or potentiometers can be used.

Although mechanical trackers can be very accurate and responsive, they restrict the user's range of motion and are poor in terms of sociability for multiple proximate users sharing the same space. They're well-suited, however, to systems that, because of the technique of force feedback they incorporate, already restrict the user's range of motion. On the other hand, they're poorly suited to some work environments, as Meyer, Applewhite, and Biocca (1991) point out in citing the Noar, Arnon, and Avnur (1987) description of the Israeli Air Force abandoning a mechanical system for fighter pilots that interfered with ejection.

Perhaps the most common use of mechanical position tracking at present is in systems such as Fake Space Lab's BOOM, which doesn't use an HMD, and in telepresence and force-feedback systems. There's a commercially available mechanical tracker (the ADL-1, manufactured by Shooting Star Technologies) that's used with some current HMD systems. Mechanical trackers don't have separate sensors and emitters, so the concept of inside-out vs. outside-in architecture doesn't apply.

Magnetic tracking systems. Magnetic position-tracking technology has been perhaps the most widely used tracking technology for virtual environments. The primary distinction between the two most common types of systems is whether they're based on alternating current (ac) emitters or direct current (dc) emitters. Both approaches, as implemented at present, use inside-out configurations (i.e., the emitter is at a fixed position in space).

Ac systems, such as the most commonly used Polhemus trackers, use three electromagnetic coils that are orthogonally collocated (wound around mutually perpendicular axes on ferrite cores) in both their emitters and sensors. When a current is fed to the emitter coils, a magnetic field is generated; this magnetic field in turn generates currents in the coils of the sensor, when it is moved through the field. The ac current is sent to the three emitters in a sequence, with each state of this sequence producing currents in the three sensor coils (which vary with distance between the sensor and emitter). The nine currents induced during the three-state cycle are processed using an algorithm that models the behavior of magnetic fields in order to calculate position and orientation of the sensor. This position and orientation information (which is, in fact, calculated from the change between successive measurements of these nine currents) is sent from the tracker to the host computer at a constant update rate.

Aside from distortion of the magnetic field caused by eddy currents induced in ferromagnetic objects in the region of the ac tracker, Meyer, Applewhite, and Biocca (1992) point out that the emitters for the common ac magnetic trackers often contain imperfections that cause their own distortions in the magnetic field, and that the manufacturer measures these and corrects them in hardware or software. Recommended sources for more information on ac magnetic tracking systems are Raab, Blood, Steiner, and Jones (1979); Meyer, Applewhite, and Biocca (1992); Kalawsky (1993); and Krieg (1993).

Dc magnetic tracking systems have been developed more recently than ac systems, and they are somewhat less sensitive to the presence of ferromagnetic objects in the environment. Like the emitter in ac systems, the dc emitter has orthogonally collocated electromagnetic coils wrapped around a core. A four-state cycle is used, during which direct current is sequentially pulsed to each of the emitter coils in the first three states and there's no current applied in the fourth state. Each pulse produces a static magnetic field in the steady state that's reached after settling the perturbation caused by the rising edge of the dc pulse.

As implemented in the commercially available Ascension trackers, one hundred cycles occur per second, with each state lasting for 2.5 ms of a four-state cycle's 10 ms. The dc receiver has three orthogonally wrapped coils, and a fourth coil that's wrapped around a cylinder in the center of the cube. Bhatnagar (1993) mentions subtracting the earth's magnetic field to calculate position, and Kalawsky (1993) discusses using a lookup table in EEPROM for corrections in nonorthogonalities in the orientation of the coils, as well as other details of implementation.

Magnetic tracking systems are all active systems, as they require emitters to function. Commonly used magnetic systems use inside-out architecture, though outside-in is technically possible.

Acoustic tracking systems. Acoustic trackers typically use ultrasonic frequencies, although audible frequencies could theoretically be used. The three main approaches to acoustic tracking are time of flight, time delay, and phase-coherent systems. Acoustic waves, which are differences in pressure that travel through the air at approximately 1,140 feet per second (just over 1 foot per millisecond), are generated in acoustic trackers by an emitter. In ultrasonic systems, the emitter generally uses a piezoelectric crystal to transduce an electrical signal to a mechanical force and thus act as a speaker and generate acoustic waves; you can use the voltage or frequency applied to the piezoelectric crystal to control the amplitude and frequency of the acoustic waves it produces. The sensor also contains a transducer, generally a piezoelectric crystal, which converts mechanical energy from acoustic waves back to electrical energy (i.e., it acts as a microphone).

Time-of-flight systems emit acoustic waves in pulses at known times, and measure the time it takes for a wave to travel from emitter to sensor. This time measurement can be converted to a distance measurement that, if there were only a single sound source and a single sensor, would define a sphere of equidistant locations at which the sensor could be positioned with respect to the emitter. By using three emitters separated in space, the three different time measurements in reaching the sensor define a single point in space at which the sensor can be located (i.e., the intersection point of the three spheres).

There are two approaches to time-of-flight systems, the pitch-catch approach and the echo approach. In pitch-catch systems, the time measured is that required for the acoustic wave to travel directly from emitter to sensor; in echo systems, the emitter and sensor are usually placed together, and the time measured is that required for the acoustic waves to travel to a target and echo back. Because of the speed at which acoustic waves travel, data rates are lower in pitch-catch systems if the tracked object is farther from the emitter. Not only is this true in the case of echo systems, but the elapsed travel time is twice as great.

Time-delay systems emit acoustic waves continually, but vary the waves in a pseudo-random way so there aren't cycles over a period of time that could correspond to the time it takes for the signal to travel from emitter to sensor. The received signal is compared to time-delayed versions of the transmitted signal, and the time it took for the signal to travel from emitter to sensor (and hence the distance between them) is calculated from this comparison.

Applewhite (1993) points out that time-delay systems have high data rates (since, unlike time-of-flight systems it isn't necessary to pause between pulses), and are robust (many points of data are compared in calculating position), but they're also impractical except in very small-volume tracking tasks due to the processing required to compare emitted and sensed signals and the memory needed to store the emitted signal.

Phase-coherent systems emit acoustic waves continually, and these waves are (unlike those emitted in time-delay systems) periodic. You can compare the phase of the emitted and received signals by using their zero crossings. Like a time-delay system, you use the time difference between these signals to calculate distance. In the case of a phase-coherent system, however, the calculated time difference must be shorter than the period of one wave cycle. This is a very small time difference and corresponds to a very small difference in distance, but phase-coherent systems calculate changes only in the position between successive measurements and cumulate these to the initial position. Given a high enough data rate, the user won't move so far between samples that a given position displacement will correspond to a difference in transmission time greater than the duration of one wave cycle.

Applewhite (1993) points out that once errors occur in phase-coherent systems (e.g., zero-crossings occur that are not correctly determined), they're cumulative; since only relative position calculations are made, there's no way to use subsequent measurements to correct errors. These errors in a phase-coherent system are known as *phase unwrapping errors*.

Time-of-flight, time-delay, and phase-coherent systems all require emitters, so they're all active systems, but the echo (vs. the pitch-catch) approach doesn't require that either the sensor or the emitter be on the tracked object. Thus, acoustic trackers can be outside-in, inside-out, or, in the case of echo systems, neither.

Optical tracking systems. Given the large number of optical trackers that have been constructed, there has been notably less use of optical trackers in VR systems than you might expect, with the exception of experimental systems and the 2-D video image processing used in artificial reality systems such as Myron Krueger's VideoPlace (Krueger 1985, 1989, and 1991) and the Vivid Group's Mandala (Wyshynski and Vincent 1993). Among the experimental systems with optical trackers, one that has received much attention is the University of North Carolina's optical ceiling tracker (Wang 1990; Wang, Azuma, Bishop, Chi, Eyles, and Fuchs 1990; Wang, Chi, and Fuchs 1990; Azuma and Ward 1991; Ward, Azuma, Bennett, Gottschalk, and Fuchs 1992).

Optical tracking systems can be passive or active, and they can be inside-out or outside-in. One approach is a beacon system, which can also be inside-out or outside-in, and uses the fixed distance between optical elements that emit light (active) or reflect light (passive) to calculate the position of objects. Another approach, an optical pattern recognition system, uses known geometry about the objects to be tracked (like beacon systems), but doesn't require special optical elements to emit or reflect light. These systems use image processing technology to calculate position by comparing known characteristics about object geometry to images transduced by video cameras at known locations; this is computationally intensive, however, and 6-DOF systems of this type aren't yet common. A third approach, laser ranging, passes laser beams through a diffraction grating and creates a diffraction pattern on the object to be tracked, which is transduced via video camera and used to calculate the object's position. Laser-ranging systems have been used for robot vision systems, but not yet in VE systems.

Other approaches to tracking. Although mechanical, acoustic, magnetic, and optical technologies have been the main approaches to position tracking for virtual environments, there are other potential approaches that have been less explored. One of these is gyroscopic systems, which, though they can't determine absolute position, can sense change in motion. Gyroscopic technology has some potential advantages, e.g., it doesn't require line of sight and could potentially offer large-working-volume, tetherless tracking. On the other hand, because it doesn't determine absolute position, errors are compounded and an unacceptable amount of "drift" could quickly develop. Because each of the more commonly used tracking approaches has shortcomings in addressing certain demands (as discussed in the following sections), tracking systems that combine the different technologies have been recommended (e.g., by Applewhite), but not yet widely implemented.

Issues and requirements

From a perceptual point of view, problems with position tracking can lead to a number of difficulties for the user. Lag (or latency) can contribute to overall system latency, which has been suggested as one cause of cybersickness in users. Poor registration can lead to usability problems, especially in augmented reality systems, where correct positioning of text and graphics that are superimposed on real-world objects is crucial to their usefulness. Poor accuracy and resolution can make the fine motions required in some control tasks (such as telepresence surgery) difficult or impossible. Poor robustness can cause problems in the real environments in which applications will be used—e.g., in offices with lots of metal, computer monitors, and ultrasonic noise.

Accuracy/resolution. For position trackers, *resolution* refers to the smallest movement that can be detected by the system, while *accuracy* describes how close the reported position is to the actual position. A system can have high resolution and be inaccurate, but low resolution necessarily limits accuracy. Mechanical systems have good accuracy and resolution, as do acoustic time-of-flight and time-delay systems. Acoustic phase-coherent systems have excellent resolution, but might not have good accuracy due to phase unwrapping errors. Optical systems have decreased accuracy and resolution with greater distance between the fixed sensors or emitters and the object being tracked, whether the system is passive or active; some optical systems have attempted to address this by using multiple emitters or sensors. Magnetic systems also have good accuracy and resolution when sensors and emitters are close, and diminished accuracy and resolution when they're farther apart; their accuracy is also reduced if there are metallic objects in the area.

Responsiveness. *Responsiveness* in position-tracking systems can be conveyed in terms of several parameters, described by Meyer, et al. (1992) as sample rate, data rate, update rate, and lag. They define *sample rate* as the rate at which sensors are checked for data, *data rate* as the number of computed positions per second, *update rate* as the number of new position coordinates reported by the tracking system to the host computer per second, and *lag* (also known as *latency*) as the delay between the movement of a remotely sensed object and the report of its new position. Sample rate often exceeds data rate because sensors are checked more often than position is calculated; if the tracking system processes raw data to reduce jitter or predict motion, the update rate might not directly reflect measured position.

Adelstein, Johnston, and Ellis (1992) point out that, while spatial and temporal components of VE systems (e.g., resolution/accuracy and responsiveness) are often examined in isolation, there are important interactions not typically captured in the specifications given by manufacturers. In particular, Adelstein et al. created a test-bed apparatus with a motorized swing arm to which they attached sensors of various magnetic (ac and dc) and ultrasonic trackers, and used a procedure in which tracker reports were collected while the arm swung back and forth pendulum-style. The trackers exhibited distinct dynamic responses that couldn't have been deduced from manufacturers' specifications. I recommend Adelstein et al.'s paper for its insights into latency issues for trackers.

Robustness. *Robustness* is the capability of a position tracker to function error-free in spite of the "noise" (some of it unpredictable) found in the environment in which it's used. "Noise" means different things to different types of trackers. For magnetic trackers, it's the presence of metallic objects that interfere with magnetic fields; ferromagnetic objects can distort the emitted field by creating eddy currents. For optical systems, it's temporary obstructions and ambient lights; for acoustic systems, it might come in the form of ultrasonic sounds in the environment, such as those emitted by computer monitors, or those produced by unexpected causes such as jangling keys. Thus, robustness requires addressing different technology-specific challenges for different tracking technologies.

Registration. *Registration* is the relationship between real and reported position and orientation. The quality of registration is distinct from the quality of resolution and accuracy, as Meyer et al. (1992) point out, since even a system that has generally good resolution and accuracy can accumulate errors that cause the reported position to drift from the actual position. In many cases, good registration isn't essential because users can mentally adjust for drift without even being conscious they're doing so. But for some applications, especially those augmented reality applications in which computer-synthesized text and graphics must be superimposed on and integrated with real-world objects, the quality of registration is crucial. A small discrepancy between the position at which things should be displayed and where they are displayed with respect to the real world (especially in the case of visual and haptic display) might undermine the value of the system for the task at hand.

Working volume and sociability. *Working volume*, also known as *range of operation*, is the volume within which a system can track position, either at all (in the case of a mechanical system) or within the resolution and accuracy that has been specified (in the case of other types of systems). *Sociability* has been described alternately as the ability of a system to track either multiple users or multiple objects in the same working volume. Note that, from the perspective of the tracking system, tracking a single user with multiple points (fingers, hands, legs, head, etc.) requires sociability in the sense that this is a "multiobject" problem. *Collateral effects* are the effects that one tracked object has on the reported position of another tracked object; these can come in the form of sensors occluding other sensors, magnetic fields affecting other magnetic fields, optical emitters interfering with other optical emitters, or linkages of one mechanical tracker colliding with those of another mechanical tracker.

Evaluation

Position-tracking technologies should be evaluated in the context of the environment in which they're actually to be used so, for example, noise and its effect on the tracker can be accurately assessed. The report of tests by Adelstein, Johnston, and Ellis (1992) is instructive in terms of issues pertaining to dynamic vs. static use of trackers. Filtering by position trackers to minimize jitter was found by Adelstein, et al. to increase lag and, for some applications, jitter might actually be preferable to lag. Unfortunately, manufacturers of current trackers generally don't allow the developer to control whether filtering is turned on or off. A summary of position-tracking technologies is given in Table 4.1.

Instrumented Gloves and Suits

Instrumented gloves, also called *hand-gesture interface devices, virtual hand controllers,* or *datagloves* (although the latter is trademarked by VPL) use bend-sensing technologies to detect the "posture" of the hand. By combining position-tracking technology with bend-sensing technology and graphically representing transduced information about finger flexion and hand position and orientation, a virtual hand can be represented in the virtual environment. This virtual hand can not

TABLE 4.1 Position Tracking Technologies

Tracker technology	Accuracy/ resolution	Responsiveness	Robustness	Registration	Working volume/ sociability
Mechanical	Excellent	Excellent	Good	Good	Poor working volume; very poor sociability; does not support occlusion
ac magnetic	Good over small volume, less good over larger volume	Medium, effect of eddy currents slows down responsiveness, as does filtering	Affected by presence of ferromagnetic objects and electromagnetic noise in the 8–1,000 Hz range (e.g., from power lines, transformers, CRTs)	Should be reasonably good in small volume quiet environment, but few reports	Moderately good working volume; increasing signal strength increases distortions; fair sociability; supports occlusion very well
dc magnetic	Good over small volume, less good over larger volume	Better than ac systems, but still slowed by emitter field distortions and filtering	Less sensitive to effects of ferromagnetic objects, but still susceptible to electromagnetic noise	Should be reasonably good in small volume quiet environment, but few reports	Moderately good working volume; increasing signal strength increases distortions; fair sociability; supports sensor occlusion very well
Acoustic time of flight; pitch catch	Very good over small working volume	Moderate to poor, depending on distance (fewer positions per second can be calculated over larger volumes)	Very vulnerable to acoustic noise; disturbances in the air can also have an effect	Unreported	Fairly good working volume, but loss of accuracy; good sociability; negatively affected by sensor occlusion, which produces errors
Acoustic time of flight, echo	Good	Moderate to poor, depending on distance (worse than pitch catch)	Very vulnerable to acoustic noise, effects from disturbances in the air	Unreported	Working volume/ accuracy trade-off as with pitch-catch systems (but at half the distance); good sociability; sensor occlusion causes errors
Acoustic time delay	Very good	Would be good, except computational demands are so great that time-delay systems are not yet practical	Should be, excellent, as decisions are made on many data points	Should be quite good	Impractical at present except for extremely small volumes due to computational demands; sensor occlusion causes errors

TABLE 4.1 Position Tracking Technologies (Continued)

Tracker technology	Accuracy/ resolution	Responsiveness	Robustness	Registration	Working volume/ sociability
Acoustic phase coherent	Very good (better than acoustic time-of-flight systems)	Good	Good, higher data rates than TOF make them less vulnerable to noise	Poor, these are especially vulnerable to accumulation of cumulative error, since absolute distance is not measured	Problematic with large working volumes due to cumulative error over zero crossings; fair sociability; sensor occlusion causes errors
Optical beacon, inside-out	Very good, decreases with larger working volume	Excellent	Good, some might be affected by changes in ambient light	Good	Large working volume is practical with multiple emitters, though at cost of complexity; sensor occlusion is fatal
Optical beacon, outside-in	Very good, decreases with larger working volume	Potentially excellent (existing systems such as SELSPOT are not real-time)	Good, some might be affected by changes in ambient light	Few reports	No benefit from multiple emitters, so there is accuracy/volume trade-off; sensor occlusion is fatal
Optical pattern recognition	Very good, decreases with larger working volume	Excellent (if processing is sufficiently fast)	Good under controlled conditions, but changes in ambient light can cause problems	Few reports	Sensor occlusion is fatal
Optical laser ranging	Very good, decreases with larger working volume	Excellent (if processing is sufficiently fast)	Problem with ambiguities in interpreting projected diffraction patterns on concave surfaces	No reports	Problematic with large working volume due to loss of accuracy; sensor occlusion is fatal

TABLE 4.1 Position Tracking Technologies (Continued)

Tracker technology	Accuracy/ resolution	Responsiveness	Robustness	Registration	Working volume/ sociability
Gyroscopic	Motion rather than absolute position is determined, so any errors become compounded ("drift")	No reports	Unreported, though should be immune to the kinds of "noise" that affect other tracking technologies	No reports (but "drift" could cause problems)	Excellent, practically unlimited; no sensor occlusion/line-of-sight problems; no interference from other users

SOURCE: Adapted from Meyer, Applewhite, & Biocca (1992)
Presence: Teleoperators and Virtual Environments vol. 1 No. 2, M.I.T. Press

only mimic the motion of the user's hand, but it can grab and manipulate objects in the virtual environment, and make gestures that the system recognizes.

Instrumented suits use the same bend-sensing technology in combination with position trackers to capture the user's full-body motion. Although these instrumented suits (also known as *datasuits*, although this is trademarked by VPL as well) have been much discussed, they're still rare and quite expensive at present.

Technologies

Several approaches have been used to sense bending and capture joint flexion. One of these, used by VPL in its DataGlove (Zimmerman, Lanier, Blanchard, Bryson, and Harvill 1987) is to use fiber-optic cables attached to a lycra glove and to determine joint flexion by measuring the amount of light that passes through the cables. The more the finger (and hence, the cable) is bent, the less light passes through the cable; the theory behind light propagation through fiber-optic cables is reviewed in Kalawsky (1993).

The Power Glove, a controller for video games created by Mattel, used a lower-cost technology based on measuring strain with flexible polyester strips covered by a special ink. Another type of flex sensor is used in a glove created by Jim Kramer that uses bend sensors at each joint of the hand. Mechanical exoskeleton-based devices like those produced by Exos can also be used to measure joint flexion and, while they're physically more cumbersome, they're well suited to providing force feedback.

Although this review of the technologies used in instrumented gloves and suits is brief, any technology that isn't overly cumbersome and can be used to measure bending is applicable, and I believe that additional technologies will be found to be useful when more work on instrumented gloves and suits is done.

Issues

Issues to be considered with respect to instrumented suits and gloves include robustness, accuracy and resolution, calibration requirements, hygiene, and how encumbering they are. While these technologies are expensive, it's worth considering the issue of "handedness," since many laboratories purchase only a single glove. There has been some preliminary research on using different haptic input devices on the dominant and nondominant hands, but the choice of whether to use one or two instrumented gloves and, if one, whether it should be worn on the dominant or nondominant hand will certainly be application-dependent, according to what tasks the user must perform in the virtual environment.

A functionally similar alternative to using bend-sensing gloves and suits is to use a large number of position trackers to keep track of position and orientation of the many points on the hand and body. This approach has been used by researchers at Boeing, who want to represent a technician's body in the virtual environment as he or she attempts to perform maintenance and repair procedures on a designed (but not yet built) aircraft (Esposito 1993).

Evaluation

Evaluating the accuracy and resolution of instrumented gloves and suits is fairly straightforward, at least in concept, and not task-dependent. It can be accomplished by bending the glove or suit in measured ways and observing how this flexion is transduced and reported by the glove or suit's bend-sensing technology. A related issue is how many joints and what types of flexion are measured, and this can be easily ascertained. Update rate and latency is also straightforward to evaluate, but won't be discussed because it hasn't proven to be a problem with instrumented gloves and suits; flex sensors, mechanical exoskeletons, and light can all be used to provide rapid reports of flexion by the user.

Robustness and encumbrance rely on carefully analyzing the demands of the task. You need to consider factors such as how frequently users will put on and take off the gloves or suit, how long they'll wear them, what kind of environment they'll be worn in, and what tasks will be performed in them. Anecdotal reports have suggested that early commercially available instrumented gloves were so lacking in robustness that they wouldn't withstand even two to three days of use in a highly trafficked public exhibition. You must also consider hygiene in this sort of application, though for many other applications, an evaluation of hygiene simply comes down to whether there's any way to clean the gloves or suit.

Calibration requirements may also not be straightforward. There are three levels at which calibration can be considered:

- Will users have to calibrate the gloves or suit the first time they use them? (The answer is almost always yes.)
- Will users have to recalibrate the gloves or suit every time they put them on again?
- Will users have to recalibrate them during the course of a single session?

While the idea of having to recalibrate even within a single session might seem excessive, Kalawsky (1993) points out that some types of instrumented gloves, as they're worn and heat up (and the users perspire), tend to slip and go out of calibration. For a while, the users can continue to make gestures that can be recognized by the system by adapting their hand motion, using the feedback from the system to guide them, but at some point the change required can no longer be compensated for and recalibration will be necessary. I want to point out that, in the case described by Kalawsky, the glove is likely being used with a highly constrained vocabulary of gestures and that, with a richer gesture vocabulary, the glove going out of calibration would more quickly become intolerable and more frequent recalibration would be required. Not all designs of instrumented gloves have this problem.

One other issue that should be evaluated with respect to instrumented gloves is whether this is the best technology for accomplishing the tasks demanded of users. Although instrumented gloves are closely associated with virtual environments due in large part to the early days of VPL, it isn't clear, if the task is to navigate through an environment, for example, that the best technology for accomplishing this task is an instrumented glove that must be trained to recognize arbitrary gestures associated with "flying forward" and "flying backward." On the other hand, if grabbing and manipulating objects is required, an instrumented glove might be a good choice of technology. A summary of instrumented glove technologies that have been used to date is given in Table 4.2.

Locomotive Input

Like dexterous handmasters, there are locomotive devices that can be used as both input and output devices, though, in general, they haven't been commonly used in VE systems. Systems such as stationary bicycles, stair-climbers, and passive treadmills let users pedal or walk, and this is sensed and used as input to navigate in the virtual environment. Stationary bicycles and treadmills have been used with VEs in systems at the University of North Carolina at Chapel Hill, for example (Brooks, et al. 1992). The goal of these input devices is to both provide a natural way to navigate and give users the illusion of moving around a large area when in fact they remain within a small (or at least confined) space.

Current commercially available equipment (mostly designed as exercise machines) clearly has certain limitations; for example, users can walk only in one direction on a typical treadmill, although circular treadmills have been developed at Brandeis University and Brown University (Durlach and Mavor, Eds. 1995).

The UNC Chapel Hill steerable treadmill, suggested as a navigation device by James Lipscomb, added bicycle handlebars to a nonmotorized treadmill to allow users to steer and walk through the virtual environment; sensors were also added to measure the users' movements. The UNC team developed this treadmill as an input device to be used in traversing an architectural walk-through, but it had some problems. The treadmill was found to be stiff and couldn't be modified to make it truly easy for walking and, as a result, users' stride length was only ⅔ of their normal stride. To compensate, the UNC team mapped treadmill movement to VE movement

TABLE 4.2 Instrumented Glove Technologies

	Strain gauges	Optical fibers	Exoskeleton with Hall position sensors	Conductive ink sensors	Gloveless gesture recognition
Principle of operation	Flexion produces change in resistance between pair of strain gauges; resulting voltage changes are measured by Wheatstone bridge	Flexion produces attenuation of light transmitted from LEDs and carried through the optical fibers to phototransitors	Flexion causes exoskeleton joints to flex, and the angles of these joints are measured by Hall position sensors	Flexion causes change in density of carbon particles in conductive ink, resulting in measured change in electrical resistance	Hand position and movement is captured by video system, and image processing is used to recognize hand position
Advantages	High resolution, comfortable, light	Fairly comfortable and light	Very high-resolution sensing, quite robust, lends itself very well to force feedback	Low cost	Unencumbered
Disadvantages	Fairly high cost (other disadvantages, if there are any, are not yet reported)	Relationship between joint movement and sensed light is nonlinear; optical fibers damaged easily	Exoskeleton weight might produce fatigue (though they are becoming lighter), and could interfere with some activities; mechanical complexity and high cost	Resolution is poor	Require line of sight, and image processing could be computationally demanding
Product that uses technology	Jim Kramer/Virtual Technology Cyberglove	VPL DataGlove	EXOS, Inc. Dexterous Hand Master	Mattel PowerGlove	None—but research systems, e.g., at AT&T
Reference	Burdea & Coiffet (1994)	Zimmerman, et al. (1987)	EXOS product literature, Burdea & Coiffet (1994)	Pausch (1991), Kalawsky (1993)	Segan (1993)

so the viewpoint in the virtual world was moved forward ⅔ the measured distance of users' stride. Although this resulted in the number of steps required to cross a room being correct, it proved frustrating for users, who found it was too slow a way to explore and grew fatigued with the exercise, and the UNC team retired its treadmill (Brooks, et al. 1992).

Although sensor/force-feedback systems worn on the feet could, in theory, permit users to walk in arbitrary ways through the virtual environment, such devices haven't yet been developed and publicly demonstrated. Other forms of locomotive input, such as climbing, swimming, and rowing, have also not been explored for their use in virtual environments.

VACTORs

In a graphical virtual environment, how is the appearance of users represented? In particular, how are users' face and facial expressions represented? In single-user systems, this might not be an issue, but in multiuser systems it usually is, for a couple of reasons. The need to represent facial information about users stems from the need to identify other participants and the importance of facial expression in communication. Facial appearance is normally a major cue to identifying others, but early prototypes of multiuser virtual environments have used color, shape, or even texture-mapped photographs on relatively static graphic figures to aid in identification of other users. This doesn't make up for losing the communicative function of facial expressions. A solution to this problem is the capture of facial gesture and representation of it through performance animation.

Technologies that capture facial gesture are still scarce, expensive, and encumbering, but are expected to become more widespread, less expensive, and more convenient to use. An alternative to them is to incorporate live images captured by video cameras of other users, but this presents problems. In the case of current artificial reality systems, in which the user's viewpoint is static, the video presented is 2-d, and the users do not wear HMDs because they see images projected onto a video screen, it is easy to transmit live images of another user's face. But in systems in which users' faces are obstructed by HMDs, images presented are 3-d, and the viewer can arbitrarily change position and orientation (and hence, viewing perspective), this is not an option. Therefore, this section will describe performance animation via the technology that is described as "VACTORs."

It should be noted that there are other movement-sensing technologies for the facial area possible, for example, sensors to measure bite/jaw clenching, but these are typically only used for people with motor disabilities.

Technologies

VACTOR technology requires that a device that senses the position and movement of the face (and the facial muscles) be worn. At present, there are few manufacturers of this specialized sensing hardware, and a lack of technical articles describing the underlying sensing technology.

The sensed facial expressions, motions, and gestures are used to create computer-generated imagery and, in particular, control animation of digital computer characters. As implemented at present, this process involves creating a hierarchical database of characteristics of the modeled character and precomputed animated movements that are then saved as separate data files and used as morph targets. A performance animation system matches the user's facial movements to morph targets, and generates and renders the animation sequence. This approach limits the number of expressions possible, although you can create expressions that are combinations of several morph targets. It does, however, permit images to be rendered at up to 30 frames per second with current technology, even if the characters and morphing are complex (Joslin 1993).

Issues

Current facial sensing technology is quite encumbering, and not easily used with HMDs. In addition to the limitations on expression due to the previously described approach, it isn't entirely a natural or intuitive interface; actors typically control the devices, and there's some learning involved in using facial expressions to select morph targets. While VACTOR technology is a very impressive use of sensor and animation technology for entertainment purposes (e.g., letting a cartoon character interact with a live audience), no empirical studies have produced evidence that it conveys information helpful to computer supported cooperative work, or for anything other than entertainment purposes. While it's easy to imagine future development of a technology that produces less cartoon-like images, there's no practical solution in sight to make the animated image that of the user's face.

Evaluation

Since VACTOR technology is currently used only for performance animation entertainment purposes, there's much that must be evaluated to determine its value. This includes usability and learning time for novices, selection of user representation, and use and value in multiuser applications for communication between participants.

Eye Tracking

Why incorporate eye tracking in VE systems? The eye's point of regard can be used for intentional user input, for example, to select objects in the virtual environment. Jacob (1991) gives a good overview on the use of eye tracking for intentional user input to computer-human interfaces, and points to its use for selecting objects, displaying additional details about a selected object, moving objects, and controlling text and menus, for example, controlling scrolling text in a window, selecting which window is active in a multiwindow display, and choosing commands from a menu.

In addition, since foveal vision has a much higher resolution than parafoveal and peripheral vision, a system that keeps track of the user's point of regard could direct most of the power of the graphical rendering and display system to presenting detail to the foveal region. This, however, would require very low-latency tracking and very fast system response to the tracking data. For the laser retinal scanning technology developed at the HIT Lab by Kollin (1993) to be used in a VE application, you'd also need eye tracking in order to control the image projected onto the retina and the angle of the projecting device. Some forms of eye tracking also provide information such as pupil dilation, which can be used to monitor physiological effects, e.g., cybersickness and workload.

Several approaches have been used in eye tracking and, although it's already more than 20 years old, Young and Sheena (1975) contains an excellent survey of these approaches. They take advantage of a variety of physical characteristics of the eye, including the potential difference of up to 1 mV between the cornea and retina, differences in electrical impedance with the position of the eyes, the shape of the corneal bulge, and reflective and optical landmark properties of various parts of the eye. Jacob (1991) emphasizes that it isn't the eye-tracking technology itself that has been the barrier to its more widespread use in human-computer interfaces, but rather the human factor research for suggesting effective (natural and unobtrusive) ways to incorporate users' eye movements into their dialog with the computer.

Technologies

Among the eye-tracking techniques used are electro-oculography, in which electrodes are put around the eyes to measure potential differences due to cornea-retina potential; corneal reflectance, in which the position of the eye is calculated by measuring reflection of a source light on the cornea; optical pupil or limbus tracking, in which you process a video image of the eye to calculate eye position using the pupil or limbus as a landmark; and Double Purkinje image tracking, which tracks the reflections that form as an image passes from cornea to lens and lens to vitreous humor. There are also a variety of contact lens methods that use specially designed contact lenses that fit tightly on the eye (and don't move and slip as do normal contact lenses) to calculate eye position via reflection of a source light by mirror surfaces on the lenses (the "optical lever" method), or by measuring voltage from nearby electromagnetic coils induced in tiny wire coils embedded in the lenses. All of these technologies are described well by Young and Sheena (1975).

Issues

For determining point of regard, i.e., the orientation of the eye in space and what elements of the visual scene are being fixated or scanned, many of the eye-tracking techniques require head tracking in combination with measurement of the eye position relative to the head, and Young and Sheena discuss some head tracking techniques. Of course, in VE systems using HMDs, head position is already tracked whether or not eye tracking is included. However, many of the eye-tracking techniques are obtrusive or not conducive to use with an HMD with optical elements placed close to the eyes.

Young and Sheena compare eye-tracking technologies, and indicate problems with specific methods. Among the problems with some of the technologies that would interfere with their use in virtual environment systems are user discomfort, head stabilization, calibration setup time, user training, unacceptability of glasses or contact lenses, and insufficient speed of response. Refer to Young and Sheena's work for more details on specific problems with each of the tracking methods.

In terms of using tracked eye movements for user input, Jacob (1991) cites issues related to the Midas Touch problem, calibration and configuration, accuracy and range, preprocessing raw data, and fixation recognition.

The Midas Touch problem results, for example, if eye position is naively used as a direct substitute for a mouse in a conventional computer interface; everywhere users look, commands are issued, even if they intend only to visually scan the display to see what's there. The normal experience of vision is that you can look around without causing things to happen, and this capability should be preserved in a VE system that incorporates eye tracking.

The calibration and configuration issue refers to practical problems in using eye-tracking technology:

- Many eye-tracking systems are designed to be used by a subject in an experiment, but require the assistance of an experimenter to perform the required calibration procedure (individual users trying to calibrate the equipment run into the difficulty that, in order for them to look at the calibration equipment's control panel, the eye is no longer fixed on the calibration target).
- Users tend to be aware of their eyes being tracked, and feel self-conscious (as though they're being watched).
- Calibration procedures tend to put eye trackers into proper calibration over part of (rather than all of) the range of possible tracked eye positions, and additional calibration within smaller regions might be preferable.

I'd like to add that, based on my personal experience, proper calibration of eye-tracking equipment is a more tricky procedure than you might imagine, and at least with some tracking technologies, differences in the dimensions of the user's face, whether or not the user wears glasses, and characteristics of the user's eyelids and eyes make for calibration problems that it takes experience to overcome.

The accuracy and range issue refers to the fact that, with most eye-tracking technologies, the range over which the eye can be accurately tracked is less than the total range over which it can move, and accuracy isn't usually better than the approximately one degree of the fovea's width.

Preprocessing raw data filters out noisy data and attempts to pull out the user's conscious intentions from the continuous jittery series of tracker readings (which are expected due to the normally jittery nature of eye movements); although this is useful, it can contribute to latency.

The fixation recognition issue refers to the problem of extracting intentional components of eye movements and using these recognized components as input in the human-computer interaction. Fixation recognition turns out to be more of a challenge than you might imagine, due to the discrepancy between how we think we're moving our eyes and their actual (more complex) movements.

Due to the jittery nature of eye movement and the consequent limitations of tracker resolution, Ware and Mikaelian (1987) found that the eye tracker as an input device worked well for rapidly selecting targets as long as their size wasn't too small, but that it was rapid and more error-prone at selecting objects below this size threshold. Note that this, as well as the other cited studies, were performed with subjects using conventional screen-based computer interfaces rather than virtual environments. At the time of writing, little has been done with eye tracking in VEs. I recommend Jacob (1991) as a source for more information on the human factor issues pertaining to using eye tracking in human-computer interaction.

Evaluation

Eye-tracking technologies themselves can be evaluated in terms of vertical and horizontal accuracy (resolution), measurement range (vertical and horizontal), speed or frequency response and latency, obtrusiveness (acceptability of glasses and contact lenses, discomfort, and interference with normal vision), problems with variation of users (e.g., eye color) and calibration and setup time and difficulty. As noted previously in the Ware and Mikaelian study, human performance with eye-tracking equipment could involve the interaction of these factors, e.g., problems with resolution or calibration might make tracking equipment slower to use for certain tasks.

Biosignal Processing

Biocontrollers use biosignal processing as an input technology from human to computer, and thus let the user control elements of the virtual environment system through bioelectric signals. Two types of these bioelectric signals that have been used in biocontrol systems are myoelectric (electrical activity associated with muscle movement) and cerebroelectric (electrical activity associated with brain signals). A special case of myoelectric signal control is the biosignals associated with eye movement. Myoelectric signals have been used with biocontrollers for gaze-controlled interfaces and to allow users with physical disabilities to control interfaces; cerebroelectric signals (also known as *brain-evoked response potential*) have been studied, especially by the military (Gembicki and Rousseau 1993) as a means of input, but have been little used to date.

Technologies

A biocontroller has three stages (Lusted, Knapp, and Lloyd 1993):

- Detecting the bioelectric signal
- Processing the acquired signal, including programmable gains, filters, and pattern recognition
- Mapping the signal to output code, e.g., for control of devices

The programmability of gains and filters is particularly significant because, in the case of myoelectric biosignal processing for disabled users, the biocontroller can be adjusted for the muscular activity level of individual users. Biocontrollers can also be used for gesture recognition and motion detection.

Issues

One of the appeals of biocontrollers is their potential for low latency. In the case of brain-evoked response potential, if the signal processing is sufficiently fast, it has the potential to be the fastest way for humans to control computers. In the case of the military fighter pilot, being able to spot a target and think "fire at it" saves the time involved in initiating and executing any motor events that would conventionally be involved. Similarly, since the bioelectric signals that instigate eye movements necessarily precede the movements themselves, a biocontrol system with sufficiently fast signal processing could be faster than any tracking technology based on detection of eye movement.

An issue of biocontrol systems is individual differences and the need for training. Cerebroelectric signals appear to be quite different from person to person and require training time to be able to recognize even a very limited vocabulary (up, down, right, left, yes, and no, for example). Myoelectric signals have been used without system training, but anecdotal reports suggest that there's actually some user training that occurs as the user learns to control the device and becomes better at it through time.

Evaluation

Accuracy, reliability, and repeatability are particularly of concern when using devices that capture biosignals for user input. In the example given of a fighter pilot using brain-evoked response potential, a "misrecognition" could be catastrophic. In the case of using myoelectric eye movement signals for gaze-controlled interfaces, the accuracy must be sufficiently great (e.g., in selecting text or graphical objects) to be useful. Temporal properties of biocontrollers should also be evaluated, as lag between the user's bioelectric signal and the biocontroller's response could impair usability and usefulness. But especially for users with impaired motor capabilities for whom there are few options, biocontrol systems offer great promise.

Haptic Devices

Haptic input devices for VE systems are, in some cases, much like other haptic input devices (e.g., joysticks, trackballs, keyboards, and mice). But how are they different? Two instances stand out. First, with conventional computer systems, it's often assumed that the user can, if necessary, look at the input device, although for expert use (e.g., touch-typing or skillfully playing a video game with a joystick) it's generally assumed that this is unnecessary. In HMD-based virtual environment systems in which sensory input from the real world is excluded, the user can't look at the haptic devices without interrupting the task and removing the HMD. Therefore, the designer of haptic devices for virtual environments should assume that the devices will be used by touch alone. The other difference between haptic input devices for conventional computer systems and those for virtual environments is that the latter typically have more degrees of freedom, allowing movement in three dimensions and, frequently, changes in orientation (yaw, pitch, and roll).

Buxton (1989) presents a good overview on haptic input, and includes a taxonomy of input devices based on the number of dimensions in which they operate and the properties (position, motion, and/or pressure) that they sense. He points out that similar types of devices (e.g., joysticks) might have less in common with each other than they do with other types of devices with similar functionality. He also considers categories of representative tasks (pursuit tracking, target acquisition, dragging, tracing, etc.) and notes that the choice of input technology for a given task can greatly influence the difficulty of accomplishing the task.

Technologies

Haptic input devices can sense position, motion, or pressure. Position-sensing haptic input devices for virtual environments are exemplified by 3-D joysticks, or the variety of position-tracked 3-D devices recently manufactured by companies such as Division. An example of motion-sensing haptic input devices for virtual environments are 3-D trackballs, which detect relative motion but not absolute position.

Pressure-sensing haptic input devices for virtual environments are exemplified by the SpaceBall, an isometric device that senses pressure and torque without moving.

Haptic input devices can be general-purpose devices (e.g., a 3-D mouse) or special-purpose devices suitable to only one application. Although the latter are often excluded from discussion of haptic devices, they have a rich history in vehicular simulators, in which real controls, such as those in a real cockpit, are presented to the user. A disadvantage to this approach is that it's costly and not easily reconfigurable.

General-purpose haptic input devices can also be used to control virtual devices such as virtual sliders, knobs, wheels, and buttons. The design of such virtual devices is discussed by Loftin, Engelberg, and Benedetti (1993).

Issues

While special-purpose devices such as cockpit displays in vehicular simulators can maximize veridicality (and presumably maximize positive transfer in offline training and rehearsal tasks), their cost and difficulty in reconfiguring is a serious drawback.

Brooks (1988) points out that, to his surprise, most of the applications developed at the University of North Carolina, Chapel Hill have required considerably more than 6 DOF for haptic input. For example, their GRIP molecular fitting system has 22 DOF mapped onto 15 joysticks, sliders, and dials, which are used for tasks such as positioning and orienting an amino acid molecule, setting the torsion angles of its side chains, and viewing positions and angles.

Haptic input devices are being used for a variety of functions in virtual environments, ranging from navigation to selection. It isn't clear what devices will work best for these functions, although ongoing experiments (such as those by Colin Ware and his colleagues) with specific devices could lead to generalized theories.

Evaluation

An evaluation of haptic input devices must include an examination of their intuitiveness to users and the learning time involved in mastering them; users' speed, accuracy, and error rate and fatigue using them; and their task-specific performance.

Gesture Recognition and Predictive Tracking Software

Gesture recognition and predictive tracking are examples of processing user input that's typically done in software (another example, discussed elsewhere, is that of speech recognition). These are necessary for recognizing a user's gestural commands with an instrumented glove (or an unencumbered user's commands with a video tracker), and compensating for latency of trackers.

Gesture recognition

Fairchild (1993) describes three possible types of user input gestures: position, dynamic, and coordinated gestures. Position gestures are based on the state of the input device (where the device in this case can even be the position of the user's unencumbered hand that's being captured by video camera), irrespective of time.

Dynamic gestures incorporate tracking in time to define their meaning. Coordinated gestures use the interaction of states of multiple sensors through time to define their meaning. Baudel and Beaudouin-Lafon (1993) see two approaches to using gestures: manipulating objects directly and using a gestural command language, which they call the *sign language paradigm*. This is analogous to the earlier categorization of gestures as object manipulations and commands (Zimmerman, Lanier, Blanchard, Bryson, and Harvill 1987). They note that, like speech recognition, gesture recognition is a complex problem.

Baudel and Beaudouin-Lafon note two issues inherent in gestural communication. It typically involves using more muscles than does keyboard input or speech, and (they warn) might therefore produce fatigue. Also, gestural languages aren't self-revealing (unlike, for example, pull-down menus that reveal available commands). They also note problems with systems created to date, such as:

- Discomfort and tethering associated with instrumented gloves that have often been associated with gesture recognition systems
- Capturing all user hand motion and lack of a technique to differentiate user gesture input intended for the system from other motion prevents the user from hand movement associated with other devices or communication with other people
- Difficulties with segmentation necessary to recognize dynamic gestures

Predictive tracking and filtering of tracker data

Like gesture recognition, predictive tracking and filtering of tracker data involves processing data rather than acquiring it. Friedmann, Starner, and Pentland (1993) note three problems that arise in the synchronization of user motion, rendering, and sound:

- Noise in position tracker measurements
- Length of the processing pipeline (i.e., total system latency)
- Unexpected interruptions caused by operating system activity or network contention

The result of these problems (depending on their magnitude) is that using the raw output of position sensors might result in undesirable system performance, and one strategy to cope with these problems is filtering tracker data and predictive tracking.

The premise of tracker data filtering and predictive tracking is that a user's motions have certain characteristics, and a sufficiently frequent sampling of the user's position will produce succeeding measurements that have nonarbitrary relationships (as well as permitting interpolation between sampled positions). An obvious example is that you wouldn't expect the position of the user's head to go from being stationary to being several feet away in a 60th of a second, and return to the original stationary position in another 60th of a second. Therefore, the single sensor measurement that's several feet away from the preceding and subsequent measurements can be taken to be noise. Similarly, you can average sensor readings with previous measurements to produce smoothed measurements, calculate the velocity of a user's motions from these measurements, and use the calculation to predict future positions at fixed time intervals.

Simply smoothing measurements and predicting future positions produces problems if the user moves quickly or suddenly changes velocity. Friedmann, Starner, and Pentland (1993) describe using Kalman filtering to better perform predictive tracking in the face of these problems. Azuma (1995b) gives a very clear description of Kalman filtering in the context of virtual environments and augmented reality systems, and points out its advantages over an alternative optimal linear estimation approach, Wiener filtering.

Speech Recognition

Speech recognition and understanding is an entire field in and of itself, so I'll discuss it here only to point to issues relevant to using it as an input technology in a VE system. The general challenges of speech recognition are discussed in Parsons (1986), who notes that the phonetic typewriter, which was the dream of the 1950s, has yet to be created, and points out four types of problems that must be addressed in speech recognition:

- Talker variations (Individual differences between speakers)
- Ambiguity, or a lack of one-to-one mapping between acoustic and phonemic variables, which humans deal with by drawing on their knowledge of language and of the subject matter being discussed
- Variations in an individual's speech, which includes carelessness, phonetic variations, coarticulation (in which the sounds of speech vary depending on their relationship to other speech sounds), and temporal variations
- Noise and interference

Speech understanding adds additional difficulties and ambiguities; note for example the importance of context in determining whether a speaker has said "The sun's rays meet" or "The sons raise meat." Humans are remarkably good at dealing with the difficulties in understanding speech and can, for example, restore missing syllables and words that are selectively masked by noise in continuous speech. In order to do this, humans use several types of knowledge: semantic knowledge (general knowledge about the subject matter), syntactic knowledge (the rules of language that specify allowable sequences of words), lexical knowledge (familiarity with topic-specific vocabulary sub-section), prosodic knowledge (derivation of meaning from the variations in pitch, rhythm, and stress), pragmatic knowledge (the listener's changing world model during a conversation), and acoustic knowledge (used to restore acoustically ambiguous sounds). See White 1976 and Reddy 1976. Few of these types of knowledge are possessed by computers engaged in recognition.

In spite of the difficulties of computer speech recognition, it has several advantages, including speed (about four times faster than manual input of text), ability to function as a parallel channel (e.g., in hands-busy situations), support for freedom of motion and unplanned communication, and the fact that it's natural and doesn't require physical training (Reddy 1976). Virtual environments and teleoperation are especially good candidates for using speech as an input technology since, in typical virtual environments, real keyboards aren't visible because of the HMD and both eyes and hands are busy.

The role of speech

Speech input can play a variety of roles in virtual environments (Thomas and Stuart 1993), including commands and inquiries to the system, speaker verification, and communication between users. Commands and inquiries to the system can be used to control tasks and navigation, specify actions (operators) in combination with gesturing to specify objects (operands), give system configuration commands, and request information on system status. Speaker verification can be used for security (analogous to passwords) and as a seamless way to customize environments for a user when several known users share a VE system. For high-security environments, verification is probably best used in conjunction with other security measures in order to prevent someone else from recording the user's voice and using it to break in. Human-to-human speech communication can fulfill the same functions it does in any other human-to-human collaborative, instructional, or other activity and requires that, if users are at remote sites, the audio be transmitted and perhaps processed so it comes from appropriate locations in the listener's environment.

A good example of a system that uses speech for user-system communication is a VE system created recently by researchers at SRI International (Bletter 1993). This system uses a keyword, Simon, to tell the system that the user is addressing it. This can be followed by user commands in the categories of selection (select this and grab that), modes (reset, quit, calibrate hand, and calibrate eyes), mods (make transparent or make solid), transport (start, stop, fly forward, move up, slower, take me there, etc.), transformation (move that there), and queries (what is this?, what is that?, and where am I?).

Speech-recognition approaches and challenges

Speech recognition approaches aren't unique to VE applications, but you must consider the challenges of speech recognition when designing and implementing a VE system that uses speech as an input. Some of the issues in speech recognition systems are:

- Do they require training and are they speaker-dependent or speaker-independent?
- Do they require users to separate words by pauses or can they speak continuously in a natural way (isolated or connected speech)?
- How many words can the system recognize (vocabulary size)?
- Can the speaker say any of these words at any time and will they be recognized or not (nonmoded vs. moded)?
- What is the nature of the environment and medium in which the speech will be transmitted (noise and bandwidth)?

Speaker dependence vs. independence. Among the problems to be addressed in speech recognition is the individual differences between speakers. One solution to this problem is speaker-dependent recognition. In speaker-dependent speech recognition systems, each user must train the system, typically providing the system with multiple utterances of each word so templates can be built for each word as spoken by that speaker. Then, when the recognition system is used, the system compares utterances only to the templates created for that speaker.

Speaker-dependent systems can typically provide good recognition rates because they don't have to deal with differences between speakers. However, the training overhead for each user can be significant and might deter casual users. Speaker-independent systems have been trained on large speech databases and don't require any training by the user. They deal with differences in speaker characteristics in several ways:

- Selecting features that are stable across speakers, if the vocabulary is sufficiently small to allow this
- Incorporating multiple templates for each word
- Providing ways to process the user's speech in order to normalize it, and correct for the individual differences of speakers (Parsons 1986)

In the past, speaker-independent systems either had high error rates or extremely constrained vocabularies, but marked improvements in speaker-independent systems have occurred in the past few years and error rates are fast becoming acceptably low, even with large vocabularies.

Continuous vs. isolated word. Typical human speech presents a challenge to speech recognition systems because it's difficult to determine where one word ends and the next begins. In addition, the phenomenon of *coarticulation*, in which the way words are spoken is dependent on the words that precede and follow them, makes the recognition process more difficult, as noted previously. Isolated-word recognition systems simplify these problems by requiring the speaker to say one word at a time and to include pauses between words. While this simplifies endpoint detection and minimizes coarticulation, thus reducing the recognition complexity problem, it requires the user to speak in a very unnatural way and considerably slows down the rate of information transmission from human to machine. Continuous speech (also known as *connected speech*) recognition systems allow the user to speak more naturally, without pauses between words, and thus permit a higher human-machine transmission rate on the speech channel.

Vocabulary size and moded vs. nonmoded. Because the recognizer compares the user's spoken utterance to its word templates, the larger the vocabulary from which the user can choose the more difficult the recognition problem (i.e., assigning the correct word to a given utterance). Not only the size of the vocabulary but also the similarity and hence confusability between words make for a more difficult recognition problem (Reddy 1976). Only recently have fairly large vocabulary recognizers with acceptable accuracy been built.

In an unmoded system, all vocabulary words are available to the user at all times. One way to reduce the vocabulary size part of the recognition problem is to use a moded system. In a moded system, only subsets of the vocabulary are available to the user and these are dependent on the system's state. Conventionally, the system state (and hence the mode) is determined by the speaker's use of certain keywords. In other words, if the speaker utters a keyword, the functional vocabulary is the subset of words available within the mode entered via that keyword.

Bandwidth and noise. Two other factors, which degrade the speech signal, make the recognition problem more difficult. One of these factors is using a low-bandwidth transmission medium, such as conventional telephone lines, between the speaker and the recognizer. A considerable amount of recent research has addressed reduced bandwidth speech recognition in a non-VE context. The other factor, noise, can be introduced by the transmission medium or the speaker's environment. It's less predictable and can mask speech as well as increase the difficulty in endpoint detection.

Issues

Issues regarding speech recognition technology include how it will be used, choice of vocabulary, whether or not the system will be moded, trade-offs between speaker-dependent and speaker-independent systems, and the effects of misrecognition. Other issues specific to virtual environments are discussed in Thomas and Stuart (1993).

Evaluation

It's especially important to evaluate speech recognition systems in context, i.e., with real users using the actual vocabulary in a representative environment and trying to accomplish real tasks. The speech recognition community typically evaluates recognizers with prerecorded speech databases that are recorded under optimal, silent conditions, then endpointed and otherwise cleaned up. This is useful in comparing recognition algorithms, but not at all representative of performance by users in virtual environments. For example, a recognizer that has greater than 99% accuracy under the optimal, laboratory conditions might have far lower accuracy rates under conditions of real use. If designers mistakenly believe that fewer than 1% of user inputs won't be properly recognized, they'll pay little attention to error correction; evaluation under more realistic conditions suggests this would be a mistake.

Speech recognizers should be evaluated in terms of rates of misrecognition or rejection (in the case of a word or phrase that isn't in the recognizer's vocabulary), training time required (if any), robustness (e.g., in the presence of extraneous environmental noise), and flexibility.

Integrating Input Technologies

Integrating the different types of input technology described in this chapter is yet another issue to be considered. Technologies such as gesture, eye-gaze, and speech recognition can be combined in different ways to provide a powerful interface control.

Deixis is indicating objects and directing attention by pointing or performing another gesture (Hill and Hollan 1991). Hill and Hollan observed pointing behaviors with what they describe as complex intents (i.e., more than simply "look here"), such as interval, grouping, branching offshoot, and reference to things absent. Deixis can be used in combination with other input (e.g., speech) to shape the meaning of the other input. An example is the early MIT work of Bolt on the Put That There system.

There are more input technologies described in this chapter than have been integrated in any single computer-human interface. Experience will surely reveal different issues in how these technologies work together.

Questions

- What position-tracking technologies would you use to track multiple users in a large working volume that has intermittent ultrasonic noise?
- How could a locomotive input system capture climbing?
- How could eye tracking, biosignal processing, speech recognition, and gesture recognition be used for navigation? When would each of these be preferable?
- Are there problems analogous to the "Midas touch" problem found in gaze control that could plague input technologies other than eye tracking? What if the VE is multiuser?

Chapter 5

Output Technologies

The goal of output technologies for virtual environments is to present information to the user so it will be perceived appropriately for the task, given the considerations described in part 1 of this book, *Defining the Requirements*. Rosenberg (1993) observes that there's a useful distinction to be made between the proximal stimuli, the distal stimuli, and the perceptual hypotheses. The *proximal stimulus* is the sensory information that falls on a receptor, the *distal stimulus* is the distant source of this information, and the *perceptual hypothesis* is the inference about the distal stimulus generated by using the proximal stimulus. A *percept* is a representation of the external world produced via this perceptual hypothesis, and *perceptual constancy* is maintaining a perceptual hypothesis (e.g., that an object in the environment is a chair) in spite of changes in the proximal stimuli (e.g., because the viewer has changed position and the image striking the retina has changed).

Output technologies for virtual environments don't have to accurately reproduce the distal stimuli from the real-world objects that are to be portrayed in the virtual environment; instead, they have to present proximal stimuli that incorporate those crucial features to generate the desired percepts in the user. The output technologies that present these stimuli will be discussed in the major sections of this chapter, on visual displays, auditory displays, tactile and force feedback displays, and other displays (such as olfactory displays). They're illustrated in Figure 5.1.

Visual Displays

Displaying images to the user of a virtual environment requires an image generator (except for video from a distant teleoperated robot), an image source, and an optical system. If a visual display calls for the observer to use both eyes, it's a *binocular* display. If the same 2-D image is viewed by both eyes, the display is *monoscopic* (also known as *binoptic*); if different images are presented to the two eyes, the display is said to be *dichoptic*, and a dichoptic display that produces the effect of depth is said

128 Designing the System

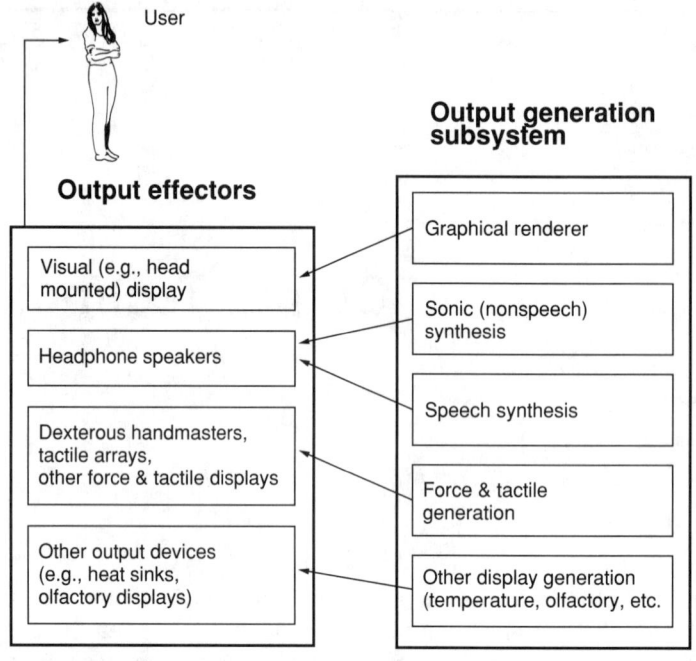

Figure 5.1 Output subsystem.

to be *stereoscopic*. Image display systems often have two lenses: the *objective lens*, which forms an image, and the *eyepiece*, which magnifies the image. When such an image display system is presented to the eyes, the *entrance pupil* is the image of the real pupil formed from the cornea's refraction, and the *exit pupil* (or *Ramsden disc*) is the circular disc of light formed from the objective lens by the eyepiece (Boff and Lincoln 1988). The available 3-D imaging systems and the 3-D visual cues they support are summarized in Table 5.1.

Image generation

The challenge of image generation for virtual environments isn't simply to render sufficient scene complexity, but to perform at a sufficiently fast speed in response to user input (such as change in head position and orientation, as measured by tracking technology) that latency is low and a sense of presence is produced. Fortunately, the graphics engines that generate images for VEs are rapidly improving in performance, driven by markets other than (and larger than) that for VE systems. Mueller (1995) summarizes the high-level issues for image generators for flight simulators (which are similar for all VE image generators) as:

- Rendering speed
- Rendering quality
- Nature of the database
- Nature of the display devices
- Additional functions assigned to the image generator

TABLE 5.1 3-D Imaging Systems and the 3-D Visual Cues They Support

	Accommodation	Convergence	Image size	Overlap	Linear perspective	Texture gradient	Aerial perspective	Shading	Horizontal parallax	Vertical parallax	Binocular disparity
HMD	Not supported	Supported	Supported	Supported	Supported	Supported	Supported	Supported	Supported	Supported	Supported
BOOM	Not supported	Supported	Supported	Supported	Supported	Supported	Supported	Supported	Supported	Supported	Supported
Stereoscopic (LCD shutter)	Not supported	Supported	Supported	Supported	Supported	Supported	Supported	Supported	Not supported	Not supported	Supported
Interactive stereoscopic (LCD shutter)	Not supported	Supported	Supported	Supported	Supported	Supported	Supported	Supported	Supported	Supported	Supported
Lenticular barrier with CRT	Not supported	Supported	Supported	Supported	Supported	Supported	Supported	Supported	Partially supported	Not supported	Supported
Parallax barrier with CRT	Not supported	Supported	Supported	Supported	Supported	Supported	Supported	Supported	Partially supported	Not supported	Supported
Slice stacking (varifocal mirror)	Supported	Supported	Supported	Not supported	Supported	Partially supported	Partially supported	Partially supported	Supported	Supported	Supported
Holographic video (MIT system)	Supported	Supported	Supported	Supported	Supported	Supported	Supported	Supported	Supported	Not supported	Supported

COURTESY: McKenna & Zeltzer (1992) *Presence: Teleoperators and Virtual Environments* vol. 1 No. 4, M.I.T. Press.

The virtual world database will be discussed in chapter 6. The display devices will be discussed in this chapter in terms of their image sources and optics, but note that, depending on the display devices used, multiple channels of video might be required (e.g., one channel for a fishtank VR system, two channels for a stereoscopic HMD, and more for a CAVE). Here, I'll focus on rendering speed and quality.

Rendering speed is important in order to give the impression of real-time display, i.e., so there isn't a discernible wait for images to be rendered. A commonly used benchmark for computer graphics hardware performance is polygons per second or polygon per frame; this is also known as the *polygon budget*. In fact, in this benchmark, polygons are actually triangles, which in practice are vertices. For an infinitely small polygon, the polygon rate would be the same as the vertex rate, but, as soon as the polygon becomes larger, the actual polygon rate includes pixel filling, which isn't incorporated in the polygons per second benchmark. So, in fact, this benchmark really refers to the number of vertices that can be projected per second. The pixel fill rate is a different issue, and refers to how long it takes to fill the pixels within the polygon. An image generator could be optimized for pixel fill rate at the cost of vertex rate, but almost all currently available image generators are optimized for vertex rate rather than pixel fill rate (Bryson 1994). A better benchmark than polygons per second is n m-pixel triangles per second. Triangles larger than m will be fill-dominated and therefore will render slower than n, while triangles smaller than m won't render any faster than n because they're floating-point-dominated (Deering 1993).

Two problems that must be addressed with high-performance image generation hardware are the large number of times per second that the frame-buffer memory must be accessed (for video scan-out and updates from the CPU) and computational demands on the main CPU due to image generation.

In order to increase the bandwidth to frame-buffer memory, Foley, van Dam, Feiner, and Hughes (1990) note approaches that have been used such as placing the frame buffer on an isolated bus and double-buffering, i.e., duplicating the frame-buffer memory so the image from one buffer is displayed (with the video controller being given uninterrupted access to this buffer) while the image in the other buffer is computed (with the CPU being given uninterrupted access to this other buffer). Foley, van Dam, Feiner, and Hughes (1990) also give a good account of the generic graphics pipeline, a logical model for the computations needed in a raster-display system.

Deering and Nelson (1993) describe some of the detailed hardware decisions that can be made on top of this generic pipeline, especially those pertaining to parallelism, both in the floating-point intensive initial stages of the pipeline, and in the drawing-intensive generation of pixels and z-buffering them into the frame buffer.

Rendering quality requirements for image generation include features such as antialiasing, texture mapping, simulating effects such as fog and haze, and being able to fade objects in and out of scenes. If the virtual world database supports level-of-detail (LOD) selection (also referred to as *multiple resolutions*), different LOD representations of a given object can be rendered based on the object's proximity to the user.

Falby, Zyda, Pratt, and Wilson (1992) discuss using hierarchical data structures that spatially partition the displayable data, allowing for the rapid culling of polygons and thus multiple resolutions of the terrain. They also describe a terrain paging algorithm that, when the user's virtual vehicle reaches the edge of the bounding box around it, frees memory from the strip of terrain in the direction opposite to where the user is traveling, and permits terrain to be paged, moving the bounding box.

The transition from one LOD representation to another can be accomplished by immediately switching from one to the other (which might create glitches and artifacts), fading one out while fading the other in (Mueller 1995), or mutating or morphing from one to the other. When an object is so distant that even the lowest LOD representation isn't useful (e.g., because it would fill too small an area of the display to be useful to the user), the object can be culled so it isn't rendered at all. Back-face culling can also reduce the number of polygons that must be rendered.

In addition to these techniques for culling polygons so fewer polygons must be rendered and blasted through the pipeline, an especially important area in terms of graphical algorithms pertinent to the high-performance demands of virtual environments is visible-surface determination (also known as *hidden-line removal* or *occlusion*). The dominant method of visible-surface determination is the widely used z-buffer algorithm developed by Catmull and described by Foley, van Dam, Feiner, and Hughes (1990). The z-buffer algorithm requires that an additional buffer be maintained that's the same size as the frame buffer. This additional buffer holds the z value of each pixel (i.e., its depth coordinate in the z axis). As polygons are scan-converted into the frame buffer, at each x,y point their z value is compared to the z value already at that point. If the new point's z value is greater (i.e., it's closer to the viewer), its color and depth replaces the old point's values in the frame buffer. Alternate visible-surface determination methods include list-priority algorithms, hybrid strategies that use list priority algorithms for static scenery and z-buffering for moving objects, and some advanced strategies specially designed for flight simulators and described by Mueller (1995).

There's much more that can be said about image generation. For example, you can use data structures such as octrees and binary space-partitioning trees to partition space, by using either mutually perpendicular planes or pairs of subspaces separated by arbitrarily positioned planes, respectively. Fortunately, the computer graphics required for image generation in VEs is one of the better researched and documented areas in this field, so I direct you to Foley, van Dam, Feiner, and Hughes (1990), who did such a good job of covering this topic that I won't provide further detail here.

Image sources

The most common image sources for visual displays in virtual environment systems are cathode ray tubes (CRTs) and liquid crystal displays (LCDs). Alternate image sources, including virtual retinal display, are also being developed. A primary consideration for these or any image source used in interactive computer graphics is its ability to change quickly. Although it's possible that either these alternate sources or some as-yet-undiscovered technology will become widespread, this is highly speculative. The vast majority of image sources used for virtual environment systems have been CRTs and LCDs, so these will be my main focus.

Cathode ray tubes. Cathode ray tubes (CRTs) are the most common display technology, and they're found widely in computer monitors. A positive high voltage (commonly 15,000–20,000 volts) accelerates a beam of electrons emitted by an electron gun towards a phosphor-coated screen, and the point on the screen that's hit by the beam emits visible light. The electron beam can be controlled and directed precisely through a focus system and a set of deflection coils that produce a magnetic field. This is analogous to focusing a beam of light except that the electrons naturally diverge because of their like charge, so the focus system must counteract this tendency. When the phosphor that coats the screen is struck by the electron beam, the light it produces decays at a given exponential rate, so the phosphor must be struck by the electron beam very frequently in order for it to appear to be constantly illuminated. The frequency with which the entire screen image is redrawn is known as the *refresh rate*.

There are different ways in which the beam can be directed to the screen. In the case of vector graphics, a display list directs the beam from endpoint to endpoint, and the refresh rate is dependent on the complexity of the displayed image. In the case of raster-scan displays, the refresh buffer explicitly stores the values of pixels, the beam is directed in a regular repetitive pattern across the screen, and the refresh rate is independent of the complexity of the displayed image. Raster-scan displays have become far more common than vector displays. In raster display devices, the horizontal scan rate describes the rate at which the beam is swept horizontally across the phosphor-coated screen.

In the case of a monochromatic CRT, the intensity of the illumination is controlled by a grid that determines the number of electrons in the beam. Resolution in a monochromatic CRT is associated with how small a point on the screen can be illuminated and how dense the scan lines are. It's also somewhat negatively dependent on brightness, in that the greater number of electrons required to produce a brighter spot on the screen tends to excite adjacent electrons (known as *bloom*).

The situation is somewhat more complex for color CRTs. The screens of color CRTs are coated with dots of phosphor that emit different colors of light (red, green, and blue), and these dots are arranged in a pattern on the screen. Shadow-mask CRTs use a metal plate near the screen with precisely placed holes (a *shadow mask*) and three electron beams that are directed at the screen in a way so each of the three can strike phosphor dots of only one color. There are less common alternatives to the shadow mask approach, such as the beam index CRT, in which a single electron beam is controlled very accurately to selectively strike phosphor spots of all three colors, as well as a kind of phosphor spot that emits ultraviolet light and precisely controls the electron beam's position. In either case, the phosphor dots are placed near enough to each other on the screen that the light they produce is seen as a mixture of their colors, but the approach used in color CRTs necessarily results in lower resolution (as well as lower brightness, especially with the shadow-mask approach) than that found in monochromatic CRTs. Refer to Foley, van Dam, Feiner, and Hughes 1990 for a good introduction to CRT displays, and Kalawsky 1993 for a description of some of the alternatives to shadow-masking.

A hybrid approach to displaying color with CRTs is to use a monochromatic CRT with some sort of color shuttering. One recently marketed CRT-based HMD separates images to be displayed into red, green, and blue fields, uses an RGB color wheel that spins at a rapid rate, and sequentially displays the three fields on the CRT, with the spinning color wheel synchronized so the red, green, or blue filter of the color wheel is in front of the CRT at the moment the appropriate field image is displayed (so that the user fuses the colors due to temporal rather than spatial proximity). This approach permits a color display with the resolution of a monochrome CRT, but the CRT must be refreshed at three times the normal rate (180 Hz, in the case of the available product), and the mechanical issues associated with a rapidly spinning color wheel must be addressed. An analogous approach replaces the color wheel with an LCD-based color shutter (and thus is a type of CRT/LCD hybrid display).

Among the problems with using CRTs in HMD displays are that they require high power consumption and aren't terribly efficient (their heat must be dissipated). There's also significant variation from CRT to CRT, so it's difficult to display images that are identical at the pixel level on CRTs for the left and right eyes (Strasser 1993).

Liquid crystal displays. Whereas CRTs emit light, liquid crystal displays (LCDs) control the light that passes through them, so they must have a light source behind them (*backlight*). LCDs consist of multiple thin layers, which include vertical and horizontal grid wires and polarizers, as well as the liquid crystal layer itself. The vertical and horizontal grid wires sandwich the thin liquid crystal layer and apply voltages that change the alignment of the molecules in the liquid crystal layer and hence their polarizing effect and the light that passes through them. The molecules maintain their alignment briefly after the voltage is withdrawn (analogous to the CRT's refresh rate), and voltage is applied to the grids in a raster-scan manner.

LCDs can be either *passive matrix* or *active matrix*, which describes whether they have a transistor at each grid point (active matrix) or not (passive matrix). The transistors, if present, change the state of the crystals quickly (and control the extent to which their state has been changed). This permits active-matrix LCDs to have faster response times. The transistors can also hold the state of the crystals at the grid point and maintain them in this state of alignment until an update changes their state; hence, active-matrix LCDs can be brighter and have more contrast than passive-matrix displays. For these reasons, active-matrix LCDs are generally preferable to passive-matrix LCDs for use in HMDs.

LCD development is currently driven by the consumer electronics market, which hasn't demanded the kind of resolution required by HMDs. Although there doesn't appear to be anything inherent in the technology that would prevent much higher-resolution miniature LCDs from being produced, current LCDs are lower in resolution than CRTs. However, they aren't variable as are CRTs and have good pixel registration; they have lower power consumption and require less heat dissipation; and they tend to be lighter weight, smaller in size, and less expensive than CRTs. LCD technology is advancing rapidly, and hopefully resolution will improve in the near future. A summary comparison of CRTs and LCDs as image sources for virtual environments is given in Table 5.2.

Retinal laser displays. Kollin (1993) has prototyped a laser display that projects images directly onto the retina. This device, the Virtual Retinal Display, was developed at the Human Interface Technology Laboratory of the University of Washington. A laser beam is deflected by high-resolution scanners and the light, which is intensity-

TABLE 5.2 Comparison of the Two Most Commonly Used Image Sources for HMDs

	CRT	LCD
Resolution	High resolution possible with current technology	Lower resolution than CRTs with current technology
Color	Inherently monochromatic (special techniques required for color)	Good
Brightness	Good (emissive devices)	Dependent upon backlighting (passive spatial light modulators)
Power consumption	Power requirements are high, efficiency is low	Power requirements are low, with most power going to backlighting
Reproducible	Variability between CRTs makes it difficult to display images that are identical on the pixel level	Variability is not a problem; LCDs can display images that are identical on the pixel level
Heat dissipation	Much heat energy must be dissipated	Less heat to dissipate, and most is from backlighting

modulated by the video signal generated by a workstation, is scanned directly onto the user's retina via an optical system. At present, the system uses an acousto-optic deflector for vertical scanning and a galvanometer for vertical scanning of a red laser beam. The current Virtual Retinal Display is a monochrome, rather high-resolution (1,000 × 1,000 pixels) display with a limited (40°) FOV, and it doesn't support head movement. The physical mechanism is still quite large, so the system can best be described as a concept demonstration. Nonetheless, the level of resolution significantly surpasses that of image sources used in commercially available HMDs, so the approach does show promise.

Light-emitting diodes, plasma, and other display technologies. Kalawsky (1993) provides a taxonomy of display technologies, of which CRTs and LCDs are but two of many. He divides image sources into direct view and projection technologies, subdivides direct view into flat panel, fiber-optic coupled, and CRT, and then further divides flat-panel displays into categories. LCDs are among a number of nonemitter flat-panel display technologies; emitter flat-panel displays include light-emitting diodes, gas discharge/plasma panels, and technologies based on electro-, photo-, and cathode luminescence. There's no shortage of possible image sources, though each source has its own limitations and problems, and few have been used yet in virtual environment systems. Table 5.3 compares characteristics of display technologies.

Optical systems

Real volumetric images have a physically identifiable location (e.g., on a screen). Artificial reality systems project real images onto viewing screens. The optical systems in visual displays for HMD-based virtual environments produce light that strikes the eyes as it would if the projected images were created by physical objects; like the images produced by bathroom mirrors and holograms, these images are known as *virtual images*. The optics in HMDs enlarge the image (so the FOV is larger) and

TABLE 5.3 Characteristics of Display Technologies

Parameter	Active matrix LCD	Direct view CRT	LED	Electroluminescent	ac & dc plasma
Spatial resolution	1,024 × 1,024 elements (512 × 512 color pixel groups)	Monochrome: 79 line pairs/cm Color: 20 line pairs/cm	12–20 elements per cm	8–20 elements per cm (research on 197 element/cm devices is ongoing)	12–24 elements per cm
Brightness	512 cdm^{-2}	Monochrome: 34 26 cdm^{-2} Color: 822 cdm^{-2}	342.6 cdm^{-2} for average area, 3,426 cdm^{-2} for single LED	102 cdm^{-2} is typical	Typical: 103–171 cdm^{-2} Possible: 1,233 cdm^{-2}
Contrast	32:1 or 17:1 under 80,000 lumen m^{-2}	Monochrome: 8:1 Color: 3:1	100:1	10:1 typical	20:1
Color	RGBG quad format or RGB delta triad	Depends on choice of phosphors	Red, green, yellow, blue (poor efficiency) possible	Depends on choice of phosphors	Neon orange; other monochrome and limited three color possible
Display size	Typical: 160 × 160 mm; maximum: 300 × 300 mm; smaller devices currently resolution-limited	Nearly unlimited; On smaller sizes, resolution is limited by phosphor granularity and spot size considerations	6" 200–300 elements; limited by power dissipation	152.4 mm with 240 × 320 pixels; 25.4 × 25.4 mm with 485 × 645 pixels	ac: 430 × 430 mm 1,024 × 1,024 pixels dc: limited to 200 columns
Aspect	±60° horizontal ±45° vertical	Unlimited, Lambertian emission	Directional, viewing angle typically 150°	4:3 viewing angle similar to conventional CRT	Wide angle
Storage/refresh	Inherent storage capability	Typical: 60 Hz; performance extended or reduced by choice of phosphor	100-Hz refresh possible; no inherent storage capability	Inherent storage capability	ac: inherent storage capability dc: no inherent storage capability
Time constants	Compatible with video rates	Dependent on choice of phosphor	Compatible with video rates	Compatible with video rates	ac: 512 pixels written in 10 ms dc: video rate
Temperature range	5° C to 55°C	–20°C to 55°C	–27°C to 55°C	–20°C to 55°C	–20°C to 55°C
Power requirements	Typical: 50 W (backlight consumes most power)	Monochrome: 50 W Color: 200 W	400 W for a 127 × 127 mm device	Typical: 10 W, 100–300 V	200–300 W 200–300 V

COURTESY: Adapted from Kalawsky (1993) *The Science of Virtual Reality and Virtual Environments* © Addison-Wesley Publishing Co., Inc.

collimate the light so the parallel rays of light appear to be from appropriately distanced objects rather than from a source that's inches from the face. In so doing, they might introduce distortion.

Also, failing to account for certain physical characteristics of both the optical system and the user could result in failure to achieve orthostereoscopy for reasons other than optical distortion in systems that present position-tracked stereoscopic images to the user (e.g., HMDs or BOOM technology).

In addition to the distortions introduced by display systems, there's a sort of distortion on the human side. Roscoe (1991) points out that, although virtual images are commonly produced by collimating light to make images appear to be at optical infinity, the viewer tends to lapse towards the resting accommodation distance (an average of about an arm's length from the viewer's face, also called *dark focus* because it's the focal distance we tend to settle on when it's too dark to see) rather than focusing on optical infinity. This causes the apparent angles of the displayed scene to shrink, and the objects within it to therefore appear to be farther away than they are. In a teleoperation task, this can have especially unfortunate consequences, as the teleoperated robot might crash into objects that the operator believes are far enough away to avoid.

Head-mounted displays. The physical design of an HMD must take into account the head geometry of the user. The HMD must be adjusted to fixed points on the head (e.g., cranium, nose bridge, etc.) in order to maintain its placement. In addition to the interpupillary distance (IPD) of users, the HMD must also accommodate facial geometry in the z axis (or "forward" direction), including 10-mm relief for clearance of the eyelashes, and additional space in front of the eye (5–10 mm). Eyeglass wearers need even more clearance; Strasser (1993) recommends > 25 mm forward and > 30 mm lateral clearance. It's also important, in the design of an HMD, that its weight not be excessive, its center of gravity not be too far from that of the head (or fatigue will result from extended use), and its durability be adequate for the intended use. Providing variable focus is optional, and it requires adjustability that's dependent on the type of optics used. For example, the image source must be moved along the Z axis for refractive and reflective systems.

There are several optical techniques for creating virtual images in HMDs, and most fit into three categories: reflective, refractive, and catadioptric. Reflective optical systems (see Figure 5.2) transmit light to reflectors, which direct the light to the eyes and might also magnify the image. Refractive optical systems (see Figure 5.3) transmit light from the image source to the eye through lenses that collimate the light. This approach was used by Eric Howlett of LEEP Optics, who developed the optical system used in many of the first HMDs. Catadioptric optical systems (see Figure 5.4) combine refractive lenses and reflectors.

Reflective systems can easily accommodate see-through capability, but they need curved image sources to create wide FOV and either off-axis reflectors (which make maintaining image quality difficult) or pancake window design, in which image sources are on opposite sides of the face from the eye to which they're presented (which incurs a high cost and the use of a beam splitter, which in turn causes a considerable loss in brightness). Refractive systems produce minimal loss of brightness

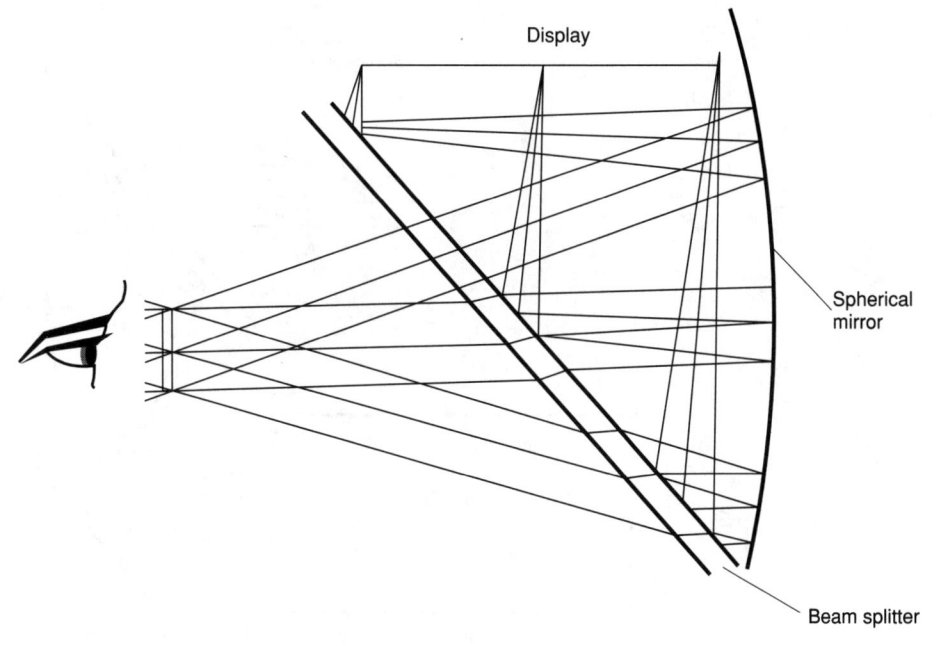

Figure 5.2 Reflective optical system.

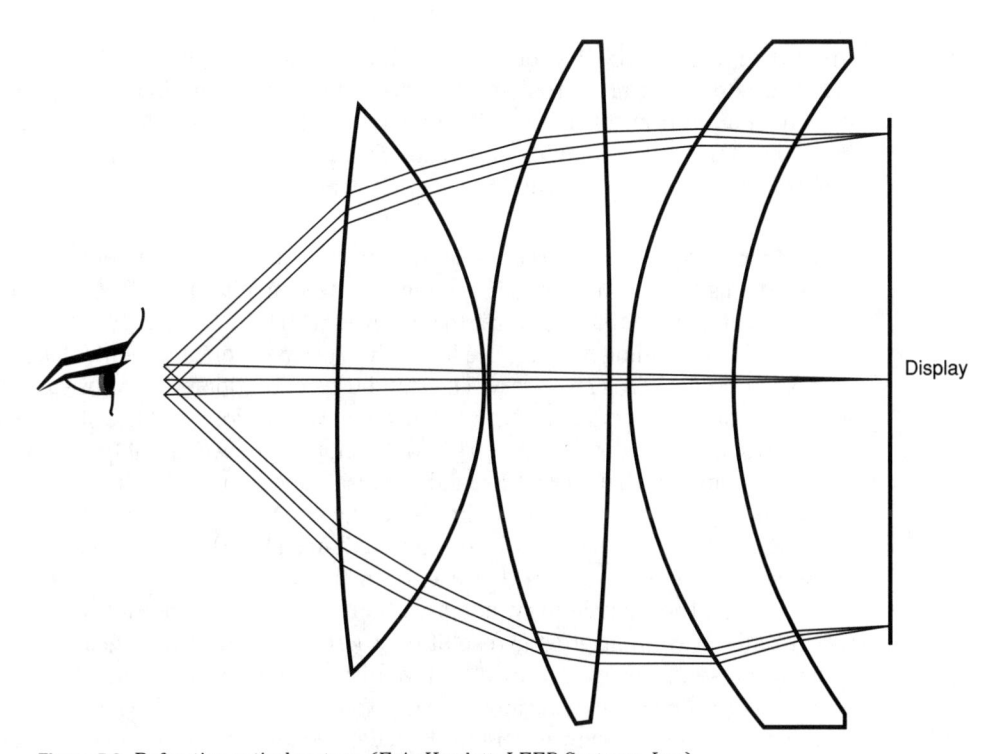

Figure 5.3 Refractive optical system. (*Eric Howlett, LEEP Systems, Inc.*)

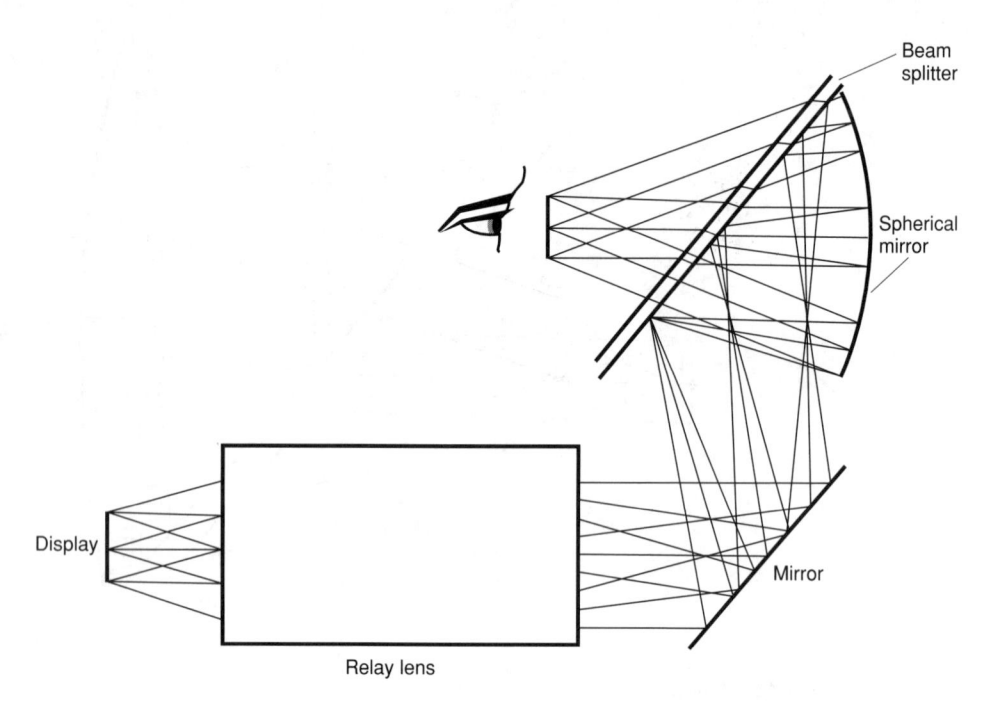

Figure 5.4 Catadioptric optical system. Note that there is a relay lens not shown in this figure.

from the image source, but produce significant distortion (in wide-FOV eyepieces). They also tend to cause problems with distribution of weight in an HMD, since their weight is all in front of the eye. Catadioptric systems can produce high-quality images, but tend to be complex and costly (Strasser 1993). A recommended general reference for more on optical systems is Bass (1995).

BOOM technology. An alternative to the HMD is a piece of equipment commonly referred to as a BOOM (binocular omni-oriented monitor). A BOOM is a viewer mounted on a stand that permits it to be moved with 6 DOF. Users bring the viewer to their face and, holding it there, use it to view the virtual environment, changing position and orientation as necessary. The stand uses potentiometers whose analog readouts are converted to digital form for mechanical position tracking. It also supports the viewer and, because users don't have to support the weight of the display device with neck muscles that easily tire (and because the weight of the device can be counterbalanced), a larger and heavier image source can be used. Current BOOM systems use CRT displays and have better resolution than all but the highest-end HMDs.

An advantage of BOOMs is that users can easily switch between their work environment and the virtual environment without having to repeatedly get into and out of an HMD. With their greater resolution, there are clear advantages of BOOM systems at present. However, they also have disadvantages: they limit the user's range of motion (as do all mechanically tracked systems), occupy at least one of the user's hands in keeping the viewer held to the face, and are currently somewhat large and costly. You must consider the type of motion in which users are engaged when in the virtual environment to determine whether BOOM technology is appropriate for an application.

Shuttered glasses. Another alternate approach to display that permits very high resolution at the expense of immersion is using shuttered glasses with a display monitor. The monitor is refreshed at a high rate with alternate left-eye and right-eye images. The shuttered glasses, synchronized to this update (e.g., via infrared transmission), alternately permit light to reach the left and right eyes, so, for example, every time a left-eye image is displayed it reaches the left eye. By alternating left-eye and right-eye images quickly enough, you fuse the images, resulting in stereoscopy.

Furthermore, using tracking technology, you can determine the position of the user and use it to display viewpoint-dependent images on the display monitor. The result is that, for others looking at the monitor, images appear to be flat and distort as the tracked user moves. To the tracked user, however, motion parallax is incorporated into the display, and objects that appear to occupy the space in front of or behind the screen maintain their positions in 3-D space, occluding each other as appropriate when the user moves.

There are alternate ways to shutter the glasses (including physical shuttering), but the most widely used technology at present is liquid crystal shutters. Starks (1992) reviews numerous approaches to constructing shutters and the patents associated with them.

Head-coupled displays that use shuttered glasses and a monitor can produce what has been called *fishtank virtual reality* (Ware, Arthur, and Booth 1993). As noted, the resolution with this approach can be high. Other advantages include the light weight of the shuttered glasses, their relatively low cost, and the ease of putting them on and taking them off. Also, you can use existing workstations and their monitors if you add appropriate software and position-tracking equipment. Disadvantages include the lack of immersion and the limited working volume for the user. Not only is the fishtank present only in the direction of the monitor, but, if the user moves too far (or the virtual object is brought too far out of the screen), part of the object will fall outside the field of the monitor, producing a clipping effect that destroys the illusion.

An attempt to address these disadvantages while still using position-tracked shuttered glasses is to surround the user with large screens. This permits an immersive virtual environment with high resolution that doesn't produce the clipping effect. It has been termed the CAVE approach and implemented by teams at the University of Illinois and at SUN Microsystems (Cruz-Neira, Sandin, and DeFanti 1993; Cruz-Neira, Sandin, DeFanti, Kenyon, and Hart 1992; Deering 1992). More than one person can be physically inside a CAVE at a given time, although only one is position-tracked to control the displayed images. The CAVE approach makes for an impressive display, but has some clear disadvantages of its own. It requires a large and costly special installation, the user is confined to the working volume between the screens, and only a single user at a time can use the CAVE and get the head-coupled stereoscopic effect.

Autostereoscopic displays and other alternatives. A large number of other approaches to stereoscopic display are provided by McKenna and Zeltzer (1992). However, few of these are applicable to head-tracked systems. A description of these alternatives is beyond the scope of this book, but I direct you to McKenna and Zeltzer's overview.

Issues and requirements

The issues and requirements for visual displays for virtual environments include orthostereoscopy, resolution, responsiveness (refresh and update rates), field of view, chromaticity and brightness, image smearing, and temporal fusion. These will be discussed in the following section, as will some issues specific to see-through HMDs.

Orthostereoscopy. I defined orthostereoscopy earlier in the book as constancy of the size, shape, and relative position of images displayed in a head-tracked HMD as they're perceived by a user who changes position and orientation. Robinett and Rolland (1992) have identified sources of error in generating correct stereoscopic images for an HMD, and a computational model that will correct (in software) for these distortions. They note that the display software in many systems ignores the optics of the system as well as the interpupillary distance (IPD) of the user, and their model addresses the need for taking these into account when generating images for an HMD. They identify incorrect convergence, decoupling of accommodation and convergence, incorrect FOV, failure to use off-center projection when needed, ignoring IPD and optical distortion, and transforming only the vertices of polygons in the presence of nonlinearities as sources of error.

Incorrect convergence is the result of misaligning the optical axes of the system. With parallel optical axes in which the axis passes through the center pixel of each screen, illuminating the central pixel of each eye's display produces the effect of a single point of light at optical infinity. Without making corrections for optical problems in software, misaligning the axes can result in images to the two eyes that are too horizontally divergent to fuse, too horizontally convergent (thus appearing close to the viewer), or vertically misaligned (*dipvergent*).

Current HMDs produce virtual images that are entirely at a fixed distance, so the decoupling of accommodation and convergence can't be corrected and the user must adapt to it. It's possible that future HMDs will incorporate servo-lens systems to adjust image plane depth in response to the user's point of regard, allowing for variable accommodation coupled with vergence. For now, however, the technical difficulties in creating such an HMD haven't been overcome (Wann, Rushton, and Mon-Williams, in press). Incorrect FOV will result if the geometric FOV used in software to create graphical perspective transformations doesn't correspond to the actual FOV of the optical system. You can correct the resulting incorrect lines of sight with subjective calibration techniques (Ellis and Nemire 1993) as an alternative to computationally modeling it correctly.

Off-center projection is necessary when the HMD is designed so the display screens are positioned perpendicular to but off-axis from the optical axis. Robinett and Rolland point out that, in this situation, an off-center perspective projection is required. Though not complex, many graphics programmers are unfamiliar with it because, in common screen-based graphics programs, the eye position of the viewer is assumed to be in front of the screen, thus the transformation is rarely useful except in VE systems.

Resolution. The resolution of visual displays is measured in different ways, all of which address the spacing of individual picture elements (pixels): the number of pixels per degree of angle subtended by the display or, equivalently, the amount of visual angle taken up by a pixel (or, formulated differently, between adjacent pixels). You need to consider requirements for resolution in terms of the requirements of the task; at present, it isn't possible to approach the resolution of the human visual system, but it also isn't necessary for most applications.

Responsiveness (refresh and update). The refresh rate of visual displays is the rate at which the image is redrawn on the display surface; this is also known as the *frame rate*. Displays that refresh at slower than the critical fusion frequency (which depends on factors such as display brightness, the brightness of ambient light, and the display's location with respect to the visual field) will cause the user to perceive flicker.

The update rate of a visual display is the frequency with which the image generator updates or modifies the image sent to the display device. The update rate is more important than the refresh rate because, even with a fast refresh rate, if an identical image is always shown for many consecutive refreshes because of a slow update rate, images will seem to move in a jerky and unnatural way. The rate of update must be sufficiently great to convey a sense of smooth motion to the user, and update rates have been associated with simulator-like sickness (Piantanida, Boman, and Gille 1993). For more on cybersickness, see chapter 3.

Field of view. The field of view (FOV) of the visual display describes, from the observer's point of view, the visual angle subtended by the display. Relevant measurements are the horizontal FOV, the vertical FOV, and the amount of binocular overlap. Roscoe (1991) points out that *optical minification*, the result of having to display a wide visual angle on a limited-FOV display, can exacerbate the underestimation of visual angles, caused by focusing on the resting accommodation distance rather than optical infinity. With wider FOV displays, images can be enlarged to reduce this problem. Anecdotal reports suggest that at least a 60° FOV is necessary to give the user of an HMD the feeling of being "in" the virtual environment (see Howlett 1990).

Color (chromaticity) and brightness. McKenna and Zeltzer (1992) note that tricolor display systems, which represent the spectrum of wavelengths by combining the three primary additive colors, cannot present the full range of colors that the human visual system is capable of distinguishing. In general, the value of using color in computer displays hasn't been as widely demonstrated as you might expect.

Image smearing. Image smearing is the phenomenon in which points on the image source don't change state quickly enough (e.g., they maintain their last assigned state for too long). The result is that when something moves in the display, a "smearing" effect is seen. Although this could result from the light of a CRT phosphor failing to decay sufficiently quickly, it has mostly been seen with early LCD displays (Kalawsky 1993), in which update rates of the crystals weren't fast enough.

Temporal fusion (flicker). The issue of critical fusion frequency was discussed earlier. Piantanida (1993) notes that the peripheral visual system is more sensitive to flicker than is the foveal visual system, which might require faster refresh rates to produce temporal fusion for wider FOV visual displays.

Issues specific to see-through displays. Augmented reality systems are said to use see-through HMDs, but there are two major implementation approaches used. While one of them involves actually seeing through the HMD (Feiner, MacIntyre, and Seligmann 1992), the other provides the effect of seeing through the display by merging video images from small video camera(s) mounted on the HMD with computer-generated images (Bajura, Fuchs, and Ohbuchi 1992).

With see-through HMDs, one issue that has to be addressed for some applications is avoiding conflicts between visual cues from the synthetic and real worlds. For example, in a system that lets the doctor see real-time ultrasound imagery that appears to be in the anatomically correct location within a pregnant patient, Bajura, Fuchs, and Ohbuchi (1992) found that simply superimposing the ultrasound images made them appear to be pasted onto the patient rather than within her. A partial solution was to superimpose a virtual hole by creating a shaded polygon pit and displaying the ultrasound imagery within the virtual hole. In their experimental system at UNC Chapel Hill, they didn't use range finding to determine the distance of objects from the viewer, so a problem with this system was that things closer to the viewer than the virtual hole but in its direction were obscured.

Evaluation

In order to evaluate visual displays, you must incorporate objective and subjective assessments. Objective assessments of optical distortion, refresh rate, FOV, and other issues are obviously of value in comparing display technologies, but users' evaluations (including their subjective assessments) provide information on whether image smearing and flicker are noticeable and whether they interfere with tasks, as well as the type of application-specific assessment given by Bajura, Fuchs, and Ohbuchi (1992) for the augmented reality display for ultrasound.

Acoustic Displays

Virtual acoustic displays present virtual auditory worlds (VAWs), generally over headphones, which provide sounds that are perceived as external to the user and that maintain their position or trajectory regardless of motion by the user. This is accomplished by synthesizing the cues that are used by humans in localizing sounds. Sounds can be presented by a virtual acoustic display not just in a horizontal plane around the user (as is done, for example, in surround sound), but anywhere in 3-D space.

In contrast to binaural sound, which provides localization cues noninteractively, a virtual acoustic display incorporates real-time interactivity, so movement by the user produces changes in the sound, maintaining the effect that the user is in the VAW. In addition to the positional nature of sounds in a VAW, the source and nature of these sounds might vary depending on the application in question.

While the nature of localization cues has been researched for more than a century, one of the cues, pinna filtering, is still a fairly young area of research, and there's still controversy regarding the cues required to produce externalization, i.e., the effect that sounds heard through headphones are external to the user's head (Durlach, et al. 1992).

Because synthesis of localization cues is a rather new area of research, there has been much recent attention to the localization of sound in virtual environments and less to the choice of sounds displayed. However, I'll also discuss the choice of sounds and representation of information through sonification and audification, audio icons, earcons, etc.

There's a useful analogy between visual and acoustic display technologies. Both involve rendering and presentation. In the case of visual displays, rendering is in terms of image generation and presentation is in terms of image source and optics. In the case of acoustic displays, rendering refers to sound synthesis and presentation is much less the focus of research than it is for visual displays, and is limited to headphones, speakers, and a third approach, within-ear monitors, which hasn't been used to date in VE systems.

Audio sources

The audio sources for virtual environments can include speech synthesis, nonspeech audio synthesis, and transduced and digitized sounds. Auditory localization cues can be synthesized and applied to each of these sources. In this section I'll describe the sources themselves, noting their advantages and disadvantages.

Speech synthesis. Speech as an output to the user can come from three sources:

- Transmitted speech from other synchronous users of the virtual environment
- Prerecorded (e.g., digitized) speech
- Synthesized speech

A significant advantage of synthesized speech over digitized speech is its flexibility (e.g., in text-to-speech conversion) because it doesn't require that anything played to the user has been prerecorded. A disadvantage is that, at present, all speech synthesizers have a mechanical sound quality and are somewhat less intelligible and comprehensible than natural human speech.

Text-to-speech synthesis takes normal text as input and, using text-to-speech rules, generates synthesized speech as output. The text-to-speech rules include analysis of text to identify word class (parts of speech) and distinguish content and function words, syntactic analysis to determine stress and intonation, and, using the syntactic analysis, calculation of properties (duration and pitch) of each syllable. These text-to-speech rules generate the sound waves of synthetic speech in a way that depends on the type of synthesis used. Three approaches to synthesis are:

- Vocal tract synthesis (in which the articulatory movements of the tongue, lips, and vocal tract areas are simulated)
- Formant synthesis (in which the known resonances associated with phonemes are used to calculate the transitions between phonemes)
- Diphone or acoustic segment synthesis (in which diphones, the segments that extend from the middle of one phoneme to the middle of the adjacent phoneme and capture the acoustic transitions across phoneme boundaries, are analyzed, stored in a library, and concatenated to produce synthetic speech)

A trade-off in approaches is how much information about speech must be stored and accessed. In spoken English, there are ~40 phonemes and ~1,600 diphones; newer synthesizers that use pronunciation dictionaries for individual words have produced dictionaries of ~100,000 words (Denes and Pinson 1993).

The stress and prosody found in natural speech tend to be lost in current speech synthesis, although several efforts at incorporating prosody have been made and there are some indications that it can improve comprehensibility.

Synthesis of nonspeech audio. A variety of approaches to the synthesis and choice of nonspeech audio in computer displays have been tried. Stuart (1993c) gives an overview of these, including sonification, auralization, automatic foley generation, and earcons. They are summarized in Table 5.4.

Sonification is the representation of data through sound. You can choose among mappings made between data parameters and sounds, which can be anything from a direct mapping between numerical values and sound parameters (e.g., from value of a stock option or temperature of an object to frequency of a tone) to a more semantic-level mapping (e.g., between selected characteristics of the data and melodic motives). Sonification hasn't yet been used in virtual environments to any significant extent, but it has been used to represent chemical spectra to visually impaired scientists, multivariate time series financial data to analysts, and medical vital signs of patients to doctors. Refer to Kramer (1993) for further information on sonification. For sonification, synthesis is essential, since no other technique provides the flexibility necessary to represent the abstract data.

Auralization, unlike sonification, is the direct presentation of data, altering only its time scale or modulating its frequency to make it more easy to perceive. This is applicable to data that already has an inherent sound, such as seismic rumble. You can use the data to synthesize an auralization display or, in some cases, process an actual recording.

Foley artists create the sounds in movies that match the actions of the actors; *automatic foley generation* is the generation of appropriate representational sounds in response to an action by the user in a computer-human interface. Users might act in unpredictable ways and yet want to hear appropriate audio response to their actions. For example, if you normally used a virtual pencil-like device to write on a virtual writing pad, but instead used it to unexpectedly hit a glass, an appropriate ringing sound would be produced. Automatic foley generation requires that the properties of objects in the virtual environment be known, and that these objects behave appro-

TABLE 5.4 Approaches to Nonspeech Audio

	Sonification	Auralization	Automatic Foley generation	Synesthetic representation	Auditory icons	Earcons	Alarms and warnings
Purpose	Represent abstract data through sound	Present data with inherent sound by changing its time scale or frequency	Create realistic sounds to match user interactions in the VE	Represent data from other sensory modalities (e.g., force) through sound	Convey system status information	Convey information about objects, operations, and interactions	Warn the user
Type of sounds	Mapped to data parameters, musical notes, or continuous range of pitches	Real-world sounds not normally perceivable without change of time scale or frequency	Everyday sounds	Mapped to data from other sense, musical notes, or continuous range of pitches	Everyday sounds, with parameters mapped to meaning	Musical; mapping of motif to meaning, musical elements combined to convey meaning	Special-purpose nonmusical sounds, such as beeps, sirens, etc.
Learning required?	Yes	Minimal if any	No	Yes	Some, but goal is for it to be minimal	Yes	Some, but goal is for it to be minimal
Sound source	Synthesis	Processed digitized audio, or synthesis	Synthesis	Synthesis	Synthesis or processed sampled sounds	Sampled sounds or synthesis	Digitized or synthesized special-purpose sounds
Issues	Recognition of patterns and anomalies in data, understanding of data parameter mapping to sound parameter	Recognition of patterns and anomalies in naturally occurring data not apparent at normal time scale/frequency	Seamless matching of unpredicted user actions in the VE to appropriate sounds	Understanding of data from another sensory modality displayed as sound	Use of everyday listening skills to minimize learning required for understanding meaning	Musical listening skills applied to auditory display; motives and associated meanings must be recognizable	Attract the user's attention in as unobtrusive a way as possible
Example	Representation of financial indicators, chemical spectra, and medical patient status information	Auralization of seismic "rumble"	User causes one object in the VE to collide with another	Force displayed as sound; NASA View system	Sonic Finder (non-VE application)	Research system by Blattner, et al.	Widespread. VE example: user is moving out of range of the position tracker
Reference	Kramer (1993)	Kramer (1993)	Darvishi, et al. (1995)	Stuart (1993) Richard, et al. (1994)	Gaver (1986)	Blattner, Sumikawa, and Greenberg (1989)	Patterson (1982)

priately. Since the number of interactions is large and there's unpredictability, audio synthesis offers the greatest flexibility for automatic foley generation (though a limited amount of it can be done with prerecorded digitized sounds). Sophisticated automatic foley generation hasn't yet been used in virtual environment systems, but promising work is underway, e.g., a system architecture described by Darvishi, et al. (1995), whose focus is on the generation of impact sounds.

Earcons use principles of musical listening and present motives (melodic phrases, i.e., pitches presented in a rhythmical sequence) to represent human-computer interface information. These have been used in interfaces other than virtual environments to represent information about computer objects (files, menus, and prompts), operations (editing, compiling, and executing), and interactions between objects and operations (editing a file). They haven't yet been used in virtual environments, and it's not clear whether or not they'll be valuable or applicable in this context. However, recent research suggests that playing earcons in parallel allows the audio message to better keep pace with human-computer interaction without compromising the ability of users to recognize their meaning (Brewster, Wright, and Edwards 1995). Because of the advantages virtual acoustic displays offer for auditory stream segregation, I think using parallel earcons in VE might be effective. They can be implemented with either synthesis or the concatenation of digitized sounds.

Synthesis of audio, while extremely flexible, and therefore preferable in the uses noted, is also computationally demanding. It also tends to produce sounds that are less realistic than digitized audio, though realism isn't always desirable.

Sampled audio. In addition to audio synthesis, sounds can be sampled and digitized. The trade-off here is that, while it requires less processing, there's less flexibility in what can be created, and a great deal more storage space is required. In addition, access time to the storage medium might be an issue if fast response time is required. On the other hand, sampling sounds is a simple process, sounds that would be complex to synthesize can be used easily if they can be sampled, and sampling permits very realistic sound displays. You can also loop samples to provide continuous background sounds (without requiring a great deal of storage space).

Transduced live audio. Transduced live audio is useful for synchronous communication between users in a multi-user networked application. It can also provide a display of audio from a remote environment to a teleoperator controlling a telerobot. The binaural nature of audio can be maintained if the telerobot has anthropomorphic ears with microphones placed in its "ear canals." And, through coupling the motion of the telerobot to that of the operator, you can create an effect nearly identical to a virtual acoustic display.

Synthesis of auditory localization cues

The area that's unique to virtual environments in terms of auditory display is the synthesis of localization cues, which has been the focus of much of the research. Like image generation, one challenge for virtual acoustic displays is to not only synthesize localization cues for sufficiently complex auditory scenes, but to do it quickly enough to maintain low latency and maintain a sense of presence.

Synthesized localization cues were described previously, but much of the focus has been on synthesizing individual anechoic sources (without incorporating the complex reverberations found in many man-made environments). This is due largely to the computational demands of calculating and synthesizing these cues.

In order to synthesize auditory localization cues, you must first measure the HRTF. This is accomplished by fitting human subjects (or, alternatively, anthropomorphic mannequin heads) with probe microphones, which are inserted deep within their ear canals, and measuring the signals that reach these microphones when sounds from a large number of locations in all directions from the listener are played in an anechoic chamber. The HRTF, as discussed in Wightman and Kistler (1989a), is a linear system that's dependent on the location of a sound source with respect to the listener's head. In current systems, the finite impulse response filters obtained from these measurements are then applied with convolutions to a sound stream that, once processed, is presented to the user (generally via headphones). I recommend Oppenheim, Willsky, and Young (1983) for a discussion of signal processing, including convolution and finite response filters.

The result of the application of these finite impulse response filters to a sound stream is that the processed sound, as heard by the listener, is very close to the sound that would be heard if it were coming from the appropriate direction in the anechoic chamber. This is illustrated in Figure 5.5.

Among the issues involved in the synthesis and rendering of these HRTFs are the following:

- The choice of listener whose HRTFs should be modeled and used (it's a laborious process to do this measurement, and nearly all current systems use either the HRTFs of a single subject measured by Wightman and Kistler or measurements from a mannequin head)
- Artifacts that can be introduced in the measurement of HRTFs
- The training time involved in becoming accustomed to localizing using "someone else's ears"
- Localization errors made by users, such as front-back reversals

Additional cues that can be incorporated into virtual acoustic display include early echoes, dense reverberation, distance effects, field patterns of sources, and Doppler effects (Burgess 1994c). Early echoes in virtual acoustic displays, like those in nonsynthetic environments, can either help or hinder localization depending on their nature (e.g., the positions of surfaces from which they occur). They're computationally intensive, unlike dense reverberation, which are similar from most locations in an enclosed space and can therefore be precomputed. Burgess notes that stereo presentation of dense reverberations is important, however, or sound sources will be perceived as external, while dense reverberations will be perceived as being intercranial. Distance effects involve the attenuation of sound with distance; different frequencies are absorbed and dispersed to different extents, and this can be modeled

148 Designing the System

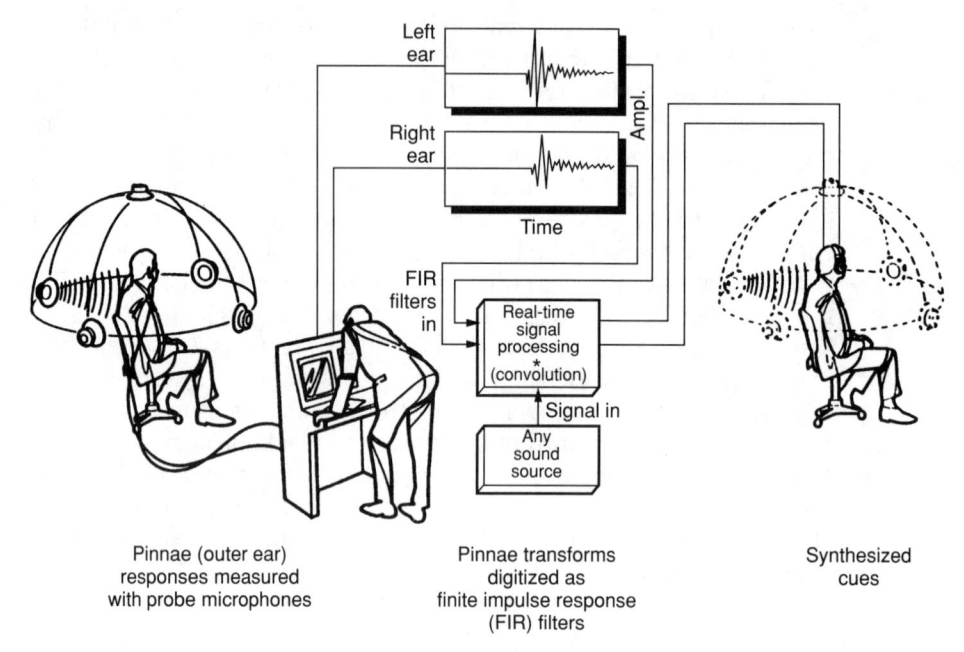

Figure 5.5 Technique for synthesizing virtual acoustic sources with measurements for the head-related transfer function. (*Elizabeth M. Wenzel, NASA Ames Research Center*)

with low-pass filters. Field patterns of sounds (directionality, e.g., a person talking doesn't transmit sound equally in all directions) have only recently been incorporated in virtual acoustic displays, and might improve veridicality; they can be modeled with precomputed filters. Doppler effects are the familiar shifting in frequency that occurs as a sound source (e.g., an ambulance siren or a train whistle) moves quickly with respect to a listener.

As described, the digital signal processing techniques necessary to synthesize HRTFs, even without nonanechoic cues, are extremely compute-intensive. The top systems use special DSP hardware, and have performance at greater than one gigaflop, according to Scott Foster of Crystal River Engineering. For more details on an example of virtual acoustic display implementation, see Chapin and Foster (1992). With continued improvements in processor performance, the computational demands of synthesizing localization cues are expected to become far less daunting. Although a more detailed description of signal processing techniques is beyond the scope of this book, refer to Begault and Wenzel (1990) and the extensive list of further references found in Stuart (1992).

Auditory presentation technologies

Unlike the presentation technology for visual displays, the technologies for presenting audio in virtual environments aren't complex. They're actually similar to the presentation technologies found commonly in music listening and other common activities. Headphone and speakers are the two most popular choices. There's also a third possible audio presentation technology, within-ear monitors, but it hasn't yet been used in virtual environment systems.

Headphones. Headphones, like those for listening to music, can be used. You should consider both the fidelity of their sound production and how much they cut out sound from the outside world.

Speakers. Because speakers can't display sound to the user without the acoustic characteristics of the listening room coming into play, and (more importantly) because they can't move with the ears of the user to produce head-tracked sound from all directions unless the listener is surrounded by speakers in all directions, they're generally not a practical alternative.

Within-ear monitors. Within-ear monitors, used at present by some musical performers, offer promise for virtual environment audio presentation. They're fit into the user's ear canal and provide very high-fidelity sound; they've been manufactured in a wireless format, leaving the listener untethered, and they very effectively cut out ambient sound from the external world. Some models require a doctor to measure the ear canal and that this measurement be used to create a custom-made mold that fits the individual's ears; others offer generically-shaped elements that can be used without custom fitting.

Super-localization

The work of Wenzel and her colleagues suggest that people can adapt to HRTFs that aren't their own. Might it also be possible for people to adapt to enhanced localization cues that would allow better than normal localization of sounds? For example, I've pointed out (Stuart 1992) that, although the barn owl with its asymmetric ears can pinpoint the location of a distant prey by sound alone (Knudsen and Konishi 1979) and although similar cues could be synthesized in a virtual acoustic display, it isn't at all clear that a human could adapt to synthesized cues like those used by the barn owl. Durlach (1991) and Durlach and Pang (1986) propose to enhance localization cues not to mimic the capabilities of other species, but to compensate for shortcomings in the human localization system—for example, by uniformly exaggerating spectral and interaural differences as though our heads and pinnae were enlarged. Adaptation to these altered sensory cues is still an area for future research. A more recent discussion of the subject that discusses some different approaches to super-localization displays is provided by Durlach, Shinn-Cunningham, and Held 1993.

Force and Tactile Feedback

Force and tactile displays for virtual environments are possible by either attaching display devices to the user (via gloves, suits, etc.) or letting the user grab or otherwise make contact with the display devices. An example of the former approach is the Dexterous Handmaster (see Figure 5.6); an example of the latter is the hand-

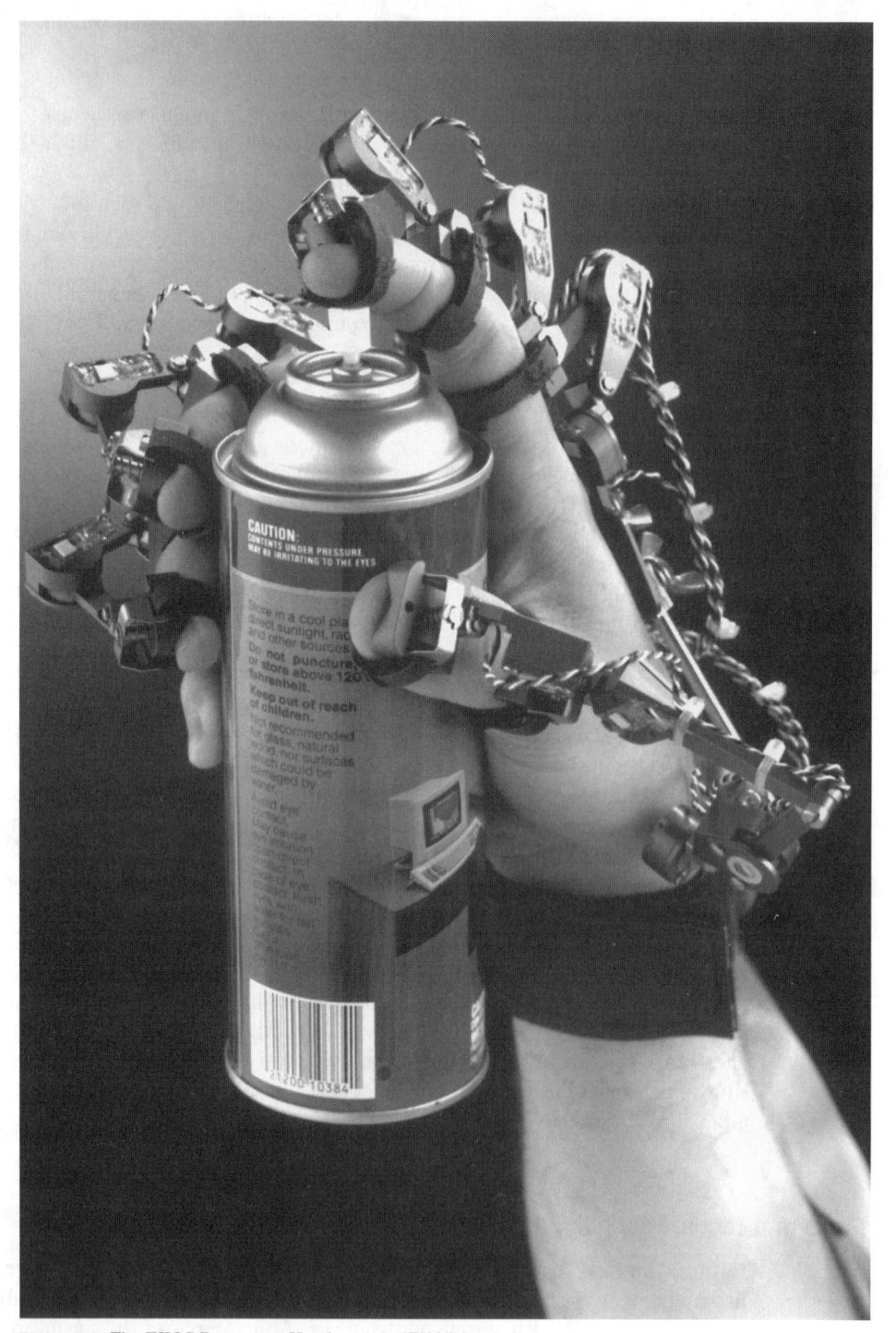

Figure 5.6 The EXOS Dexterous Handmaster. (*EXOS Inc.*)

grip-based Argonne remote manipulator used for Project GROPE at University of North Carolina, Chapel Hill (described in Brooks, Ouh-Young, Batter, and Kilpatrick 1990). Another less frequently used display that could be included in force feedback is a locomotive display, such as a stationary bicycle used as a navigation device; resistance could, for example, be increased to convey the greater force required to climb a hill.

Force and tactile displays are truly in their infancy at the time this is being written, and even certain simple percepts, such as that of a virtual rigid wall, have been difficult to produce in users (Rosenberg 1993). Unlike visual and auditory perception, haptic perception often involves active exploration, so the line between input subsystems and output subsystems is less clearly drawn. Tactile displays have been developed largely for users with disabilities for non-VE applications. Much of the development of force displays has been in the context of feedback for remote manipulation and teleoperation.

Tactile display technologies

There are several technologies that have been used to create tactile displays. Typically, tactile displays consist of two-dimensional arrays of points, each of which is a tactile stimulator, or *tactor*; these tactors can be vibro-tactile (e.g., piezoelectric, vibrating pins, or voice coil), pneumatic, electrocutaneous (electrotactile), or shape-memory alloy. Alternately, functional neuromuscular stimulation can be used to create the impression of tactile display.

Vibro-tactile displays give the impression of touch via vibration, e.g., on the fingertips. Pneumatic displays create the impression of touch by creating pressure with air rings, air jets, or air pockets that touch the user. Electrocutaneous displays create the illusion of touch by sending tiny pulses of electricity through electrodes touching the user's skin. Shape-memory alloys change shape and create the impression of touch through their pressure on the skin. Functional neuromuscular stimulation, invasive and seldom used, creates the impression of touch through direct stimulation to the neuromuscular system.

In general, the stimulus in tactile displays can be displayed in static, vibratory, or impulsive modes.

With pneumatic displays, the duration of exposure is an issue, as sensitivity decreases after an extended period of time, and the magnitude of pressure is an issue, as fingers, for example, can't sense a pressure of less than 0.2 N/cm^2, but too much pressure will produce fatigue (Shimoga 1993b).

With electrocutaneous displays, many different waveforms can be effectively used, but there's a limited range between the thresholds of sensation and pain, adaptation leads to a decrease in the subjective intensity of a given stimulus, and the electrodes must not introduce irritating or damaging ions to the skin or react chemically to produce an insulating layer between themselves and the user's skin (Kaczmarek and Bach-y-Rita 1995).

With vibro-tactile displays, the density of contactors, their area of contact with the skin, and the frequency and amplitude with which they vibrate are issues. Shimoga (1993b) suggests that contactors of cross-sectional area between 0.02 cm^2

and 8 cm² be used and placed at an optimal density, so the distance between adjacent contactors is equal to the two-point discriminating ability of the skin at that location (this distance is dependent on what area of the hand or body is chosen). Kaczmarek and Bach-y-Rita (1995) recommend that sine waves at amplitudes of at least 10 dB over threshold at frequencies between 60–250 Hz be used. Table 5.5 summarizes the advantages and disadvantages of different tactile display technologies.

TABLE 5.5 Tactile Display Technologies: A Comparative Evaluation in View of Their Suitabilities for Dexterous Telemanipulation

Features	Visual	(Pneumatic) air jets	(Pneumatic) air pockets	(Pneumatic) air rings	(Vibrotactile) blunt pins	(Vibrotactile) voice coils	(Vibrotactile) Piezoelectric	Electrotactile	FNS
Cost	high	low	low	low	med	med	med	high	high
Complexity	low	low	low	low	med	med	med	med	high
Heaviness	med	high	high	high	high	med	med	low	low
Comfort	good	fair	fair	fair	good	good	good	fair	poor
Suitability for more DOFs	good	poor	fair	fair	poor	fair	fair	good	?
Noise	none	high	med	med	high	med	med	no	no
Power requirement	low	med	med	med	high	low	high	high	high
Induction of numbness	no	low	low	low	med	med	med	high	?
Pain	no	no	no	no	some	no	no	yes	yes
Liability	none	low	low	low	med	med	med	med	high
Invasiveness	none	low	low	low	med	med	med	high	very high
Sensory substitution	yes	no	no	no	no	no	no	no	no

Copyright 1993 by IEEE, Courtesy K.B. Shimoga's "A survey of perceptual feedback issues in dexterous telemanipulation."

Force display technologies

Dexterous handmasters are force-sensing and force-display devices worn on the hands by the operator of a virtual environment or teleoperation system. In the case of teleoperation (for which dexterous handmasters have been most used in the past), the handmaster measures the movement of the user's hand (as do instrumented gloves) as well as the force applied; this input controls the movement and force exerted by the hand of a distant anthropomorphic robot. The robotic hand in turn transduces information about the objects with which it's in contact, and these forces are reproduced and displayed to the user via the handmaster. Dexterous handmasters can similarly be used to display force information in the context of virtual environments; here the controlled hand is virtual, and it interacts with synthetic objects that have force properties defined in the world database. The EXOS Dexterous Handmaster is shown in Figure 5.6.

Shimoga (1993a) notes constructional and functional requirements for dexterous handmasters. Force must be conveyed to the user's hand in some way. Two approaches for conveying this force are placing actuators at the user's finger joints and connecting remote actuators to the user's hands via tendons. Since dexterous handmasters are often used to control teleoperated robots, a constructional requirement for this application is that the robot's hand and the dexterous handmaster be kinematically identical, i.e., that they have identical link dimensions, and motion and torque ranges (the assumption, which might be questioned, is that there must be a one-to-one mapping). Other requirements include:

- Strength and durability
- Fit and calibration to different size hands
- Capability of response at sufficiently high frequency
- Sufficiently low work-to-rest ratio and force in order to avoid user fatigue
- Adequate sensitivity

Update rates are crucial for haptic displays to aid user perception. Twenty updates/second has been found marginally useful for a remote-manipulator molecular-docking display, with 60–80 updates/second necessary for good performance on hard-surface forces (Brooks, Ouh-Young, Batter, and Kilpatrick 1990). They also note problems to be solved with discontinuities in force displays, including mechanical backlash and static friction.

Rosenberg (1995) suggests some criteria for assessing a force-feedback system. The basic measure is the fidelity, i.e., how well it can reproduce haptic sensations, and this in turn is largely the result of the system's bandwidth and lack of noise. Bandwidth is particularly an issue in terms of the higher frequencies since low frequency isn't difficult in force displays. High bandwidth in force displays is generally associated with systems that have low friction and low inertia, as well as fast response actuators and fast electronics. A stiff transmission between the actuators and the user also helps convey crisp haptic display.

Noise in a force display can originate from both mechanical problems—Rosenberg (1995) gives friction, stiction, meshing gear teeth, and damping as examples—and electrical problems, such as an overly coarse quantization between analog and digital signals. Rosenberg also offers some ways to "kick the tires" of a force feedback system:

- Feel the stiffest stable virtual spring that can be generated; if the system can generate a crisp stiff spring, this is an indication of high bandwidth.
- Feel a solid surface generated by the system; a hard nonmushy surface indicates high bandwidth, and the lack of jitter or vibration indicates low noise.
- If the force display is a haptic device such as a force-feedback joystick or force-feedback pen (see Buttolo and Hannaford 1995), hold it between your fingers (which are more sensitive to vibrations than other parts of the hand), move it around when it's not powered up, and feel for smoothness (the absence of gears meshing, parts rubbing, or other friction) and lightness, or low inertia.

Temperature

Displaying temperature (regulating the temperature felt by a given area of the user's body) is a display technology that, though related to other types of tactile feedback, is in its infancy. Its applications include conveying information about temperatures in a remote environment to a teleoperator and making a virtual environment more veridical. Although not yet implemented in a virtual environment system, one technology for temperature display is discussed by Zerkus, et al. (1993).

Olfactory Display

The mechanism of smell presents special challenges to interactive displays. Smell requires that a stimulus be volatile so vaporized molecules pass through the air into the user's nasal cavity, and the chemicals themselves must be present as stimuli. This is unlike visual and auditory display, where energy can be converted into a form that simulates the sights and sounds of an environment. It isn't entirely true, though, that you must have the "real thing" to display its smell; as researchers in the perfume industry are well aware, you can combine synthesized chemicals to imitate a wide range of odors. Thus, a mechanical system that can activate and release these primary chemicals, which are physically stored in the system (e.g., in tiny capsules), could present a virtual olfactory display. Unlike visual, auditory, and haptic displays, however, an olfactory display would require that you periodically resupply the required chemicals.

It's fortunate that our sense of smell has a slow response time; although there might be mechanical limits on how quickly a system such as the one described could release the different combinations of chemicals, it shouldn't be difficult to do this quickly enough to create a realistic display in which latency isn't a problem. Cater (1992) claims that a proprietary system he's developing at the Southwest Research Institute provides "computer-selected variable-intensity" odors with a 250-msec response time, though he mentions that this is accomplished with a cartridge of "preselected and encapsulated" odors. Thus, it isn't clear how interactive his system is.

For online performance tasks such as teleoperation, a technical challenge is in developing a sufficiently fast olfactory sensing system for the robot and an encoding scheme for transmitting the olfactory information. Although there is no shortage of technologies for analysis of chemical content, the required speed makes creating the robot's olfactory sensing system particularly challenging.

Locomotive Displays

As discussed in chapter 2, motion can be passive or active, and it can be whole-body or part-body. Motion platforms can display whole-body passive motion, and force displays can display part-body active and passive motion. Locomotive displays are used for whole-body active motion. Locomotive input was discussed in chapter 4; it permits users to walk or pedal in order to navigate through a virtual environment, and experience this self-motion while confined to a limited space. As display devices rather than simple input devices, locomotive devices must be able to provide feedback to the user, changing in resistance when appropriate based on the VE. Thus, locomotive displays should combine force display with locomotive input. Most current locomotive input devices, however, don't incorporate this force display.

Inertial Displays

Inertial displays take advantage of our vestibular perception and use motion-base simulators. These motion-base simulators consist of motion platforms, a system that moves the motion platform, and a simulation that defines when and how this movement should occur. In the case of full inertial displays, centrifuges are incorporated to fully and continuously simulate the forces (including angular acceleration and G forces) that would be present, for example, in an aircraft in flight.

Full inertial displays are very expensive and complex, and typically used only for specialized vehicular simulators or for research. Partial inertial displays don't incorporate centrifuges and thus aren't capable of simulating continuous acceleration, but their movement in up to 6 degrees of freedom can convey many of the normal motion cues. There are various "tricks" that can be used to convey the intended illusions, such as G seats, which inflate and deflate to apply pressure and partially convey the feeling of G forces, and particular motion combinations that approximate the effects of other motions, such as the combination of slight forward translation and back-and-forth pitching to convey the impression of forward acceleration (Durlach and Mavor 1995).

The systems that move the motion platform are commonly mechanical, hydraulic, or pneumatic. Don't underestimate the price, size, and complexity of inertial displays, especially if you require a great degree of accuracy in the motions they produce. Motion platform vendors have told me that, especially for entertainment applications, systems that are less accurate and even have fewer than 6 DOF might suffice to produce the desired effects, at a savings in cost due to reduced complexity. However, inertial displays, though appropriate for flight simulators and public arcade installations, are too large and unwieldy at present for most virtual environment applications.

Questions

- For what kinds of virtual worlds would LOD representations in the database be useful?
- How could you incorporate eye tracking in an HMD?
- What difficulties could image smearing cause users?
- When might it be useful to combine spatialized synthetic sounds with transduced live audio? What problems could arise?
- How could you apply the idea of augmented reality to force and tactile displays? To auditory displays?
- Can you think of applications where temperature or olfactory display would be important?

Chapter 6

Computational and Supporting Technologies

As noted in previous chapters, supporting computational technology must meet performance demands unlike those of all but a very few types of systems, and there are tradeoffs that developers of non-VE applications seldom confront. Speed in generating and displaying changes in the environment in response to certain kinds of user input, especially to position-tracked changes in head position, is an example of a demand that's so great that it generally takes priority over demands for quality of the rendered image or complexity in the displayed scene. Other demands include integrating multiple (sometimes quite a few) I/O devices, synchronizing multisensory displays, and, in the case of multiuser networked environments, handling distributed simulations, which might involve contested control of objects and other user interface design challenges.

Van Dam (1994) has noted that the central concern of performance in virtual environment implementation recalls the values of vector graphics that have generally been supplanted by the values of raster graphics. He points out that, with vector graphics, only a limited number of vectors or characters can be displayed due to the need for speed in order to avoid display flicker and limiting the display list buffer size. He also notes that, even with the advent of storage tubes, while flicker stopped being a problem, the storage tubes were slow at generating images, so the updates had to be batched and sent selectively. The focus in raster graphics has evolved to photorealism and scene complexity; with virtual environment systems, these latter concerns must often be sacrificed in order to achieve the required low-lag performance. Efficient algorithms and data structures and optimized code are often crucial, and otherwise well-written modular code that isn't very efficient might not be acceptable.

System Architecture

There are both different system architectures that have been used for virtual environment systems and different ways of describing a given system architecture. In all cases, a virtual environment system incorporates a computational system with the input and output technologies described in the previous chapters. Figure 6.1 shows how the I/O components are connected. Please note that this functional description is distinct from the physical appearance of a system; at present, position-tracker vendors typically sell units that incorporate both the sensor/emitters and the polling and filtering components.

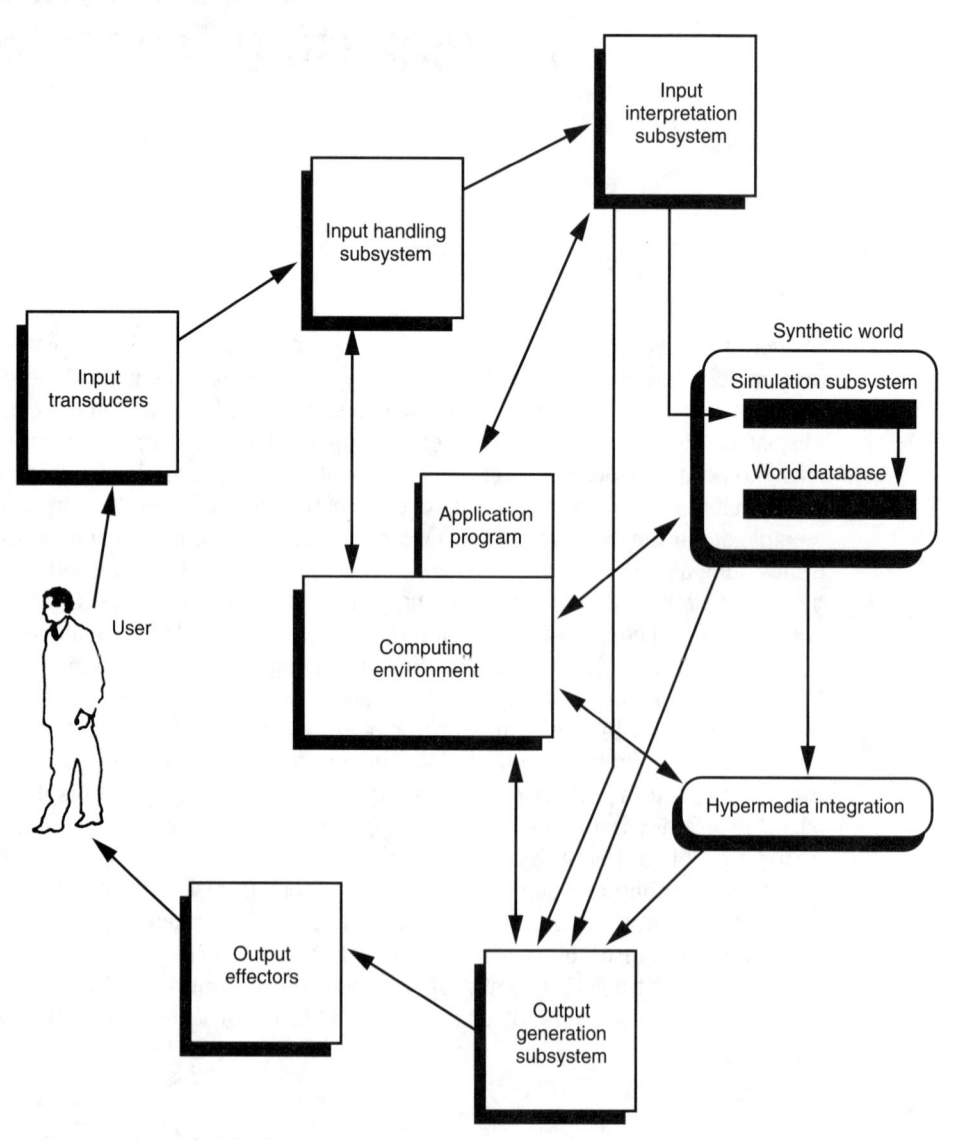

Figure 6.1 A decoupled simulation architecture.

The I/O components are practically identical whether they're connected to a VE system or a teleoperation system. Likewise, the supporting computing environment, shown in Figure 6.2, is practically identical, with the exception of a somewhat different programming environment (which controls mapping between I/O and teleoperated robot, rather than controlling simulations and facilitating model building). You can see the similarity between a virtual environment system and a teleoperation system by comparing Figures 1.1 and 1.2 back in chapter 1. More detail about the respective virtual environment and telerobotic components of these systems is illustrated in Figure 6.3.

Shaw, Liang, Green, and Sun (1992), in what they call the *decoupled simulation model* (see Figure 6.1), see VE applications as consisting of four components: computation, interaction, geometric model, presentation. In their view, the *computation* model is a continuously running simulation that periodically evaluates the state of a computational model, appropriately updates the state of the application, and, when the state of the application is consistent, sends data to the geometric model component. The computation component deals with all computations relating to the application except for presentation-related computations. The only input to the computation component is from the *interaction* component, which manages user input and coordinates output to the user. In addition to issuing user commands to the computation component, the interaction component sends the current time to the computation component in order to pace update of the application with update of the presentation to the user, i.e., synchronize simulation time with real time. The *geometric* model component receives input from the computation and interaction components, and uses this to convert data into a form suitable for display, which is in turn used as input to the presentation component. The *presentation* component is responsible for rendering images, synthesizing audio, and generating force and tactile displays; it does this by using graphical and other data from the geometric model component and user position and orientation data from the interaction component.

An advantage of Shaw et al.'s architecture, which is shared by other architectures that decouple simulation and rendering (e.g., the systems described by Pausch, Conway, DeLine, Gossweiller, and Miale 1993 and by the IBM researchers in a series of papers beginning with Lewis, Koved, and Ling 1992), is that changes of viewpoint and other user interactions, such as moving the instrumented glove on the user's hand, can be reflected as quickly as possible in the environment that's displayed to the user, even if the complexity of the simulation results in simulation-generated changes being updated more slowly.

Pausch et al. refer to these, respectively, as the *rendering frame rate* and the *simulation frame rate*. They point out that, although there's a similarity of the architecture of VPL's Body Electric to that of their system, Body Electric attaches the input devices not to the rendering component but to the application component. Because there tends to be great variability in the rates of simulation and application computation, decoupling simulation, rendering, and tying input devices to the rendering component permits more stable rendering rates and a system-to-user response that's closer to real time.

In Figure 6.1, the input interpretation subsystem sends messages directly to the output generation subsystem, as well as to the simulation subsystem. In addition,

Designing the System

Computing environment

Application program
(Application)

Operating system

- Real-time support: system-level support for timers and multilevel prioritized interrupts
- Device interfaces (proprietary vs. standard bus; device drivers and allocation)
- Memory allocation
- Interrupt vs. polling
- Single- vs. multiuser system
- Single- vs. multitasking system
- Distributed vs. centralized system

Network subsystem

- Layered network architecture (handles network protocols, passes changes in the VE caused by one user to others)
- Synchronization handler (maintains consistency of world database)

Programming environment

- World creation language
- Simulation control
- Interface to interaction software and devices
- Modeling software

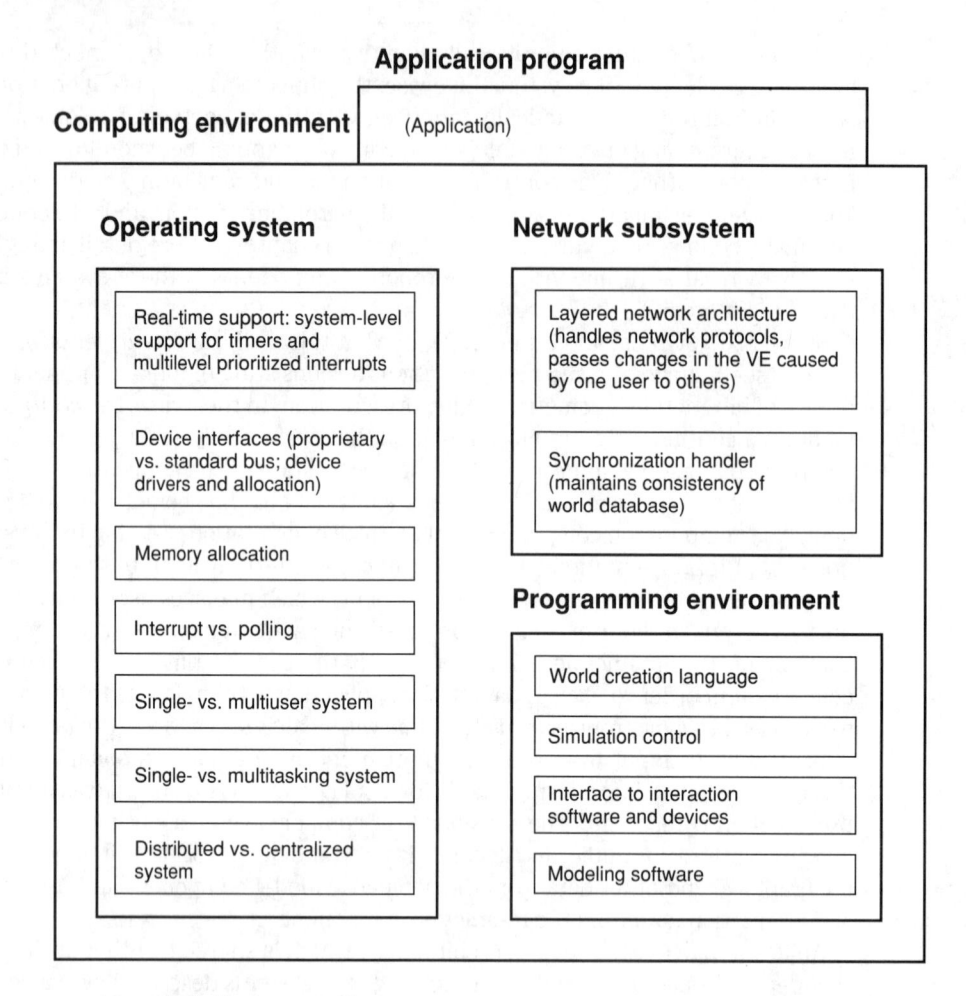

Hypermedia integration

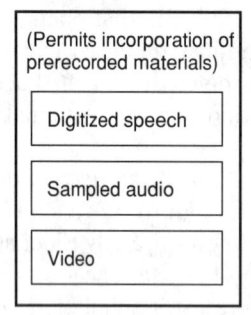

(Permits incorporation of prerecorded materials)
- Digitized speech
- Sampled audio
- Video

Figure 6.2 The computing environment and hypermedia integration subsystems.

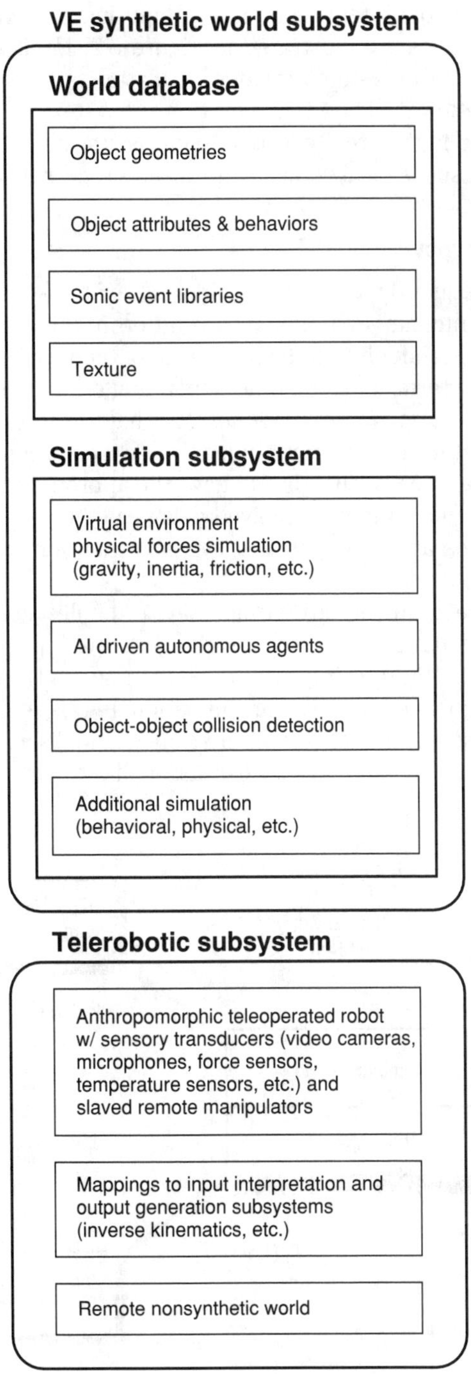

VE synthetic world subsystem

World database
- Object geometries
- Object attributes & behaviors
- Sonic event libraries
- Texture

Simulation subsystem
- Virtual environment physical forces simulation (gravity, inertia, friction, etc.)
- AI driven autonomous agents
- Object-object collision detection
- Additional simulation (behavioral, physical, etc.)

Telerobotic subsystem
- Anthropomorphic teleoperated robot w/ sensory transducers (video cameras, microphones, force sensors, temperature sensors, etc.) and slaved remote manipulators
- Mappings to input interpretation and output generation subsystems (inverse kinematics, etc.)
- Remote nonsynthetic world

Figure 6.3 The synthetic world and teleoperation subsystems.

this figure incorporates hypermedia integration. The computing environment and hypermedia integration subsystems are illustrated in Figure 6.2. Input and output technologies are similar whether the system provides simulation or teleoperation, a point made earlier. The synthetic world and teleoperation subsystems are shown in Figure 6.3. A further distinction in the architecture of multiuser systems is shown in Figures 6.4 and 6.5. Here the issue is local versus centralized processing.

Real-time requirements and minimizing latency

The term *real time* is used frequently and, on occasion, rather loosely to describe requirements for virtual environments. Real time means different things in different contexts. From a perceptual standpoint, it might mean perceived simultaneity, which means different things in terms of clock time depending on the modality and nature of the stimulus (see the section *Responsiveness*, in chapter 3). Because perceived simultaneity is important for many interactions in virtual environments (e.g., users should be able to turn their head or hands and have the appropriate visual, auditory, and haptic displays updated without perceived delay), many people feel that virtual environment applications and the operating systems that support them be real-time.

Another meaning of real time is "in very little time," say, 100 milliseconds. In this sense, real-time image generation means that images are generated quickly enough to be displayed at the chosen frame rate (e.g., 30 frames per second), rather than much more slowly and then sequenced to create an animation. In this section, I'll examine real time in yet another sense, that of computer science, and discuss real-time systems (in this computer science sense) and their relationship to virtual environment requirements.

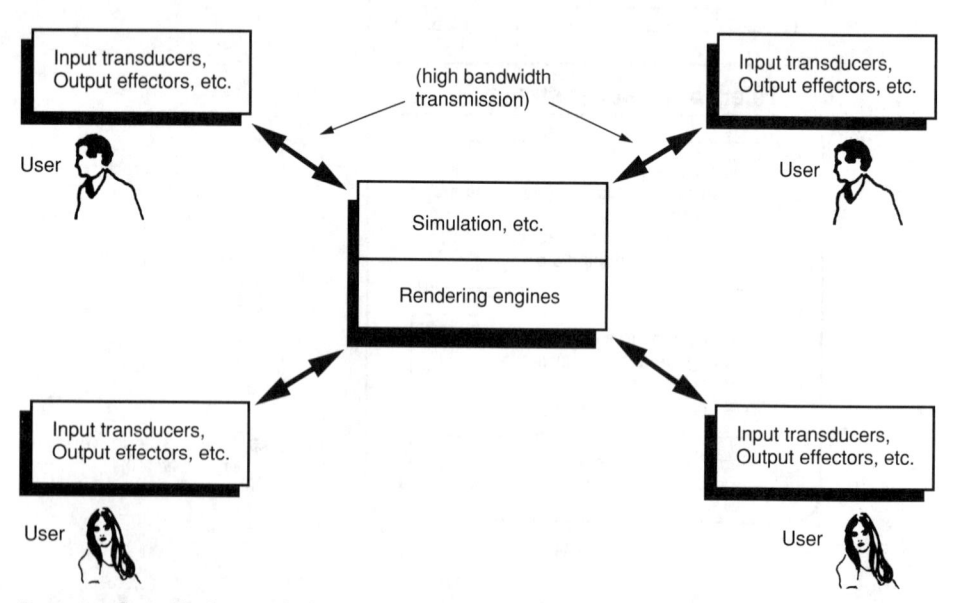

Figure 6.4 Centralized networked rendering and simulation.

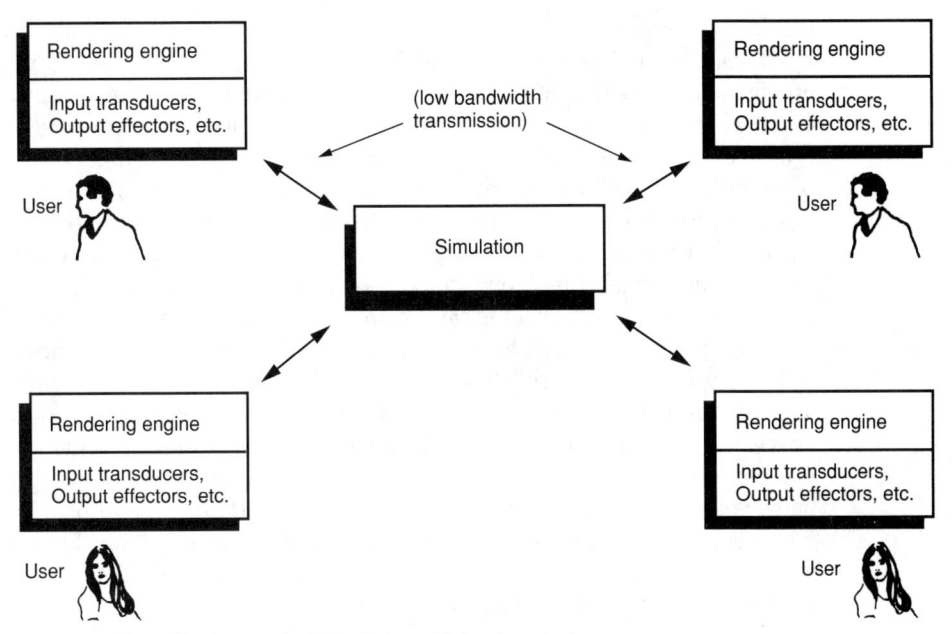

Figure 6.5 Centralized networked simulation with local rendering.

Real-time systems (also called *hard real-time systems*) have a number of distinguishing characteristics. They've been defined as systems in which not only the logical result of computations but also the time at which results are produced determine correctness of system performance. For example, coming up with the correct calculation but missing the deadline when it was required is as much a system failure as is producing an incorrect calculation (Stankovic and Ramamritham 1988). An implication of being able to guarantee meeting time constraints, another property of real-time systems, is that the system behavior be predictable.

Real-time systems should be contrasted with fast systems. Stankovic (1988) points out that the goal of a fast system is to minimize the average response time of a given set of instructions, whereas the objective of a real-time system is to meet the timing requirements of each specific task. A system might have very fast processors, high-speed buses, etc., but if it can't guarantee that a specific computation will occur with specified temporal properties, it isn't a real-time system. On the other hand, a system might have slow hardware, but be designed so a given computation will take place at a certain time; this slower system would be considered to be real-time. Although such a system would meet the definition of real time, it should be noted that, for actual real-time systems, fast performance is almost always considered essential.

In fact, a problem with real-time systems is that, in order to guarantee temporal properties of computations, many tend to underuse their available resources. Hence, one of the challenges in real-time systems is to use a high degree of resources. Typically, an application generates both time-crucial and non-time-crucial tasks; the time-crucial tasks must be handled within the given time constraints, but in order to use a high degree of resources, the non-time-crucial tasks must also be performed as quickly as possible. For highly time-crucial tasks, resources are typically preallocated.

Wloka (1995) cites several researchers who recommend not directly using time-crucial computing to reduce lag because of, for example, the gross visual errors that result in trading computational time for accuracy. Instead, he proposes using time-crucial computing to produce more consistent (i.e., nearly constant) renderer and application-dependent lag in order to allow predictive strategies to reduce lag. User input events that are time-crucial can be periodic (such as updates from position trackers) or aperiodic (such as a human input via speech or pressing a button on a haptic input device). Predictive strategies can be used for the periodic events, but less readily for the aperiodic events (although in some cases it might be possible and useful to use predictive strategies within an aperiodic event if it's of sufficient duration).

There are several approaches to reducing latency in VE systems, and the system architecture plays a role here. First, you can use faster devices, e.g., position trackers that report position more quickly and often, or faster image generators. Second, you can use predictive tracking (see chapter 4) and other predictive strategies. Finally, you can choose architectures that distribute the computational load and use multiple processors to parallelize simulation processing, handling of I/O, and rendering. In this case, a variety of schemes, discussed in Wloka (1995), can be used to minimize synchronization lag as well.

Single-processor vs. multiprocessor systems

In a sense, practically all virtual environment systems are multiprocessor—at the least, they have I/O processors as well as a central processor unit (CPU)—but not all are multiprocessor in the more commonly used sense of the term, that they have multiple CPUs. Because there are so many concurrent tasks to handle due to the variety of inputs, outputs, and computation, there's some advantage to using multiprocessor systems for the possible performance improvements. And there's nothing unique about the multiprocessor issues related to virtual environment systems; they're like other systems with a large number of input and output devices, and requirement for fast (and in some cases real-time) performance. The issues of problem decomposition, interprocessor communication, mutual exclusion, and bus arbitration are common to all multiprocessor systems.

Hardware Requirements

Hardware requirements for VE systems include processing speed and memory, as well as cost, size, and durability.

Processing and memory

In all virtual environment applications, fast processing speed is essential. This is a given. On the other hand, memory and storage requirements vary widely depending on the application. Many virtual environments are presently so simple that not much memory and storage is required. Contrast this to using virtual environments to design complex aircraft, where demands on memory and storage are great. Thus, when selecting the amount of computing power and storage requirements, you must first analyze the needs of the particular application you're designing, rather than some general standard.

Cost, size, and durability

Many of the other hardware requirements are specific to the application or environment. A computer system that costs $250,000 and must be local to the user isn't appropriate for a consumer home entertainment system; a bulky and heavy computer that must be carried around by a telephone repairperson who uses an augmented reality system for maintenance and repair of boxes that are high up telephone poles isn't appropriate; and computer hardware that's fragile or unreliable is ill-advised for a telepresence surgery system in which the lives of patients depend on system performance.

Software Requirements

There are a number of challenges that need to be solved by the software in virtual environments. There's an exceptionally high premium on performance, since latency can make a system practically unusable (see the sections *Responsiveness* and *Cybersickness*, in chapter 3). There are typically an unusually large number of I/O devices to support, which, at least with current commercially available technology, often require multiple (heterogeneous) platforms on which to run, with the platforms not even necessarily sharing the same operating system. While this permits taking advantage of the strengths of different platforms and the hardware and software available for them, it adds another level of complexity to software design. In addition, I/O technologies, as well as the software and computer hardware, is changing rapidly. It's often desirable to reuse some modules of the software, however, so developers don't always have to start from scratch.

With networked applications, the delays associated with transmission time can cause problems in the virtual environment system's interactivity; with multiuser networked applications, information that's crucial to the simulation being run can be widely distributed. The high level of computational resources that are typically required (particularly in terms of processor cycles) suggest the value of parallel computation and, although writing software for parallel processing systems is becoming more common, it's still less familiar and more challenging to many developers than writing software for serial processing systems.

Many of the human factor issues that are crucial to designing virtual environments, particularly in terms of interaction between user and system, are in need of further research (Stuart 1993a, and Thomas and Stuart 1992). Since an iterative design approach is recommended, software should support rapid prototyping. A lack of standards and integrated development environments at present often saddles the designer with the need to import data (e.g., modeled objects) created in different formats with a variety of packages, and what standards there are (e.g., MIDI, DXF, TCP/IP) are generally inadequate for the requirements of virtual environment systems. Physical simulations require not only motion and object interaction (including solid object computation and collision detection), but also that the simulations be extremely efficient and not introduce unacceptable latency. The architectural approach of decoupling the simulation is described previously in the chapter and illustrated in Figure 6.1.

Zyda, et al. (1993) make the point that, while a great deal of attention has been paid to the novel I/O devices of VE systems, "it is the software that is the hard part . . ." They divide the required software into five categories:

Interaction software. Determines the state of input devices, perhaps filters out erroneous or unlikely data, and might generate messages to the application that tell it to execute meaningful operations.

Navigation software. Interprets movement-related messages from the interaction software, and handles virtual camera viewpoint control, as well as polygon flow minimization, e.g., by removing hidden surfaces.

Communication software. Passes changes in the virtual environment caused by one user to other users, and keeps the world database consistent.

Autonomy and scripting software. Handles AI-driven autonomous agents in the environment, captures user-system interactions, and lets previously captured interactions be replayed and, perhaps, combined with real-time interaction with the system. (The latter is an idea by Zyda et al., and isn't widespread in the field.)

Hypermedia integration software. Lets prerecorded hypermedia (video and audio) be incorporated into the virtual environment.

These five categories address some of the underlying software that's used when running the virtual environment, not the software used to create it. The creation software includes modeling tools, programmer interfaces, and toolkits. Coco (1993) notes, for example, the importance of modularity, simplicity, and generality to support a rapid prototyping capability. Also relevant are real-time operating systems and software to support networking of system components, and of course the application (and world database) software itself.

The operating system

The real-time requirements discussed earlier in this chapter put additional demands on operating system software. Many of the operating systems currently used for virtual environments don't provide sufficient real-time control. Preemptable kernels, minimized context-switching times, and fast clock speeds are important; bounded latency times can also be useful or even necessary for some applications. This section discusses real-time operating systems.

A real-time operating system must manage resources in such a way as to support the environment in which real-time applications execute. Handling time-related issues is perhaps the most distinctive feature of these systems, and involves issues such as clock synchronization, time representation, and meeting time constraints. Current real-time operating systems are often "stripped-down and optimized" versions of existing time-sharing operating systems, with reduced functionality, fast context-switching, and fast response to external interrupts. They minimize the time during which interrupts are disabled, and their kernel maintains a real-time clock (Stankovic and Ramamritham 1988).

Levi and Agrawala (1990) propose an object-oriented approach to real-time system development that uses and represents time uniformly and explicitly as an integral property of all entities in the system. They suggest that this object-oriented approach will help alleviate one of the problems endemic to real-time systems: the high overhead for maintenance (e.g., the extensive testing required when any change is made to programs).

Stankovic and Ramamritham (1988) suggest an abstraction of the scheduling and synchronization problems in real-time systems that's a variation on the classic "dining philosophers" problem suggested and solved by Dijkstra. In the original formulation, five philosophers spend their lives thinking and eating, seated around a circular table on which there are five chopsticks positioned between them and a bowl of rice. They sit quietly without interacting when they're thinking. When a philosopher gets hungry, however, he attempts to pick up the two chopsticks closest to him (he can pick up one at a time), eats rice once he has both chopsticks, and, when finished, sets down both chopsticks. In the original problem, the two risks are deadlock and livelock. In Stankovic and Ramamritham's variation, the "dying, dining philosophers problem," each philosopher has a time by which he must start eating, otherwise he dies of starvation. This analogy highlights the challenge of real-time systems, since solutions to Dijkstra's formulation (e.g., allowing at most 4 philosophers to be seated at once to avoid deadlock and keeping track of chopstick requests to avoid starvation) don't solve the revised formulation.

Additional current research in real-time systems isn't limited to operating systems and also addresses the topic of object-oriented real-time systems. A number of real-time extensions to C++, such as FLEX, RTC++, and RIPE, have been written, as have other real-time object-oriented languages, such as CHAOS (Gopinath and Bihari 1993). Work on real-time databases is also being performed. These databases have strict timing constraints when responding to queries, handling transactions, and maintaining the database (Ozsoyoglu, Ozsoyoglu, and Hou 1993).

Interrupt-driven vs. polled systems

With the multiple I/O devices typical of a virtual environment system, each device can originate an interrupt request. In a polling system, all interrupts typically share a common branch address and the CPU polls interrupt sources sequentially, starting at the common branch address and basing the order of polling on priority levels assigned to the interrupt sources. A given source is polled and, if it hasn't signaled an interrupt, the next-lower-priority source is polled; this continues until an interrupt signal is found and, in turn, handled. This can be problematic in many virtual environment systems, in which there are often many interrupt requests at any given time, and the time spent polling is time not spent actually processing requests (Mano 1982). An interrupt-driven system (also known as an *event-driven system*) can also be problematic for virtual environments because of the many interrupts that can be issued at one time and the fact that temporal sequence and priorities can be crucial. These are liable to be lost in typical interrupt-driven systems. Events can have context-sensitive meanings based on the state of the user, which is difficult to interpret given a queue of interrupts (Durlach, et al. 1995).

Real-time systems are often implemented as interrupt-driven systems with priority-based scheduling (Levi and Agrawala 1990). A priority interrupt unit that's hardware-based determines the priorities of interrupt requests and, depending on the priorities of these requests, the priority interrupt unit signals the CPU that an interrupt request must be handled.

Another alternative that's useful in multiprocessor systems is a concurrent model, in which separate processes are assigned to each element in the VE, and these individual processes are like miniature polled systems, with each implemented as a thread or lightweight process that's preempted so it won't take too much time (Durlach, et al. 1995). A disadvantage that Durlach, et al. point out with this concurrent approach is that the processes might not stay in synch and, if they're forced to stay in synch, their speed is determined by that of the slowest process.

Virtual world database

The virtual world database contains descriptions of the physical and behavioral characteristics of objects in the virtual environment. These include object geometries; visual (color and texture), auditory, and haptic properties of objects, motion (velocity, direction, and acceleration) and collision properties; positions; and linkages to other objects.

Properties of the virtual environment's objects are described as its "content" by Ellis (1991), who also describes the environment as having geometry and dynamics and the environment's geometry as consisting of its dimensionality, metrics, and extent. The dimensionality is the number of terms needed to define an object's position in the virtual environment, the metrics are rules that define the space (e.g., the ordering of position vectors and definition of geodesic or straight lines in the space), and the extent describes the volume of the world, i.e., the range of values with which position vectors of objects can be associated. Finally, the virtual environment has dynamics, which are the rules of interaction and physics of the environment (Ellis 1991).

The virtual world database must keep track of the current state of the virtual environment, a more demanding challenge if multiple users are interacting with the environment. One solution to this challenge is Division's DVS system, which maintains a VL "shared data space." DVS provides separate servers (actors) to handle different elements of the user interface; each actor typically needs to access only a subset of the shared data space, and communicates with other actors through shared objects.

The virtual world database can be quite large, and you can use the structure of the database to reduce the amount of searching that's required, for example, to determine which elements are potentially visible or audible to a particular user at a particular location in the virtual environment. You can also group static elements in the environment into "patches" in the database and, rather than cull-testing each individual element, the scene manager can cull-test each patch (Mueller 1995). In addition, you can use level-of-detail (LOD) selection, discussed with respect to image generation in chapter 5, to reduce the demands on the image generation system. In order to support LOD selection, the database must be organized so each element has multiple representations ranging from much detail to very little detail; the appropriate representation is chosen based on the proximity of an element to the user of the VE system.

Programmer interface and toolkits

There are no truly standard VE toolkits or application programmer interfaces (APIs) for virtual environments at present. Although several commercial and research development tools are available, there are no clear signs that any of them will still be used within a few years, and there are problems with all of them. Therefore, rather than describe these individual products here, I'll discuss some of the key issues they reveal that are generalizable and that you should consider when designing a virtual environment system to meet specified requirements. In his technical report on APIs for VE systems, Taylor (1995) includes a review of currently available systems.

From the perspective of the application builder, four approaches to building the virtual environment have been discussed or implemented. These are:

- Text-based
- Visual programming language
- World building within the environment (sometimes described as VE-CAD)
- Automated world building

The vast majority of current virtual environments are constructed with text-based systems, and there are several factors you should consider with respect to these, including whether or not they're interpreted languages and whether or not they're object-oriented. The next most common system for constructing virtual environments is a visual programming language. Although they're much less common than text-based systems, these types of systems were popularized by VPL's Body Electric system. Systems that allow world building within the environment are much less common, although many systems allow trivial changes to the environment from within and systems are increasingly providing toolkits that allow more of this functionality. Automated world building is also a research topic in need of more work, although examples of some system-mediated design decisions can be found in Feiner, MacIntyre, and Seligmann 1992. Since the iterative design methodology I advocate might require repeated changes in response to evaluations, in the case of any of these approaches to building virtual environments, it's valuable to be able to make these changes quickly and easily, and experience the results of the changes quickly.

In text-based systems, the developer uses a text editor to create the environment. In some text-based systems, this involves using class libraries to instantiate objects; in others, it involves writing low-level C code; in others, it means invoking predefined objects and actors from a high-level scripting language.

A common problem with text-based systems, especially those that aren't in interpreted languages, is the amount of time and effort required to iteratively make minor changes in the environment. Even highly talented programmers often can't tell how the virtual environment they're creating with text will appear or behave until they try it. And, if they find that even small changes must be made, the process of returning to the text editor, making modifications, recompiling, and then running and trying the virtual environment can be laborious and time-consuming.

Visual programming languages present graphical representation on a flat screen of the code components of the system, which the developer can select, order, and connect as desired. These don't reveal anything more about how the environment will actually appear or behave than text-based systems, but the developer can create a system without as much programming skill. Bletter (1993) compares experiences between visual VE programming and text-based VE programming, based on using Body Electric (a visual programming language from VPL) and MR Toolkit (a text-based programming language from the University of Alberta). He finds that the first 90% of the prototyping effort is easy with a visual programming language and difficult with a text-based system, but the last 10% is difficult with the visual programming language and easy with the text-based system.

Device drivers

Although device drivers for input/output devices used in virtual environment systems are similar to other device drivers, the issue with virtual environment systems is the large number of input/output devices that can be used. If you're selecting a supporting development software package and are either limited in time or working with a number of other developers, it's worth considering beforehand whether it supports the devices planned for the system. Otherwise, it will be necessary to write all the device drivers for unsupported devices before prototyping the application. Coco (1993) notes the desirability of modular drivers that produce standard data streams and can be plugged into applications.

Simulation

Simulation is a field unto itself and, in many cases, the designer of a VE system will have access to an existing simulation to which the VE system provides an interface. If a complex simulation that doesn't already exist is required for the application you're developing, don't underestimate the effort involved in developing the simulation so it runs quickly enough to be used in the virtual environment. Because of the computational demands of simulations, there are clear advantages to the decoupled simulation architecture described earlier in this chapter and shown in Figure 6.1. Although distributed simulation is often discussed in the context of a multiuser system where the users are at remote locations, distributed simulation also offers advantages when a simulation is computationally demanding and can be run on one or more remote supercomputers.

An example of calculating the trade-offs involved—in this case, between doing the simulation and the rendering all on a supercomputer versus doing the simulation on the supercomputer and the rendering on a separate graphics computer—is provided by Keith Fredericks of Cray Research, Inc. (1994):

> As for data transfer rate requirements for this supercomputer to remote rendering engine link:
> I think of the supercomputer/remote workstation as a rendering pipeline. Bandwidth requirements between stages in the pipeline can be well defined. These requirements are included in articles like Akeley (1989) and Foley, van Dam, Feiner, and Hughes (1990).
> The thing that really matters is the case where you have an enormous amount of data to transmit to the front-end (graphics) workstation and the geometry is changing. This is

when this type of visualization starts to fall apart and you end up having to wait minutes for the image to be regenerated on the workstation. We did some calculations for the practical case of a system such as SGI's DGL (geometry transfer) running over Ethernet and FDDI, and compared that with image transfer over an HiPPI frame buffer. We found a CRAY rendering speed break-even point, i.e., the point at which the CRAY generating images becomes a faster method than the CRAY transferring geometry to the front end. For Ethernet the number is 6,711 triangles per sec., and for FDDI the number is 81,967 triangles per sec. This is a kind of weird comparison for several reasons, but it was based on what was currently available last year. We did not calculate the HiPPI number for the workstation because we didn't have a number for HiPPI-connected workstation performance.

Anyway, the main parameter that's required for this calculation is scene complexity (you can express this in numbers of polygons, which breaks down into 6 floating-point numbers per vertex or roughly 72 bytes per triangle at 4 bytes per float). Most supercomputer data is expressed in polygons for visualization. You might also want to use image size ($n \times n$ pixels, n bits deep) if you decide to transfer images instead of geometry.

A big question is what type of graphics task partitioning should be used. For the supercomputer case, this breaks down into the question "Should I render on the supercomputer and transfer fixed-size images over the network, or should I transfer geometry which will vary with scene complexity?" Another big question is real-time vs. postprocessing visualization. Is it possible to visualize this in real time with the available equipment? Is real time necessary, or will postprocessing do?

Although distributed simulation, e.g., on supercomputers, can be used for an application-specific simulation, it can also be used to simulate generic behaviors, such as physical properties of the world (gravity, inertia, and so forth) that can be used by many different applications. Such libraries of generic behaviors could prove quite useful to developers as they become more widespread, and decrease the overhead in the rapid prototyping component of the iterative design cycle.

Modeling

The geometric modeling of objects isn't a conceptually difficult problem, and can be performed with a variety of currently available CAD packages. The problems in this area are that modeling objects can be very time-consuming and modeling packages require that the modeling be done outside the virtual environment, often in very unintuitive ways. Two approaches to the first problem are to acquire predesigned CAD models where appropriate and use systems that permit modeling by tracing real-world objects with position-tracking technology (where the real-world object exists, is accessible, and is of a size that makes this feasible). An approach to the second problem, which can be thought of as VE-CAD, has been described (Stuart 1993b), but not yet implemented beyond the prototype stage.

Cross-platform compatibility

Being able to port software across platforms is generally advantageous, particularly so in fields that have no de facto standard platform. This is a problem area at present; almost all available development and toolkit software is device-specific, with very few vendors having ported their software to different platforms.

True portability does come at a price, since specific characteristics of the hardware can't be taken advantage of and only common operating system services can be used. For this reason, makers of video games, with their emphasis on performance with low-end computers, rarely even consider cross-platform compatibility. Attempts at a generic compute model (which decouples the model from details such as native instruction set, location of computation, CPU throughput rate, and device handling) have been advocated (Coco 1993), but haven't yet been implemented well enough to get any widespread use, even when they're available for free. As computer hardware performance improves, the portability of virtual environment software might become more feasible.

Networking

Networking serves several roles in virtual environment systems. It permits system components to be distributed (e.g., for the simulation engine to be physically separated from the rendering engine). It allows users to be physically separated from system components (e.g., for a user to control a teleoperated robot at a distance, or for users to share the resources of a remote simulation or rendering engine). And it permits multiple users to be physically separated from each other. Three network-related issues that should be considered are:

- Transmission time delays and their effects
- Types and appropriateness of network protocols used
- Local versus remote processing, and the associated implications for required bandwidth

The data transmission requirements for all the subsystems of the virtual environment system should be considered, but at present this might be too closely based on available devices rather than theoretical requirements to be useful.

Networked multiuser systems present problems in displaying objects to all users with their correct positions and orientations. In a simulated war game, for example, one participant might move a vehicle as another participant prepares to fire a weapon at it. Transmission delays could lead the participant firing the weapon to think the vehicle is still in a certain position when, in fact, the other participant has just moved it. While it seems clear that the fired weapon shouldn't succeed at hitting the vehicle in this case, what should be displayed to the person firing the weapon?

A better solution is to design the networked system so the displays for all participants are accurate. Singhal and Cheriton (1995) discuss this accuracy in terms of positional accuracy, behavioral accuracy, and structural accuracy. They suggest an approach that makes use of position history to predict future position and orientation, and they argue that their approach, which permits transmitting update packets that contain nothing but position information, reduces the demands on the network while providing better accuracy, reduced dependencies between hosts, and smoother rendering. Their paper is recommended both for the approach they describe and their review of approaches, including dead-reckoning, taken by others.

Expert system components

Expert system components have been used in various ways in virtual environments. They can be used in a simulation, e.g., to control the behavior of autonomous agents in the virtual environment. In a simulated war game, the expert system can control the behavior of a tank to make it difficult to distinguish from that of a tank controlled by another user, which is useful when there aren't a sufficiently large number of users engaged in the distributed interactive simulation at a particular time. The behavior of these autonomous agents shouldn't be distinguishable from that of human participants—not by human users of the system, nor by statistical analysis, nor by performance characteristics. The expert system can also incorporate learning, so it uses the behavior of a user and learns from it to be a "smarter" opponent or teammate.

Expert systems can also be used to control the design of a virtual environment (as opposed to the simulation). Feiner, MacIntyre, and Seligmann 1992) use a knowledge-based graphics component based on their Intent-Based Illustration System (IBIS). The illustrations this system creates are pictures that are intended to satisfy goals the knowledge-based system deduces from the user's input. Such application of expert systems to virtual environments might aid in the choice and application of visualization techniques and tools, which offers promise especially in the domains of applications for online comprehension and offline learning and knowledge acquisition.

Finally, expert systems, in combination with physiological measures of the user, can be used to dynamically control and change the virtual environment, for example to maintain a desired level of arousal in the user. This application of expert systems to virtual environments, suggested by David Zeltzer, might be especially applicable for entertainment applications, where, for example, the "story" through which the user is navigating could be made more or less scary depending on whether the user's heart rate was too low or too high.

Questions

- Are there any disadvantages to the decoupled simulation model?
- Do you see hypermedia integration as an important element in virtual environments? Why or why not?
- When would you choose each of the four approaches described for building a virtual environment?
- What criteria would you use in choosing a VE programmer's toolkit?
- Can you think of ways that expert systems could be used in virtual environments other than those described in the chapter?

Chapter 7

Objects, Behaviors, and Interactions

Given the supporting hardware, software, input, and output devices to make the virtual environment possible, what should the content of the VE itself be? A virtual environment has objects, the objects have behaviors, and there are certain kinds of supported interactions between the user and these objects (and, in a multiuser system, between users). Your design of these objects, behaviors, and interactions depends on your analysis of the application-specific requirements for the system, the issues and requirements common to VEs, and your understanding of the users, the way they do their tasks, and their environments. In turn, you'll get feedback on your design of the objects, behaviors, and interactions from evaluating prototypes (as described in part 3 of this book), and you'll use the feedback to make modifications to your initial design.

In spite of the very much application-specific nature of objects, behaviors, and interactions, this chapter will include some brief general comments about each of these items. Note that all objects in the environment are transduced rather than computer-generated in a straight teleoperation system, so for this type of system you don't need to consider the elements in this chapter.

Objects

There are many types of objects that can be incorporated into virtual environments, and you need to ask yourself several questions: "What should the geometries of these objects be?" "What should their shapes, colors, and textures be?" "What should their size and scale be?"

As discussed in chapter 3 in the section *Choice of Representation*, objects in a virtual environment can be representations that are realistic (as nearly identical as possible to their real-world counterparts), scale-altered (realistic except that their scale, either in size or in time, is altered), property-altered in a variety of ways, modality-altered (represented through a different sensory modality), iconic, reified, or abstract. Objects with which the user interacts can also provide strong cues as to their own operation and use (*affordances*) just as real-world objects do. (For more on affordances and the design of real-world objects, see Norman 1988.)

In addition, you also need to consider how the objects in a virtual environment are to be created and the choice of primitives of which the objects are composed. There are six ways to either create or acquire objects for a VE. You can:

- Define them by typing into a text editor, either entering explicit coordinates, colors, textures, auditory, force and tactile attributes, or defining objects in terms of an existing library of graphical elements, texture maps, sound files, etc.
- Create them with an existing 3-D CAD (computer-aided design) modeling program, such as AutoCAD, and then import them into the VE software.
- Base them on real-world objects you capture by tracing the real-world objects with a 3-D digitizing program.
- Obtain them from existing libraries (e.g., of CAD files).
- Automatically generate them with an algorithm that responds to user behavior, is data-driven, or functions autonomously in the VE in response to the state of the simulation.
- Allow the user to create them from within the virtual environment using what I describe as a VE-CAD system.

The graphical objects can be composed of primitives that depend on the graphics system used; Robinett (1994) gives triangles, polygons, spheres, NURBs, bitmaps, and volumes as examples.

Behaviors

What behaviors can the objects in the virtual environment exhibit? Objects can exhibit a large spectrum of behaviors, depending on the needs of the application. Objects can be designed to change sound, feel, color, visual texture, and shape, either in response to user action or the state of the simulation. They can be made to grow larger or smaller. They can be modified to become either more spongy or resilient. The sounds they make can be designed to change pitch, timbre, volume, and rhythm. They can be made to move or to be movable in different ways. They can have weight in the VE, exhibit inertia, and drop in response to gravity. They can be made to bend, shatter, or be separated into discrete pieces. They can either exhibit the property of space exclusion (not being allowed to occupy the same space in the VE as another object), or be allowed to pass through other objects.

You can design objects to interact with other objects in the environment in various ways. They can collide, bounce off of each other, work together, and be attachable to each other. They can, in response to user action or the state of the simulation, undergo metamorphosis as a plant flowering, a building collapsing, a log burning, or a crystal forming. They can serve as tools to interact with other objects in the world. They can serve as devices to transport other objects in the VE or the user from place to place.

Objects can have intelligence and incorporate machine learning. They can exhibit self-modifying behavior, using the behavior of users, behavior of other objects, and results of interaction with other objects as stimuli. They can learn not only from passive observation of examples (e.g., searching for patterns and regularities in these stimuli), but also through active experimentation, in which they instigate actions to observe the effects of these actions. Little has been done so far in the area of machine learning within virtual environments, but some of the motivations to develop more intelligent objects for certain applications seem compelling. Even in the case of an entertainment application, self-modifying behavior by objects within the virtual environment could result in the VE evolving so it's different each time a user enters it.

You can also design objects, by defining their properties, to behave appropriately even when they're involved in unpredicted interactions. An example of this is the automatic foley generation discussed in chapter 5.

Interactions

How can users interact with objects in the virtual environment? At a minimum, all virtual environments let users move through the virtual world. If this is all they can do, the system is what might be thought of as a simple architectural walk-though, even if it's immersive. Most VEs permit interactions beyond simple user navigation. Other interactions that the design might make possible include the user selecting objects; grabbing and moving the objects; removing or "deleting" objects; opening objects (e.g., a door or a box); and pushing, hitting, or throwing objects (e.g., in a game of racquetball or squash).

Mine (1995b) organizes the fundamental interactions possible in a virtual environment into four fundamental forms, with a fifth derived form. These fundamental forms are movement, selection, manipulation, and scaling; the derived form is virtual menu and widget interaction. Two other possible interactions not mentioned by Mine (1995b) are modification of object and world properties, and object creation. Mine categorizes interaction techniques as direct user interaction (e.g., hand tracking, eye tracking, gesture recognition, and pointing), physical controls (e.g., buttons, dials, joysticks, sliders, steering wheels, and other haptic devices), and virtual controls (these can take a wide variety of forms; examples are discussed in Loftin, Engelberg, and Benedetti 1993).

Movement

Navigation approaches and techniques are discussed earlier in the book, as are input methods for navigation (see Tables 3.1 and 3.2 in chapter 3). Position-tracked real-world movement can move the user within the VE, and the mapping between real and virtual movement can be either one to one or scaled (e.g., so the movement of 12 centimeters in the real world produces movement of 12 microns in a bacterial simulation or 12 kilometers in a planetary terrain simulation). This type of navigation, which would be described in my classification scheme as "relative motion through tracked head and body movement," has the following disadvantages:

- Working volumes in most current systems are limited by position-tracking technology, and therefore the area within which the user can move in the VE through this type of input is limited.
- Depending on the nature of the VE, users might become disoriented, or "lost in space," without clear reference points with which to orient themselves. Other input methods and navigation styles avoid this problem, but, in all methods of input to control relative motion, the direction of motion and the speed of motion must be controlled.

The direction of relative motion can be controlled via the direction the user's head is facing, the direction in which the user's eyes are directed, or the direction the user's hand is pointing; it can also be specified by the user's interaction with physical or virtual controls.

Mine (1995b) notes that, while pointing with the hand or a hand-held device to control direction allows flexibility (e.g., to fly in one direction while looking in other directions), this type of action can confuse novice users who don't entirely understand the relationship between hand orientation and flight direction; an alternative is the crosshairs method in which a cursor, commonly positioned at the user's fingertip, is placed in line visually with the point to which the user wants to fly. This method, however, which requires calculation of the vector from the user's eyes to fingertip, also requires that the user continue pointing in a direction and not look around. So, in addition to the reduced flexibility in terms of the user's looking around the VE, it could also produce arm fatigue.

Controlling the direction of motion by tracking the direction in which the user's head is facing or the user's eyes are directed shares the disadvantage of the crosshairs method, that the user can't freely look around while flying towards a destination in the virtual environment. Orbital mode is an alternative way to view objects from different angles; as summarized by Mine from J. Chung's 1994 UNC Ph.D. thesis, an object of interest always appears in front of users in orbital mode, but the orientation of the user's head controls the angle from which the object is viewed. The result is that users can observe the object from different viewpoints as would be possible if they actually moved around it.

Controlling the direction of motion by using physical or virtual controls has the disadvantage that users might first be required to understand the mapping between manipulation of controls and movement in the environment. However, using controls is certainly a better solution in cases where a simulated vehicle has such controls.

The direction in which a user can move can be constrained. Unconstrained motion can lead to disorientation, and for some applications it's useful to constrain motion. For example, in an application that requires visualizing the signal quality of radio transmissions to and from an automobile as it drives along a road in a certain terrain, it makes sense to constrain the user to travel along the road path that could be driven by the real automobile in the terrain that's being simulated. The extra demands on the user to control a 6 DOF automobile and keep it along the road in all degrees of freedom would probably distract from the visualization task at hand.

There are several alternatives for controlling the speed of motion. You can set a fixed speed for flying through the environment, or multiple fixed speeds from which the user can choose (e.g., via gesture or button selection on a haptic device). There can also be a fixed rate at which the user accelerates during flight through the VE. Variable-speed flight is possible, and can be controlled by physical or virtual controls, e.g., by hand position. Mine (1995b) illustrates two schemes for this in which the distance of the user's hand from his head controls the speed of movement in the direction the user is pointing, either in a linear manner (the speed increases linearly as the distance from head to hand increases) or in a "three-zone" manner (the user's hand can be in one of three zones, which is determined by its distance from the user's head; the closest zone produces deceleration, the middle zone produces constant speed, and the furthest zone produces acceleration).

Selection

Techniques for selecting objects can be local or "at a distance." Local techniques require that the object to be selected is within reach of the user; the user can then move a position-tracked hand or a haptic device-controlled cursor to within the object's region and use a selection gesture, speech command, or other action for selection. In the case of local techniques, the selection action is on-off in nature; it simply issues the command that the region within which the hand or cursor is positioned should be selected or deselected. At-a-distance techniques for selection involve identifying the object to be selected by naming it, gazing at it, pointing at it (e.g., with a virtual flashlight or pointing device), choosing it from a menu, or directing a cursor through the environment (via physical or virtual control devices, gestures, or voice commands) until it's in the region of the object.

Manipulation

Manipulating an object in a VE consists of moving its position or changing its orientation. Users can do this by grasping the object as though it were a real object in the real world; the mapping between the distance moved by the user's hand in the real world and the distance moved by the object in the virtual world can be 1:1 or some other ratio, e.g., in order to let the user position a small object more precisely than would otherwise be possible given the limits of human motor control. As a substitute for this hand-grasping approach to manipulation, a haptic device such as a 3-D mouse can be used to select the object and move it, as though the mouse were the user's hand. Manipulation can also encompass dropping an object or throwing it in the virtual environment.

Besides manipulating via grasping an object (or using a haptic device as a surrogate for the hand), you can manipulate objects via speech commands or by using virtual or physical control devices. The manipulation can be unconstrained or it can be constrained, e.g., by preventing an object from being moved through other objects.

Scaling

Scaling always requires that there be a center of scaling, i.e., a point from which objects move when the environment is scaled up and towards which objects move when the environment is scaled down. You can also use dynamic scaling in order to move within the virtual environment. Mine (1995b) points out that this can be accomplished through a sequence of three steps:

1. Scale the environment down until it's small enough that the user can reach the intended destination.
2. Move the center of scaling to the intended destination.
3. Scale the environment back up to its original size.

Virtual widget and menu interaction

Another type of interaction also involves selecting and moving objects, but the objects are tools or control devices within the VE. So you can design tools or control devices, for example, that the user can turn (in the case of wheels or dials), flip (in the case of switches), push (in the case of buttons), or select (in the case of menu items).

Modification of object and world properties

Other interactions that can be supported by the design of the VE involve the user modifying various objects in the environment. These modifications include changing the shapes of the objects (bending them, twisting them, etc.), changing the size of objects, changing their color and texture, changing the sounds they make, and changing the forces they generate.

Object creation

In the case of what I call a VE-CAD system, the user can also create objects within the VE. As mentioned in chapter 1, 3DM and Conceptual Design Space are two research systems that support VE-CAD. You can create objects by modifying basic objects (selected via menu options, spoken commands, etc.), selecting vertices from a grid and indicating the height to which objects should be extruded (as in Conceptual Design Space), shaping objects with your hands, or using a gestural language (as well as speech commands) to indicate object properties at a higher level of abstraction.

Questions

- How could the affordances Norman describes for real-world objects be applied to VE objects?
- What are some useful kinds of behaviors not mentioned in this chapter for objects in VEs?
- How could users who don't have programming skills define or modify the behaviors and interactions in a VE?
- If you constrain the movement of users in the virtual world, what should happen if the users' real-world movement doesn't stay within these constraints?
- In what kinds of applications would at-a-distance selection techniques be most useful? Could they be used (i.e., would they have meaning) in teleoperation?
- Dynamic scaling as a method to move within the VE is unlike any way we move in the real world. Can you think of other interactions that would be useful in a virtual world, though they're impossible in the real world?

Chapter 8

Design Trade-Offs

I've mentioned numerous design trade-offs in previous chapters of this book. In some ways, nearly everything you do in designing a virtual environment seems to involve compromises, given the state of current technology and the demands in addressing our sophisticated perceptual/motor capabilities. It's important to make the correct decisions when faced with these compromises. In this chapter, I'll focus on some of the most important design trade-offs.

General-Purpose vs. Special-Purpose VE Systems

A high-level design question that must be answered is whether to use a general-purpose virtual VE hardware system (and application software written for it) or whether to design a special-purpose system with custom-built specially configured hardware. At present, there are few if any general-purpose commercially available systems for some of the "flavors" of VE systems. For example, nearly all teleoperation and CAVE systems are currently custom-made. There are, however, commercially available general-purpose immersive HMD-based systems. It's certainly easier in many ways to obtain such a system and write application software for it. However, you must carefully consider whether such a general-purpose system can meet the demands of the application. If not, you should custom-configure or custom-build your hardware to meet the identified requirements, and write application software for the special-purpose hardware system.

Degree of Encumbrance and Choice of "Flavors"

Another high-level design decision is what type or "flavor" of VE system to use. Immersive HMD-based systems tend to be encumbering—the user typically has instrumented glove(s) or dexterous handmasters and other force displays, an HMD that occludes the real-world environment in which the system is used, and cabling that connects position trackers, the HMD, and other display devices to the system. Such a system can provide very rich multisensory cues, but might not be practical if the user needed to be aware of things going on in the surrounding real-world environment, or if there were frequent interruptions that required taking off and putting back on all the display equipment.

In contrast, an artificial reality system is completely unencumbering, and lets users move in and out of the system seamlessly. However, along with these advantages is the disadvantage that the cues provided are necessarily less rich and less multisensory; there's no practical way to provide force and tactile feedback in an unencumbered system (except by requiring the user to grab on to some device) and, while virtual acoustic display is possible with wireless transmission to headphones or within-ear monitors and unencumbered position tracking, this hasn't been implemented in any known artificial reality system. Stereoscopy is also sacrificed in current artificial reality systems.

Vehicular simulators and CAVEs are large and expensive, and the virtual environment in fishtank VR systems fills only as wide a field of view as the screen size permits (and displays only in the direction of the monitor). Each type of VE system has disadvantages as well as advantages, which must be weighed in light of analyzing the user, environment, and tasks for which the application will be used.

Degree of Customizability for the Individual User

Some of the individual physiological differences between users have been discussed. People have different interpupillary distances, different shaped pinnae and consequently different head-related transfer functions, different sized hands, and different ways of performing a gesture. In addition, users can have different preferences in modality and choice of representation, and other preferences related to cognitive style.

The advantages of allowing customizability includes better user performance (e.g., fewer auditory localization errors), greater system performance (e.g., accuracy at recognizing individually trained gestures), fewer user problems (e.g., less visual fatigue from using an HMD setting that doesn't match the user's own IPD), and greater user satisfaction (e.g., being able to choose preferred representations of information).

The disadvantages of allowing this customizability is the greater complexity associated with it and the overhead in getting users set up to begin a session. As pointed out in chapter 3, you need to distinguish between the customization and calibration done once for each user and that which is required at every session in which a user is engaged. You should also consider how often and for what duration a user will make use of the application when making the design decision as to how much customizability to incorporate into a system.

Responsiveness vs. Image Quality vs. World Complexity

One of the most crucial design trade-offs for a VE system is between responsiveness, image quality, and world complexity. Brooks (1988) sees real-time motion, complex world models, and high-quality images as three aims that not only can't be simultaneously addressed with current hardware, but will always require trade-offs, regardless of future improvements in hardware. He favors prioritizing them so objects always move realistically at the expense of everything else; image resolution, quality, and model complexity can be sacrificed as the user moves objects, and improvements in image quality (detail, resolution, antialiasing, etc.) can automatically occur as soon as the user stops moving objects. He also feels that, in order to preserve the illusion of reality, jumps and discontinuities in the displayed images must be avoided.

Brooks, Airey, Alspaugh, et al. (1992) provide an example by describing specific trade-offs between the complexity of models (and rendering requirements) and the speed of the system (lag, frame rates, etc.). Whether or not Brooks is correct that advances in hardware and software will never result in a lack of need for these trade-offs, these decisions are certainly crucial given the state of current technology!

Sharing Resources vs. Bandwidth

While there are obvious advantages to sharing computational resources across a network (including the cost savings to each user or user site of not having to own and maintain the dedicated machines), there are design trade-offs here as well. There is a cost associated with the higher bandwidth required as the amount of shared computational resources (and hence network usage) increases, and there's also latency in transmission time. Such a system might also be more complex due to the synchronization required because of network latency. Although you need to base your decision on the specific needs of the application you're designing, there might be future trends in what's most common, influenced by the progress and cost in network technologies versus that in computational technologies.

Optimization vs. Cross-Platform Compatibility

Because of the limits of current computational technology and the performance demands for responsiveness (and, to a lesser extent, image quality and world complexity), developers often do a great deal of optimization for a particular platform that's used in a VE system. This optimization results in the software performing better on the machine for which it's written, but not being portable to other platforms. In many non-VE applications, this sort of optimization has fallen out of favor as processing speed has increased. Imagine computational power increasing to the point that writing portable code would generally be preferred to optimizing for a certain platform. This, unfortunately, isn't yet the case for many VE applications.

Specific Technologies

Finally, I'll review some of the design trade-offs you must consider with respect to the individual-component technologies of VE systems. I'll focus on trade-offs concerning HMDs, position trackers, acoustic displays, and physical and virtual devices.

HMD trade-offs

A central decision concerning HMDs is whether to maximize field of view or resolution. Because of the nature of the optics involved, which must spread the pixels displayed on a relatively small image source so the image is larger and its light collimated, the resolution of HMDs is necessarily lower than it would be if the image source were not displayed in an HMD and, instead, held at arm's length from the eyes. You must decide how much resolution to sacrifice in order to have a wider FOV in the HMD.

As Piantanida, Boman, Larimer, Gille, and Reed (1992) point out, the display technologies used in most HMDs were developed for other applications, such as LCDs designed for camcorder viewfinders. These displays present a limited number of pixels and, if the visual angle they subtend (because of the optics system used in the HMD) increases, there's an accompanying decrease in resolution (because there are fewer pixels per degree of visual angle). Thus, if the display device presents a fixed number of pixels, the wider the FOV the lower the resolution. Although this trade-off would still come into play with display devices that present many more pixels, it might have less impact than it does given the limitations of current image sources, permitting both wide FOV and high resolution.

At present, there's also a trade-off with HMDs between image quality (the combination of resolution and FOV) and complexity, as well as cost, of the HMD. By starting with a large (and heavy) image source, it's possible for an HMD to have higher resolution without sacrificing adequate FOV. The problem with this is that the HMD would be too heavy to wear if it supported such an image source. One approach used in current very high-end HMDs is to carry the image from such an image source to the HMD over a large number of bundled fiber-optic cables. Not only are these HMDs very expensive, but the thin fiber-optic cables can be damaged rather easily. In terms of the optical systems I've described, the greater complexity of catadioptric systems is apparent. Even color comes at a cost in HMDs, so that some military applications use HMDs that are black and white but have higher resolution.

Tracker trade-offs

There are quite a few trade-offs you must choose between regarding position trackers. As pointed out in chapter 4, Adelstein, Johnston, and Ellis (1992) found that filtering with position trackers to minimize jitter increased lag (and many manufacturers of position trackers don't allow the developer to control whether filtering is turned on or off). Therefore, there's a trade-off between stability and latency, and this decision should be based on the needs of the application.

Another trade-off involves working volume versus complexity. A system such as the University of North Carolina's optical ceiling tracker can support a large working volume if it has a great many sensors (or emitters, depending on whether it's an outside-in or inside-out system), but there's cost associated with this, as well as greater demands associated with handling, processing, and interpreting all the data coming in from the tracking system.

Passive tracking is appealing because users can be totally unencumbered, but most passive systems require line of sight, a trade-off that may create problems unless there are a great many sensors (which, again, makes for greater complexity). Although it's often assumed that trackers must track all six degrees of freedom, for some applications it's worth considering the simplicity (and perhaps cost savings) of having fewer DOF tracking if some of the degrees of freedom aren't necessary.

Finally, the issue of noise and what sort of environmental conditions will hurt tracker performance results in a trade-off. Each tracker technology has its own version of noise, which doesn't affect other tracker technologies. For magnetic trackers it's metallic objects that interfere with magnetic fields, for optical trackers it's temporary obstructions and ambient light, for acoustic systems it's ultrasonic sounds that can come, for example, from computer monitors or jangling keys. By combining tracker technologies, you can mitigate the effects of these different noises, but combining tracker technologies introduces more complexity and cost to the system.

Acoustic display trade-offs

Trade-offs regarding virtual acoustic displays include veridicality vs. cost and complexity, as well as choosing between the types of sounds to display and whether they should be presented over headphones or speakers. The most veridical display would involve as many spatialized sound sources as required (which might be a very large number in some simulations), and would allow many reflections and nonanechoic cues to be incorporated, all synthesized using HRTFs of the actual users. Spatializing a large number of simultaneous sound sources is very computationally demanding, as is generating (and spatializing) anything beyond first-order reflections. There's also some overhead in measuring and using the HRTFs of each individual user; for many purposes, generic HRTFs might suffice.

Speech and nonspeech audio both have their merits and both can be included within a virtual environment, so there's no need to decide between one or the other. But such a decision might be required for displaying a particular kind of information, and here there are trade-offs. Some types of nonspeech audio require that the user learn a mapping between sound and meaning that isn't necessary for speech, but nonspeech audio can also reduce the ambiguity found in spoken language by assigning unique meanings to individual sounds, and it allows many different sounds and sound parameters to be modified and presented simultaneously.

Whether the audio is speech or nonspeech, another trade-off involves whether it should be synthesized or digitized. As synthesis technology becomes more powerful, the advantages of digitized audio might decrease. At present, however, digitized speech is more natural-sounding and more comprehensible than synthesized speech, and digitized nonspeech audio is also more natural-sounding. Digitized audio takes up more storage space in the system, while synthesized audio requires more processing resources. Although sampler technology allows the pitch and duration of digitized audio to be controlled (defining sounds in terms of their attack, decay, sustain, and release), synthesized audio wins out in the flexibility it offers, e.g., in automatic foley generation and creating sounds not precisely planned for.

Headphones are generally superior to speakers for virtual acoustic displays, since they can move with the user's head, don't require the user to remain in any "sweet spot," and don't require taking into account acoustical characteristics of the real environment in which the user is situated. The one trade-off in this case is that speakers allow the user to be unencumbered—really an advantage only if other display technologies, such as the visual display, don't already encumber the user.

Physical vs. virtual devices

If control devices will be used by participants in the virtual environment, should they be real physical devices or virtual devices? In an immersive HMD system in which the user can move around, the registration must be accurate to even let the user find and manipulate physical devices; in a vehicular simulator, physical devices in a physical cockpit are the norm, and users can see their own hands and arms as well as the physical devices to be manipulated. The big advantage of real physical devices is their veridicality: they look, feel, and respond exactly as they should. Virtual devices are less veridical—especially at present in terms of the force and tactile feedback that can be provided to users who manipulate these devices—but they can be modified and reconfigured in software much more quickly, easily, and inexpensively than physical devices.

Questions

- Which design trade-offs discussed in this chapter will go away with improvements in hardware? Which will remain?
- What are some of the differences between general-purpose and custom-built VE systems? When would the extra effort required to custom build a system be worthwhile?
- Can you think of ways in which a VE system could automatically customize itself to its user without requiring calibration, training, specifying choices in modality and representation, or other explicit actions by the user?
- Do you agree with Fred Brooks' opinions on trade-offs between responsiveness, image quality, and world complexity? Why or why not?
- When might sharing computational resources across a network be worthwhile? When would an HMD with wider FOV but lower resolution be a good choice? What advantages does nonspeech audio offer over speech? Under what circumstances would physical control devices be preferable to virtual devices?

Part 3

Evaluating the System

You can't underestimate the importance of evaluating your design. If the system you've designed is to be deployed for its intended application, it will be evaluated; the only question is whether you or someone else will evaluate an early prototype and use it to modify and improve the design, or if the end users of the deployed product will perform the evaluation, when it's too late to improve the design. The iterative design philosophy espoused in this book strongly suggests that you evaluate prototypes and actively use the results to improve your design before deploying the application.

There are three levels on which you should evaluate your VE system, and each of these has a chapter devoted to it. These levels are system performance, usability, and value for the task/application. Finally, I'll discuss using the results of these evaluations to redesign the system, making modifications to improve system performance, usability, and usefulness for the task/application until you've achieved acceptable performance in each of these areas.

Chapter

9

System Performance

Overall system performance can be evaluated in a number of ways once a prototype is developed. For example, although you can consider each of the elements in the system that contribute to latency, the final evaluation of the system's cumulative latency also reveals the effects of the interaction between system components. Perhaps the most tricky part of evaluating system performance in the iterative design methodology is that you must evaluate the system performance of a prototype, rather than that of the final implementation of the system, so you must pay careful attention to how closely each element of the prototype's system performance that's measured reflects the performance of the final system.

In this chapter, I'll discuss some of the elements of system performance you should evaluate, including latency, display update rate, synchronizing spatial and temporal cues, robustness and fault tolerance, registration, and working volume.

Total Latency

As noted previously in the section in chapter 3, *Responsiveness*, total latency is, in general, the accumulation of lag introduced by each system component required to generate the system response: the data rate and update rate of position trackers; the time spent by the host computer in processing tracker position, running the simulation, and rendering the graphical, sonic, and tactile images (i.e., the update rate of the computer); the refresh rate of display devices; and the cumulative transmission time.

The objective measurement of the total latency requires the timed mechanical measurement of inputs and their corresponding outputs. For example, the user makes a mechanical action that can be detected by input transducers (such as movement of a position tracking sensor, or flexion of an instrumented glove), and the time between this action and the related change in display by output effectors (e.g., change in the scene displayed in the HMD or sound displayed through headphones) is measured.

These measurements should be taken under a range of conditions, in terms of complexity of the scene displayed, number of users accessing resources (in a multiuser system), multiple simultaneous inputs, and different simulation scenarios.

As an example, here's an analysis of total latency in a relatively simple (but effective) prototype. The prototype was designed and implemented by David Burgess, currently at Interval Research Corp., while he was at the Georgia Institute of Technology. This prototype accepts only one type of input—the position-tracked movement of the user's head and of a mallet—and produces only one type of output—spatialized nonspeech audio through headphones.

In this prototype, the Virtual Drum Kit (Burgess 1994a), users are situated in a virtual auditory environment and can move a position-tracked mallet through space. As the mallet crosses the surface of a cone-shaped region of space surrounding the user, a drum sound is triggered from the appropriate location. This prototype incorporates modeled percussive sources (which use a sound generator, an auditory field pattern, and an algorithm that controls user interaction), synthesis of HRTF cues (via digital filters running on the CPU of a SUN Sparc machine), and modeled listening environment (incorporating stereo reverberation and atmospheric dispersion). The total latency, from the time the user strikes the surface of the virtual drum until the time the associated sound is played over the headphones, is 240 ms.

Burgess notes that most of the various delays are adjustable and involve trade-offs. One such trade-off involves performing more motion extrapolation using predictive tracking to reduce latency, but this would run the risk of overshooting the actual tracker positions (for example, a movement of the mallet towards the virtual drum surface might cause the sound of the drum to be heard even if the user stops the movement in midswing before reaching the drum with the mallet). This system allows the designer to easily adjust the parameters. Here is an account by Burgess (1994b) of total latency and its causes:

> Polhemus latency: 100 ms
> Comment: This delay is inherent in the tracker technology we're using. Faster tracking systems are available, but they're more expensive.
>
> Latency due to buffering between threads within the demo software: 50 ms
> Comment: Smaller buffers result in break-up of the signal during periods of high activity, because the buffers run empty in the time it takes to compute new filter and synthesizer parameters.
>
> Latency due to buffering in the audio device driver: 140 ms (average)
> Comment: If unchecked, the audio device driver's buffering latency can be as much as 5 seconds. We used a "hack" to periodically check the number of buffered audio samples and busy-wait when the buffer held more than 140 ms worth of data. Busy-waiting was controlled by a periodic signal from the Polhemus polling thread. Since we received this signal only once every 100 ms, we couldn't afford to let the buffer drain more than this amount. We're working on a better latency control scheme, which should allow us to shave about 100 ms from this latency.
>
> Motion extrapolation: 50 ms
> Comment: Motion extrapolation was first-order. We used a fast clock to time-tag tracker

samples and estimate tracker velocity. To extrapolate motion, we just multiply velocity by the extrapolation time. There are some much better extrapolation schemes, but we didn't have time to implement them. These better schemes could buy us another 50 ms to 100 ms.

Total latency: 100 ms + 50 ms + 140 ms − 50 ms = 240 ms
Comment: If you want actual sample counts, the sample rate was 32 kHz, so 50 ms = 1,600 samples and 140 ms = 4,480 samples. The /dev/audio buffers appear to be nearly a megabyte in size.

This example demonstrates both some trade-offs and the need to evaluate total system latency. The largest source of latency in this example, buffering in the audio device driver, might not have been predicted before the system was prototyped.

Once you objectively measure the total system latency, you can compare it to the requirements specified for responsiveness. In addition, you might expect latency, if it's a problem, to affect measurements of usability and value for the task/application, so keep this in mind in interpreting those measurements if you find significant latency when evaluating a prototype.

Display Update Rate

Display update rate is the frequency with which successive visual images appear on the display. Although display update rate contributes to total latency, it should be examined individually as well. Especially in visual displays, where insufficient display update can create the effect of a series of still pictures rather than the fusion of a continuous animated scene, the update rate might be a problem apart from its effect on latency and should, like latency, be measured under a range of conditions, including those that tax the computational resources of the rendering engine.

Synchronizing Spatial and Temporal Cues

First, a caveat about this requirement: real-world cues aren't perfectly temporally synchronized, either objectively or perceptually. Because light travels more quickly than sound, for example, the image of an event generally reaches an observer before the sound of the event, especially if the event is distant. When you take into account the time involved in perceptually processing different stimuli, the situation becomes even more complex. For a good account of this issue, I direct you to Piantanida (1994), who points out that, from a perceptual point of view, "real time" can even be negative since, for example, an expectation of movement can cause perceived visual effects prior to the movement itself. An example where the discrepancy is obvious in the real world is when you see distant lightning before hearing the associated thunder.

With these factors in mind, synchronization of spatial and temporal cues is still a system performance issue, but *synchronization* should generally be interpreted in terms of the user's perception. Two exceptions to this would be in some offline training and rehearsal applications that require the timing of stimuli to match real-world timing rather than perceptually synchronous timing, and in some online performance tasks with teleoperated robots, where simply presenting transduced cues as quickly as possible is sufficient.

Robustness and Fault Tolerance

Robustness is highly application-specific. First, the metrics pertinent to robustness must be defined for the application in question, which has to do with the environment in which the application will be used and the nature of the users. Metrics include robustness in the face of load (e.g., heavy processing through simultaneous demands by multiple users or a great deal of simultaneous input from multiple devices), adverse environmental conditions (cold, heat, humidity, vibration, and radiation), and use/misuse. A system's weak links in terms of robustness might also be in the interrelationship between components or in individual components themselves. An example faced by those who presently exhibit virtual environment systems to the public (such as museums and conference exhibitors) is that individual components of the transducer and effector subsystems, such as HMDs and instrumented gloves, aren't designed and manufactured to meet the demands and abuse by the public. An HMD costing many thousands of dollars can be destroyed if it's dropped, and an instrumented glove might not withstand more than a couple of days of use in such conditions.

Fault tolerance isn't generally a feature of virtual environment systems at present, but will be required for real deployment of applications such as telepresence surgery. You can use simulated system problems (crashes, network failures, and misuse that puts the system into undesirable states) to evaluate the fault tolerance, though admittedly it's difficult to foresee and simulate all potential problems.

Registration

Although registration was previously discussed in the context of position tracking, registration in relationship to total system performance might involve additional cumulative inaccuracies. Recalling that I defined *registration* as the relationship between real and reported position and orientation in the context of position trackers, on a system level you can consider registration to be the relationship between where objects *should* be displayed and where they *are* displayed. Thus, not only inaccuracies in tracking but also inaccuracies introduced algorithmically and via display technologies (such as optical distortion in HMDs) contribute to cumulative inaccuracies in registration.

Perhaps the two most demanding types of systems in terms of registration are teleoperation systems and augmented reality systems. In teleoperation systems, inaccuracies in registration can produce a situation where the user, in response to displayed information, makes a movement in space and, due to registration inaccuracies, the teleoperated robot makes a movement to a somewhat different position in space, with potentially catastrophic results (e.g., in the case of telepresence surgery). In augmented reality systems, inaccuracies in registration will cause synthetic information (such as computer-generated graphical images) to be misaligned with real information (such as a visual image of the real world viewed through a see-through HMD); if this problem is sufficiently bad, the system could be unusable. You can measure system registration by comparing the location of objects as they should be displayed and objects as they are displayed, with the particular measurement technique dependent on the type of system and display devices.

Working Volume

Although the working volume of a system is closely related to the working volume of its position tracker, total working volume should be evaluated if it's different. Factors that can make total working volume different than that of the individual position tracker include using multiple position trackers or multiple sensors, or emitters distributed through the area to enlarge the working volume, and using limited-distance transmission media (tethered cables or wireless transmission) between transducers/effectors and the rest of the system.

Questions

- How can you determine whether latency found in a prototype will be present in the final deployed system?
- Were you surprised by the analysis of latency and its causes in the Virtual Drum Kit? What lessons can be learned from this analysis?
- How can you objectively determine how well force cues and visual cues are synchronized spatially and temporally? Would a subjective evaluation of this suffice?
- Take an application of your choice and list all the challenges it would pose to system robustness. How can you test how well the system would handle each of these challenges? Are there any that couldn't adequately be tested in the prototype stage?

Chapter 10

Usability

Early predictions that virtual reality would make the interface vanish and spell the end of usability problems were clearly overly optimistic. Anyone who watches a novice user first try to use a haptic device or instrumented glove to navigate in a virtual environment will get a first-hand glimpse of the usability problems that remain. Like other human-computer interfaces, evaluating usability, including error rates, workload, task completion, and learning, can contribute to improved design. In addition, usability issues unique to virtual environments, in particular cybersickness, should be evaluated. The usability evaluation approaches I'll discuss in this chapter are summarized in Table 10.1.

Evaluation Processes

Several approaches have been used to evaluate the usability of human-computer interfaces and these can generally be applied to virtual environment systems, although few currently have. These approaches include empirical evaluation, analytic modeling, and techniques such as heuristic evaluation and cognitive complexity analysis (Kieras and Polson 1985). Because the analytic modeling approaches generally haven't been validated for users performing tasks with virtual environment interfaces, they're more of a research area than an applicable group of evaluation tools at present.

For now, empirical evaluation is the most useful and reliable approach for evaluating the usability of virtual environments. When prototyping the virtual environment, you can bring representative users in for a lab study, in which they attempt to complete designated tasks with the system. Techniques you can use include videotape analysis, automatic data collection, think-aloud protocol, Likert-like questionnaires, open-ended interviews, and physiological monitoring. You can measure simulator-like sickness (cybersickness), error rates, workload, task completion rates and times, subjective response, learning (and learning time), and retention of acquired knowledge about the interface over the course of time. First I'll discuss the techniques.

TABLE 10.1 Usability Evaluation Approaches

	Real-time observation by experimenter	Videotape analysis	Think-aloud protocol	Automation data collection	Likert-like questionnaires	SWAT (subjective workload assessment technique) scales	SSQ (simulator sickness questionnaire)	Open-ended interviews	Physiological monitoring and testing
Task completion	Good, unless tasks are completed too quickly to record	Excellent	N/A	Excellent	N/A	N/A	N/A	N/A	N/A
Error rates	Fair to poor (if errors occur, they will often be too rapid to record)	Excellent	N/A, except useful for clarifying user intent	Good if error can be pulled out of data	N/A	N/A	N/A	N/A, except useful for clarifying user intent	N/A
Time to complete task	Possible	Excellent	N/A	Excellent if there is a way to detect start of task	N/A	N/A	N/A	N/A	N/A
Learning	Good	Good	Good	Good	Good at identifying subjective impression of ease of learning	N/A	N/A	Can be used to note whether learning is seen as difficult	N/A

Workload	N/A unless workload experiment (e.g., dual task) is included	N/A unless workload experiment (e.g., dual task) is included	N/A	N/A	N/A	Excellent	N/A	N/A	Very good if correct factors are measured
Supports novices and experts	Good (some subjects must use system enough to gain expertise)	Good (some subjects must use system enough to gain expertise)	Good (some subjects must use system enough to gain expertise)	Good (some subjects must use system enough to gain expertise)	Good (some subjects must use system enough to gain expertise)	N/A	N/A	Good (some subjects must use system enough to gain expertise)	N/A
Subjective response by user	Some subjective response might be observed, though this is not the purpose	Some subjective response might be observed, though this is not the purpose	Some subjective response might be observed, though this is not the purpose	N/A	Excellent	N/A (except as applied to workload)	N/A	Excellent	N/A
Cyber-sickness	Fair (only severe cases can be noted; ataxia can be noted afterwards)	Fair (only severe cases can be noted)	Fair (only in severe cases will user interrupt verbal protocol)	N/A	N/A	N/A	Excellent	Users can mention symptoms if they were sufficiently severe	Excellent if correct factors are measured

TABLE 10.1 Usability Evaluation Approaches (Continued)

	Real-time observation by experimenter	Videotape analysis	Think-aloud protocol	Automation data collection	Likert-like questionnaires	SWAT (subjective workload assessment technique) scales	SSQ (simulator sickness questionnaire)	Open-ended interviews	Physiological monitoring and testing
Other physiological aftereffects	Possible if postsession observation is part of experimental protocol	N/A	N/A	N/A	N/A	N/A	SSQ focus is on cyber-sickness, though other aftereffects might be noted	Fair (for subjective self-assessment of symptoms)	Excellent
Ideas for improvements	N/A	N/A	N/A unless they arise in user's comments	N/A	N/A	N/A	N/A	Excellent	N/A

Videotape analysis

By videotaping representative users carrying out tasks in the prototyped virtual environment system, you can go back and review the tapes to collect objective data that occurs too quickly in real time to be noted. This includes data on the errors that users make, choices made when there are multiple ways to complete a task, the success of users in completing a task and the time required to do so, verbal self-reports by users, and the learning that occurs as subsequent tasks are performed with the interface.

I've found that, on occasion, the library of evaluation videotapes created during the course of the iterative design process has proven useful for studying an aspect of the human-computer interaction that proves to be important, even though I didn't attend to it at the start of the study. Another practical point to keep in mind is that videotapes should capture not only the users as they perform the tasks, but also the virtual environment as experienced by the users, and that the evaluation system should allow easy synchronization of these captured materials for a subsequent review. SMPTE time-stamping the videotapes from a common SMPTE time-code generator is recommended for this.

Automatic data collection

Automatic data collection requires that the virtual environment system itself capture information about the user's interaction. For example, a trace of the user's position tracker, instrumented glove, and haptic input device data can be saved. This trace can then determine errors and task completion rates, although it's particularly useful for time-related events (e.g., task completion times), as it saves you from having to transcribe and determine these from videotape.

Since the system has to calculate the user's position and orientation in the environment, user-object collisions, and other interactions anyway, capturing this information from the system allows you to more efficiently determine some measures. However, two issues to consider with respect to automatic data collection are:

- How difficult will it be to design and implement software that analyzes the copious generated data, and how well can the user's high-level actions be derived from this raw data?

- Is there a way to automatically collect this data without placing a burden on the VE hardware that could affect system performance (e.g., latency) and consequently affect user behavior?

Think-aloud protocol

Although there has been much criticism of classical introspective verbal reports, think-aloud protocol avoids many of these problems. Users verbalize their thoughts and experiences with the human-computer interface as they occur. The think-aloud approach avoids problems associated with keeping thoughts in memory or retrieving them from memory after the fact.

Three general criticisms of this approach are the effect-of-verbalization argument, the incompleteness argument, and the epiphenomenality or irrelevance argument.

The first posits that verbalizing about a task as it's performed requires some of the user's cognitive resources and therefore changes the nature of the task itself. The second argues that the user might fail to verbalize much of the information passing through short-term memory that's significant in performing the task. The third argument is that the user might verbalize activities that occur in parallel with the task but that aren't relevant to it (Ericsson and Simon 1984). In spite of these criticisms, the think-aloud approach is of value if useful information can be acquired through it, such as disambiguations of users' intentions, which aren't possible by simply observing the users as they attempt to perform a task.

The think-aloud approach could be particularly problematic, however, when applied to some types of virtual environments. Thinking aloud might mask or distract the user from the auditory component of systems that use a virtual acoustic display. Thinking aloud will almost certainly interfere with the speech recognition component of a virtual environment system (as it will with communicating verbally with other users in a multiuser VE system). This protocol isn't particularly suited to perceptual and motor tasks, where users tend to neither be aware of nor verbalize lower-level thought processes. Finally, I speculate that users in virtual environments make particularly high use of their resources, which makes the effect-of-verbalization problem a larger one than it is for many other tasks.

Likert-like questionnaires

Likert-like questionnaires are rating scales with which users retrospectively express their subjective satisfaction with specified aspects of the human-computer interface. Typically, users circle numbers (such as 0–10), for example to rate an item such as ease of learning the interface. Responses might be requested to the following sorts of questions:

```
Learning to operate the system:
difficult                                              easy
0     1     2     3     4     5     6     7     8     9     10

You can navigate in the virtual environment in a straightforward manner:
never                                                  always
0     1     2     3     4     5     6     7     8     9     10

Selecting an object in the virtual environment and determining that the object
has been selected:
difficult                                              easy
0     1     2     3     4     5     6     7     8     9     10

Remembering the names and using speech commands:
difficult                                              easy
0     1     2     3     4     5     6     7     8     9     10
```

A Likert-like questionnaire that has been studied for reliability is the Questionnaire for User Interface Satisfaction (QUIS) created at the Human-Computer Interaction Laboratory at the University of Maryland (Chin, Diehl, and Norman 1988). Although many of its questions are aimed at typical screen-based human-computer interfaces (and aren't applicable to virtual environment tasks), a colleague and I have adapted it for use with a speech recognition-based interface, and I believe it could serve as a good model for a questionnaire that evaluates user subjective response to a virtual environment system.

Two things to keep in mind when using this type of Likert-like scale are that it's better at capturing users' higher-level subjective impressions than details of the human-computer interaction (which users might not be aware of), and it can be used only after the fact and hence relies on users' memories—so they might not recall certain things, or might be especially influenced either by the last interactions that occurred before filling out the questionnaire or by atypical interactions that are especially memorable.

Open-ended interviews

In open-ended interviews, the evaluator asks some prepared open-ended questions that let users express observations and subjective comments that wouldn't be captured with a Likert-like questionnaire. The evaluator can ask follow-up questions in response to the users' answers to further elicit their impressions. It's important for the evaluator to convey a sense of impartiality rather than advocacy to users so they feel comfortable expressing both positive and negative criticisms of the interface (this attitude on the part of the evaluator is actually important throughout the evaluation, and encourages full expression by users in think-aloud and questionnaire response, as well). Users can also suggest solutions as well as expressing problems during open-ended interviews.

Physiological monitoring

Physiological monitoring is an adjunct to the methods of assessing usability described previously. You can monitor pupil dilation, galvanic skin response, heart rate, respiration, blood pressure, and other physiological signs to detect stress, pleasure or displeasure, and signs of simulator-like sickness. Many of these measures require somewhat intrusive or distracting technologies, however, which emphasizes the difference between the laboratory evaluation environment and the environment in which the system will really be used.

Alternatives to usability studies

There are a variety of alternatives to laboratory usability studies that have been developed to assess the usability of conventional human-computer interfaces. None have yet been used successfully to assess the usability of virtual environments, so I'll just describe them briefly, as techniques that could become practical in the future.

Analytic models have been used to predict the performance of conventional human-computer interface operators, such as telephone operators, while they're using workstations and simultaneously interacting with customers. Building on the work of Card, Moran, and Newell (1983), these modeling techniques include CPM-GOMS (critical path method goals, operators, methods, and selection rules), EPIC, and SOAR. They predict different things; CPM-GOMS predicts the time required for experts to complete well-practiced tasks, while SOAR uses production rules in order (among other things) to model learning. In order to be applied successfully to predicting performance of users in virtual environment systems, these techniques require more research and understanding of how users interact with the systems.

Other approaches, such as heuristic evaluation, assume that human factor experts can identify many of the usability problems with an interface simply by looking at it and considering its design in terms of established principles. But there's more that must be understood about human factor issues pertinent to virtual environments before such procedures can be used with any reliability for virtual environments. (For this reason, these alternatives are not included in Table 10.1).

Factors to Measure

In evaluating usability, you must determine whether users can complete tasks using the VE system. You'll want to examine their error rates in doing so, and perhaps how long it takes them to accomplish these tasks. You must also examine how easily and quickly they can learn to use the interface, and what workload it entails. You'll also want to examine how experts use the interface compared to novices, and how users feel subjectively about it. You should give users a chance to voice any ideas or suggestions for improvements, as these could be useful. And you should determine whether users experience cybersickness or any physiological after-effects.

Task completion

A most rudimentary but important measure to assess is whether representative users of the system can accomplish the tasks they're called upon to accomplish using a prototype of your design. When your system is deployed, will its real users have to read dense manuals explaining its use? If not, you should minimize the amount of explanatory materials you give the subjects of your evaluation; it's better to give them less (rather than more) written material than real users will have. If it's reasonable to expect them to accomplish tasks with no supporting written materials about using the interface, try having them use the interface with no explanatory materials. Expecting users to consult written manuals is particularly problematic in the case of virtual environments with visual displays (e.g., HMDs) that cut out the surrounding world, as the users have to repeatedly don and doff the display technology in order to read and then apply the materials from the manuals.

Will your system have a one-on-one human tutor to teach every one of its users how to use the VE interface? If not, it would be best for the evaluator in your usability studies not to coach the subjects, either. In the worst case, they could be coached only if they reach a total dead end in which they can't perform crucial tasks with the interface, and this should certainly be noted and should be a matter of concern to you as the designer.

Given an evaluation without coaching (unless it will always be present for new users of the deployed system) and a minimum of written support materials, task completion should be rather straightforward to measure. Provide the users in your study with a series of tasks (representative of what the system will really be used for), and make sure the evaluator records whether each of these tasks is attempted and completed. The evaluator can note this as the evaluation proceeds, or observe it after the fact by reviewing a videotape or analyzing automatically collected data. Anything less than very high task completion rates should be a cause for concern, especially if the system is expected to be usable by novices.

Errors

The evaluator can record errors as users attempt to complete tasks with the prototype, or after the fact through videotape analysis and automatic data collection. From personal experience, I'll warn you to be wary of trying to record all errors as the evaluation proceeds without having some backup mechanism (such as videotape) to record the process. Unlike task completion, which is usually quite easy to observe and record as an evaluation proceeds, errors sometimes happen in bursts and are difficult to reconstruct—and they're all the more so if the evaluator has to both observe users' actions and record errors.

Also, consider what you're classifying as an error prior to running subjects. A strict approach would consider an error to be any user action that doesn't move the user towards the goal state for the task being performed. This means that many actions that are exploratory and don't cause any subsequent problems are termed errors, and the evaluator must be able to assess the user's goal. Two ways to do this are to have a very highly structured evaluation process where users follow a predetermined set of instructions to accomplish an ordered set of tasks, and to get information from users (e.g., through verbal protocol analysis) about what they're trying to accomplish.

This approach to errors has an obvious shortcoming: it doesn't distinguish between user actions that simply don't advance the user towards the goal state and those that cause more severe difficulties. In an online performance task, more severe errors would include actions that cause damage to the teleoperated robot or to objects in the remote environment. In offline training and rehearsal tasks, more severe errors would include user actions that have adverse consequences in the real world, for example, injuring a patient in surgery or damaging a piece of equipment that the operator is attempting to repair. In any of the categories of tasks, a user action that puts the system into a state from which the user finds it difficult or impossible to recover would be a more severe error. Given the importance of these more severe types of errors, I recommend that, in addition to recording an overall error rate (e.g., "the user's error rate was 4.5% on a predetermined set of 12 tasks"), you also categorize the error types, paying special attention to the more severe errors.

Although the errors referred to here are user errors, the usability evaluation process permits a close examination of system performance, including performance when unforeseen sequences of (perhaps errorful) actions are taken. This can reveal implementation flaws that can then be fixed. If these implementation flaws interfere with user actions, they can confound the process of measuring user error rate (e.g., the system doesn't behave properly and users respond with actions that don't advance them towards the goal state). This is unfortunate if the experimenter is concerned with a carefully controlled study, but it's far preferable to discover system problems during the prototype/evaluation phase rather than when the system is deployed.

Task completion time

With many applications, task completion times are a less important factor to measure than are task completion rates or errors. In addition, there might be differences between the environment of the evaluation laboratory or site and the real environment in which the virtual environment will be used (as well as in the state of mind of the subjects being evaluated) that could make the task completion times measured during evaluations less than entirely indicative of what they would be for the deployed system. Given this, task completion time should probably be noted mainly to identify areas that cause users considerable confusion, to identify performance on time-crucial tasks if the application requires such tasks, and to note a decrease in task completion times as an indicator of learning. The best techniques for measuring task completion times are automatic data collection and transcription of time-stamped or time-coded videotape.

Learning

A subsequent section in this chapter, *Novice vs. expert behavior*, distinguishes between novices using a system and experts doing so. You should also evaluate a virtual environment application in terms of how well it supports learning to use the interface. While the learning involved is different than, for example, learning arcane UNIX commands, you can observe navigation, gestural and speech commands, and other aspects of interaction with the interface, and measure the learning.

Really well-designed systems can facilitate the transition from novice to expert. You can best evaluate the novice-expert shift by observing novices repeatedly using the system and noting how their behavior evolves and the problems they have in developing expert skills. You can measure the learning of general interface skills (e.g., navigating and making recognized gestures) and of application-specific knowledge and skills.

Workload

The concept of mental workload is much-studied, but there's considerable disagreement about its definition. Cognitive psychologist researchers want to assess and evaluate a class of difficulties experienced by users as they perform a task. The difficulties aren't those in which the user lacks the necessary knowledge, capabilities, or motivation required to perform the task, but rather those in which some aspects of the user-task interaction cause the demands of the task to exceed the user's capacity to deliver (Gopher and Donchin 1986). Human beings have a limited capacity to process and respond to information and, as a task is made more difficult, more of this capacity is used; if the demands of the task exceed this capacity, the performance will degrade.

Workload describes the amount of the user's capacity that's required to perform the task. These capacity-related performance decrements are believed to be caused by limitations of the human information processing system; attempts to model the human cognitive resources have produced several conceptual frameworks that are beyond the scope of this work to discuss. Nevertheless, to the extent that workload is measurable and consistent, it can be used as an empirical measure of interface design.

Note that, in the case of mental workload, *less* isn't necessarily better. Only in the case of tasks where workload is high enough to risk decrements in performance is it considered a crucial element of usability. The remainder of this section will discuss assessing the workload for tasks in which the workload experienced by the operator of the VE system is a crucial issue in the system's usability.

There are a very large number of techniques that have been developed to measure mental workload but, as O'Donnell and Eggemeier (1986) point out, most of them can be categorized as subjective measures, performance-based measures, and physiological measures. These measures vary in their appropriateness to different types of tasks and can be judged in terms of sensitivity, diagnosticity, intrusiveness, implementation requirements, and operator acceptance. I'll summarize them here with respect to their applicability to tasks in virtual environments. O'Donnell and Eggemeier (1986) offer an excellent overview of these techniques, and are the primary source for the remainder of this section.

Subjective measures rely on the assumption that users will experience increased capacity expenditure as requiring more effort or exertion, and be able to accurately report this experience on one of a variety of rating measures, known as *subjective workload assessment techniques* (SWAT) scales. Often, these are administered in the form of numerical scales or "card sorts," which are used to make comparative ratings. Although they've been found to be sensitive to different levels of capacity expenditure, they're poor at discriminating whether resources used are perceptual, motor, or what are termed "central processing." They're often administered after the task is completed and, when done in this way, are nonintrusive, simple to implement, and generally well-accepted by users. Other subjective measures include magnitude estimation and paired comparisons. Among the shortcomings of subjective techniques are that issues related to administering them, such as the delay between users performing a task and rating the workload associated with it, can influence the workload reported, and that several confounding factors, such as external demands and expectations, can influence the workload experienced by users.

Performance-based measures consist of primary task measures and secondary task methods. You can use primary task measures to judge whether or not users are experiencing an overload of capacity, and they're nonintrusive because users don't have to modify behavior in any way to accommodate them. But their diagnosticity is poor because they can be used only to determine whether there's overload, and not what part of the user's processing system is being overloaded. Secondary task methods require users to perform a subsidiary task in addition to the normal primary task. These dual-task measures are intrusive, but they can measure reserve capacity as well as determine the level of load on different components of the user's processing system.

Physiological measures, such as electroencephalograms (EEGs) and measuring pupil dilation, the static tension of muscles, and cardiac functions, vary in their intrusiveness, though they're generally less intrusive than dual-task measures. You can use them to assess workload in nonoverload situations, and some of them (e.g., EEGs) are thought to be able to discriminate, to some extent, the level of load on different components of the user's processing system.

Novice vs. expert behavior

Novices and experts typically use computer systems in very different ways, which is probably also the case with virtual environment systems, although research hasn't yet addressed the issue. I'm distinguishing between novices and experts here in terms of using the system, not in terms of task domain knowledge.

System designers have often become experts at using a system by the time it's prototyped and evaluated with representative users; they have a deep knowledge and understanding of the system that novices don't share, and it's often a real surprise to them to witness the usability problems experienced by novices.

Usability studies generally emphasize novice behavior, both for principled reasons (if novices can't successfully use the system, it might be a failure, since there won't be a body of users who can develop into experts), and for pragmatic ones (it's a simpler and less costly endeavor to bring in novices and observe their first use of a system than it is to get people to continue coming to the lab and using the system until they develop expertise).

This emphasis, however, might have the unfortunate side effect of encouraging systems that are easy for novices to use, but don't provide the functionality and shortcuts required for satisfactory use by experts. Most current virtual environment systems are designed for novices and don't offer greater functionality for experts (although the support of expertise could offer benefits; see, for example, Stuart 1993b). Systems should be evaluated in terms of their usability for both novices and experts, as well as how well they facilitate the acquisition of expertise.

Subjective impressions

Evaluations of interfaces often have as their focus objectively measurable criteria such as task completion rates and errors, but subjective impressions of users are worth collecting as well. In the case of some applications (e.g., entertainment), a virtual environment will never be used if its intended users don't find it subjectively appealing. For other applications, if users enjoy using a VE system, they might be more motivated to spend time with it; time on task, in turn, might result in learning and the development of greater skills, as noted in the section *Affect* in chapter 2.

Cybersickness

Cybersickness (simulator-like sickness) was discussed in chapter 3. Since theories of simulator sickness are still not sufficiently well developed to either predict whether it will occur or design virtual environment systems that entirely avoid the problem, you need to evaluate it with a prototyped system to determine its nature, severity, and impact on performance of the task. Kennedy et al. (1992) have designed a factor analysis scoring key, the Simulator Sickness Questionnaire, for evaluating cybersickness in terms of what they see as its three main components: oculomotor stress (eyestrain), nausea, and disorientation. Kennedy et al. also believe that the three main components are associated with different simulator problems, so the results of their questionnaire can point to interface areas that need improvement.

Other physiological after-effects

Among other physiological effects that are of concern are visual after-effects. Studies from the University of Edinburgh, for example, indicate that a commercially available HMD can harm vision (see the section *Visual Impairment* in chapter 3). One hypothesis is that these effects aren't intrinsic to HMDs, but are the result of improperly calibrating the HMD to the user's visual system (e.g., adjusting the interpupillary distance).

You must determine whether or not to evaluate visual and other physiological after-effects with a carefully calibrated system. I recommend that you consider how the system will really be used when making this decision. If users will typically use a poorly calibrated HMD, I recommend that you evaluate the effects of the system on them without making special adjustments to the HMD. On the other hand, if users have their own high-end HMDs that no one else will use and each HMD is very carefully calibrated to its user, similar calibration should be used during the evaluation.

Questions

- Create a Likert-like questionnaire for an online performance application. In what ways might this differ from a Likert-like questionnaire used for communication or entertainment applications?
- Why might think-aloud protocol be less obtrusive than physiological monitoring in some cases? What types of information might one method provide that the other wouldn't?
- If you're familiar with one of the analytic modeling techniques mentioned, what additional research would be necessary before it could reliably be used to predict performance of users in virtual environments?
- In what cases would it be useful to classify all actions that don't advance the user towards the goal state as errors? How would you decide what error rate is acceptable?
- Why might it be especially challenging to find a subsidiary task to use for secondary task method assessment of workload in a virtual environment? What kinds of subsidiary tasks might be viable?
- Give examples of interaction techniques that would be valuable for experts but inappropriate for novice users of a VE. Are there any of these a novice could perform by accident? If so, should such accidents be prevented? How?
- Do you agree that a poorly calibrated HMD should be used in evaluations if that's what will typically be available to real users? Why or why not?
- Can you think of other ways for users to contribute ideas for improving a system besides the methods outlined in this chapter?

Chapter 11

Value for Task and Application

In order to evaluate the value of a virtual environment system for the application for which it's designed, it's necessary to first define criteria on which the value will be judged. Since a task analysis will already have been done during the process of defining requirements, one approach is to evaluate the system by analyzing its success for each subtask. In the example earlier in the book of a virtual environment system for individual combat training (see the section *Application-Specific Requirements* at the end of chapter 3), you could judge, on a requirement-by-requirement basis, whether the system supported the task. For example, the system was "highly successful at training assessment of physical terrain with respect to cover and concealment, highly successful at training the reading of navigation aids, moderately successful for practicing communication among trainees, not successful at training control and manipulation of weapons," and so forth.

A shortcoming of this subtask-by-subtask approach to evaluating the value of the system for the application is that it assumes, in some cases mistakenly, that users will do things the same way they have in the past, only somewhat better because of the virtual environment system. This approach misses the mark when the system is valuable for the application because users can do things with it that they couldn't do before or accomplish tasks in ways they couldn't previously. Take, for example, a visualization system for network planning that permits planners to base decisions on types of information that weren't previously available or that couldn't previously be understood, e.g., due to volume and complexity. With such a system, they might be able to make better planning decisions, and it would be a mistake to evaluate the value of the system simply on how it helped them accomplish subtasks they already perform.

Note two other problems regarding evaluation of the value of the system for the application. First, a laboratory evaluation, though it can assess system performance and usability quite well, might not give the entire picture when it comes to assessing the value for the application. To complete the picture, it might be necessary to observe the system in real use in the real work setting. Yet there are often good reasons not to deploy an unfinished product in a real work setting, especially if there are still system performance and usability problems to be solved. I recommend that, once the prototype performs acceptably and is usable, you run a very small-scale "friendly user" field trial, if possible, to further evaluate the value for the application.

The second problem is that value for the application means very different things for different task domains. Therefore, I'll briefly discuss assessing a system's value for each category of application. Even within each category, however, criteria for this value is highly application-specific.

Online Performance

For online performance applications, many of the measures of value are immediate. Can the teleoperator successfully control the remote robot and use it to complete repairs in a hazardous (e.g., undersea or radioactive) location, and is the time necessary to train such an operator reduced? Can the surgeon perform a telepresence surgery operation on a remote patient as well or better than available local surgeons? Do the repairpeople using augmented reality displays repair the telephone crossboxes more quickly and with fewer errors than their colleagues who aren't using augmented reality systems? Can a user with motor and sensory disabilities use a synesthetic display and biocontrol transducers to better perform navigation and control tasks in the real world?

Other possible benefits are less immediately measurable. An example would be whether the long-term health of teleoperators controlling remote robots to clean up hazardous waste sites is better than that of their colleagues who are doing the cleanup on-site and wearing protective gear.

Offline Training and Rehearsal

Offline training and rehearsal applications should be evaluated primarily in terms of positive and negative transfer. After using the virtual environment system to practice a task, does the user perform the task better in the real world than others who haven't trained in the virtual environment? Does training in the virtual environment produce better real-world performance than alternative training approaches? Is the safety higher and is the cost of training in the virtual environment lower than alternatives? Are there negative impacts of alternative training approaches that training in the virtual environment doesn't incur? Are there any negative effects of training in the virtual environment on real-world performance?

Online Comprehension

Online comprehension applications aren't always easy candidates for controlled study, but they should be evaluated primarily in terms of giving insight to the user and facilitating the user's understanding of the subject domain. In the case where the experimenter has a set of data from which certain known insights should be drawn, you can run a laboratory study that compares users of the virtual environment system exploring the data with others who are exploring the data in other ways. Such a controlled study can examine how many of the insights each group arrives at, how much time it takes to reach these insights, and how the members of each group understand the data.

It's less clear that online comprehension applications can be evaluated in terms of data for which the desired insights aren't already known. How would you determine whether or not a molecular visualization system gives a biochemist insight into a possible new cancer-fighting drug without letting chemists spend extensive time using the system?

Offline Learning and Knowledge Acquisition

Like online comprehension, you can evaluate offline learning and knowledge acquisition applications in terms of the insight they give users of the system compared to a control group who doesn't use the virtual environment. The difficulty in evaluating offline learning and knowledge acquisition applications is that users might require extensive use of the system in order to synthesize the cumulative experience and understanding. Evaluating these applications, then, should involve users returning to the laboratory repeatedly to use the system over an appropriate length of time, and subsequent evaluation of the abstractions the users have formulated from the experience.

Online Design

For an online design application, the success of the application can be judged by whether it allows its users to do their jobs better. In other words, if the users of the system come up with better designs using the system than they do without it (or they come up with equally good designs more quickly), the value of the application is demonstrated. In terms of evaluating online design applications, the challenge is getting representative users to tackle a real though tractable design problem in the evaluation session, or finding "toy" problems that will meaningfully measure the usefulness of the application for real design tasks.

Entertainment

Entertainment applications are far different to evaluate than the other categories described in this section. The sole value of the system is for users to enjoy themselves while using it. Evaluation in this case is more in the marketing domain than in the scientific domain. Will users pay to use (or purchase) this system? How much? Does the system continue to give them enjoyment after repeated use? What can be done to make it more enjoyable?

Communication

The difficulty in evaluating the value of a virtual environment system in facilitating communication is that communicating with new media often develops in unforeseen ways. In order to truly judge the value of such a system, it's necessary to let people use it over the course of time and to observe the patterns of behaviors and usage that develop. A laboratory evaluation can judge how well the system supports people communicating in a certain way about a given task, but it can't predict these evolving behaviors and uses. This is a case, therefore, where an extended field trial, with participants who want to communicate with each other for a variety of purposes, is an appropriate approach in evaluating the system.

Tools for Researching Human Perceptual-Motor Capabilities

The value of a virtual environment system that's designed to conduct research on human perceptual-motor capabilities should be evaluated in terms of its ability to control, at the appropriate level of precision, the variables that are being researched, and facilitate good data collection by the researcher. Although there might be a tendency to evaluate the system in terms of the first particular experiment for which it's used, there are two other longer-term factors you need to evaluate in order to judge its value for related tasks. First, since such a system can be used to study different characteristics of human performance, you need to consider the flexibility in applying it to other studies. Second, because the psychologists using the system for research won't necessarily be, or have constant access to, strong programmers, you need to consider the ease of adjusting variables and modifying prototypes with the system.

Questions

- Return to the application-specific task analysis you performed after chapter 3 and describe how to evaluate a prototype on a task-by-task basis for this application.
- Which categories of application seem best suited to a value-for-the-task evaluation in the prototype stage? Would some categories require a field trial for this evaluation?
- How could you evaluate positive and negative transfer in an offline training and rehearsal application if the task being trained is hazardous?
- Do you agree that online comprehension applications are difficult to evaluate if the insights they're designed to help reveal aren't already known? How could you evaluate such a system?

Chapter

12

Using the Results of the Evaluation

Evaluating the prototype will reveal information about system performance, usability, and value for the task/application, which can be used in iterating the requirements definition/design/prototype phases of the iterative design process. Although Figure I.4 in the Introduction shows using the results of an evaluation to revise the definition of requirements, you can also use these results directly to modify the system design or redo the prototype. The challenge you'll face is to determine from the evaluation results what to revise and how to revise it. In addition, you should establish performance that's considered acceptable for each area of evaluation; at the point the acceptable performance is achieved, the system can be developed past the prototype to the deployment stage. Even in the development for deployment, other forms of evaluation, such as field testing the beta version, can continue in order to confirm that the results of the laboratory evaluation are applicable to the deployed system in the user's real environment.

In the following sections, I'll present a sampling of some possible evaluation findings and how you can use them to revise the definition of requirements, the design of the system, and the implementation of the prototype.

System Performance

From one perspective, you need to use and act on the results of a system performance evaluation only to the extent that they impact the usability or value of the system for the application. System performance statistics will be cited, for example, when comparing competitive products (and this is certainly appropriate and necessary if the products are subsystems, such as position trackers, graphics engines, or DSP cards). But, for this discussion, I'll assume that the system performance evaluation has identified system problems that affect usability or value for the task/application (or are so obvious that it's clear that they will).

Total acceptable latency should be roughly predictable given the human performance issues discussed in chapter 2 and the nature of the tasks that must be performed. Different latencies can be tolerated in displays for different senses (to take an extreme case, a latency of several seconds that wouldn't be a problem in an olfactory display would be entirely unacceptable in a visual display). Different kinds of applications also have different demands with respect to latency. An online performance (e.g., teleoperation) application must have low enough latency that changes in the environment (whether caused by the remote robot or independent of it) can be detected and reacted to sufficiently quickly; an offline training and rehearsal application must have low enough latency that users can learn a skill without adapting to latency that would cause negative transfer in performing the skill in the real world. Other applications, such as different types of visualization, might be less demanding of low latency.

There's still a need, however, to evaluate the effects of latency in the context of a user working with a prototyped application. If the prototype's latency is sufficiently low to meet the functional requirements and the results of this evaluation show a need for lower latency, you can use these results to revise or refine the functional requirements (and, in turn, modify both the system design and the prototype). If the prototype doesn't meet the functional requirements for latency, you must determine whether it's the result of a problem in design or an artifact of the way the prototype was implemented (which won't be present in the deployed system).

Display update rates and synchronization of spatial and temporal cues should be rather straightforward to measure, and you should revisit design and implementation of the prototype if there are problems in these areas. Robustness and fault tolerance might be less simple to evaluate, but problems, as with those related to registration and working volume, should suggest that you analyze the causes of these problems, which in turn should indicate where redesign is needed.

Usability

Problems identified in the evaluation of usability might include the failure of users to complete tasks or an excessive time required to do so, errors, excessive workload, difficulties in learning to use the interface, failure to support expert as well as novice behavior, negative subjective impressions, cybersickness, and other physiological after-effects.

Unless system problems or prototype bugs interfere, failure to complete the task suggests problems in the design; note where users get stuck and give up, interview them to find out what misimpressions or confusions came into play, and modify the design accordingly. If task completion time is excessively high, identify whether instructions are unclear to users or if they're having perceptual/motor difficulties with tasks, and modify the design accordingly. The nature and frequency of errors can suggest whether there are problems with choice of representation, interaction techniques, or the user's understanding of the task. Workload-related problems should suggest that the amount required of the user is too great in terms of working memory, information to be perceived, or time-crucial tasks to accomplish. If users become dissatisfied as they acquire expertise, you can interview them and find out what features they think would be desirable for expert users and what qualities of the virtual environment become annoying or frustrating over the course of time. You can also observe the transition between novice and expert behavior, which might help you see ways to facilitate learning and the novice-to-expert shift. Note instances of cybersickness and other physiological after-effects if they occur. If cybersickness is a problem, consult Kennedy et al. (1992) to identify which of the main components of cybersickness are present, use this knowledge to identify the cause of the cybersickness, and change the system to mitigate the problem.

Value for the Task and Application

If an evaluation of the prototype shows less value than expected for the tasks and application for which the system is designed, it's crucial to understand why this is so. Is the system performance or usability interfering with the system's usefulness? In this case, you should either reassess the requirements or redesign the system, as discussed previously.

But what if system performance and usability aren't obstacles and the usefulness of the system is still not as great as expected? It's especially important to work closely with users in order to understand what's going on. Were there flaws in the task analysis that are only now revealed? In this case, users can help clarify these flaws and what's required to make the system more useful. Are there factors in the environment (physical, work, or social environment) that weren't revealed in the earlier analysis of user, task, and environment, but are proving to be obstacles in using the system? Again, the users themselves are the best source of clarification, and their feedback can help you determine what changes are needed to make the system more useful.

Finally, an evaluation might not reveal problems; it might, in fact, show that the system provides great benefits for the tasks and application. If any of the following are true:

- an online performance application permits tasks to be accomplished successfully in the real world
- an offline training and rehearsal system improves the user's performance of the practiced tasks when later performed in the real world
- an online comprehension system leads to an understanding or insight into the problem domain during the user's interaction with the system
- an offline learning and knowledge acquisition application produces useful knowledge and experience that's subsequently synthesized into abstract knowledge
- an online design application leads to improved designs of objects or environments
- an entertainment system provides enjoyment to its users
- a communication application facilitates the sharing of ideas or communication between its users
- an application for research on human perceptual-motor capabilities leads to new findings

then the goals of the application are achieved and the design has been proven a success. This is the most important test. Even some shortcomings, for example in system performance, can be tolerated if benefits for the tasks and application are revealed. You can then use the results of such a successful evaluation as needed to gain support, funding, and user buy-in for deployment of the system.

Questions

- The prototype crashes several times during evaluations, and you're concerned that these robustness problems might affect your deployed system. What should you do?
- Your evaluation reveals that users of your online performance system for teleoperation are experiencing workload-related difficulties. How can you use these results to improve the system?
- Can you think of a case where difficulties users experience navigating in the virtual world would prove beneficial for the application and shouldn't result in redesign?
- Users of your entertainment-oriented prototype find it very enjoyable to use, though many of their actions when using the system are in fact errors. Would you modify the system in hopes of reducing the error rate? Why or why not? What kinds of errors might concern you?

Chapter

13

Conclusion

I'll conclude this book with some comments on the design process, the design team, the tools and implementation technology, and areas for future research.

The Design Process

Designing should be iterative: define your requirements; design the system; create a prototype; evaluate; then revise the requirements, design, and prototype until the evaluation is satisfactory. There are still too many areas in need of further research to assume that you'll "get it right" the first time; in fact, you might need to revise even the specified requirements in response to observing system performance and user behavior.

Designing a successful virtual environment application is presently a difficult process; it requires both top-down and bottom-up design, since problems at any level can undermine the usability and value of the application. The iterative design approach lets you consider many factors (perceptual, motor, cognitive, and affective capabilities; nature of the user, task, and environment; and both requirements common to virtual environments and those that are task-specific) in specifying the requirements. You then use these requirement specifications when designing the system and subsequently selecting and purchasing or creating component technologies. Although you might need to revise the specifications and design in response to the results of evaluating a prototype with representative users, the process puts the designer "in the ballpark," and then offers guidance in what to look for when making revisions.

The Design Team

Experience in building virtual environments doesn't yet provide a clear prescription for the successful design team. On one hand, there are a very large set of skills required, in areas including computer graphics; digital signal processing; algorithms and code optimization; simulation; operating systems and computer architecture; perceptual psychology; human factors; electrical, optical, and mechanical engineering; modeling; designing graphical, auditory, and force displays, and knowledge of the application domain. This large set of skills suggests the value of large and very interdisciplinary design teams. On the other hand, Bryson (1994) has noted that the success of most virtual environment projects has been due to one or two people on the development teams mastering all levels of the system. Over the next several years, the cumulative experience of design teams around the world should be instructive in suggesting what kinds of teams are successful in designing virtual environments.

Tools and Implementation Technology

Currently available tools and technologies for implementing virtual environments are in a relatively primitive state, which makes the implementation process especially difficult. Designing a successful virtual environment application involves finding a way to effectively use currently available technologies with all their limitations in order to usefully solve some problem or accomplish some task. Some of these limitations are:

- Position trackers with small working volumes, inadequate robustness, and problems of latency and poor registration
- HMDs with very poor resolution, somewhat limited FOV, and encumbering form factor
- Virtual acoustic displays that require a great deal of computational resources to simulate a small number of sources with even simple modeling of first-order reverberation
- Force and tactile displays, which are in their infancies, with limited functionality
- Image generators that can't provide low-latency rendering of head-tracked complex scenes and thus require severe trade-offs between performance and scene complexity
- Limited real-time capabilities of operating systems in widespread use
- Inadequate software development tools and environments

As these limitations and problems with current technologies are solved, some of the obstacles to virtual environment design and implementation will be removed. There will still be difficult design decisions, but the overhead in building prototypes to try out alternatives will be reduced.

The current common practice of building and modifying virtual environments by writing code with a text editor, compiling the code (which, in the case of complex environments, can be rather time-consuming), running the code only to find an obvious problem with the virtual environment, returning to the text editor to modify the code, recompiling, and so on is especially inefficient. Creating objects in different packages and importing them in a format that's compatible with the virtual environment application development software is also time-consuming. It will be interesting to see whether improvements in visual programming languages lessen the problems noted by Bletter (1993) and whether systems that permit development of virtual environments from within the environment fulfill the promise they appear to offer.

Future Research and Development

In terms of development, it has become a cliché to say that the VisiCalc of virtual environments—an application that so clearly and compellingly proves its value for a task of importance to a large number of people that it spurs major efforts at improving and commercializing the technology—has not yet been found. Perhaps there won't be a single such application that drives the development of virtual environment systems, but instead, a variety of specialized applications (e.g., surgical training, controlling teleoperated robots in hazardous environments, and financial visualization) that prove valuable.

Alternately, it's possible that such a large market will develop for entertainment applications that they'll spur the creation and mass production of much improved component technologies at greatly reduced costs, and the availability of these technologies will promote their use in a variety of applications, even those where their added value is small (like using color monitors for conventional screen-based computer systems). Still another possibility is that virtual environment systems could entirely change the way most of us work together and learn, and that major paradigm shifts in the way computer-supported cooperative work and education are carried out could affect beyond what we imagine when we think of specific applications. Balancing these optimistic views is the possibility that VE systems will prove to have limited usefulness for many potential applications because of persistent problems, for example, with cybersickness.

Although this speculation suggests that not a single future for virtual environment applications can be foreseen, a great deal of further research in many areas is required for any of the scenarios. Much of this research, which has been alluded to throughout the book as I've discussed different aspects of the design process, will have practical consequences to VE designers of the future. The areas for this research include perceptual, motor, and cognitive psychology; system architecture; input and display technology; networking; many types of software that have been discussed; and how to best design virtual environments for specific applications. Specific examples of these areas include:

- Efficient algorithms for sound synthesis and computer graphics
- High-performance rendering engines
- Real-time systems
- Communication protocols
- Distributed interactive simulations
- Numerous human factor issues (described further in Stuart, 1993a)

- More robust tracking technology that supports lower-latency, higher-resolution, better registration tracking in larger working volumes
- Improved display technologies including higher-resolution image sources
- Improved optics for HMDs
- Improved force and tactile display technologies
- Improved application programmer interfaces with toolkits that offer cross-platform compatibility

In addition, the development of more successful applications will provide further insights into task-specific requirements. For an entire book that outlines areas for future research, see the National Research Council Committee on Virtual Reality Research and Development's report (Durlach, N.I. and Mavor, A.S., eds. 1995).

Although there have been a few leaps forward in the field of virtual environments (with Ivan Sutherland's early work a prime example), much of the progress is incremental. I sincerely hope that you find useful information and ideas in this book that help you both design successful applications and systems, and make original contributions that help advance the field.

Appendix

This appendix provides pointers to sources of currently available VE technologies. They're listed in the order of vendors carrying hardware components, software, then finally complete VE systems. The list isn't exhaustive, but intended as a starting point for those who want more information on specific products. Because the state of the technology is changing rapidly, I haven't included the details and specifications of current models here. For current information, you can contact the vendors listed in this appendix for their latest product information.

Updated Information

You can also contact me for periodically updated information in a variety of forms (including electronic). These include a very extensive bibliography of VE literature (it's fast-growing and would already have filled more than half the size of this book), contact information for VE researchers and developers, and information about commercially available VE technologies and who manufactures them. I'll send you a list of what's available, when it was last updated, prices, and available formats if you send a self-addressed stamped envelope marked "list of available VE updates" to me at:

Rory Stuart
P.O. Box 391
Pomona, NY 10970-0391
USA

I invite you to send any comments, corrections, requests, or suggestions to me at this address as well.

Consider the Specifications Carefully

It's important that, in some cases, you don't accept the specifications provided by vendors uncritically. For example, Adelstein, Johnson, and Ellis (1992) found dynamic response performance by position trackers that's quite unlike the static response provided by vendors, by using a procedure they developed for testing the devices with a motorized rotary swing arm. For many applications, the dynamic response performance is more pertinent than static response to your wisely selecting a tracker.

Unfortunately, although there have been a few rigorous independent studies testing the specifications of certain commerically available VE products (such as Adelstein et al), in many cases the only source of information is the vendor specifications, which, as noted, you should read with a critical eye.

Position Trackers
Mechanical

Shooting Star Technology
52023 Yale Road, RR1
Rosedale, B.C.
VOX 1X0 Canada
Phone: 604-794-3364
Fax: 604-794-3139
Contact: Bill Chernoff

Magnetic

Polhemus Laboratories, Inc.
1 Hercules Drive
P.O. Box 560
Colchester, VT 05446
Phone: 802-655-3159
Fax: 802-655-1439
Contact: James C. Krieg

Ascension Technology Corp.
P.O. Box 527
Burlington, VT 05402
Phone: 802-860-6440
Fax: 802-860-6439
Contact: Jack T. Scully

Acoustic

Logitech
6505 Kaiser Drive
Fremont, CA 94555
Phone: 510-795-8500
Fax: 510-792-8901
Contact: Ron McClure

Optical

Adaptive Optics Associates, Inc.
54 Cambridge Park Drive
Cambridge, MA 02140-2308
Phone: 617-864-0201
Fax: 617-864-5855

Instrumented Gloves and Suits

Virtual Technologies
2175 Park Blvd.
Palo Alto, CA 94306
Phone: 415-321-4900
Fax: 415-321-4912
Contact: Jim Kramer

Greenleaf Medical Systems
2248 Park Blvd.
Palo Alto, CA 94306
Phone: 415-321-6135
Fax: 415-321-0419
Contact: Walter Greenleaf

Abrams/Gentile Entertainment, Inc.
244 West 54th Street, 9th Floor
New York, NY 10019
Phone: 212-757-0700
Fax: 212-765-1987
Contact: Chris Gentile

VACTORs

SimGraphics Engineering Corp.
1137 Huntington Drive
S. Pasadena, CA 91030
Phone: 213-255-0900
Fax: 213-255-0987
Contact: Steve Glenn

Eye Trackers

ISCAN Inc.
125 Cambridgepark Drive
Cambridge, MA 02140
Phone: 617-868-5353
Fax: 617-868-9231
Contact: Alan Kielmar or Rikki Razdan

Applied Science Labs
335 Bear Hill Road
Waltham, MA
Fax: 617-890-7966
Contact: Chuck Valois

Biosignal Input

BioControl Systems, Inc.
430 Cowper Street
Palo Alto, CA 94301
Phone: 415-329-8494
Fax: 415-329-8498

Haptic Devices

Ball-type 3-D input devices

CIS Graphics, Inc.
18 Pelham Rd.
Salem, NH 03079
Phone: 603-894-5999
Contact: Sandra LaCoss

Spaceball Technologies, Inc.
600 Suffolk Street
Lowell, MA 01854
Phone: 508-970-0330

3-D mice

Gyration, Inc.
12930 Saratoga Ave.
Building C
Saratoga, CA 95070
(408)-255-3016

SimGraphics Engineering Corp.
1137 Huntington Drive
S. Pasadena, CA 91030
Phone: 213-255-0900
Fax: 213-255-0987
Contact: Steve Glenn

Logitech
6505 Kaiser Drive
Fremont, CA 94555
Phone: 510-795-8500
Fax: 510-792-8901
Contact: Ron McClure

Other 3-D input devices

Digital Image Design Inc.
170 Claremont Avenue
New York, NY 10027
Phone: 212-222-5236
Fax: 212-864-1189
Contact: Brad Paley

Speech Recognition

PureSpeech, Inc.
100 Cambridge Park Dr.
Cambridge, MA 02140
Phone: 617-441-0000
Fax: 617-441-0001
Contact: Benjamin Chigier

BBN
150 Cambridge Drive
Cambridge, MA 02140
Phone: 617-873-3000
Fax: 617-873-3776

Covox, Inc.
675 Conger St.
Eugene, OR 97402
Phone: 503-342-1271
Fax: 503-342-1283

Dragon Systems, Inc.
320 Nevada St.
Newton, MA 02160
Phone: 617-965-5200
Fax: 617-527-0372

Image Generators

Silicon Graphics Computer Systems
2011 N. Shoreline Blvd.
Mountain View, CA 94039-7311
Phone: 415-964-1980
Fax: 415-961-0595
Contact: Josh Mogal

Evans & Sutherland
600 Komas Drive
P.O. Box 59700
Salt Lake City, UT 84158
Phone: 801-582-5847
Fax: 801-582-5848
Contact: Jeff Edwards

Sun Microsystems
MS UMTV18-211
2550 Garcia Avenue
Mountain View, CA 94043
Phone: 415-336-3017
Fax: 415-336-1525
Contact: Mike Deering

HMDs

Virtual Research
3193 Belick Street, Suite #2
Santa Clara, CA 95054
Phone: 408-748-8712
Fax: 408-748-8714
Contact: Bruce Bassett

LEEP Systems Inc.
241 Crescent Street
Waltham, MA 02154
Phone: 617-647-1395
Fax: 617-647-1109
Contact: Eric Howlett

CAE Electronics Ltd.
A CAE Industries Ltd. Company
C.P. 1800 Saint Laurent
Quebec, Canada H4L 4X4
Phone: 514-341-6780
Fax: 514-341-7699

Appendix

Nissho Electronics Corp.
Advanced Electronics Systems Division
70301 Tsukiji, Chuo-ku
Tokyo 104
Japan
Phone: 81-3-3544-8452
Fax: 81-3-3544-8284

Liquid Image Corp.
659 Century Street
Winnepeg, Manitoba R3H OL9
Canada
Phone: 204-772-0137
Fax: 204-772-0239
Contact: Shannon O'Brien

n-Vision Inc.
7915 Jones Branch Drive
McLean, VA 22102
Phone: 703-506-8808
Fax: 703-903-0455

Kaiser Electro-Optics Inc.
2572 Loker Avenue W.
Carlsbad, CA 92008
Phone: 619-438-9255
Fax: 619-438-6875

RPI Advanced Technology Group
P.O. Box 14607
San Francisco, CA 94114
Phone: 415-495-5671
Fax: 415-495-5124

Virtual Reality Inc.
485 Washington Avenue
Pleasantville, NY 10570
Phone: 914-769-0900
Fax: 914-769-7106
Contact: Nelson Merritt

FORTE Technologies
1057 East Henrietta Rd.
Rochester, NY 14623
Phone: 716-427-8595
Fax: 716-427-8595
Contact: Paul Matthews

VictorMaxx Technologies
501 Lake Cook Road, Suite 100
Deerfield, IL 60015
Phone: 708-267-0007
Fax: 708-267-8669

Virtual I/O
100 Lenora Street, Suite 600
Seattle, WA 98121
Phone: 206-382-7410
Fax: 206-382-0570

W-Industries
Virtuality House
3 Iswin Road
Brailsford Industry Park
Leicester, LE1 5WD
United Kingdom
Phone: 0533 542 127
Contact: Jonathan Waldern

O.I.P. NV/SA
Westerring 21
B-9700 Oudenaarde
Belgium
Phone: 33-55-333-811
Fax: 33-55-316-895

General Reality Co.
170 S. Morrison Ave.
San Jose, CA 95126
Phone: 408-289-8340
Fax: 408-289-8258
Contact: Arthur Zwern

VRontier Worlds of Stoughton Inc.
809 E. South Street
Stoughton, WI 53589
Phone: 608-873-8523
Fax: 608-877-0575
Contact: Brad Burnett

Hughes Training Inc./Link Division
P.O. Box 1237
Binghamton, NY 13902-1237
Phone: 607-721-4356
Fax: 607-721-5600

BOOMs

Fake Space Inc.
4085 Campbell Avenue
Menlo Park, CA 94025
Phone: 415-688-1940
Fax: 415-688-1949
Contact: Mark Bolas

LEEP Systems Inc.
241 Crescent Street
Waltham, MA 02154
Phone: 617-647-1395
Fax: 617-647-1109
Contact: Eric Howlett

Shuttered Glasses

76StereoGraphics Corp.
2181 E. Francisco Blvd.
San Rafael, CA 94901
Phone: 415-459-4500
Fax: 415-459-3020
Contact: Wil Cochran

3D TV Corp.
Stereoscopic Video
Box Q
San Rafael, CA 94913-4316
Phone: 415-479-3516
Fax: 415-479-3316
Contact: Michael Starks

NuVision Technologies, Inc.
1815 NW 169th Place, Bldg. 3060
Beaverton, OR 97006
Phone: 503-614-9000
Fax: 503-614-9100

Tektronix Inc.
P.O. Box 500 MS 46-557
Beaverton, OR 97077
Phone: 503-627-6499
Fax: 503-627-1070

Binaural Audio Transducers

HEAD acoustics GmbH
Kaiserstrabe 100
D-5120 Herzogenrath 3
Germany
Phone: 2407-5770
Fax: 2407-57799

Virtual Acoustic Displays

Crystal River Engineering Inc.
12350 Wards Ferry Road
Groveland, CA 95321
Phone: 209-962-6382
Fax: 209-962-4873
Contact: Scott Foster

Bo Gehring
318 W. Galer St.
Seattle, WA 98119
Phone: 416-963-9188

Tactile Displays

Xtensory Inc.
140 Sunridge Drive
Scotts Valley, CA 95066
Phone: 408-439-0600
Fax: 408-439-8845
Contact: Paul S. Cutt

TiNi Alloy Co.
1144 65th St.
Oakland, CA 94608
Phone: 415-658-3172
Contact: A. David Johnson

Begej Corp.
5 Claret Ash Road
Little, CO 80127
Phone: 303-932-2186

TeleSensory
N. Bernardo Ave.
Mountain View, CA
Phone: 415-960-0920

Unitech Research, Inc.
702 N. Blackhawk Dr.
Madison, WI 53705
Phone: 608-238-5244

Thermal Displays

CM Research
2437 Bay Area Blvd. #234
Houston, TX 77058
Phone: 213-488-3598
Contact: Mike Zerkus

Force Displays

Force-feedback gloves

EXOS Inc.
2A Gill Street
Woburn, MA 01801
Phone: 617-933-0022
Fax: 617-933-0303
Contact: Beth Marcus

Advanced Robotics Research Ltd. , NARRC
University Road
Salford M5 4PP
United Kingdom
Phone: 44-61-745-7384
Contact: Robert J. Stone

Other force display devices

Cybernet Systems Corp.
1919 Green Road
Suite B-101
Ann Arbor, MI 48105
Phone: 313-668-2567
Fax: 313-668-8780
Contact: Heidi N. Jacobus

Immersion Corp.
3350 Scott Blvd. , Bldg. 30
Santa Clara, CA 94054
Phone: 408-653-1160
Fax: 408-654-9360
Contact: Louis Rosenberg

Motion Platforms

McFadden Systems, Inc.
11835 E. Smith Avenue
Santa Fe Springs, CA 90670
Phone: 310-948-4414
Fax: 310-948-1291
Contact: Michael B. Rogers

Trailcraft
Toronto, Canada
Phone: 905-450-1144
Contact: Barry Reed

Moog Inc.
Motion Systems Division
East Aurora, NY 14052-0018
Phone: 716-687-4000
Fax: 716-687-4467
Contact: Bill Egger

CineMotion International, Ltd.
29 High Street, HamptonWick
Kingston upon Thames, Surrey KT1 4DA
United Kingdom
Phone: 4481-943-5223
Fax: 4481-944-9991

Denne Developments Ltd.
7 Lyndon Gate, China Crest Road
Bournemouth BH2 SLW
United Kingdom
Phone: 0202-752206
Fax: 0202-769550

Sarcos
261 East 300 South, Suite 150
Salt Lake City, UT 84111
Phone: 801-531-0559
Fax: 801-531-0315

VE Toolkits and Simulation Software

Division Inc.
Suite 101 Seaport Court
Redwood City, CA 94063
Phone: 415-364-6067
Fax: 415-364-4663

Autodesk Inc.
2320 Marinship Way
Sausalito, CA 94964
Phone: 415-332-2344
Fax: 415-491-8303

Sense8 Corp.
4000 Bridgeway, Suite 101
Sausalito, CA 94965
Phone: 415-331-6318
Fax: 415-331-9148
Contact: Thomas Coull

VREAM, Inc.
2568 N. Clark St. #250
Chicago, IL 60614
Phone: 312-477-0425
Fax: 312-477-9702
Contact: Edward LaHood

StrayLight Corporation
150 Mount Bethel Rd.
Warren, NJ 07059
Phone: 908-580-0086
Fax: 908-580-0092
Contact: Tony Asch

Virtus Corp.
117 Edinburgh Street, Suite 204
Cary, NC 27511
Phone: 919-467-9700
Fax: 919-460-4530

MicronGreen Inc.
1240 N.W. 21st Avenue
Gainesville, FL 32069
Phone: 904-376-1529
Fax: 904-376-0466

Dimension International
Zephyr1, Calleva Park
Aldermaston, Berkshire RG7 4QZ
United Kingdom
Phone: 011-44-734-810-077
Fax: 011-44-734-816-940
Contact: Ian Andrew

3-D Modeling Software

MultiGen., Inc.
550 S. Winchester Blvd., Suite 500
San Jose, CA 95128
Phone: 408-261-4100
Fax: 408-261-4101
Contact: Cindi A. Christian

Mira Imaging Inc.
2257 South, 100 East Suite 1A
Salt Lake City, UT 84106
Phone: 801-466-4641
Fax: 801-466-4699

Coryphaeus Software
985 University Ave., Suite 31
Los Gatos, CA 95030
Phone: 408-395-4537
Fax: 408-395-6351

Networking Software

Mak Technologies
380 Green St.
Cambridge, MA 02139
Phone: 617-876-8085
Fax: 617-876-9208
Contact: Warren Katz

Virtual Universe Corp.
Suite 510
700 4th Ave. S.W.
Calgary, Alberta T2P 3J4
Canada
Phone: 403-261-5652
Fax: 403-237-0005
Contact: Jim Durward

Note that there's also quite a bit of noncommercial software available on the Internet.

Augmented Reality Systems

Various custom-made see-through HMDs have been fabricated by research groups. Columbia University has used the Private Eye, available from:

Reflection Technology
240 Bear Hill Road
Waltham, MA 02154
Phone: 617-890-5905
Fax: 617-890-5918

Artificial Reality Systems

Artificial Reality Corporation
55 Edith
Vernon, CT 06066
Phone: 203-871-1375
Contact: Myron Krueger

The Vivid Group
317 Adelaide Street W. #302
Toronto, Ontario M5V 1P9
Canada
Phone: 416-340-9290
Fax: 416-348-9809
Contact: Vincent John Vincent

Fishtank VR Systems

Sun Microsystems
MS UMTV18-211
2550 Garcia Avenue
Mountain View, CA 94043
Phone: 415-336-3017
Fax: 415-336-1525
Contact: Mike Deering

CAVEs

There are no commercial off-the-shelf CAVEs available at present. CAVEs have been built by researchers at the University of Illinois at Chicago, and by SUN Microsystems.

Teleoperation Systems

Many teleoperation systems have been expensive custom-designed systems, for example for the military, and aren't commercially available.

Telepresence Research
320 Gabarda Way
Portola Valley, CA 94028
Phone: 415-854-4420
Fax: 415-854-3141
Contact: Scott Fisher

Sarcos
261 East 300 South, Suite 150
Salt Lake City, UT 84111
Phone: 801-531-0559
Fax: 801-531-0315

Glossary

AC/A ratio Describes the relationship between vergence and accommodation and is expressed as change in (accommodative) vergence in prism diopters per unit change in accommodation in diopters. The AC/A ratio must be within a certain range for binocular vision without double images.

accommodation Change in the thickness of the eye's crystalline lens induced by the eye's muscles, in order to focus an image on the retina.

accommodation/vergence mismatch In natural viewing conditions, accommodation and vergence work together so you can view an object at any distance. Virtual images, e.g., presented via an HMD, might create a mismatch by requiring vergence but presenting all images at optical infinity so accommodation isn't required.

acoustic reflex A contraction of muscles attached to the conducting bones of the middle ear that reduces the amount of sound that reaches the inner ear; this protective reflex happens in response to loud noises.

acoustic tracking Position-tracking approach that uses acoustic waves to determine an object's position and orientation.

actuator The mechanism that controls the motion of a robot, or any device or mechanism that produces mechanical force.

adaptation A perceptual or perceptual-motor change in response to a stimulus. Adaptation might involve changing the perceptual sensitivity to stimuli (e.g., the visual system becomes more sensitive to light with exposure to darkness) or changing the perceptual-motor system to reduce conflicting cues between sensory and/or motor modalities.

aerial perspective Also known as *atmospheric attenuation*, this is a monocular visual cue for depth that gauges relative distance by using the effects of the scattering and absorption of light by the atmosphere; a nearer object will have more color saturation and brightness contrast (and thus appear bluer) than a more distant object.

amplitude The magnitude of pressure variations, e.g., of sound waves.

anechoic chamber A controlled sound environment constructed to eliminate echoes by using sound-dampening materials on all surfaces. Anechoic chambers are used, for example, to measure HRTFs.

anosmia A complete absence of the sense of smell.

artificial reality A system of the type originated by Myron Krueger, in which the user's image is projected onto a screen and surrounded by synthetic objects, and the user interacts with these objects by moving, thus bringing his image in contact with the objects on the screen.

ataxia An inability to coordinate the actions of voluntary muscles. For example, locomotive ataxia is a condition where walking is uncoordinated. Locomotive ataxia is one symptom that has been observed in cybersickness.

auditory localization The process of determining the location of a sound source by using acoustic cues.

auditory scene analysis Retrieving mental descriptions of the sources of sound from a complex mixture of acoustic energy.

auditory stream segregation The process of grouping sequential sounds (such as a series of tones) into a single perceived event.

augmented reality The integration of computer-generated synthetic stimuli with real-world stimuli from the user's surroundings. Often thought of in terms of see-through HMDs that overlay text and graphics on real-world images, augmented reality can also use other sensory modalities, such as an auditory display that combines synthetic sounds with sounds in the user's environment.

auralization The direct auditory presentation of data, altering only the time scale or modulating the frequency to make it more easy to perceive. Auralization is applicable only to data that already has an inherent sound, such as seismic rumble.

autonomy Defined by Zeltzer (1992) as "a qualitative measure of the ability of a computational model to act and react to simulated events and stimuli . . . ," autonomy is the ability of the objects and processes simulated in the virtual environment to exhibit independent behaviors, whether in response to the state of the simulation or to user actions.

autostereoscopic displays Visual displays that are three-dimensional in appearance but don't require special viewing aids (such as HMDs or shuttered glasses) in order for the user to perceive the stereoscopic effect.

autotelic Having no purpose other than its own use, e.g., an entertainment application's only purpose is to bring its user the enjoyment of using it.

azimuth Horizontal position with respect to the viewer's head, expressed as the angular distance along the horizontal plane from a fixed reference point.

behavioral animation By defining behaviors associated with objects, the objects in virtual environments (or other computer graphics applications) can change their position, orientation, shape, color, texture, transparency, and other properties.

binaural A sound signal as it reaches two ears. Binaural recordings are typically made by using an anthropomorphic mannequin head with a microphone placed in each of its ear canals.

binocular disparity The difference in the images that fall on the two eyes; this difference is used in stereopsis.

binocular display A display that requires that the viewer use both eyes, whether the eyes receive identical or different images.

binoptic display *See* monoscopic display.

bio-signal processing Biosignal processors use sensors that detect bioelectric signals associated with muscle contractions or brain waves, and process these signals, detecting patterns or particular elements of the signals and using them to control interaction in the virtual environment.

BOOM (binocular omni-oriented monitor) A viewing device mounted to a stand that allows it to be moved in 6 degrees of freedom. Using mechanical position tracking, the stand sends position and orientation information to the computing system, and the user, who holds the viewer to his face, can use it to view the virtual environment.

brain-evoked response potential (BERP) Used as a source of input in biocontrol systems, this is the measured cerebro-electric activity associated with specific thoughts. Using BERP would, for example, permit users to select an object by thinking of it. Since current pattern recognition permits only a limited number of BERP commands, users might need to think in terms of specific directions to move a cursor to the location of the desired object and then select it; also, an individual must train the recognition system.

brightness The subjective impression of the intensity of light, also used to describe the subjective impression of sound timbres, i.e., the content of upper partials in a sound.

catadioptric Catadioptric optical systems, used in HMDs, combine refractive lenses and reflectors.

cathode ray tube (CRT) The most common display technology used in computer monitors, CRTs rely on emission of light by points on a phosphor-covered screen as they're struck by a beam of electrons. CRTs require high power consumption and are low in efficiency, hence their heat must be dissipated.

CAVE An enclosure that surrounds a user with large screens that project images that are viewed through shuttered glasses to provide stereoscopy and are coupled to the user's head-tracked movements.

cochlea A spiral-shaped fluid-filled structure in the inner ear that conveys vibrations to a membrane (the basilar membrane) contained within it.

cocktail party phenomenon The ability to discriminate individual conversations in a noisy environment such as a cocktail party. This phenomenon depends on localization cues perceived with binaural hearing.

collateral effects The effects that one tracked object can have on the position of another object as reported by a position-tracking system.

collimated Light rays are collimated if they're optically adjusted to be parallel.

collision detection A variety of algorithms are available to determine whether objects in a VE or other 3-D graphical environment come in contact with each other.

computer-supported cooperative work (CSCW) Collaborative work between individuals that's carried out with the support of communications and computing technology. CSCW is a field of study that has its own Association for Computing Machinery annual conference and has come to encompass a range of activities and tools, from desktop video-conferencing to collaborative text editing to work with shared virtual environments.

cones The visual receptors in the eye that are packed most densely in the fovea and are used to see color and resolve fine detail.

connectivity The ability for sites or users to connect on a network to a shared virtual environment, and hence the capability of a system to permit users at remote physical locations to share a common VE. For the ability of a system to allow multiple users at the same physical location to share a virtual environment, *see* sociability.

contrast (visual) The difference in luminance between viewed regions.

convergence Rotating the eyes inward. *See* vergence.

convolution A signal-processing technique that involves the summation of shifted unit sample responses, used to apply finite impulse response filters to sound streams in virtual acoustic displays in order to spatialize sounds.

critical band A frequency region (of about one third of an octave) in which the energy of different sounds is summed; masking tends to happen especially between sounds within the same critical band.

critical fusion frequency The threshold frequency at which temporal fusion occurs, i.e., flicker is no longer perceived as individual changes in luminance but is fused perceptually into a continuous image.

cross-platform compatibility The capability of software written for one system or platform to be run on a different system or platform.

CSCW *See* computer-supported cooperative work.

cutaneous perception *See* tactile perception.

cutaneous receptors Numerous types of receptors located under the surface of the skin; these receptors are specialized to detect different stimuli, e.g., lateral skin stretch, object shape, and vibration.

cybersickness (simulator-like sickness) A constellation of symptoms, including nausea, oculomotor discomfort, and disorientation, that might result from the use of a virtual environment system.

degree of interest distortion An intentional departure from veridicality, this is an approach offered by Fairchild (1993) to reducing the perceived complexity of VEs and helping users focus on a particular area of interest.

degree of virtuality The extent to which sensory input that's perceivable by the user is synthetic (computer-generated) vs. real.

degrees of freedom (DOF) The number of ways in which an object can move, i.e., the number of axes around which it can change in orientation or along which it can change in position.

dexterous handmaster Force-sensing and force-display devices worn on the hands of the operator of a virtual environment or teleoperation system.

dichoptic stimulus Visual stimulus to the eyes that's different for one eye than for the other.

dichotic stimulus Auditory stimuli to the ears that's different for one ear than for the other.

diopter The inverse of the distance from a viewed object to the eye in meters, this is the measure that expresses accommodation.

diotic stimulus Auditory stimulus that's identical for both ears.

display update rate The frequency with which an image generator updates or modifies an image sent to the display device.

Distributed Interactive Simulation protocol (DIS) Adopted by the IEEE as a standard for shared networked simulations, this protocol supports interaction in a shared networked virtual environment (e.g., by users in different types of vehicular simulators) via network packets (known as Protocol Data Units or PDUs) that are periodically sent by each participant and also sent in the event of a state change. Dead-reckoning is used to reduce the required bandwidth.

DOF *See* degrees of freedom.

Donder's line Expresses the AC/A ratio for symmetrical convergence on a target as it approaches the viewer along the midline.

Doppler effect The shifting in frequency that occurs as a sound source (e.g., an ambulance siren or a train whistle) moves quickly with respect to a listener.

earcons Developed by Blattner, Sumikawa, and Greenberg (1989), they use nonspeech tones or short sequences of tones as building blocks to create messages using a formal syntax.

egocentric viewpoint A point of view where the user of a VE system perceives the virtual environment in relationship to some part of his or her body. Think of this as a "first person" viewpoint.

elevation Vertical position with respect to the viewer's head, it's expressed as the angular distance along the vertical plane from a fixed reference point.

engagement Users' subjective sense of being deeply involved and occupied with what they're doing. This involves paying attention to the immediate experience and not being distracted by thoughts of other things; a very strong level of engagement is associated with a variety of traits, such as losing track of time, which have been collectively described as *flow*.

entrance pupil When viewed from image space, this is the image of the aperture stop that's formed by all the lenses that precede it, i.e., on the object side of the stop.

Euler angles A set of angles that describe orientation of a body with respect to reference axes. *See* yaw, pitch, and roll.

everyday listening The type of listening we do when we attend to the attributes of a sound's source (e.g., the size of a can that's hit by a rock, how full the can was, and how hard the rock was thrown) rather than the pitch, rhythm, and timbre of the sound. Everyday listening is contrasted to musical listening.

exit pupil When viewed from image space, this is the image of the aperture stop that's formed by all the lenses that follow it.

expert system A system that, within a limited problem domain, uses heuristics and a knowledge base to perform the kind of cause-and-effect reasoning that would be carried out by a human expert in that domain.

externalization The perception that a sound is coming from a position in space that's outside the listener's head.

eyepiece The lens in an image display system that magnifies the image formed by the objective lens.

eye tracking Determining the direction of a user's gaze, which can be accomplished by using a variety of techniques.

fault tolerance The ability of a system to recover from errors caused by, e.g., adverse conditions or unexpected input from other systems, and continue to function properly.

Fiber Distributed Data Interface (FDDI) A local area network standard, similar in many ways to a token ring, with a 100-Mbps data rate.

field of view (FOV) The part of space you can see immediately, without moving your head or eyes. The FOV is also referred to as the *visual field*. In terms of a visual display, the FOV is the visual angle subtended by the display.

finite impulse response (FIR) filters Nonrecursive discrete-time filters. They're nonrecursive because they compute a function using the current and previous value, rather than previously computed values, discrete-time because they're applied to a continuous signal only at the discrete times measured at a fixed sampling rate, and finite because the impulse response is nonzero only during a finite time slice. FIR filters are obtained from measurements of HRTFs and are used to spatialize sound in virtual acoustic displays.

fishtank VR A phrase coined by Colin Ware, Kevin Arthur, and Kellogg Booth (1993) to describe systems in which a perspective projection system coupled to the head position of the user displays stereoscopic images of a 3-D scene on a monitor. This type of system has also been called *desktop VR* (Paley 1993).

Fitts' law The linear relationship between movement duration and the index of movement difficulty (the logarithmic transformation of target distance divided by target width) observed by Paul Fitts. This relationship has been found to apply to a great variety of movements.

Fletcher-Munson curve Loudness, though primarily affected by amplitude, is also affected by frequency. The Fletcher-Munson curve shows the amplitude of sine waves at different frequencies that are perceived as equal in loudness.

flicker Pulsed change in luminance that's produced by many sources, such as videotapes, computer monitors, and other displays.

flight simulator A vehicular simulator used to train pilots, it typically has a real cockpit with real controls. The pilot manipulates these controls, which causes images projected on screens in the cockpit (that represent cockpit windows) to change appropriately in response. Similarly, flight simulators typically incorporate motion platforms, which cause the cockpit to change in position and orientation in response to the pilot's steering maneuvers.

Foley A Foley artist produces the sounds (sound effects) associated with actions, e.g., of movie characters. Automatic Foley generation requires synthesizing the sounds associated with unpredictable interactions within a virtual environment, based on properties of the objects involved.

force feedback Force applied to the user's hand or other body parts (by devices such as dexterous handmasters) in response to user actions or simulation events.

force perception The perception of mechanical forces applied to the body, which depends on sensitivity to the muscular opposition used to resist these forces.

fovea The region in the eye in the center of the retina that has the highest concentration of cones. This area of ~1–2 degrees is where the finest visual resolution takes place.

foveal vision Vision in the foveal region, i.e., the normal high-resolution vision we experience when we direct our eyes towards an object of interest.

frequency The rate at which a signal varies. In acoustics, for example, frequency is the rate at which pressure varies in the medium conducting a sound.

fusion interface Combines synthetic and real controls. For example, a fusion interface for flight simulation would combine real and virtual cockpit controls.

gesture recognition When a computer applies pattern recognition to identifying symbolic meaning in predefined shapes and movements (e.g., of a user's hand).

God's-eye viewpoint Also known as the *exocentric viewpoint*, this is defined in terms of an external coordinate system and allows users to perceive a scene from above.

goniometer Developed for medical measurement of the range of motion of joints, these are instruments that measure angles.

GROPE A system incorporating force feedback, this was created at the University of North Carolina at Chapel Hill to display molecular forces to biochemists and permit molecular docking (fitting together molecules based on their structures).

haptic perception The broad category that encompasses tactile (or cutaneous) perception, including perception of temperature, and kinesthetic/force perception.

head-mounted display (HMD) Is worn by a user to present head-coupled virtual images. Its optical system collimates light (generally coming from two small image sources) and the head tracker tracks the position and orientation of the user's head.

head-related transfer function (HRTF) Function that describes the transformation of an acoustical signal from its source in space to the ear canal. This direction-dependent filtering includes the acoustical effects of pinna filtering.

head tracking Using position-tracking technology to track the position and orientation of the user's head. In a VE system, this is used to perform real-time updating of the displays to each sensory modality.

highlighting The way light is reflected off certain (e.g., curved) surfaces, conveying the three-dimensionality of a scene; it's used as a monocular visual depth cue.

HMD *See* head-mounted display.

HRTF *See* head-related transfer function.

hydraulic actuator A hydraulic actuator uses force transferred via water pressure to produce movement, e.g., of a motion platform.

immersion Although different meanings have been attached to the term, I define it as the presentation of sensory cues that convey perceptually to users that they're surrounded by the computer-generated environment. Thus, immersion is an objectively quantifiable phenomenon that can be described by measures such as visual field of view, auditory localization cues, directions from which force reflection can be displayed, and the range of orientations supported by tracking.

inertial display A display that moves the user's body in order to convey information to the vestibular sense.

instrumented glove Uses some type of bend-sensing technology to detect and report the posture of the hand. In addition, instrumented gloves typically use position-tracking technology, and this information is combined and used to present a virtual hand in the VE that mimics the user's hand and can manipulate objects in the VE.

interactivity Encompasses both the frequency, range, and significance of user choices in interacting with the system, as well as the tight coupling of head-tracked (and other) user input with a multisensory display.

interaural level difference (ILD) The difference in volume of the sound reaching the two ears, ILD is one cue used in auditory localization.

interaural time difference (ITD) The difference in time of a sound reaching both ears, ITD is an auditory localization cue.

interposition A monocular visual cue for depth, this is the phenomenon of an object closer to the viewer obstructing the view of an object that's farther away. It's also known as *occlusion*, *obscuration*, and *contour interruption*.

interpupillary distance (IPD) The distance between the centers of the pupils of the eyes when the eyes are directed along parallel axes, as they are when converged to optical infinity. IPD varies from individual to individual, and should be considered when you're designing or choosing an HMD.

intrinsic motivation Motivation that comes from actually performing a behavior or an activity rather than from any extrinsic reward.

I/O An abbreviation for input/output.

I/O bandwidth The amount of information that can pass from user to system and from system to user; it can be considered in terms of each sensory modality.

IPD *See* interpupillary distance.

iterative design A process of defining requirements, designing a system or application, prototyping it, evaluating the prototype with representative users, using the results of the evaluation to modify the design or redesign, and repeating the process until acceptable performance is achieved.

just noticeable difference (JND) The smallest reliably detectable change in a stimulus.

Kalman filtering Sampling tracking sensor data at known times and combining this data with a model of motion to estimate true position and predict true position at a specified future time.

kinesthetic perception The perception of the movement, position, and torque of limbs and other body parts.

kinesthetic sense The awareness of the position of your own body parts, their direction and rate of movement, and the force produced by muscular contractions; this sense depends on and is closely related to kinesthetic perception.

lag *See* latency.

laser retinal scanning *See* retinal laser display.

latency Also known as lag, the total delay time between a user action and the system responding to this action. Latency is the cumulative delay caused by each system component required to generate the system response, which is typically introduced by the data rate and update rate of position trackers; the time spent by the host computer in processing tracker position, running the simulation, and rendering the graphical, sonic, and tactile images; the refresh rate of display devices; and cumulative transmission time.

level-of-detail (LOD) selection If the virtual world database is organized to contain different representations of objects with different degrees of detail, you can choose which LOD representation to render based on the distance between the object and the user in the virtual environment.

light-emitting diode (LED) An element of a visual display device that uses semiconductor diodes to convert electrical energy to light.

Likert-like questionnaire Rating scales with which users retrospectively express their subjective satisfaction (choosing responses on a numbered scale) with specified aspects of a human-computer interface.

linear perspective A monocular visual cue for depth, the phenomenon of parallel lines, such as railroad tracks, appearing to converge as they recede from the viewer. Linear perspective applies not only to parallel lines, but to component parts of any object appearing to converge as they become more distant.

liquid crystal display (LCD) Visual display devices that apply voltages to grid wires, which change the alignment of the molecules in the liquid crystal layer and hence their polarizing effect. This controls the light from a source (the *backlight*), which passes through and reaches the viewer. Current LCDs have lower resolution than CRTs, but have lower power consumption; require less heat dissipation; and tend to be lower in weight, smaller in size, and lower in cost.

locus of control In the context of VE systems, this is the location of content creation and control, i.e., the person or organization who has the power to create and control the content of virtual environments.

LOD *See* level of detail.

long-term memory (LTM) Holds the user's knowledge, which is encoded, stored, and retained through time. In contrast, *see* short-term memory.

looming The rapid visual changes in angular size and texture density that occur as an object quickly approaches an observer, this produces avoidance and other reactions, indicating that the viewer perceives the object as rapidly approaching.

loudness The psychoacoustical term for a subjective impression that roughly corresponds to amplitude, but varies also with frequency and bandwidth.

masking Obscuring the spectral components of some sounds with other sounds.

master-slave teleoperation Controlling a robot's motion with your own motion. The robot, which might be anthropomorphic, mimics your motions, at a minimum your hand and arm motions.

mechanical tracking A position-tracking system that physically connects the user to the tracker, which is at a known reference point, and mechanically measures position by using jointed linkages.

metathetic Perceptual dimensions that vary in quality rather than in intensity (e.g., pitch and color).

minimum audible angle The smallest change in position of a sound source that's detectable by a listener, measured in an anechoic chamber with the listener's head held motionless.

model human processor Cognitive psychology perspective in which perceptual, cognitive, and motor operations are seen in terms of information processing. The model human processor represents human-computer interaction in analytic modeling. Refer to Card, Moran, and Newell 1983.

monocular cues Visual cues for depth that don't depend on oculomotor or binocular disparity cues, i.e., visual cues for depth you can use if you look with only one eye and were insensitive to focusing.

monoscopic display A monoscopic display, also known as a binoptic display, is one in which the same 2-D image is viewed by both eyes.

motion parallax The difference in relative motion in the visual field of objects that are nearer and farther from a moving observer. For example, if one looks out from a moving car, the distant mountains appear to move much more slowly than do the closer telephone poles.

motion platform A physical platform which supports the user and moves to provide vestibular cues. Motion platforms are typically used with vehicular simulators.

multimedia system Typically, systems that have prerecorded digitized video, audio, text and graphics that are hyperlinked. Because the source materials are prerecorded, there are fixed choices available to the user, e.g., a scene can only be viewed (or sounds heard) from certain prerecorded positions and angles.

musical listening Musical listening is the type of listening we do when we attend to pitch, rhythm, and timbre. It is contrasted to "everyday listening."

natural language system Although the precise and formal syntax used in computer languages is quite different from the informal and often ambiguous syntax of normal human language, a natural language system permits a computer to translate between these two types of languages, and react appropriately to normal human speech.

navigation Navigation is the process of getting from place to place in the virtual environment, and assumes the user's volition and planning in the process.

negative transfer When associations with previously stored information cause interference in learning to do a new task or use a new system. Also when practicing with a simulation results in unintended and detrimental behavior when the task is performed in the real world.

objective lens The lens in an image display system that forms the image. *See also* eyepiece.

oculomotor cues Visual depth cues the observer gets by attending to the visual system's state of muscular tension in converging and focusing the eyes.

offline learning and knowledge acquisition Applications of VE technology in which users acquire knowledge and experience using the VE that they can later synthesize into more abstract knowledge.

offline training and rehearsal Applications of VE technology in which users practice tasks with the VE that they later perform in the real world.

olfactory display The presentation of chemical stimuli as cues to the sense of smell.

olfactory perception The perception of odor, which lets us gather information about chemical events in the environment through our sense of smell.

online comprehension Applications of VE technology in which the user understands or gains insight into the VE while interacting with it.

online design Applications of VE technology where an individual or collaborative group designs objects or environments.

online performance Applications of VE technology where the user uses the VE to accomplish tasks in the real world (e.g., via teleoperation).

operating system The underlying system that controls a computer's resources and provides a layer of abstraction on which applications can be built without dealing with all the specifics of particular hardware being used.

optical tracking Position-tracking systems that use light to determine the position and orientation of tracked objects.

orthostereoscopic display A visual display that produces stereoscopy by presenting different images to each eye (binocular disparity) and doesn't introduce distortions to the images. In the case of the transduced visual images used in teleoperation, an orthostereoscopic display would maintain the accurate correspondence of the size, shapes, and relative positions of displayed objects to real-world objects.

panorama The ability (with the viewer's head movement incorporated) of a display to surround the viewer, thus adding a temporal element and head movement to immersion.

PC (Pacinian) receptors A type of cutaneous receptor used to detect vibration.

photopic High levels of light (e.g., during the day) in which cones are the primary visual receptors and the eye is light-adapted.

piezoelectric display Conveys the impression of touch by converting electrical forces to mechanical forces and applying these mechanical forces to the surface of the user's skin.

pinnae The outer ears.

pinna filtering The direction-dependent distortion (spectral filtering) of incoming sound signals by the outer ear, used in auditory localization.

pitch In the context of position tracking, a change in orientation that involves movement around the lateral axis.

pneumatic actuator Produces mechanical force driven by gas, e.g., air pressure.

pneumatic display Creates the impression of touch by creating pressure with air-to-air rings, air jets, or air pockets that touch the user.

position tracking Determines the position and orientation of users of a VE system. Head tracking tracks the position and orientation of the user's head; position tracking is also used both with instrumented gloves to track hand position and orientation, and with full-body tracking systems.

positive transfer When associations with previously stored information aid in learning to do a new task or using a new system.

precedence effect The first arriving signal in a reverberant environment takes perceptual precedence, which allows the many temporally separated sounds to be perceptually fused into a single source.

predictive tracking Uses available sensed information from a position-tracking system to predict a position at a given future time.

presence Generally associated with the sense of "being in" a place. Although researchers in the field offer different definitions, I define presence as the subjective sense by users that they're physically in a virtual environment. Although presence is subjective, you can measure it objectively, for example by observing responses to the visual looming of a large, fast-approaching virtual object.

prosody The melody and rhythm of speech.

prothetic Perceptual dimensions that vary in intensity rather than in quality (e.g., loudness or brightness).

proximity-luminance covariance A monocular visual cue for depth, this is a tendency to perceive more brightly illuminated parts of a scene as being closer than are other parts of the scene.

quaternions Algebraic structures that can represent all possible orientations, and one of several ways to represent orientation. You can multiply them to represent changes in orientation and, unlike Euler angles, they don't require that you specify the order in which rotations around each axis occur.

reaction time (RT) The duration of time between the presentation of a stimulus and the beginning of the subject's response.

real time Real time has different meanings to people in different fields. To computer scientists, real-time systems are systems in which not only the logical result of computations but also the time to produce results determine system performance. To psychologists, real time means perceived simultaneity (which means different things depending on the modality and nature of the stimulus). Finally, real time is used loosely to mean "very quickly" (i.e., in 100 milliseconds or less).

reconfigurability The ability of a system to be modified. You could, for example, modify an easily reconfigurable system built for one application to be used for another application without a great deal of time and effort (or hardware).

reflective Reflective optical systems, used in HMDs, transmit light to reflectors, which direct the light to the eyes and might also magnify the image.

refractive Refractive optical systems, used in HMDs, transmit light from the image source to the eye through lenses that collimate the light.

refresh rate The frequency with which an entire screen image is redrawn.

registration The accuracy with which reported/displayed position and orientation correspond to physical position and orientation.

reification The representation of something abstract as a concrete physical object. An example would be representing probabilities or financial indicators as solid geometric objects that vary in color and size.

representation of the user How users appear to themselves in the virtual environment, and how they appear to other users.

resolution The level of precision and detail with respect to a sensor (e.g., how precisely can a position tracker identify position), a display (what level of detail can the display present), and perceptual or motor activity (e.g., what level of visual acuity can be resolved or how precisely a movement can be made).

responsiveness The ability of a system to minimize the time between a user's input and the system's response; i.e., the lower the system's latency, the higher is its responsiveness.

retinal laser display A visual display that scans the light from a laser beam directly on the user's retina, it was first prototyped at the Human Interface Technology Laboratory at the University of Washington.

reverberation After an original direct sound and its early reflections have ended, the vibrations excited by the original signal, late reflections, and scattering that prolong the sound are known collectively as reverberation.

robustness A measure of the system's ability to withstand the conditions in which it will be used, including environmental conditions such as heat or noise and handling by users (e.g., of instrumented gloves).

rods The rod-shaped visual receptors in the eye that are distributed outside the fovea and are sensitive to dim light.

roll A change in orientation that involves movement around the longitudinal axis.

SA I and SA II receptors Among the types of cutaneous receptors found in the skin of the fingertips, these are slowly adapting receptors thought to detect, respectively, object shape and lateral skin stretch.

saccade A type of eye movement that consists of short fast jumps from one point of regard to another.

scaling errors These occur when cues to the visual, auditory, and haptic systems change to different degrees in response to a given motion. Scaling errors are especially difficult to adapt to.

scotopic Low levels of light (e.g., at night) in which rods are the primary visual receptors used and the eye is dark-adapted.

servo system A feedback system that controls the motion of mechanical devices.

shape-memory alloy One of a group of substances that recover their shape after being deformed if they're heated.

short-term memory (STM) Holds the information upon which mental operations "obtain their operands and leave their outputs" (Card, Moran, and Newell 1983). Although there has been some debate about the existence of a separate short-term memory structure, STM is characterized by the rapid decay of its contents if they aren't rehearsed, and its small capacity (7, plus or minus 2, chunks).

shuttered glasses Provide stereoscopy by alternately letting in light to one eye and then the other, synchronized to the refresh rate of a monitor that alternately displays left and right eye images. This shuttering (and the alternate images) must occur at such a high rate that the images are fused by the viewer.

SIMNET A simulator networking project sponsored by DARPA that permitted different types of vehicular simulators (e.g., a helicopter and tank simulator) to interact in a shared virtual environment.

simulator-like sickness *See* cybersickness.

sociability The capability of a system to permit multiple users to share a virtual environment, often associated with users sharing the same physical space; for systems that allow users at remote physical locations to share a virtual environment, *see* connectivity.

sonification The representation of data through sound.

space-exclusion A property generally found in the real world that objects can't occupy the same space at the same time; objects can exhibit the property of space-exclusion in a VE.

speaker-dependent Speech recognition that's based on templates built on the individual user's speech, so users must individually train the system on their own speech.

speaker-independent Speech recognition system that's trained on a large speech database, and doesn't require any training by users.

speaker verification A system that identifies speakers by the distinctive qualities in their voices.

spectral integration When different spectral components of simultaneously heard complex sounds are grouped and associated with their sources.

speech recognition When a computer applies pattern recognition to acoustic signals produced by human speakers to determine their linguistic content.

speech synthesis When a computer converts text to acoustic signals to produce recognizable speech.

stability The lack of jitter or oscillation in the position of objects in the virtual environment.

stereopsis Perceiving visual depth by using binocular disparity, i.e., the difference in the image that reaches the two eyes.

stereoscopic display A visual display that presents different images to the two eyes in order to produce the effect of stereopsis in the viewer.

superlocalization It's thought that enhanced cues might allow users to localize better in a VE than in the real world. For example, enhanced auditory localization cues might allow auditory superlocalization.

synchronization The temporal control of processes so they remain in step with each other.

synesthetic representation Displaying stimuli that would normally be perceived with one sensory modality in a different modality. For example, you could synthetically present force and tactile information to a user in the form of an auditory display.

synthetic environment A computer-generated environment in which a user can navigate and interact with objects.

tactile feedback When a system conveys the impression of touch to a user; this is accomplished by stimulating the surface of the user's skin.

tactile perception The perception of stimuli (whether mechanical, thermal, or electrocutaneous) on the surface of the skin; it makes use of the numerous types of cutaneous receptors located under the surface of the skin.

teleoperation One way a human operator can control a remote robot: the robot's transducers display the remote environment to the human, and the human's motions control the robot's motions. This coupling creates the impression that the human is present at the robot's location.

telepresence Although defined somewhat differently by people in the CSCW community, telepresence is generally taken by the VE community to mean the sense of being physically present at a remote teleoperator site (Barfield, et al. 1995).

temporal fusion Above certain frequencies, a rapid series of discrete events are perceptually fused, i.e., perceived to be one continuous event. For example, still images, projected in a motion picture, are perceived as a continuous movie rather than a series of individual frames.

textural gradient A monocular visual cue for depth, the apparent change in a pattern's density with distance (e.g., grass in a field or tiles on a floor).

texture mapping The mapping of a 2-D image onto the surface of graphical objects to provide fine textural detail at a relatively low computational cost.

transduction Converting energy from one form to another with transducers. Transduction can occur when our sensory receptors convert energy from environmental stimuli into neural activity, or when energy from environmental stimuli is captured and encoded by mechanical sensors in a teleoperator system.

transmission time The absolute duration of time from transmission until reception of a signal.

trigeminal chemoreception Also known as *common chemical sense*, this is a response other than taste or smell to chemical stimuli, and is characterized by the sensitivity of mucosal surfaces to chemical irritants such as pepper. For obvious reasons, it isn't a widely chosen sense modality for computer-human interaction.

ultrasonic tracking Acoustic position tracking using waves in the ultrasonic frequencies. Ultrasonic tracking is used in three types of systems: time-of-flight, time-delay, and phase-coherent.

update rate The number of times per second that reports are issued or new images displayed. For a position tracker, the update rate is the frequency with which the tracker issues a new report of position and orientation of a tracked object; for a visual display, it's the frequency with which successive visual images appear on the display.

usability The ease with which a human can use and learn a human-computer interface.

VACTOR Technology that measures facial expressions and movements via a device worn on the face, and uses sensed facial expressions to control the facial expressions of animated digital computer characters.

vehicular simulators They provide physical cockpits (often on motion platforms) with images projected on the cockpit's screens, and the images and the motion of the cockpit respond appropriately to the user manipulating the cockpit controls.

ventriloquist effect When there are conflicts between visual and auditory localization cues, vision predominates, so a sufficiently compelling visual cue can make a sound appear to come from somewhere other than its true source. Perhaps related to this effect is the tendency to make front-to-back errors in localizing virtual acoustic display-produced sounds in the absence of corresponding visual cues.

vergence The inward or outward rotation of the eyes that occurs so the eyes' lines of sight intersect at the distance of a viewed object.

veridicality The accuracy with which the virtual environment reproduces real objects, the user's actions, and the environment it models.

vestibular sense Detects movements of the head by sensing head rotations, gravity, and linear accelerations.

vestibulo-ocular reflex A reflex that moves the eyes in a compensatory way in the direction opposite to that of head or body movement in order to maintain visual fixation. You can suppress this reflex in order to follow an object that rotates with the head.

viewpoint How users perceive their location, i.e., the perspective on the virtual environment presented to users.

virtual acoustic display Displays that synthesize the cues in auditory localization to provide sounds (generally over headphones) that the user perceives to be external and to maintain their position or trajectory regardless of the user's motion.

virtual environment (VE) An interactive computer-generated environment presented by a virtual environment system.

virtual environment (VE) system A human-computer interface that provides interactive, immersive, multisensory, 3-D, synthetic environments to its users.

virtual image Unlike a real image, which has an identifiable location on a viewing screen, a virtual image has an apparent location to the viewer due to the optical system used, but doesn't have a real physical location in space.

virtual reality (VR) The popular expression for what is generally referred to in the technical field as *virtual environment*.

voice coil Voice coils, used in moving-coil loudspeakers (where the interaction between magnetic field and current causes them to move between pole pieces and generate sound waves), are one of the technologies in tactile displays.

von Frey hair A calibrated filament used to study cutaneous perception of step function stimuli.

within-ear monitors Fit by users into their ear canals, these monitors are a high-fidelity audio technology.

working volume Also known as *range of operation*, the volume within which a system can adequately track position.

workload (mental workload) Although there's no single precise definition, it's the amount of a person's information processing capacity required to perform a task.

yaw Change in orientation that involves movement around the vertical axis.

Bibliography

Ackerman, D. (1990). *A Natural History of the Senses*. New York: Random House.

Adelstein, B.D., Johnston, E.R., and Ellis, S.R. (1992). A testbed for characterizing dynamic response of virtual environment spatial sensors. *Proceedings of UIST '92: The Fifth Annual ACM Symposium on User Interface Software and Technology*. Nov. 15–18, Monterey, CA. 15–22.

Akeley, K. (1989). The Silicon Graphics 4D/240GTX Superworkstation. *IEEE Computer Graphics and Applications*. July.

Andersson, R.L. (1993). A real experiment in virtual environments: A virtual batting cage. *Presence: Teleoperators and Virtual Environments*. 2(1). Cambridge, MA: MIT Press. 16–33.

Anstis, S.M. (1974). A chart demonstrating variations in acuity with retinal position. *Vision Research*. 14, 589–592.

Applewhite, H.L. (1993). Acoustic positioning systems. *Virtual Reality Systems: Applications, Research and Development*. vol. 1 no. 1. New York: SIG-Advanced Applications.

Applewhite, H.L. (1991) Position Tracking in Virtual Reality. *Piltdown Technical Report 91-04*. Beaverton, OR: Piltdown Inc.

Azuma, R.T. (1995a). A survey of augmented reality: SIGGRAPH '95 course notes. To be published in *Course Notes 9: Developing Advanced Virtual Reality Applications*. ACM SIGGRAPH 1995 (Los Angeles, CA, 6–11 August).

Azuma, R.T. (1995b). Predictive tracking for augmented reality. *Technical Report TR95-007*. UNC-Chapel Hill Department of Computer Science.

Azuma, R. and Ward, M. (1991). Space Resection by Collinearity: Mathematics behind the Optical Ceiling Head-Tracker. *Technical Report TR91-048*. UNC-Chapel Hill Department of Computer Science. November 1991.

Bajura, M., Fuchs, H., and Ohbuchi, R. (1992). Merging virtual objects with the real world. *Computer Graphics*. vol 26, no. 2, July. 203–210.

Barfield, W., Zeltzer, D., Sheridan, T., and Slater, M. (1995). Presence and performance within virtual environments. In W. Barfield and T.A Furness III (eds.) *Virtual Environments and Advanced Interface Design*. New York: Oxford University Press. 473–513.

Bass, M., ed. (1995). *Handbook of Optics*. New York: McGraw-Hill, Inc.

Batteau, D.W. (1967). The role of the pinna in human localization. *Proceedings of the Royal Society of London*. B168, 158–180.

Baudel, T. and Beaudouin-Lafon (1993). Charade: remote control of objects using free-hand gestures. *Communications of the ACM*. vol. 36, no. 7. 29–35.

Begault, D.R. and Wenzel, E.M. (1990). Techniques and Applications for Binaural Sound Manipulation in Human-Machine Interfaces. *NASA TM-102279* (later published in 1992, *The International Journal of Aviation Psychology*. 2(1):1–22).

Benford, S., Bowers, J., Fahlen, L.E., Greenhalgh, C., and Snowdon, D. (1995). User embodiment in collaborative virtual environments. *Proceedings of the CHI '95 Conference on Human Factors in Computer Systems*. New York: ACM. 242–249.

Bertelson, P. and Radeau, M. (1981). Cross-modal bias and perceptual fusion with auditory-visual spatial discordance. *Perception and Psychophysics*. 29. 578–584.

Biocca, F. (1992). Communication within virtual reality: Creating a space for research. *Journal of Communication*. vol. 42, no. 4. 5–22.

Bibliography

Blattner, M.M., Sumikawa, D.A., and Greenberg, R.M. (1989). Earcons and icons: Their structure and common design principles. *Human Computer Interaction.* vol. 4. 11–44.

Blauert, J. (1983). *Spatial Hearing: The Psychophysics of Human Sound Localization* (J.S. Allen, trans.). Cambridge, MA: MIT Press.

Bletter, N. (1993). VR applications and the software used to create them. Presentation at Virtual Reality Systems Fall '93. New York City: SIG-Advanced Applications. October 21.

Boff, K.R., and Lincoln, J.E. (1988). *Engineering Data Compendium: Human Perception and Performance.* Wright-Patterson AFB, OH: AAMRL.

Bolas, M. T. (1994). Human factors in the design of an immersive display. *IEEE Computer Graphics and Applications.* vol. 14, no. 1. 55–59.

Bostrom, M., Singh, S.K., and Wiley, C.W. (1993). Design of an interactive lumbar puncture simulator with tactile feedback. *VRAIS '93: 1993 IEEE Virtual Reality Annual International Symposium.* Piscataway, NJ: IEEE. 280–286.

Bowman, D. (1995). *Conceptual Design Space.* Available at World Wide Web site http://www.cc.gatech.edu/gvu/virtual/CDS.

Bregman, A.S. (1990). *Auditory Scene Analysis.* Cambridge, MA: MIT Press.

Brewster, S. Wright, P.C., and Edwards, A.D.N. (1995). Parallel Earcons: Reducing the length of audio messages. *Int. J. Human-Computer Studies.* 43. 153–175.

Brody, A.R., Jacoby, R., and Ellis, S.R. (1992). Extravehicular activity self-rescue using a hand-held thruster. *Journal of Spacecraft and Rockets.* vol. 29, no. 6, November–December. 842–848.

Brooks, F. P. Jr. (1988). Grasping reality through illusion-interactive graphics serving science. *Proceedings of the CHI '88 Conference on Human Factors in Computer Systems.* New York: ACM. 1–11.

Brooks, Jr., F.P., Airey, J., Alspaugh, J., Bell, A., Brown, R., Hill, C., Nimscheck, U., Rheingans, P., Rohlf, J., Smith, D., Turner, D., Varshney, A., Wang, Y., Weber, H., and Yuan, X. (1992). Six Generations of Building Walkthrough: Final Technical Report to the National Science Foundation. *UNC Technical Report TR92-027.* Chapel Hill, NC: Dept. of Computer Science, University of North Carolina.

Brooks, F.P. Jr., Ouh-Young, M., Batter, J.J., and Kilpatrick, P.J. (1990). Project GROPE: Haptic displays for scientific visualization. *Computer Graphics.* vol. 24, no. 4, August. 177–185.

Bryson, S. (1994). Introduction in Pausch, R., van Dam, A., Robinett, W., and Bryson, S. *Implementing Virtual Reality. CHI '94 Tutorial #25.* Conference on Human Factors in Computing Systems. April 24–28. Boston, MA: ACM.

Bryson, S. and Levit, C. (1992). The virtual windtunnel. *IEEE Computer Graphics and Applications.* 12(4). 25–34.

Burdea, G. and Coiffet, P. (1994). *Virtual Reality Technology.* New York: John Wiley and Sons.

Burgess, D. (1994a). 3-D Interactive Percussion: The virtual drum kit. *CHI '94 Human Factors in Computing Systems Conference Companion.* New York, NY: ACM. 45–46.

Burgess, D. (1994b). Personal communication (electronic) on latency. May 6.

Burgess, D. (1994c). Implementing Audio in Virtual Environments. Presentation to NYNEX Science and Technology, White Plains, NY. May 13.

Butterworth, J., Davidson, A., Hench, S., and Olano, T.M. (1992). 3DM: A three-dimensional modeler using a head-mounted display. *Computer Graphics.* 25(2). 135–138.

Buttolo, P. and Hannaford, B. (1995). Pen-based force display for precision manipulation in virtual environments. *VRAIS '95: IEEE Virtual Reality Annual International Symposium.* Piscataway, NJ: IEEE. 217–224.

Buxton, B. (1989). *The Pragmatics of Haptic Input. Tutorial #16 Notes. CHI '89.* New York: ACM.

Buxton, W., Gaver, W., and Bly, S. (1989). *The Use of Non-Speech Audio at the Interface. Tutorial #10. CHI '89.* New York: ACM.

Calhoun, G.L., Valencia, G., and Furness, T.A. (1987). Three-dimensional auditory cue simulation for crew station design/evaluation. *Proceedings of the Human Factors Society 31st Annual Meeting.* Santa Monica, CA: Human Factors Society. 1398–1402.

Calvin, J., Dickens, A., Gaines, B., Metzger, P., Miller, D., Owen, D. (1993). The simnet virtual world architecture. *VRAIS '93: 1993 IEEE Virtual Reality Annual International Symposium.* Piscataway, NJ: IEEE. 450–455.

Card, S.K., Moran, T.P., and Newell, A. (1983). *The Psychology of Human-Computer Interaction.* Hillsdale, NJ: Lawrence Erlbaum.

Carroll, J.M. and Thomas, J.C. (1988). Fun. *SIGCHI Bulletin.* Vol 19, no. 3. New York: ACM. 21–24.

Cater, J.P. (1992). The nose have it! (letter to the editor). *Presence: Teleoperators and Virtual Environments.* Fall 1992, 493–494.

Chang, S., Tan, H., Eberman, B., and Marcus, B. (1993). Sensing, perception, and feedback for VR. Presented at *Virtual Reality Systems Fall '93.* New York: SIG-Advanced Applications.

Bibliography

Chapin, W.L. and Foster, S.H. (1992). Virtual environment display for a 3D audio room simulation. Presented at *SPIE '92 Stereoscopic Displays and Applications*. February 13.

Chin, J.P., Diehl, V.A., and Norman, K.L. (1988). Development of an instrument measuring user satisfaction of the human-computer interface. *Proceedings of the CHI '88 Conference on Human Factors in Computer Systems*. New York: ACM. 213–218.

Clark, F.J. and Horch, K.W. (1986). Kinesthesia. In K.R. Boff, L. Kaufman, and J. P. Thomas (eds.) *Handbook of perception and human performance*. vol. 1, 13:1–13:62. New York: Wiley.

Coco, G.P. (1993). The Virtual Environment Operating System: Derivation, Function and Form. Unpublished Master's Thesis, Department of Computer Science and Engineering, University of Washington. Available by FTP from the University of Washington.

Cornsweet, T.N. (1970). *Visual Perception*. San Diego: Harcourt Brace Jovanovich.

Cruz-Neira, C., Sandin, D.J., and DeFanti, T.A. (1993). Surround-screen projection-based virtual reality: The design and implementation of CAVE. *Computer Graphics (SIGGRAPH '93 Proceedings)* vol. 27, 135–142.

Cruz-Neira, C., Sandin, D.J., DeFanti, T.A., Kenyon, R.V., and Hart, J.C. (1992). The CAVE: Audio visual experience automatic virtual environment. *Communications of the ACM*. vol. 35, June, 64–72.

Cytowic, R.E. (1993). *The Man Who Tasted Shapes*. New York: G.P. Putnam's Sons.

Darvishi, A., Munteanu, E., Guggiana, V., Schauer, H., Motavalli, M., and Rauterberg, M. (1995). Designing environmental sounds based on the results of interaction between objects in the real world. *Human-Computer Interaction: Proceedings of Interact '95*. London: Chapman and Hall. 38–42.

Deering, M.F. (1993). Data complexity for virtual reality: Where do all the triangles go?. *VRAIS '93: 1993 IEEE Virtual Reality Annual International Symposium*. Piscataway, NJ: IEEE. 357–363.

Deering, M. F. (1992). High resolution virtual reality. *Computer Graphics*. vol 26, no. 2. July. 195–202.

Deering, M.F. and Nelson, S.R. (1993). Leo: A system for cost effective 3D shaded graphics. *Computer Graphics (SIGGRAPH '93 Proceedings)*. vol. 27. 101–108.

Denes, P.B. and Pinson, E. N. (1993). *The Speech Chain: The Physics and Biology of Spoken Language*. New York: W.H. Freeman.

Division, Ltd. (1994). *Virtual Design Environment: dVS Technical Reference*. Bristol, UK: Division, Limited.

Durlach, N.I. (1991). Auditory localization in teleoperator and virtual environment systems: Ideas, issues, and problems. *Perception*. 20. 543–554.

Durlach, N.I. and Colburn, H.S. (1978). Binaural Phenomena. In E.C. Carterette and M.P. Friedman (eds.) *Handbook of Perception IV: Hearing*. New York: Academic Press. 365–466.

Durlach, N.I. and Mavor, A.S., eds. (1995). *Virtual Reality: Scientific and Technological Challenges*. Report by the National Research Council Committee on Virtual Reality Research and Development. Washington D.C.: National Academy Press.

Durlach, N.I. and Pang, X.D. (1986). Interaural magnification. *Journal of the Acoustical Society of America*. 80. 1849–1850.

Durlach, N.I., Rigopulos, A., Pang, X.D., Woods, W.S., Kulkarni, A., Colburn, H.S., and Wenzel, E.M. (1992) On the externalization of auditory images. *Presence: Teleoperators and Virtual Environments*. Spring, 1992. 251–257.

Durlach, N.I. and Sheridan, T.B. (1990). Introduction in Human Machine Interfaces for Teleoperators and Virtual Environments. *NASA Conferences Publication 10071*. CA: NASA Ames Research Center.

Durlach, N.I., Shinn-Cunningham, B.G., and Held, R.M. (1993). Supernormal auditory localization. I: General background. *Presence: Teleoperators and Virtual Environments*. vol. 2, no. 2. 89–103.

Ebenholtz, S.M. (1992). Motion sickness and oculomotor systems in virtual environments. *Presence: Teleoperators and Virtual Environments*. 1(3). 302–305.

Ellis, S.R. (1994). What are virtual environments? *IEEE Computer Graphics and Applications*. 17–22.

Ellis, S.R. (1993). Keynote speech at *Virtual Reality Systems Fall '93 Conference*. New York: SIG-Advanced Applications.

Ellis, S.R. (1991). Nature and origin of virtual environments: a bibliographical essay. *Computer Systems in Engineering*. 2(4). 321–347.

Ellis, S.R. (1991b). *Pictorial Communication in Virtual and Real Environments*. London: Taylor and Francis.

Ellis, S.R. and Nemire, K. (1993). A subjective technique for objective calibration of lines of sight in closed virtual environment viewing systems. *Society for Information Display International Symposium Digest of Technical Papers*. volume XXIV. Playa Del Ray, CA: Society for Information Display. 487–490.

Ellis, S.R., Tyler, M., Kim, W.S., and Stark, L. (1992). Three dimensional tracking with misalignment between display and control axes. *SAE Transactions, Journal of Aerospace*. 100-1. 985–989.

Bibliography

Ericsson, K.A. and Simon, H.A. (1984). *Protocol Analysis: Verbal Reports As Data*. Cambridge, MA: The MIT Press.

Esposito, C. (1993). Industrial Strength VR. Keynote address at Virtual Reality Systems' Fall '93 Conference. New York: SIG-Advanced Applications.

Fahlen, L.E., Stahl, O., Brown, C.G., and Carlsson, C. (1993). A space based model for user interaction in shared synthetic environments. *Human Factors in Computing Systems: INTERCHI '93 Conference Proceedings*. New York: ACM 43–48.

Fairchild, K.M. (1993). Information management using virtual reality-based visualizations, in A. Wexelblat (ed.) *Virtual Reality: Applications and Explorations*. San Diego, CA: Academic Press.

Falby, J.S., Zyda, M. J., Pratt, D.R., and Wilson, K.P. (1992). Educational and technological foundations for the construction of a 3D virtual world. *VR Becomes a Business: Proceedings of Virtual Reality '92*. Westport, CT: Meckler. 190–208.

Feiner, S. and Beshers, C. (1990). Worlds within worlds: Metaphors for exploring n-dimensional virtual worlds. Proceedings of the *ACM SIGGRAPH Symposium on User Interface Software and Technology*. 76–83.

Feiner, S., MacIntyre, B., and Seligmann, D. (1992). Annotating the real world with knowledge-based graphics on a see-through head-mounted display. *Proc. Graphics Interface '92*. Vancouver, Canada. May 11–15, 78–85.

Fisher, S.S., Wenzel, E.J., Coler, C., and McGreevy, M.W. (1988). Virtual interface environment workstations. *Proceedings of the 32nd Annual Meeting of the Human Factors Society*. Anaheim, CA. 91–95.

Foley, J.D. (1987). Interfaces for advanced computing. *Scientific American*. 10/87. 127–135.

Foley, J.D., van Dam, A., Feiner, S.K., and Hughes, J.F. (1990). *Computer Graphics: Principles and Practice*. 2nd edition. Reading, MA: Addison-Wesley.

Foley, J.M. (1991). Stereoscopic distance perception, in Ellis, S.R. (ed.) *Pictorial Communication in Virtual and Real Environments*. London: Taylor and Francis. 558–566.

Fredericks, K. (1994). Personal communication (electronic) on use of Cray supercomputer for virtual environment simulation with separate renderer. April 20.

Friedmann, M., Starner, T., and Pentland, A. (1993). Device synchronization using an optimal linear filter, in R.A. Earnshaw, M.A. Gigante, and H. Jones (eds.) *Virtual Reality Systems*. London: Academic Press Limited. 119–132.

Fry, D. B. (1979). *The Physics of Speech*. Cambridge, England: Cambridge University Press.

Furness III, T.A. (1986). The Super Cockpit and its human factors challenges. *Proceedings of the Human Factors Society 30th Annual Meeting*. Santa Monica, CA: Human Factors Society. 48–52.

Garner, W.R. (1949). Auditory signals, in *A Survey Report on Human Factors in Undersea Warfare*. Washington, D.C.: National Research Council. 201–217.

Gaver, W.W. (1986). Auditory icons: using sound in computer interfaces. *Human-Computer Interaction*. 2. 167–177.

Gembicki, M. and Rousseau, D. (1993). Naval applications of virtual reality. *Virtual Reality 93 Special Report* by AI Expert. 67–72.

Gershenfeld, N. (1991). The Hypercello Project. Invited lecture at IBM's T.J. Watson Research Center, NY.

Gopher, D. and Donchin, E. (1986). Workload: an examination of the concept, in K. R. Boff, L. Kaufman, and J. P. Thomas (eds.) *Handbook of perception and human performance*. vol. 2, 41:1–41:48. New York: Wiley.

Gopinath, P. and Bihari, T. (1993). Concepts and examples of object-oriented real-time systems, in Y.H. Lee and C.M. Krishna (eds.) *Real-Time Systems*. Los Alamitos, CA: IEEE Computer Science Press. 123–135.

Gould, J.D. and Lewis, C. (1983). Designing for usability: key principles and what designers think. *Proceedings ACM CHI '83 Conference on Human Factors in Computing Systems*. 50–53.

Gulick, W.L., Gescheider, G.A., and Frisina, R.D. (1989). *Hearing: Physiological Acoustics, Neural Coding, and Psychoacoustics*. New York: Oxford University Press.

Haas, M.W. and Hettinger, L.J. (1993). Applying virtual reality technology to cockpits of future fighter aircraft. *Virtual Reality Systems: Applications, Research and Development*. vol. 1, no. 2. New York: SIG-Advanced Applications. 18–26.

Hardy D. and Healy, M. (1993). Constructive and virtual interoperation: A technical challenge. *Virtual Reality Systems: Applications, Research and Development*. vol. 1, no. 2. New York: SIG-Advanced Applications. 12–17.

HEAD Acoustics (circa 1990, no date given). Computer-Aided Classification of Sound Events, Taking Into Account the Psychoacoustic Characteristics of Human Hearing. Herzogenrath, Germany: HEAD Acoustics GmbH.

Bibliography

Heilig, M.L. (1955). El cine del futuro: The cinema of the future. *Espacios*. Mexico. Reprinted in *Presence: Teleoperators and Virtual Environments*. 1(3). Cambridge, MA: MIT Press. 279–294.

Held, R. and Durlach, N. (1991). Telepresence, time delay and adaptation. In Ellis, S.R. (ed.) *Pictorial Communication in Virtual and Real Environments*. London: Taylor and Francis. 232–246.

Hezel, P.J. and Veron, H. (1993). Head-mounted displays for virtual reality. *Society for Information Display International Symposium Digest of Technical Papers*. volume XXIV. Playa Del Ray, CA: Society for Information Display. 909–911.

Hill, W.C. and Hollan, J.D. (1991). Deixis and the future of visualization excellence. *Proceedings of the IEEE Visualization Conference*. San Diego, CA.

Hirose, M., Hirota, K., and Kijima, R. (1992). Human behavior in virtual environments. *Proceedings of the SPIE, The International Society for Optical Engineering*. volume 1666. *Human Vision, Visual Processing, and Digital Display III*. Bellingham, WA: SPIE. 548–559.

Howard, I.P. (1991). Spatial vision within egocentric and exocentric frames of reference. In Ellis, S.R. (ed.) *Pictorial Communication in Virtual and Real Environments*. London: Taylor and Francis. 338–358.

Howlett, E.M. (1990). Wide angle orthostereo. *Proceedings of the SPIE Conference*. Santa Clara, CA. February, 210–223.

Jacob, R.J.K. (1991). The use of eye movements in human-computer interaction techniques: What you look at is what you get. *ACM Transactions on Information Systems*. vol. 9, no. 3. 152–169.

Joslin, A. (1993). Interactive dinosaur welcomes visitors to Tokyo hotel. *Virtual Reality Systems: Applications, Research, and Development*. vol. 1, no. 1. New York: SIG-Advanced Applications. 14–15.

Kaczmarek, K.A. and Bach-y-Rita, P. (1995). Tactile displays, in W. Barfield and T. A. Furness III (eds.) *Virtual Environments and Advanced Interface Design*. New York: Oxford University Press. 349–414.

Kalawsky, R. S. (1993). *The Science of Virtual Reality and Virtual Environments*. Reading, MA: Addison-Wesley.

Kennedy, R.S., Lane, N.E., Lilienthal, M.G., Bernbaum, K.S., and Hettinger, L.J. (1992). Profile analysis of simulator sickness symptoms: Application to virtual environment systems. *Presence: Teleoperators and Virtual Environments*. 1(3). 295–301.

Kieras, D.E. and Polson, P.G. (1985). An approach to the formal analysis of user complexity. *International Journal of Man-Machine Studies*. vol. 22. 365–394.

Kleiss, J.A. and Hubbard, D.C. (1993). Effects of three types of flight simulator visual scene detail on detection of altitude change. *Human Factors*. vol. 35, no. 4. 653–671.

Knudsen, E.I. and Konishi, M. (1979). Mechanisms of sound localization in the barn owl (Tyto alba). *Journal of Comparative Physiology*. 1133. 13–21.

Kolasinski, E.M. (in press). Simulator sickness in virtual environments. ARI Technical Report. Alexandria, VA: U.S. Army Research Institute for the Behavioral and Social Sciences.

Kollin, J. (1993). A retinal display for virtual-environment applications. *Society for Information Display International Symposium Digest of Technical Papers*. vol. XXIV. Playa Del Ray, CA: Society for Information Display. 827.

Kramer, G., ed. (1993). *Proceedings of the first International Conference on Auditory Display*. Reading, MA: Addison-Wesley.

Kramer, J. and Leifer, L. (1989). The Talking Glove: A speaking aid for non-vocal deaf and deaf-blind individuals. *Proc. RESNA 12th Annual Conf*. Louisiana. 471–472.

Krieg, J.C. (1993). Motion tracking: Polhemus technology. *Virtual Reality Systems: Applications, Research and Development*. vol. 1, no. 1. New York: SIG-Advanced Applications. 32–36.

Krueger, M.W. (1991). *Artificial Reality II*. Reading, MA: Addison-Wesley.

Krueger, M.W. (1989, June 27). Real time perception of and response to the actions of an unencumbered participant/user. U.S. Patent 4 843 568 (filed 1986, April 11).

Krueger, M.W. (1985). VIDEOPLACE: An artificial reality. *Proceedings ACM CHI '85 Conference on Human Factors in Computing Systems*. 35–40.

Laurel, B. (1986a). *Toward the Design of a Computer-Based Interactive Fantasy System*. Ph.D. dissertation, Ohio State University.

Laurel, B. (1986b). Interface as mimesis, in D.A. Norman and S. Draper (eds.) *User Centered System Design: New Perspectives on Human-Computer Interaction*. Hillsdale, NJ: Lawrence Erlbaum.

Levi, S.T. and Agrawala, A.K. (1990). *Real Time System Design*. New York: McGraw-Hill, Inc.

Levison, W.H. and Pew, R.W. (1993). Use of Virtual Environment Training Technology for Individual Combat Simulation. *BBN Systems and Technologies Inc./ United States Army Research Institute Technical Report 971*. February.

Lewis, J.B., Koved, L., and Ling, D.T. (1991). Dialogue structures for virtual worlds. *Proceedings of the CHI '91 Conference on Human Factors in Computer Systems*. New York: ACM. 131–136.

Li, L.C.H. (1993). Virtual reality and telepresence applications in space robotics. *Virtual Reality Systems: Applications, Research and Development* 1(2). 50–56.

Lindsay, P. H. and Norman, D.A. (1972). *Human Information Processing*. New York: Academic Press.

Lion, D., Rosenberg, C., and Barfield W. (1993). Overlaying three-dimensional computer graphics with stereoscopic live motion video: Applications for virtual environments. *Society for Information Display International Symposium Digest of Technical Papers*. volume XXIV. Playa Del Ray, CA: Society for Information Display. 483–486.

Lipton, L. (1991). *The Crystal Eyes Handbook*. Stereographics Corporation.

Liu, A., Tharp, G., and Stark, L. (1992). Depth cue interaction in telepresence and simulated telemanipulation. *Proceedings of the SPIE, The International Society for Optical Engineering*. volume 1666, Human Vision, Visual Processing and Digital Display III. Bellingham, WA: SPIE. 541–547.

Loftin, R.B., Engelberg, M., and Benedetti, R. (1993). Virtual controls in interactive environments: A virtual physics laboratory. *Society for Information Display International Symposium Digest of Technical Papers*. volume XXIV. Playa Del Ray, CA: Society for Information Display. 823–826.

Lusted, H. S., Knapp, R.B., and Lloyd, A. (1993). Biosignal processing and biocontrollers. *Virtual Reality Systems*. vol 1, no. 1. New York: SIG-Advanced Applications. 38–39.

Mann, R., Rowell, G., Conati, F., Tetwsky, A., Ottenheimer, D., and Antonsson, E. (1981). Precise, rapid, automatic 3D position and orientation tracking of multiple moving bodies. *Proceedings of the VIII International Congress of Biomechanics*. Nagoya, Japan.

Mano, M.M. (1982). *Computer System Architecture*. Englewood Cliffs, NJ: Prentice-Hall.

McCauley, M.E. and Sharkey, T.J. (1991). Spatial orientation and dynamics in virtual reality systems: lessons from flight simulation. *Proceedings of the Human Factors Society 35th Annual Meeting*. Santa Monica, CA: Human Factors Society, 1348–1352.

McGovern, D.E. (1991). Experience and results in teleoperation of land vehicles, in Ellis, S.R. (ed.) *Pictorial Communication in Virtual and Real Environments*. London: Taylor and Francis. 182–195.

McGreevy, M.W. (1993). Virtual reality and planetary exploration, in A. Wexelblat (ed.) *Virtual Reality: Applications and Explorations*. San Diego, CA: Academic Press.

McKenna, M. and Zeltzer, D. (1992). Three dimensional visual display systems for virtual environments. *Presence: Teleoperators and Virtual Environments*. 1(4). Cambridge, MA: MIT Press. 421–458.

Mershon, D. H. and King, L.E. (1975). Intensity and reverberation as factors in the auditory perception of egocentric distance. *Perception and Psychophysics*. 18. 409–415.

Meyer, D.E., Abrams, R.A., Kornblum, S., Wright, C.E., and Smith, J.E.K. (1988). Optimality in human motor performance: Ideal control of rapid aimed movements. *Psychological Review*. 95. 340–370.

Meyer, D.E., Smith, J.E.K., Kornblum, S., Abrams, R.A., and Wright, C.E. (1990). Speed-accuracy trade-offs in aimed movements: Toward a theory of rapid voluntary action, in M. Jeannerod (ed.) *Attention and Performance XIII*. Hillsdale, NJ: Lawrence Erlbaum. 173–226.

Meyer, K., Applewhite, H.L., and Biocca, F. A. (1991). The ultimate tracker: A survey of position trackers. *Piltdown Technical Report 91-05*. Beaverton, OR: Piltdown Inc. December. Subsequently published in *Presence: Teleoperators and Virtual Environments*. vol. 1, no. 2. Spring 1992. 173–200.

Mine, M. (1995a). ISAAC: A virtual environment tool for the interactive construction of virtual worlds. *UNC Chapel Hill Computer Science Technical Report TR95-020*.

Mine, M. (1995b). Virtual environment interaction techniques. *UNC Chapel Hill Computer Science Technical Report TR95-018*.

Mon-Williams, M., Wann, J.P., and Rushton, S.K. (1993). Binocular vision in a virtual world: Visual deficits following the wearing of a head-mounted display. *Ophthalmic and Physiological Optics*. 13. 387–391.

Mowbray, G.H. and Gebhard, J.W. (1961). Man's senses as information channels, in H.W. Sinaiko (ed.) *Human Factors in the Design and Use of Control Systems*. New York: Dover. 115–149.

Mueller, C. (1995). Architectures of image generators for flight simulators. *UNC Chapel Hill Computer Science Technical Report TR95-015*.

Noar, D., Arnon, O., and Avnur, A. (1987). A lightweight innovative Helmet Airborne Display and Sight (HADAS). *Display System Optics, SPIE Proceedings*. vol. 778. 89–95.

Norman, D.A. (1988). *The Design of Everyday Things*. New York: Doubleday.

O'Donnell, R.D. and Eggemeier, F.T. (1986). Workload assessment methodology, in K.R. Boff, L. Kaufman, and J. P. Thomas (eds.) *Handbook of perception and human performance*. vol. 2, 42:1–42:49. New York: Wiley.

Olzak L.A. and Thomas, J.P. (1986). Seeing spatial patterns, in K.R. Boff, L. Kaufman, and J. P. Thomas (eds.) *Handbook of perception and human performance*. vol. 1, 7:1–7:56. New York: Wiley.

Oppenheim, A.V., Willsky, A.S., and Young, I.T. (1983). *Signals and Systems*. Englewood Cliffs, NJ: Prentice-Hall, Inc.

Ozsoyoglu, G., Ozsoyoglu, Z.M., and Hou, W.C. (1993). Case-DB: A real-time database management system, in Y.H. Lee and C.M. Krishna (eds.) *Real-Time Systems*. Los Alamitos, CA: IEEE Computer Science Press. 199–216.

Paley, W.B. (1993). Immersion or desktop virtual reality? *Virtual Reality Systems: Applications, Research, and Development*. vol. 1, no. 1. New York: SIG-Advanced Applications. 18–20.

Paradiso, J.A. and Gershenfeld, N. (in press). Musical applications of electric field sensing. To be submitted to *Computer Music Journal*.

Parsons, T.W. (1986). *Voice and Speech Processing*. New York: McGraw-Hill, Inc.

Patterson, R.R. (1982). *Guidelines for Auditory Warning Systems on Civil Aircraft*, paper no. 82017. London: Civil Aviation Authority.

Pausch, R. (1994). The software development environment, in Pausch, R., van Dam, A., Robinett, W., and Bryson, S. *Implementing Virtual Reality. CHI '94 Tutorial #25. Conference on Human Factors in Computing Systems*. April. Boston, MA: ACM. 24–28.

Pausch, R. (1991). Virtual reality on five dollars a day. *Proceedings of the CHI '91 Conference on Human Factors in Computer Systems*. New York: ACM. 265–270.

Pausch, R., Conway, M., DeLine, R., Gossweiller, R., and Miale, S. (1993). Alice and DIVER: a software architecture for building virtual environments. *INTERCHI '93 Adjunct Proceedings: Conference on Human Factors in Computing Systems*. New York: ACM, 13–14.

Piantanida, T.P. (1994). What is "real time," "real space?" *Virtual Reality Systems: Applications, Research, and Development*. vol. 1, no. 3. New York: SIG-Advanced Applications. 68–70.

Piantanida, T.P. (1993). Tuning sensory and psychological factors to enhance virtual reality. Unpublished presentation at the DPMAEF Conference on Synthetic Environments. McLean, VA. March 31.

Piantanida, T.P., Boman, D., and Gille, J. (1993). Human perceptual issues and virtual reality. *Virtual Reality Systems: Applications, Research, and Development*. vol. 1, no. 1. New York: SIG-Advanced Applications. 43–52.

Piantanida, T.P., Boman, D., Larimer, J., Gille, J. and Reed, C. (1992). Studies of the field-of-view/resolution tradeoff in virtual reality systems. *Proceedings of SPIE, The International Society of Optical Engineering*. volume 1666, Human Vision, Visual Processing and Digital Display III. Bellingham, WA: SPIE. 448–456.

Pimentel, K. and Teixeira, K. (1993). *Virtual Reality: Through the New Looking Glass*. Blue Ridge Summit, PA: Windcrest/McGraw-Hill, Inc.

Poston, T. and Fairchild, K.M. (1993). Virtual Aristotelean physics. *VRAIS '93: 1993 IEEE Virtual Reality Annual International Symposium*. Piscataway, NJ: IEEE. 512–518.

Psotka, J., Davison, S.A., and Lewis, S.A. (1993). Exploring immersion in virtual space. *Virtual Reality Systems: Applications, Research and Development*. 1(2). New York: SIG-Advanced Applications. 70–82.

Raab, F.H., Blood, E.B., Steiner, T.O., and Jones, R.J. (1979). Magnetic position and orientation tracking system. *IEEE Transactions on Aerospace and Electronic Systems*. 15:5. AES. 709-718.

Reddy, D.R. (1976). Speech recognition by machine: a review, in N. Rex Dixon and Thomas B. Martin (eds.) *Automatic Speech and Speaker Recognition*. New York: IEEE Press. 56–86.

Regan, D.M., Kaufman, L., and Lincoln, J. (1986). Motion in depth and visual acceleration, in K. R. Boff, L. Kaufman, and J. P. Thomas (eds.) *Handbook of Perception and Human Performance*. New York: John Wiley and Sons. Chapter 19.

Regian, J.W., Shebilske, W.L., and Monk, J.M. (1992). Virtual reality: an instructional medium for visual-spatial tasks. *Journal of Communication*. vol. 42, no. 4. Autumn. 136–149.

Rheingold, H. (1991). *Virtual Reality*. New York: Summit.

Richard, P., Burdea, G., Gomez, D., and Coiffet, P. (1994). A comparison of haptic, visual and auditive force feedback for deformable virtual objects. Submitted to *ICAT '94 The Fourth International Conference on Artificial Reality and Tele-Existence*. Tokyo, Japan.

Robinett, W. (1994). Designing virtual worlds, in Pausch, R., van Dam, A., Robinett, W. and Bryson, S. *Implementing Virtual Reality. CHI '94 Tutorial #25, Conference on Human Factors in Computing Systems*. April 24–28. Boston, MA: ACM.

Robinett, W. (1992). Synthetic experience: a taxonomy, survey of earlier thought, and speculations on the future. *University of North Carolina, Chapel Hill tech report TR92-022*. Subsequently published as Synthetic experience: A proposed taxonomy. *Presence: Teleoperators and Virtual Environments*. Spring. 229–247.

Robinett, W. and Rolland, J.P. (1992). A computational model for the stereoscopic optics of a head-mounted display. *Presence: Teleoperators and Virtual Environments*. Winter. 45–62.

Roscoe, S.N. (1991). The eyes prefer real images, in Ellis, S.R. (ed.) *Pictorial Communication in Virtual and Real Environments*. London: Taylor and Francis. 577–585.

Rosen, J.M. (1991). Surgical simulation: From flight simulation to virtual reality. *Virtual Worlds: Real Challenges*. Papers from SRI's 1991 Conference on Virtual Reality. 43–50.

Rosenbaum, D.A. (1991). *Human Motor Control*. San Diego, CA: Academic Press, Inc.

Rosenberg, L.B. (1995). How to assess the quality of force-feedback systems. *The Journal of Medicine and Virtual Reality: Computers, Imagery, Photonics, and Robotic Applications*. vol. 1, no. 1. New York: Virtual Reality Solutions. 12–15.

Rosenberg, L.B. (1993). Perceptual design of virtual haptic sensations. To appear in *Proceedings of Virtual Reality Systems Fall '93 Conference*. New York: SIG-Advanced Applications.

Rushton, S.K., Mon-Williams, M., and Wan, J.P. (1994). Binocular vision in a bi-ocular world: New generation head-mounted displays avoid causing visual deficit. *Displays*. vol. 15, No. 4. 255–260.

Satava, MD, FACS, Col. R.M. (1993). Virtual reality surgical simulator: the first steps. *Proceedings of Virtual Reality Systems '93*. New York: SIG-Advanced Applications. 41–50.

Schiffman, H.R. (1990). *Sensation and Perception: An Integrated Approach*. New York: John Wiley and Sons.

Sedgwick, H.A. (1988). Space perception, in K. R. Boff, L. Kaufman, and J. P. Thomas (eds.) *Handbook of perception and human performance*. vol. 1, 21:1–21:57. New York: Wiley.

Segan, J. (1993). Controlling computers with gloveless gestures. Presentation at Virtual Reality Systems '93. New York City, March 15.

Shaw, C., Liang, J., Green, M., and Sun, Y. (1992). The decoupled simulation model for virtual reality systems. *Proceedings of the CHI '92 Conference on Human Factors in Computer Systems*. New York: ACM. 321–328.

Sherrick, C.E. and Cholewiak, R.W. (1986). Cutaneous sensitivity, in K. R. Boff, L. Kaufman, and J. P. Thomas (eds.) *Handbook of perception and human performance*. vol. 1, 12:1–12:58. New York: Wiley.

Shimoga, K.B. (1993a). A survey of perceptual feedback issues in dexterous telemanipulation, Part I: finger force feedback. *VRAIS '93: 1993 IEEE Virtual Reality Annual International Symposium*. Piscataway, NJ: IEEE. 263–270.

Shimoga, K.B. (1993b). A survey of perceptual feedback issues in dexterous telemanipulation: Part II. finger touch feedback. *VRAIS '93: 1993 IEEE Virtual Reality Annual International Symposium*. Piscataway, NJ: IEEE. 271–279.

Singhal, S.K. and Cheriton, D.R. (1995). Exploiting position history for efficient remote rendering in networked virtual reality. *Presence: Teleoperators and Virtual Environments*. 4(2). Cambridge, MA: MIT Press. 169–193.

Sowa, J.F. (1984). *Conceptual Structures: Information Processing in Mind and Machine*. Reading, MA: Addison-Wesley.

Speeter, T.H. (1992). Transforming human hand motion for telemanipulation. *Presence: Teleoperators and Virtual Environments*. 1(1). Cambridge, MA: MIT Press. 63–79.

Srinivasan, M.A. (1990). Tactual interfaces: The human perceiver. *Human Machine Interfaces for Teleoperators and Virtual Environments*. NASA Conference Publication 10071. Moffett Field, CA: National Aeronautics and Space Administration.

Stankovic, J.A. (1988). Real-time computing systems: The next generation, in J.A. Stankovic and K. Ramamritham *Hard Real-Time Systems*. Washington D.C.: Computer Science Press of IEEE. 14–37.

Stankovic, J.A. and Ramamritham, K. (1988). Introduction in J.A. Stankovic and K. Ramamritham *Hard Real-Time Systems*. Washington D.C.: Computer Science Press of IEEE. 1–11.

Starks, M. (1992) Stereoscopic video and the quest for virtual reality: An annotated bibliography of selected topics, in Merritt, J (ed.) *Stereoscopic Displays and Applications II: Proceedings of SPIE*. vol. 1457.

Stevens, K.A. (1991). Perceptions of three-dimensionality, in Ellis, S.R. (ed.) *Pictorial Communication in Virtual and Real Environments*. London: Taylor and Francis. 449–459.

Strasser, A. (1993). Head-Mounted Display Engineering. *VRAIS Tutorial Notes #4. Presented at VRAIS '93: 1993 IEEE Virtual Reality Annual International Symposium*. Seattle, WA. September 18.

Stuart, R. (1993a). Human factors and virtual reality: A perspective. *Society for Information Display International Symposium Digest of Technical Papers*. volume XXIV. Playa Del Ray, CA: Society for Information Display. 901–904.

Stuart, R. (1993b). Creative Improvisational Design in Virtual Environments: Users as Virtuoso Collaborative World-Builders. *Pace University Technical Reports #66*. White Plains, NY: Pace University School of Computer Science and Information Systems.

Stuart, R. (1993c). Sonic Issues: Audio display from the simple beep to sonification and virtual auditory environments, in Marchese, F. (ed.) *Understanding Images*. TELOS Springer-Verlag. 283–307.

Stuart, R. (1992). Virtual auditory worlds: an overview. VR Becomes a Business: *Proceedings of Virtual Reality '92*. Westport, CT: Meckler. 144–166.

Stuart, R., Desurvire, H., and Dews, S. (1991). The truncation of prompts in phone-based interfaces: using TOTT in evaluations. *Proceedings of the Human Factors Society 35th Annual Meeting*. Santa Monica, CA: Human Factors Society. 230–234.

Stuart, R and Thomas, J.C. (1991). The implications of education in cyberspace. *Multimedia Review*. vol. 2, issue 2. Summer. 17–27.

Sturman, D.J. and Zeltzer, D. (1994). A survey of glove-based input. *IEEE Computer Graphics and Applications*. vol. 14, no. 1. 30–39.

Sutherland, I.E. (1965). The ultimate display. *Proceedings of IFIP 65*. 2. 506–508, 582–583.

Sutherland, I.E. (1968). A head-mounted three-dimensional display. 1968 Fall Joint Computer Conference. *AFIPS Conference Proceedings*. 33. 757–764.

Taylor II, R.M. (1995). Requirements and availability of application programmer's interfaces for virtual-reality systems. *Technical Report TR95-009*. UNC-Chapel Hill Department of Computer Science.

Taylor II, R.M., Robinett, W., Chi, V.L., Brooks Jr., F.P., Wright, W.V., Williams, R.S. and Snyder, E.J. (1993). The Nanomanipulator: A virtual reality interface for a scanning tunneling microscope. *Computer Graphics, SIGGRAPH '93 Proceedings*. vol. 27. 127–134.

Tharp, G., Liu, A., French, L., Lai, S., and Stark, L. (1992). Timing considerations of helmet mounted display performance. *Proceedings of the SPIE, The International Society for Optical Engineering*. volume 1666, Human Vision, Visual Processing, and Digital Display III. Bellingham, WA: SPIE. 570–576.

Thomas, J.C. and Stuart, R (1993). Speech technology and virtual reality. *Virtual Reality Systems: Applications, Research, and Development*. vol. 1, no. 1. New York: SIG-Advanced Applications. 53–59.

Thomas, J.C. and Stuart, R. (1992). Virtual reality and human factors. *Proceedings of the Human Factors Society, 36th Annual Meeting*. Santa Monica, CA: Human Factors Society. 207–210.

Urdang, E. and Stuart, R. (1992). Orientation enhancement through integrated virtual reality and geographic information systems. *Virtual Reality and Persons with Disabilities*. California State University, Northridge. March 18–21. 55–62.

van Dam, A. (1994). Perspectives on virtual reality, in Pausch, R., van Dam, A., Robinett, W., and Bryson, S. *Implementing Virtual Reality. CHI '94 Tutorial #25, Conference on Human Factors in Computing Systems*. April 24–28. Boston, MA: ACM.

Wallach, H. (1939). On sound localization. *Journal of the Acoustical Society of America*. 10. 270–274.

Wang, J.F. (1990). A Real-time Optical 6D Tracker for Head-mounted Display Systems. *Technical Report TR90-011*. UNC-Chapel Hill Department of Computer Science, March.

Wang, J., Azuma, R., Bishop, G., Chi, V., Eyles, J., and Fuchs, H. (1990). Tracking a head-mounted display in a room-sized environment with head-mounted cameras. *Proceedings: SPIE '90 Technical Symposium on Optical Engineering and Photonics in Aerospace Sensing*. Orlando, FL, 1290.

Wang, J., Chi, V. and Fuchs, H. (1990). A real-time optical 3D tracker for head-mounted display systems. *Computer Graphics: 1990 Symposium on Interactive 3D Graphics*. 24(2). 205–215.

Wann, J.P., Rushton, S.K., and Mon-Williams, M. (in press). Natural problems for stereoscopic depth perception in virtual environments. *Vision Research*.

Ward, M, Azuma, R., Bennett, R., Gottschalk, S., and Fuchs, H. (1992). A demonstrated optical tracker with scalable work area for head-mounted display systems. *Proceedings of 1992 Symposium on Interactive 3D Graphics*. Cambridge, MA, 43–52.

Ware, C., Arthur, K., and Booth, K.S. (1993). Fishtank virtual reality. *Human Factors in Computing Systems: INTERCHI '93 Conference Proceedings*. New York: ACM. 37–42.

Ware, C. and Mikaelian, H.H. (1987). An evaluation of an eye tracker as a device for computer input. *CHI + GI 1987 Conference Proceedings: Human Factors in Computing Systems and Graphics Interface*. New York: ACM. 183–188.

Warren, D.H., Welch, R.B., and McCarthy, T.J. (1981). The role of visual-auditory "compellingness" in the ventriloquism effect: Implications for transitivity among the spatial senses. *Perception and Psychophysics*. 30. 557–564.

Waterworth, J.A. (1982). Man-machine speech "dialogue acts." *Applied Ergonomics*. vol. 13, no. 3. 203–207.

Weghorst, S., Prothero, J., Furness, T., Anson, D., and Reiss, T. (1994). Virtual images in the treatment of Parkinson's disease akinesia. *Medicine Meets Virtual Reality II. Interactive Technology and Healthcare: Visionary Applications for Simulation, Visualization, and Robotics*. San Diego, CA: Aligned Management Associates. 242–243.

Welch, R.B. (1978). *Perceptual Modification: Adapting to Altered Sensory Environments*. New York: Academic Press.

Welch, R.B. and Warren, D.H. (1986). Intersensory interactions, in K.R. Boff, L. Kaufman and J.P. Thomas (eds.) *Handbook of perception and human performance*. vol. I: *Sensory processes and perception*. New York: Wiley. 25–1, 25–36.

Wells, M. J. (1989). Obtaining new perspectives with head-coupled simulators. *Symposium at 33rd Annual Human Factors Society Meeting.* Denver, CO. October 16–20.

Wenzel, E.M. (1992). Localization in virtual acoustic displays. *Presence: Teleoperators and Virtual Environments.* 1(1). Cambridge, MA: MIT Press. 80–107.

Wexelblat, A. (1993). The reality of cooperation: Virtual reality and cscw, in A. Wexelblat (ed.) *Virtual Reality: Applications and Explorations.* Cambridge, MA: Academic Press.

White, B.W., Saunder, F.A., Scadden, L., Bach-y-Rita, P., and Collins, C.C. (1970). Seeing with the skin. *Perception and Psychophysics.* vol. 7. 23–27.

White, G. M. (1976). Speech recognition: A tutorial. In N. Rex Dixon and Thomas B. Martin (eds.), *Automatic Speech and Speaker Recognition.* New York: IEEE Press. 87–100.

Wickens, C.D. and Baker, P. (1995). Cognitive issues in virtual reality, in W. Barfield and T A. Furness III (eds.) *Virtual Environments and Advanced Interface Design.* New York: Oxford University Press. 514–541.

Wickens, C.D., Todd, S., and Seidler, K. (1989). *Three-dimensional displays: Perception, implementation, applications.* CSERIAC SOAR-89-01. Wright-Patterson AFB, OH: CSERIAC.

Wightman, F.L. and Kistler, D.J. (1989a). Headphone simulation of free-field listening I: Stimulus synthesis. *Journal of the Acoustical Society of America.* 85. 858–867.

Wightman, F.L. and Kistler, D.J. (1989b). Headphone simulation of free-field listening II: Psychophysical validation. *Journal of the Acoustical Society of America.* 85. 868–878.

Wloka, M.M. (1995). Lag in multiprocessor virtual reality. *Presence: Teleoperators and Virtual Environments.* 4(1). Cambridge, MA: MIT Press. 50–63.

Woodson, W.E. (1981). *Human Factors Design Handbook.* New York: McGraw-Hill, Inc.

Wulfeck, J.W. and Zeitlin, L.W. (1962). In R. Gagne (ed.) *Psychological Principles in System Development.* New York: Holt, Rinehart, and Winston. 115–156.

Wyshynski, S. and Vincent, V.J. (1993). Full-body unencumbered immersion in virtual worlds, in A. Wexelblat (ed.) *Virtual Reality: Applications and Explorations.* San Diego, CA: Academic Press.

Wyszecki, G. and Stiles, W.S. (1982). *Color Science: Concepts and Methods, Quantitative Data and Formulae.* New York: John Wiley and Sons.

Young, L.R. and Sheena, D. (1975). Survey of eye movement recording methods. *Behavior Research Methods and Instrumentation.* vol 7, no. 5. 397–429.

Zeltzer, D. (1992). Autonomy, interaction, and presence. *Presence: Teleoperators and Virtual Environments.* 1(1). Cambridge, MA: MIT Press. 127–132.

Zerkus, M., Becker, B., Ward, J., and Halvorsen, L. (1993). Temperature sensing in virtual reality and telerobotics. *Virtual Reality Systems: Applications, Research and Development.* 1(2).

Zimmerman, T.G., Lanier, J., Blanchard, C., Bryson, S., and Harvill, Y. (1987). A hand gesture interface device. *CHI + GI 1987 Conference Proceedings: Human Factors in Computing Systems and Graphics Interface.* New York: ACM. 189–192.

Zimmerman, T.G., Smith, J.S., Paradiso, J.A., Allport, D., and Gershenfeld, N. (1995). Applying electric field sensing to human-computer interfaces. *Proceedings of the CHI '95 Conference on Human Factors in Computer Systems.* New York: ACM. 280–287.

Zyda, M.J., Pratt, D.R., Falby, J.S., Lombardo, C., and Kelleher, K.M. (1993). The software required for the computer generation of virtual environments. *Presence: Teleoperators and Virtual Environments.* 1(4). Cambridge, MA: MIT Press. 130–140.

Author Index

A

Ackerman, D., 41
Adelstein, B.D., 105, 106, 184, 221
Agrawala, A.K., 167, 168
Airey, J., xxvii, 8, 183
Akeley, K., 170
Alspaugh, J., xxvii, 8, 183
Andersson, R.L., 11
Anstis, S.M., 26
Applewhite, H.L., xxix, 14, 73, 99, 100, 101, 102, 103, 104
Arnon, O., 101
Arthur, K., 139
Avnur, A., 101
Azuma, R.T., 80, 104, 121

B

Bach-y-Rita, P., 39, 46, 83, 151, 152
Bajura, M., 72, 142
Baker, P., xxiii, xxv, 8, 9, 11, 57, 70
Barfield, W., 72
Bass, M., 138
Batteau, D.W., 33
Batter, J.J., xxvii, 39, 84, 151, 153
Baudel, T., 120
Beaudouin-Lafon, 120
Begault, D.R., 148
Bejczy, A., 9
Benedetti, R., 77, 119, 177
Benford, S., 71, 72
Bennett, R., 104
Bertelson, P., 55
Beshers, C., 11
Bhatnager, 102

Bihari, T., 167
Biocca, F., xxix, 13, 14, 73, 99, 101, 102
Bishop, G., 104
Blanchard, C., xxix, 109, 120
Blattner, M.M., 145
Blauert, J., xxix, 34
Bletter, N., 66, 122, 170, 219
Blood, E.B., 102
Bly, S., 31
Boff, K.R., 18, 20, 26, 28, 37, 38, 40, 44, 46, 48, 49, 50, 74, 128
Boman, D., 81, 184
Booth, K.S., 139
Bostrom, M., 11
Bowman, D., 12
Bregman, A.S., 31
Brewster, S., 146
Brody, A.R., 8
Brooks, Fred P. Jr., xxvii, 8, 11, 39, 75, 76, 79, 84, 111, 112, 119, 151, 153, 182, 183
Brown, C.G., 71
Bryson, S., xxix, xxxii, xxxiv, xxxvi, xxxviii, 12, 109, 120, 130, 218
Burdea, G., 69
Burgess, David, 147, 190
Butterworth, J., 12
Buttolo, P., 154
Buxton, W., 31, 118

C

Calhoun, G.L., xxix
Calvin, J., 11
Card, S.K., 49, 50, 56, 57, 201

Author Index

Carlsson, C., 71
Carroll, J.M., 57, 58
Cater, J.P., 41, 154
Chang, S., 36, 38
Chapin, W.L., 148
Cheriton, D.R., 172
Chi, V., xxvii, 104
Chin, J.P., 200
Cholewiak, R.W., 37, 39
Chung, J., 178
Clark, F.J., 38, 39
Coco, G.P., 78, 166, 170, 172
Coiffet, P., 69
Colburn, H.S., 34
Coler, C., xxviii, xxix
Conway, M., 159
Cornsweet, T.N., 21
Cruz-Neira, C., 67, 139
Cytowic, R.E., 78

D

Darvishi, A., 146
Davison, S.A., 57, 70
Deering, M.F., 130, 139
DeFanti, Thomas A., xxviii, 67, 139
DeLine, R., 159
Desurvire, H., 53
Dews, S., 53
Diehl, V.A., 200
Dijkstra, 167
Donchin, E., 204
Doppler, Christian, 35
Durlach, N.I., xxvi, xxix, 33, 34, 69, 111, 143, 149, 155, 167, 168, 220

E

Ebenholtz, S.M., 81
Eberman, B., 36, 38
Edison, Thomas, 58
Edwards, A.D.N., 146
Eggemeier, F.T., 205
Ellis, Steve R., xxviii, xxx, 3, 8, 15, 19, 23, 32, 55, 59, 65, 105, 106, 140, 168, 184, 221
Engelberg, M., 77, 119, 177
Ericsson, K.A., 200
Esposito, C., 71, 110
Evans, David, xxvi
Eyles, J., 104

F

Fahlen, L.E., 71
Fairchild, K.M., 65, 74, 75, 76, 77, 119
Falby, J.S., 130
Feiner, S., xxxiii, 9, 11, 72, 73, 130, 131, 132, 142, 169, 170, 173
Fisher, Scott, xxviii
Fitts, Paul, 48
Foley, J.D., xxxiii, 130, 131, 132, 170
Foley, J.M., 25
Foster, Scott H., xxix, 148
Fredericks, Keith, 170
French, L., 28
Friedmann, M., 120, 121
Frisina, R.D., 33
Fry, D.B., 52
Fuchs, H., 72, 104, 142
Furness, Tom A., xxvii, xxix

G

Gaver, W., 31, 32
Gebhard, J.W., 44
Gembicki, M., 117
Gershenfeld, N., 9
Gesheider, 33
Gille, J., 81, 184
Gopher, D., 204
Gopinath, P., 167
Gossweiller, R., 159
Gottschalk, S., 104
Gould, John, xxx, xxxi, xxxii
Green, M., 159
Griffith, D. W., 66
Grimes, Gary, xxix
Gulick, W.L., 33

H

Haas, M.W., 68
Hannaford, B., 154
Hardy, D., 5
Hart, J.C., 67, 139
Harvill, Y., xxix, 109, 120
Healy, M., 5
Heilig, Morton, xxvi, 74, 99
Held, R.M., 69, 149
Henning, 41
Hettinger, L.J., 68
Hezel, P.J., 25, 29

Hill, W.C., 125
Hirose, M., 46, 47
Hirota, K., 46
Hollan, J.D., 125
Horch, K.W., 38, 39
Hou, W.C., 167
Howard, I.P., 43, 70
Howlett, Eric, xxviii, 65, 136, 141
Hughes, J.F., xxxiii, 130, 131, 132, 170

J

Jacob, R.J.K., 8, 114, 115, 116
Johnston, E.R., 105, 106, 184, 221
Jones, R.J., 102
Joslin, A., 113

K

Kaczmarek, K.A., 39, 46, 83, 151, 152
Kalawsky, R.S., xxviii, 25, 102, 109, 111, 142
Kaufman, L., 21, 25, 40
Kennedy, R.S., 206, 215
Kenyon, R.V., 67, 139
Kieras, D.E., 195
Kijima, R., 46
Kilpatrick, P.J., xxvii, 39, 84, 151, 153
Kim, W.S., 55
King, L.E., 34
Kistler, Doris J., xxix, 34, 147
Knapp, R.B., 117
Knudsen, E.I., 149
Kolasinski, E.M., 81
Kollin, J., 114, 133
Konishi, M., 149
Koved, L., 159
Kramer, Jim, 29, 50, 109, 144
Krieg, J.C., 102
Krueger, Myron, xxvii, 40, 104

L

Lanier, Jaron, xxviii, xxix, 109, 120
Larimer, J., 184
Laurel, Brenda, 74
Leifer, L., 50
Levi, S.T., 167, 168
Levison, W.H., 8, 92, 93
Levit, C., 12
Lewis, Clayton, xxx, xxxi, xxxii

Lewis, J.B., 159
Lewis, Peter, 58
Lewis, S.A., 57, 70
Liang, J., 159
Lincoln, J.E., 18, 20, 21, 25, 26, 28, 37, 38, 40, 44, 46, 48, 49, 50, 74, 128
Lindsay, P.H., 31, 57
Ling, D.T., 159
Lion, D., 72
Lipton, L., 21
Liu, A., 28
Lloyd, A., 117
Loftin, R.B., 11, 77, 119, 177
Lusted, H.S., 117

M

Machover, 9
MacIntyre, B., 9, 72, 73, 142, 169, 173
Mallock, 33
Mano, M.M., 167
Marcus, B., 36, 38
Mavor, A.S., 111, 155, 220
McCarthy, T.J., 54
McGovern, D.E., 9
McGreevy, Michael W., xxviii, xxix, 12
McKenna, M., 21, 140, 141
McLean, W.B., 33
Mershon, D.H., 34
Meyer, K., xxix, 14, 48, 49, 73, 99, 101, 102, 105, 106
Miale, S., 159
Mikaelian, H.H., 116
Mine, M., 12, 177, 178, 179, 180
Minsky, Margaret, 39
Mon-Williams, M., 81, 82
Monk, J.M., 57
Moran, T.P., 49, 50, 56, 57, 201
Mowbray, G.H., 44
Mueller, C., 128, 131, 168

N

Nelson, S.R., 130
Nemire, K., 65, 140
Newell, A., 49, 50, 56, 57, 201
Noar, D., 101
Norman, D.A., 31, 57, 176, 180
Norman, K.L., 200

O

O'Donnell, R.D., 205
Ohbuchi, R., 72, 142
Olzak, L.A., 26
Oppenheim, A.V., 147
Ouh-Young, M., xxvii, 39, 84, 151, 153
Ozsoyoglu, G., 167
Ozsoyoglu, Z.M., 167

P

Pang, X.D., 149
Paradiso, J.A., 9
Parsons, T.W., 121, 123
Pausch, R., 159
Pavel, 72
Pentland, A., 120, 121
Pew, R.W., 8, 92, 93
Piantanida, T.P., 29, 43, 81, 142, 184, 191
Pimentel, K., xxvi
Polhemus, xxviii
Polson, P.G., 195
Poston, T., 76
Pratt, D.R., 130
Psotka, J., 57, 70

R

Raab, F.H., 102
Radeau, M., 55
Ramamritham, K., 163, 166, 167
Reddy, D.R., 121, 122, 124
Reed, C., 184
Regan, D.M., 21, 25
Regian, J.W., 57
Richard, P., 78
Robinett, Warren, xxvii, xxviii, 58, 65, 78, 140, 176
Rolland, J.P., 65, 140
Roscoe, S.N., 136
Rosen, J.M., 11
Rosenbaum, D.A., 50, 54
Rosenberg, L.B., 38, 72, 127, 151, 153, 154
Rousseau, D., 117
Rushton, S.K., 81, 82

S

Sandin, Daniel J., xxviii, 67, 139
Satava, R.M., 9
Sayre, Rich, xxviii
Schiffman, H.R., 24, 27, 35, 41, 42
Sedgwick, H.A., 21, 22
Segan, J., 52
Seidler, K., 19, 21, 24
Seligmann, D., 9, 72, 73, 142, 169, 173
Shaw, C., 159
Shebilske, W.L., 57
Sheena, D., 20, 114, 115
Sheridan, T., xxvi
Sherrick, C.E., 37, 39
Shimoga, K.B., 38, 39, 47, 151, 153
Shinn-Cunningham, B.G., 149
Simon, H.A., 200
Singhal, S.K., 11, 172
Slater, M., 72
Snowdon, D., 71, 72
Snyder, E.J., xxvii
Sowa, J.F., 42
Speeter, T.H., 47, 65
Stahl, O., 71
Stankovic, J.A., 163, 166, 167
Stark, L., 28, 55
Starks, M., 139
Starner, T., 120, 121
Steiner, T.O., 102
Stiles, W.S., 26
Stoker, Carol, 5, 73
Strasser, A., 136, 138
Stuart, Rory, xx, 6, 7, 12, 32, 35, 51, 58, 74, 77, 78, 79, 122, 124, 148, 149, 165, 171
Sturman, D.J., xxviii, xxix
Sumikawa, D.A., 145
Sun, Y., 159
Sutherland, Ivan, xxvi, xxvii, xxviii, xxx, 83, 101, 220

T

Tan, H., 36, 38
Taylor, R.M. II, xxvii, 169
Teixeira, K., xxvi
Tharp, G., 28
Thomas, J.C., 6, 7, 40, 57, 58, 74, 77, 79, 122, 124, 165
Thomas, J.P., 26
Thomson, 33
Todd, S., 19, 21, 24
Tyler, M., 55

U

Urdang, E., 7

V

Valencia, G., xxix
van Dam, A., xxxiii, 69, 130, 131, 132, 157, 170
Veron, H., 25, 29
Vincent, V.J., 104

W

Wang, J., 104
Wann, J.P., 81, 82
Ward, M., 104
Ware, C., 116, 117, 139
Warren, D.H., 54, 55
Waterworth, J.A., 53
Weghorst, S., 9
Welch, R.B., 54, 55
Wells, M.J., 66
Wenzel, Elizabeth, xxviii, xxix, 8, 67, 148
Wexelblat, A., 5
White, B.W., 37, 121
Wickens, C.D., xxiii, xxv, 8, 9, 11, 19, 21, 22, 23, 24, 25, 57, 70
Wightman, Fred L., xxix, 34, 147
Wiley, C.W., 11
Williams, R.S., xxvii
Willsky, A.S., 147
Wilson, K.P., 130
Wloka, M.M., 69, 164
Woodson, W.E., 47
Woodworth, 49
Wright, P.C., xxvii, 146
Wulfeck, J.W., 44
Wyshynski, S., 104
Wyszecki, G., 26

Y

Young, L.R., 20, 114, 115, 147

Z

Zeitlin, L.W., 46
Zeltzer, David, xxviii, xxix, 21, 77, 140, 141, 173
Zerkus, M., 154
Zimmerman, Tom, xxix, 101, 109, 120
Zyda, M.J., 130, 166

Subject Index

3-D space, position and orientation in, xxxiv-xxxvi

A

absolute motion, 75
acoustic displays, 142-149, 185
  audio sources, 143-146
  auditory presentation technologies, 148-149
  manufacturers, 228-229
  super-localization, 149
  synthesis of auditory localization cues, 146-148
acoustic tracking, xxx, 102-103
  manufacturers, 222
alarms, 145
applications, xxv
  categories, 10
  communication, 13, 211-212
  defining, 8-13
  entertainment, 12, 211
  environment for, 13-15
  offline learning/knowledge acquisition, 11-12, 211
  offline training/rehearsal, 11, 210
  online comprehension, 11, 210
  online design, 12, 211
  online performance, 9, 11, 210
  requirements for, 63-94
  tools for researching human perceptual-motor capabilities, 13, 212
Argonne E-3 remote manipulator, xxvii
Aristotelean physics, 76-77
arms (*see* hands and arms)
artificial reality, xxiii, xxvii, 233
atmospheric attenuation, 22
audio (*see also* acoustic displays; auditory perception; speech recognition; speech synthesis)
  nonspeech, 144-146
  sampled, 146
  transduced live, 146
auditory icons, 145
auditory perception, 29-35
  complex acoustic environments, 34
  damage caused by sound, 82
  duplex theory, 33
  ear characteristics, 30-32
  interaural level difference, 32-33
  interaural phase difference, 33
  interaural time difference, 33
  motion cues, 34-35
  pinna filtering, 33-34
  types of listening, 32
  virtual environments and, 35
auditory scene analysis, 31
auditory stream segregation, 31
augmented reality, xxiii, 233
auralization, 144, 145
automatic foley generation, 144, 145
autonomy, 77

B

bandwidth, 130, 183
  input/output, 73-74
  speech recognition and, 124
binaural audio transducers, 228
binocular disparity, 24

268 Subject Index

binocular field of view, 25
binocular omni-oriented monitor (BOOM), xxiii, 138-139
  manufacturers, 227-228
biosignal processing, 117-118
  manufacturer, 223
bloom, 132
boresighting, 80
brightness, 135, 141
burns
  electrochemical, 83
  thermal, 83

C

calibration, 79-80, 90
  gloves, 110
cathode ray tube (CRT), 131-133
CAVE systems, xxiii, 139, 233
cerebroelectric signals, 117
cocktail party effect, 35
cognition, 56-57
collateral effects, 106
color, 135, 141
color perception, 27
computation model, 159
computer-aided design (CAD), 171, 180
computers, 157-173
  costs, 165
  environment and hypermedia integration subsystems, 160
  hardware requirements, 164-165
  memory, 164
  real-time systems, 162-164
  single-processor vs. multiprocessor systems, 164
  software requirements, 165-173
  system architecture, xx, xxi, 158-164
configurations
  inside-out vs. outside-in, 100
  reconfigurability of systems, 68, 85, 88
connectivity, 64
contour interruption, 22
contrast, 135
costs, 91
  building VE applications, 84
  computer system, 165
critical flicker frequency, 21
critical fusion frequency, 21
customization, 79-80, 90, 182
cybersickness, 80-81, 206

D

databases, virtual world, 168
DataGlove, xxix, 109
DataSuit, xxix
decoupled simulation model, 159
Defense Advanced Research Projects Agency (DARPA), 4
degree of virtuality, 72-73, 89
deixis, 125
design, xxx-xxxiv
  degree of customizability, 182
  degree of encumbrance, 181-182
  display tradeoffs, 184-186
  general-purpose vs. special-purpose systems, 181
  levels, xxxii
  optimization vs. cross-platform compatibility, 183
  process, xxxii-xxxiii, 217
  prototypes, xxxiii-xxxiv
  responsiveness vs. image quality vs. world complexity, 182-183
  sharing resources vs. bandwidth, 183
  team of qualified persons, 217-218
  tools and implementation technology, 218-219
Dexterous Handmaster, 153
diopter, 20
display update rate, 191
displays
  acoustic, 142-149
    audio sources, 143-146
    auditory presentation technologies, 148-149
    manufacturers, 228-229
    super-localization, 149
    synthesis of auditory localization cues, 146-148
  autostereoscopic, 140
  binocular, 127
  BOOM technology, xxiii, 138-139, 227-228
  cathode ray tubes, 131-133
  characteristics of various technologies, 135
  dichoptic, 127
  force, 149-150, 153-154, 229-230
  head-mounted, xxiii, xxvi, 4, 28-29, 136-138, 184
    manufacturers, 225-227

see-through, 142
size/weight considerations, 84, 91
inertial, 155
liquid crystal, 133
locomotive, 155
monoscopic, 127
motion, 83
olfactory, 154-155
optical systems, 134, 136
power requirements, 135
recommended, 59-60
retinal laser, 133-134
see-through, 142
shuttered glasses, 139-140
size, 135
stereoscopic, 128
tactile, 149-152
   electrocutaneous, 151
   evaluation chart, 152
   manufacturers, 229
   pneumatic, 151
   vibro-tactile, 151
temperature range, 135
thermal, manufacturer, 229
visual, 127-142
   brightness, 141
   color, 141
   evaluating, 142
   field of view, 141
   image generation, 128-131
   image smearing, 141-142
   issues/requirements, 140-142
   resolution, 141
   responsiveness, 141
   temporal fusion, 142
Doppler effect, 35
duplex theory, 33

E

earcons, 145, 146
ears (*see* auditory perception)
electrical shock, 83
electromagnetic spectrum, 19
engagement, 65-66, 85
environments
   degree of virtuality and integration in real, 72-73
   physical, 13-14
   social, 14-15
   virtual (*see* virtual environments)

work, 14
evaluation process, 195-207
   alternatives to usability studies, 201-202
   automatic data collection, 199
   cybersickness, 206
   error recording, 203
   guidelines, 196-198
   learning curve, 204
   mental workload, 204-205
   novice vs. expert behavior, 206
   open-ended interviews, 201
   physiological after-effects, 207
   physiological monitoring, 201
   questionnaire, 200-201
   subjective impressions, 206
   system performance, 213-214
   task completion report, 202-203
   task completion time, 204
   usability, 214-215
   users verbalizing comments, 199-200
   value of task/application, 215-216
   videotape analysis, 199
eyes (*see* visual perception)
eye tracking, 114-117
   manufacturers, 223

F

fault tolerance, 192
field of view, 25-26
   visual displays, 141
fishtank VR systems, xxiii, 139, 233
Fitts' law, 48
flicker, 21, 142
flight simulators, xxvi
FLYBAR system, xxix
force displays, 149-150, 153-154
   manufacturers, 229-230
frame rate
   rendering, 159
   simulation, 159
fusion, 21

G

Gehring Auditory Localizer, xxix
gesture recognition, 119-121
glabrous skin, 36
glasses, shuttered, 139-140, 228

gloves, xxviii, 106, 109-111
  DataGlove, xxix, 109
  evaluating, 110-111
  instrumented technologies, 112
  issues/considerations, 110
  manufacturers, 222-223
  Power Glove, 109

H

hand-gesture interface devices (*see* gloves)
hands and arms, 47-51
  aimed movements, 48-49
  grasping, 49-50
  key-pressing, 50
  playing musical instruments, 50-51
  sign language, 50
  size, 47
  strength, 47
  tapping, 50
  virtual environments and, 51
  writing/drawing, 50-51
haptic devices, 118-119
  manufacturers, 223-224
haptic perception, 35-40
  force and kinesthetic perception, 38-39
  tactile perception and, 36-38
  virtual environments and, 39-40
head-mounted display (HMD), xxiii, xxvi, 4, 28-29, 136-138, 184
  manufacturers, 225-227
  see-through, 142
  size/weight considerations, 84, 91
headphones, 149
head-related transfer function (HRTF), 4, 34, 147
health and fitness
  auditory damage, 82
  awareness of surrounding environment, 82-83
  burns, 83
  cybersickness, 80-81, 206
  disease transmission, 82
  injury from motion displays, 83
  physiological after-effects of VEs, 207
  shocks, 83
  skin irritation, 83
  visual impairment, 81-82

hearing (*see* auditory perception)
highlighting, 23
hue, 27
hyperspace, 75

I

IEEE, 5
image generators, 128-131
  manufacturers, 225
images
  rendering speed, 130
  smearing in visual displays, 141-142
  sources for visual displays, 131-134
immersion, 65-67, 85, 88
  mixed systems, 67
  quantifying, 67
impulse function, 37
inertial displays, 155
input technologies, 76, 97-125
interactivity, 74
interaural level difference (ILD), 32-33
interaural phase difference, 33
interaural time difference (ITD), 33
interposition, 22
interpupillary distance (IPD), 136, 140

J

joysticks, 118

K

keyboards, 118
kinesthetic perception, 38-39
kinetic occlusion, 22

L

lag (*see* latency)
latency, 69, 189-191
learning, 57
light-emitting diode (LED), 134
linear perspective, 22
liquid crystal display (LCD), 133
locomotion, 51-52, 111-112
locomotive displays, 155
locus of control, 77-78, 87
looming, 25

M

magnetic tracking, xxx, 101-102
  manufacturers, 222
mechanical tracking, xxx, 101
  manufacturers, 222
Midas Touch, 115
motion
  absolute, 75
  relative, 75
motion cues, 24, 34-35
motion parallax, 24, 139
motion platforms, manufacturers, 230-231
motor skills, 18, 47-54, 212
  eye movement/expressions, 53
  facial movement/expressions, 54
  hands/arms, 47-51
  locomotion, 51-52
  speech, 52-53
mouse systems, 224
multimedia systems, xx
multisensory systems, 74, 89
musical listening, 32
myoelectric signals, 117

N

navigation techniques, 74-76, 86, 90, 177-179
  input methods, 76
networking, 172
  software, 232
noise, speech recognition and, 124
nose (*see* olfactory perception)

O

objects, 175-176
  abstract, 79
  behaviors of, 176-177
  creating, 180
  geometric modeling of, 171
  iconic, 78
  interactions with, 177-180
  manipulating, 179
  modality-altered, 78
  modifying, 180
  movement, 177-179
  property-altered, 78
  realistic, 78
  reified, 79
  representation of, 78-79
  scaling, 78, 179-180
  selecting, 179
  tools/control devices, 180
obscuration, 22
occlusion, 131
olfactory displays, 154-155
olfactory perception, 40-43
  benefits of using in VEs, 42
  nose characteristics, 40-42
  virtual environments and, 42-43
operating systems, 166-167
optical tracking, xxx, 103-104
  manufacturers, 222
orthostereoscopy, 140-141
output technologies, 127-156

P

perception
  auditory, 29-35, 82
  dimensions of, 18
  haptic, 35-40
  kinesthetic, 38-39
  modes of, 18
  olfactory, 40-43
  tactile, 36-38
  vestibular system, 43-44
  visual, 19-29, 81-82
periodic function, 37
phototropic vision, 19
physics
  Aristotelean, 76-77
  of virtual environments, 76-77, 87
pinna filtering, 33-34
plasma, 134
polygon budget, 130
position tracking, xxx, 98-106, 184-185
  accuracy/resolution, 105
  active vs. passive systems, 100
  categories, 99
  evaluating, 106
  inside-out vs. outside-in configurations, 100
  manufacturers, 222
  registration, 106
  responsiveness, 105
  robustness, 105
  role of, 99-100

272   Subject Index

position tracking *continued*
　　technologies, 100-101, 107-109
　　working volume/sociability, 106
Power Glove, 109
predictive tracking, 120-121
presence, 65-66
prosody, 52
proximity-luminance covariance, 22
Pseudophone, xxix

R

range of operation, 106
refresh rate, 132, 135
registration, 73, 86, 89, 192
　　position tracking systems, 106
relative motion, 75
rendering frame rate, 159
resolution, 26-27, 68, 85, 88
　　position tracking systems, 105
　　spatial, 135
　　visual displays, 141
responsiveness, 69, 85, 182-183
　　position tracking systems, 105
　　visual displays, 141
retinal laser display, 133-134
robustness, 70, 85, 192
　　gloves, 110
　　position tracking systems, 105

S

safety, 80-83, 87, 91
scotopic vision, 19
senses (*see also* perception)
　　adaptation to, 55-56
　　characteristics of, 44-47
　　ears/hearing, 29-35, 82
　　eyes/vision, 19-29, 53-54, 81-82
　　interactions with, 54-55
　　nose/smell, 40-43
　　skin/touch, 35-40
　　virtual environments and, 55
Sensorama Simulator, xxvi
shadow mask, 132
shadows, 22
sign language, 50
SIMNET, 4-5
simulation frame rate, 159
skin, tactile perception and, 36-38
smell (*see* olfactory perception)

sociability, 88
　　position tracking systems, 106
software
　　autonomy, 166
　　communication, 166
　　cross-platform compatibility, 171-172
　　database, 168
　　device drivers, 170
　　expert systems, 173
　　hypermedia integration, 166
　　interaction, 166
　　interrupt-driven vs. polled systems,
　　　　167-168
　　modeling, 171, 232
　　navigation, 166
　　network, 172, 232
　　operating systems, 166-167
　　programmer interface and toolkits,
　　　　169-170
　　scripting, 166
　　simulation, 170-171, 231-232
sonification, 29, 144, 145
SpaceBall, 119
speakers, 149
spectral integration, 31
speech, 52-53
　　as a communication medium, 52
　　in human-computer interaction, 53
　　physical production of, 52
　　role of, 122
　　virtual environments and, 53
speech recognition, 121-124
　　bandwidth, 124
　　continuous vs. isolated words, 123
　　evaluating systems, 124
　　manufacturers, 224-225
　　noise, 124
　　speaker dependence vs. independence, 123
　　vocabulary size and moded vs. non-moded, 123-124
speech synthesis, 143-144
stability, 69-70, 85
step function, 37
suits, 106, 109-111
　　evaluating, 110-111
　　issues/considerations, 110
　　manufacturers, 222-223
synchronization, 191
synesthetic representation, 145

T

tactile displays, 149-152
  electrocutaneous, 151
  evaluation chart, 152
  manufacturers, 229
  pneumatic, 151
  vibro-tactile, 151
teleoperation system, xxii, 5, 161, 233-234
teleportation, 75
textural gradients, 22
thermal displays, manufacturer, 229
touch (*see* haptic perception)
touch sensors, xxix
trackballs, 118, 223-224
tracking systems, xxx, 98-106, 184-185
    (*see also* position tracking)
  acoustic, xxx, 102-103
  magnetic, xxx, 101-102
  manufacturers, 222
  mechanical, xxx, 101
  optical, xxx, 103-104
  predictive, 120-121
transformation, 75

U

users, 3-13
  affect of VEs on, 57-58
  aptitude of, 7
  evaluating virtual environments (*see* evaluation process)
  individual physiological differences of, 7
  multiple, 64
  novices vs. experts, 6-7
  remote vs. proximate, 5-6
  representation of, 71-72, 86, 89
  single vs. multiple, 4-5
  with disabilities, 7-8

V

VACTOR technology, 54, 97, 113-114
  manufacturer, 223
ventriloquist effect, 54
vergence, 24, 53
veridicality, 64-65, 85
vestibular illusions, 44
vestibular system, 43-44
viewpoints, 70-71, 86, 88
  egocentric vs. God's eye, 70-71
virtual auditory world (VAW), 142-143
Virtual Drum Kit, 190
virtual egocenter, 70
virtual environments (VEs)
  applications, xxv
  definition/description, xix-xxiii
  evaluation process, 195-207
  future research/development, 219-220
  history, xxv-xxx
virtual hand controllers (*see* gloves)
virtual interface environment workstation (VIEW), xxviii
virtual reality, xxviii
Virtual Retinal Display, 133
vision
  phototropic, 19
  scotopic, 19
visual displays, 127-142
  brightness, 141
  color, 141
  evaluating, 142
  field of view, 141
  image generation, 128-131
  image smearing, 141-142
  image sources, 131-134
  issues/requirements, 140-142
  resolution, 141
  responsiveness, 141
  temporal fusion, 142
visually coupled airborne systems simulator (VCASS), xxvii
visual perception, 19-29
  accommodation, 23
  binocular disparity and stereopsis, 24
  brightness and contrast, 27-28
  color, 27
  cues and performance, 28
  depth cues, 24-25
  eye movement, 20, 53-54
  field of view, 25-26
  human eye characteristics, 19-21
  impairment, 81-82
  looming, 25
  monocular depth cues, 21-23
  motion cues, 24
  oculomotor cues, 23-24
  resolution, 26-27
  vergence, 24
  virtual environments and, 28-29

W
warnings, 145
within-ear monitors, 149
working volume, 106, 193
workload, 204-205

Y
Young-Helmholz theory, 27

ABOUT THE AUTHOR

Rory Stuart is a member of the technical staff at NYNEX Science & Technology, Inc., where he leads the Virtual Reality Project. He has also served as editor-in-chief of the quarterly journal *Virtual Reality Systems.* Stuart writes technical papers on VR and has chaired several important conferences on the subject. He holds a master of science degree from Pace University, where his thesis was named "Thesis of the Year" in 1994 by the School of Computer Science & Information Systems. He is also an accomplished jazz composer and guitarist, who has been called by *Jazz Times* "perhaps THE most innovative straight-ahead jazz guitarist to emerge in years."